コンプレックス・エイジ

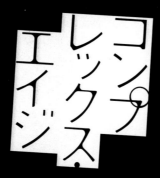

Complex age

Yui Sakuma

1

C O N T E N T S

Complex age

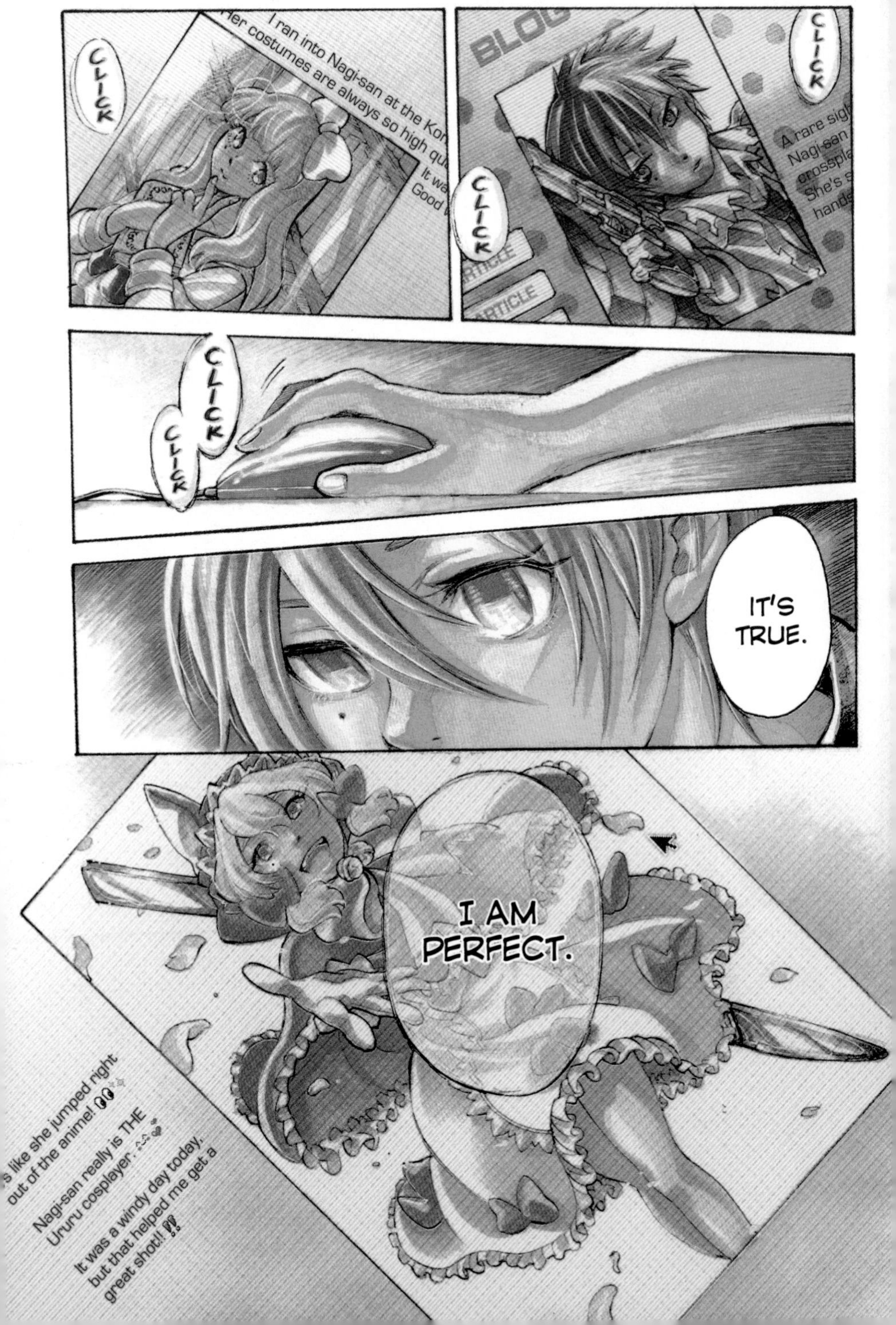

CLICK
BLOG
A rare sigh
Nagi-san
crosspla
She's s
hands
CLICK
ARTICLE
ARTICLE
CLICK
I ran into Nagi-san at the Kon
Her costumes are always so high qu
It wa
Good
CLICK
CLICK
IT'S TRUE.
I AM PERFECT.
s like she jumped right out of the anime!
Nagi-san really is THE Ururu cosplayer.
It was a windy day today, but that helped me get a great shot!!

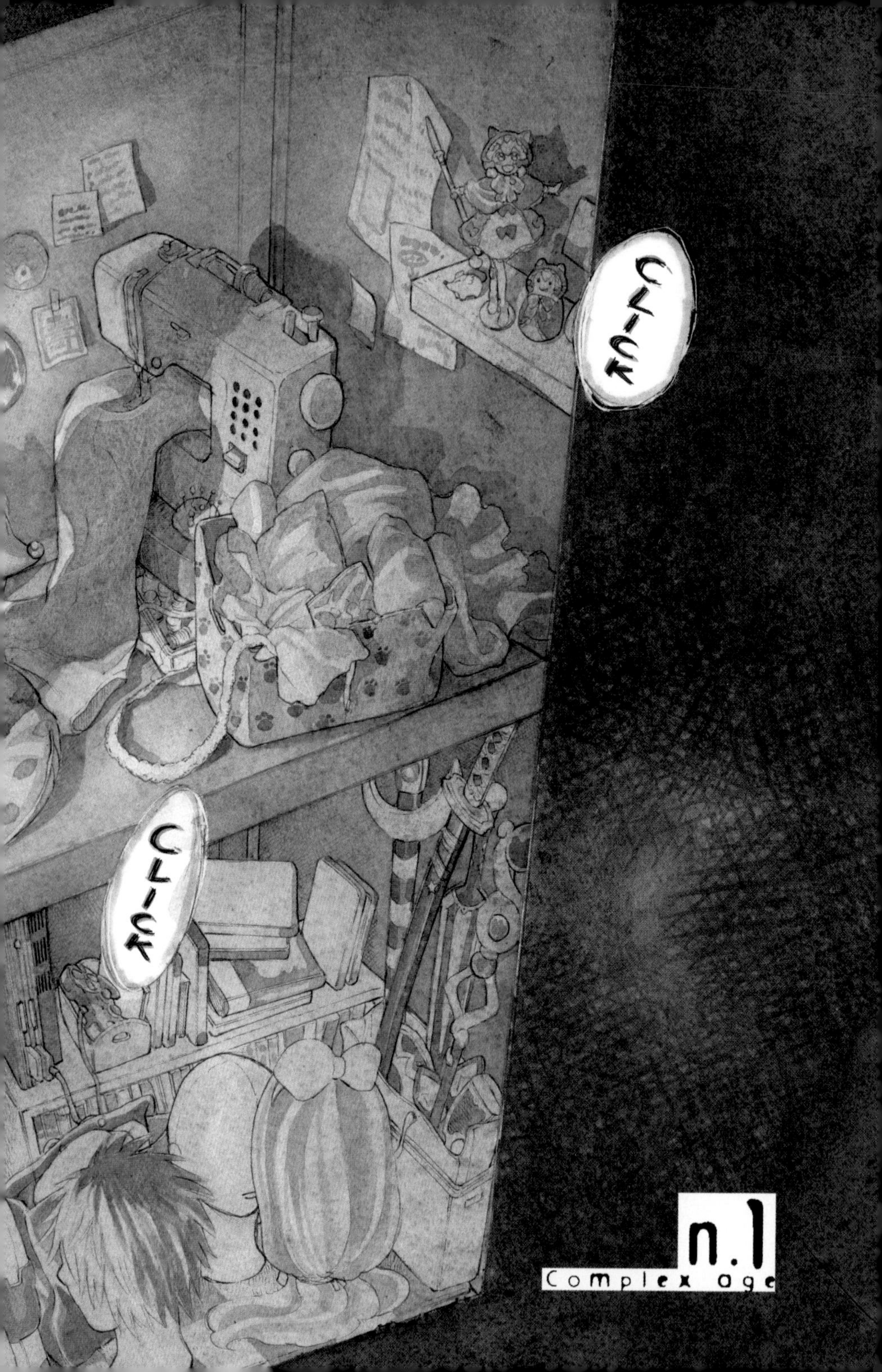
CLICK
CLICK
n.1
Complex age

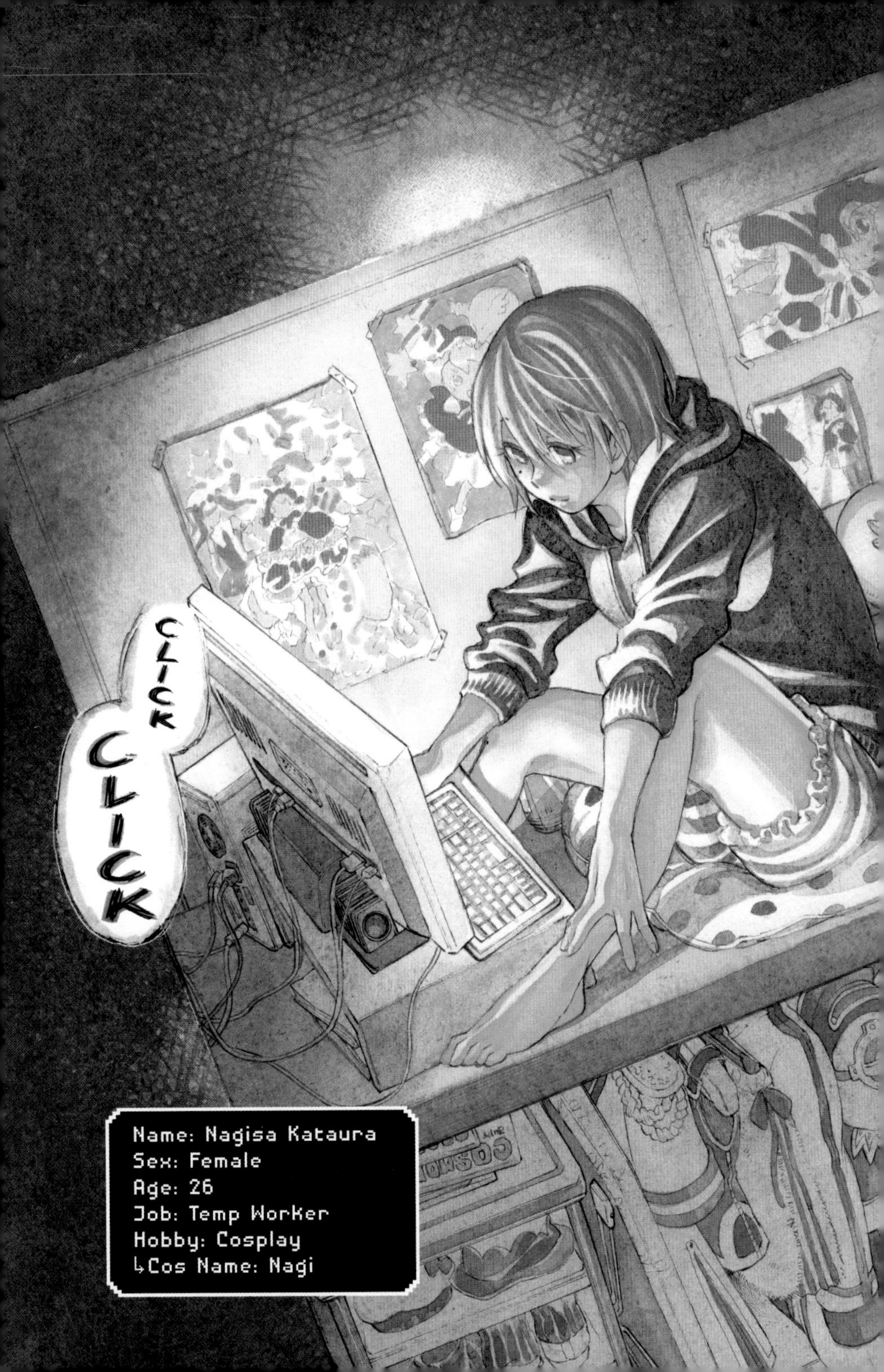
CLICK
CLICK
Name: Nagisa Kataura
Sex: Female
Age: 26
Job: Temp Worker
Hobby: Cosplay
↳Cos Name: Nagi

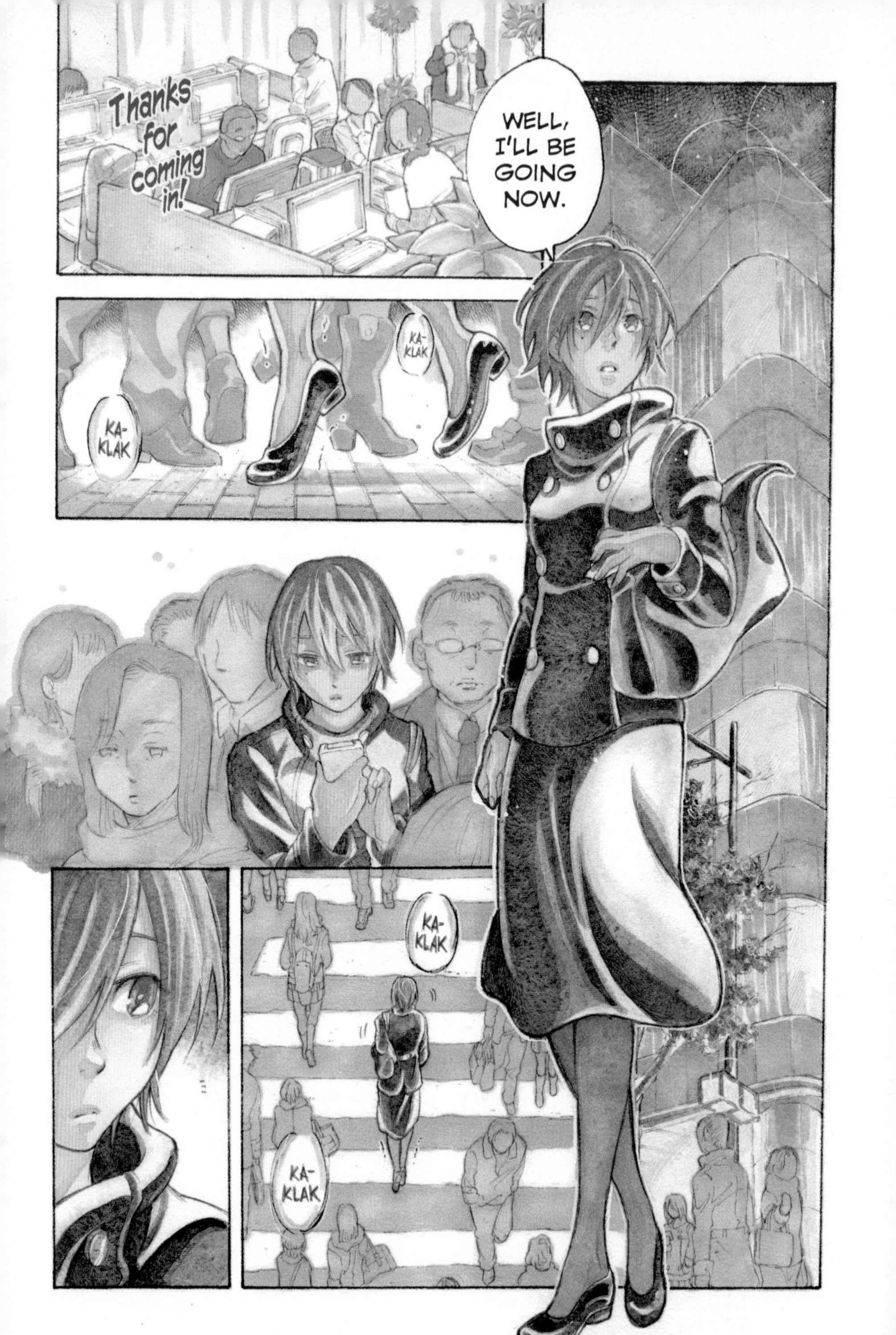
WELL, I'LL BE GOING NOW.
Thanks for coming in!
KA-KLAK
KA-KLAK
KA-KLAK
KA-KLAK

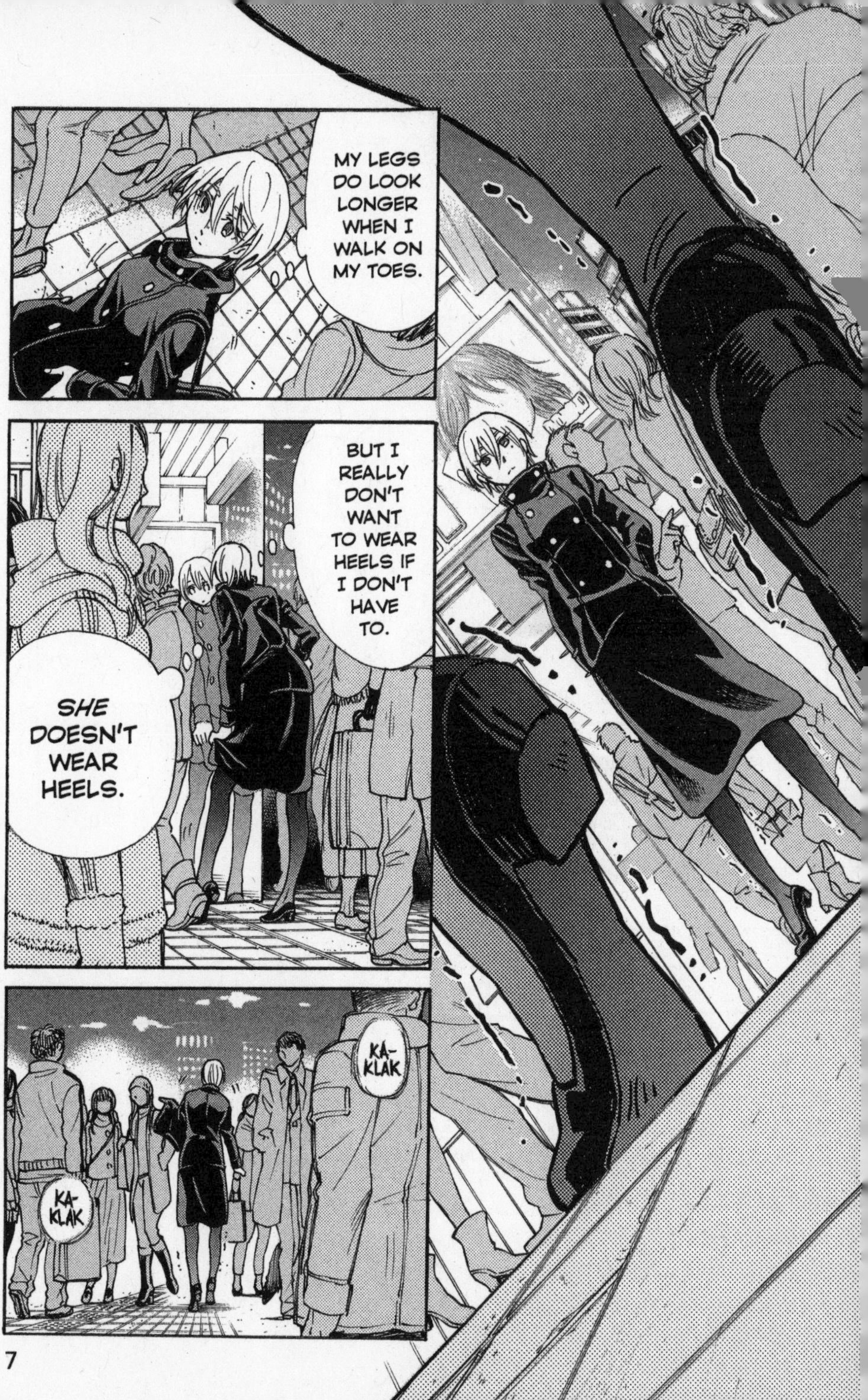
MY LEGS DO LOOK LONGER WHEN I WALK ON MY TOES.
BUT I REALLY DON'T WANT TO WEAR HEELS IF I DON'T HAVE TO.
SHE DOESN'T WEAR HEELS.
KA-KLAK
KA-KLAK

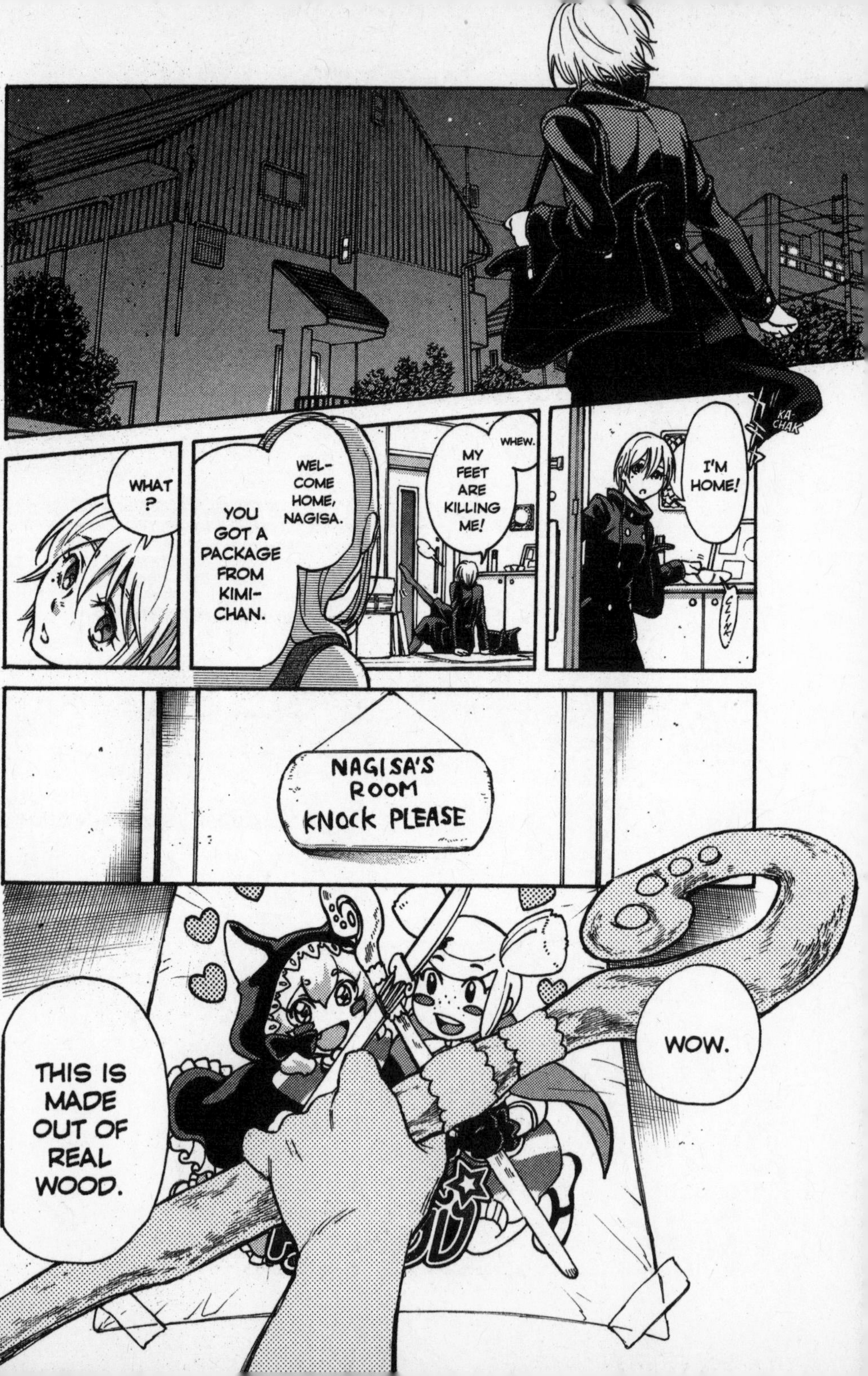
KA-CHAK
I'M HOME!
CLINK
WHEW.
MY FEET ARE KILLING ME!
WEL-COME HOME, NAGISA.
YOU GOT A PACKAGE FROM KIMI-CHAN.
WHAT?
NAGISA'S ROOM
KNOCK PLEASE
WOW.
THIS IS MADE OUT OF REAL WOOD.

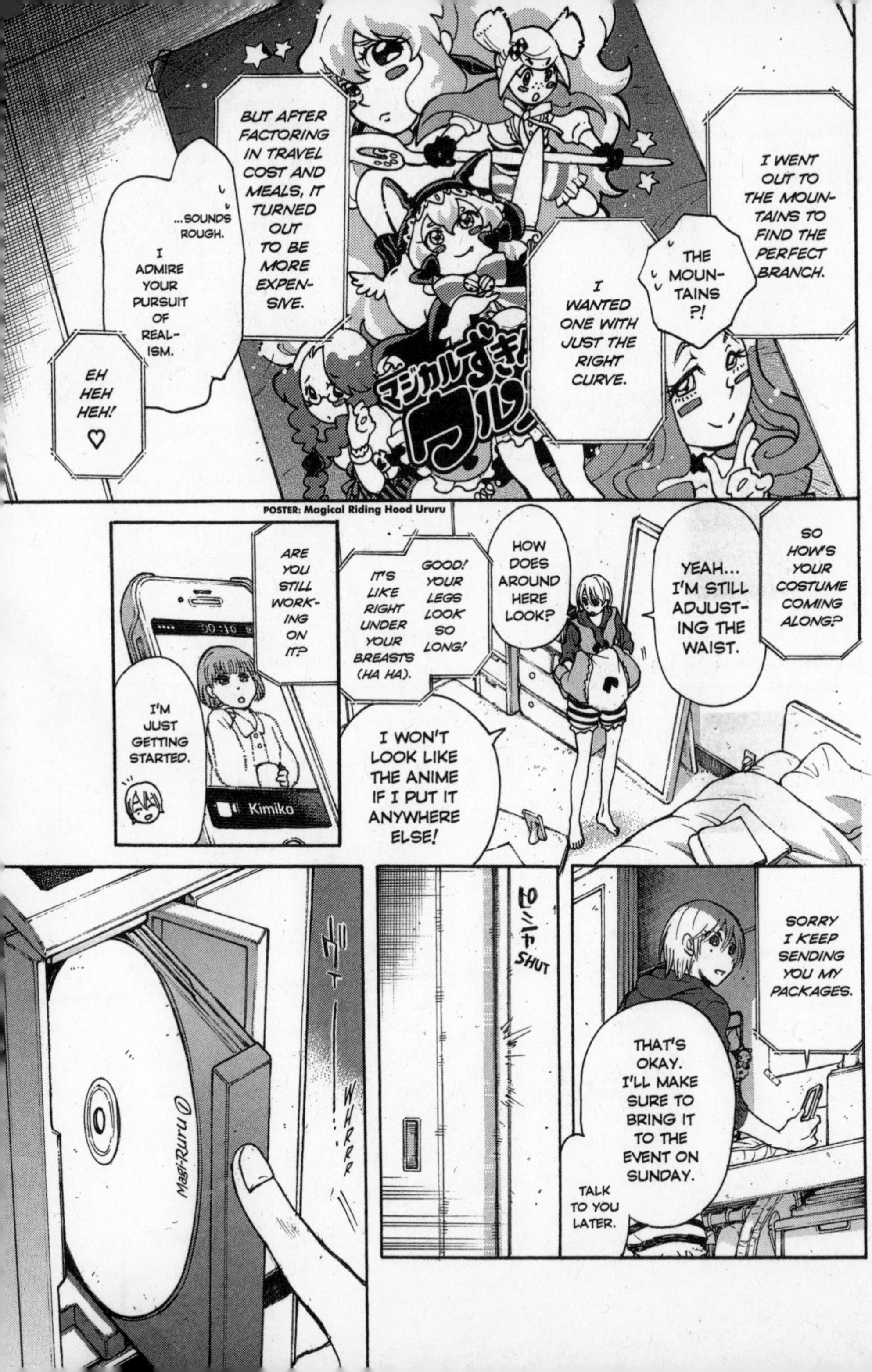
I WENT OUT TO THE MOUNTAINS TO FIND THE PERFECT BRANCH.
THE MOUNTAINS?!
I WANTED ONE WITH JUST THE RIGHT CURVE.
BUT AFTER FACTORING IN TRAVEL COST AND MEALS, IT TURNED OUT TO BE MORE EXPENSIVE.
...SOUNDS ROUGH.
I ADMIRE YOUR PURSUIT OF REALISM.
EH HEH HEH! ♡
SO HOW'S YOUR COSTUME COMING ALONG?
YEAH... I'M STILL ADJUSTING THE WAIST.
HOW DOES AROUND HERE LOOK?
GOOD! YOUR LEGS LOOK SO LONG!
IT'S LIKE RIGHT UNDER YOUR BREASTS (HA HA).
I WON'T LOOK LIKE THE ANIME IF I PUT IT ANYWHERE ELSE!
ARE YOU STILL WORKING ON IT?
I'M JUST GETTING STARTED.
Kimiko
SORRY I KEEP SENDING YOU MY PACKAGES.
THAT'S OKAY. I'LL MAKE SURE TO BRING IT TO THE EVENT ON SUNDAY.
TALK TO YOU LATER.
ピシャ
SHUT
WHRRR
Magi-Ruru ①
POSTER: Magical Riding Hood Ururu

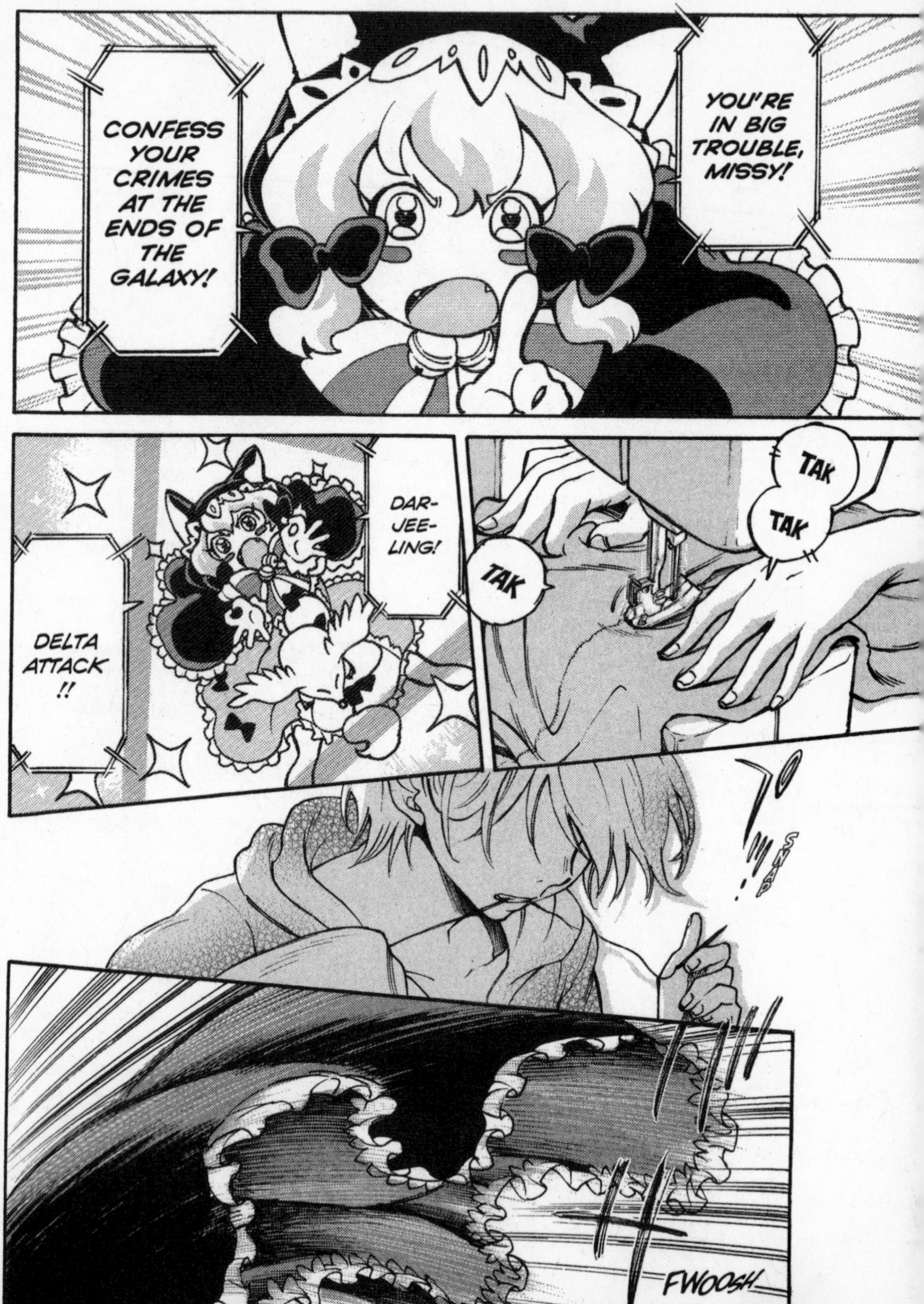
YOU'RE IN BIG TROUBLE, MISSY!
CONFESS YOUR CRIMES AT THE ENDS OF THE GALAXY!
TAK
TAK
TAK
DAR-JEE-LING!
DELTA ATTACK !!
SNAP
FWOOSH

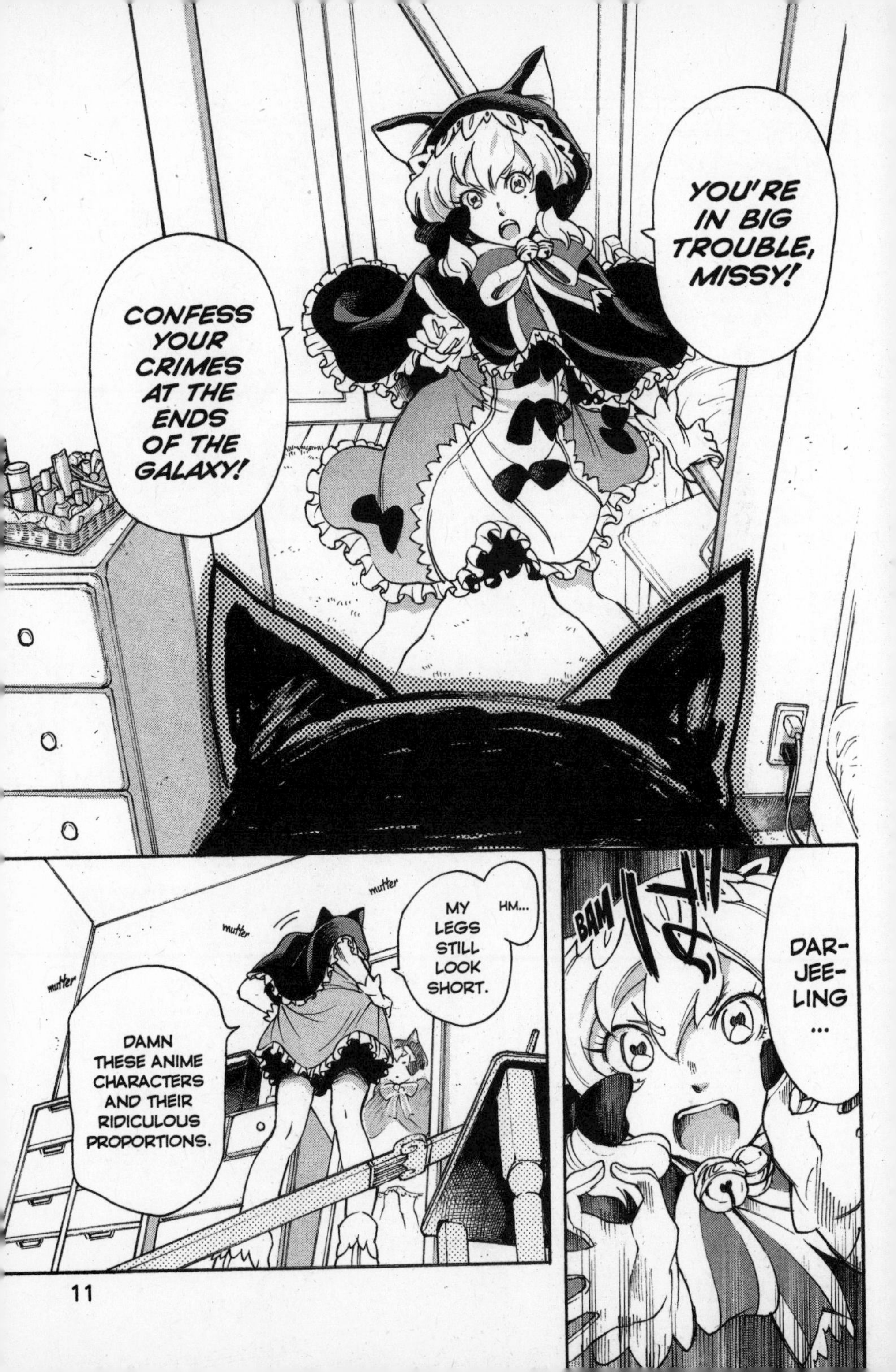
YOU'RE IN BIG TROUBLE, MISSY!
CONFESS YOUR CRIMES AT THE ENDS OF THE GALAXY!
BAM
DAR-JEE-LING ...
HM...
MY LEGS STILL LOOK SHORT.
mutter
mutter
mutter
DAMN THESE ANIME CHARACTERS AND THEIR RIDICULOUS PROPORTIONS.

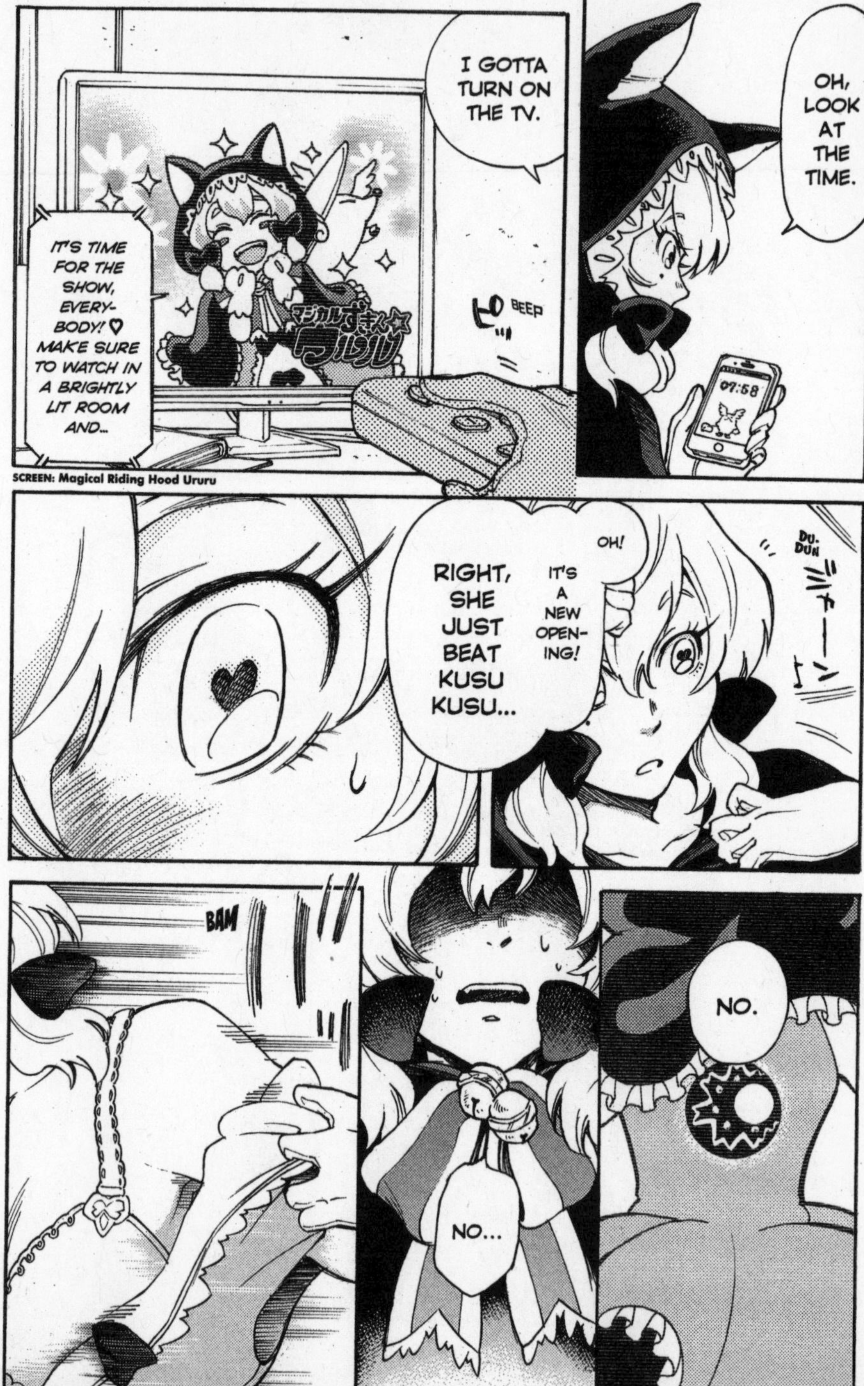
OH, LOOK AT THE TIME.
I GOTTA TURN ON THE TV.
BEEP
IT'S TIME FOR THE SHOW, EVERYBODY! ♡ MAKE SURE TO WATCH IN A BRIGHTLY LIT ROOM AND...
マジカルずきん☆ウルル
SCREEN: Magical Riding Hood Ururu
DU-DUN
ジャーン
OH! IT'S A NEW OPENING!
RIGHT, SHE JUST BEAT KUSU KUSU...
NO.
NO...
BAM

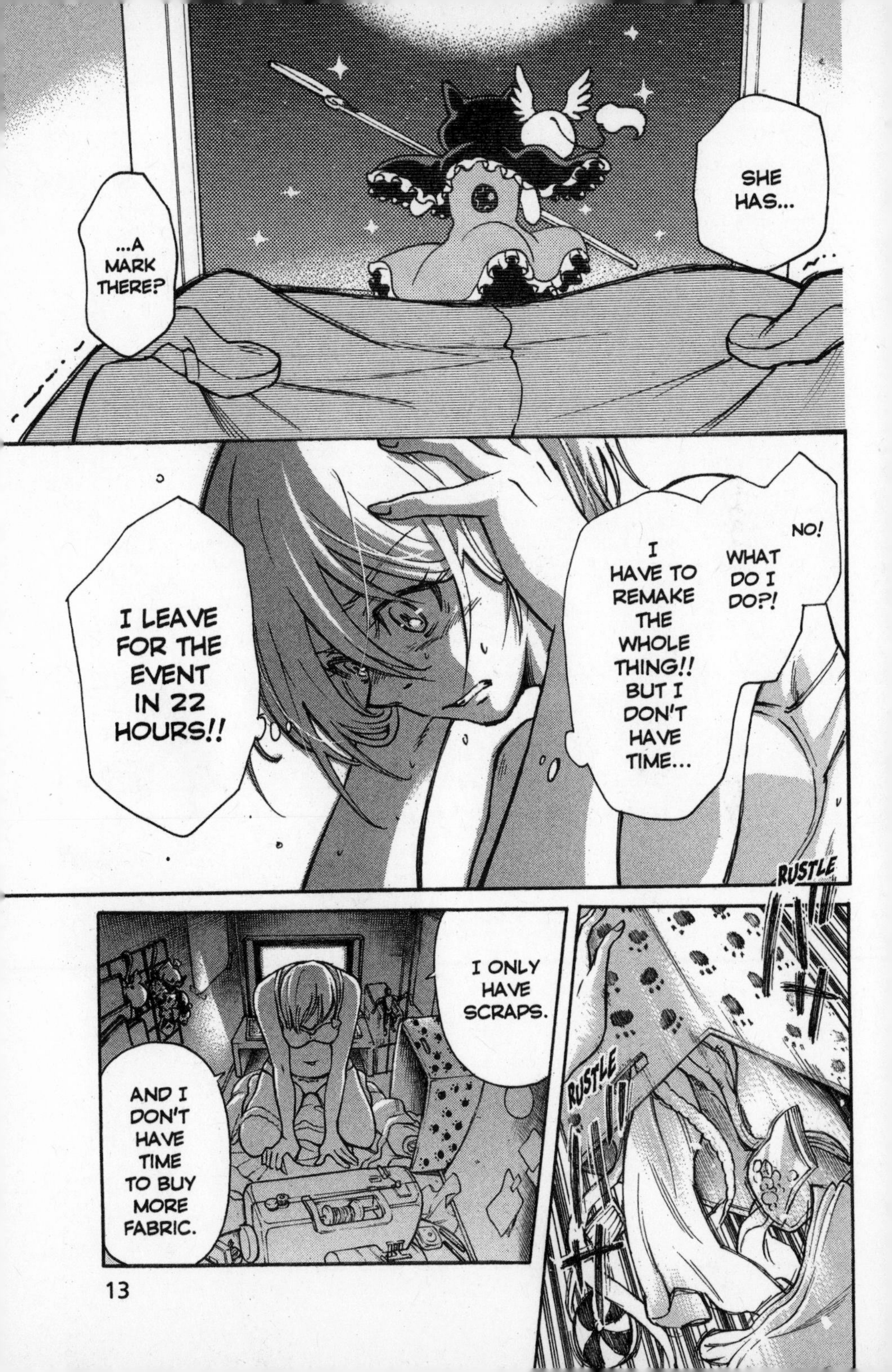
SHE HAS...
...A MARK THERE?
NO! WHAT DO I DO?!
I HAVE TO REMAKE THE WHOLE THING!! BUT I DON'T HAVE TIME...
I LEAVE FOR THE EVENT IN 22 HOURS!!
RUSTLE
RUSTLE
I ONLY HAVE SCRAPS.
AND I DON'T HAVE TIME TO BUY MORE FABRIC.

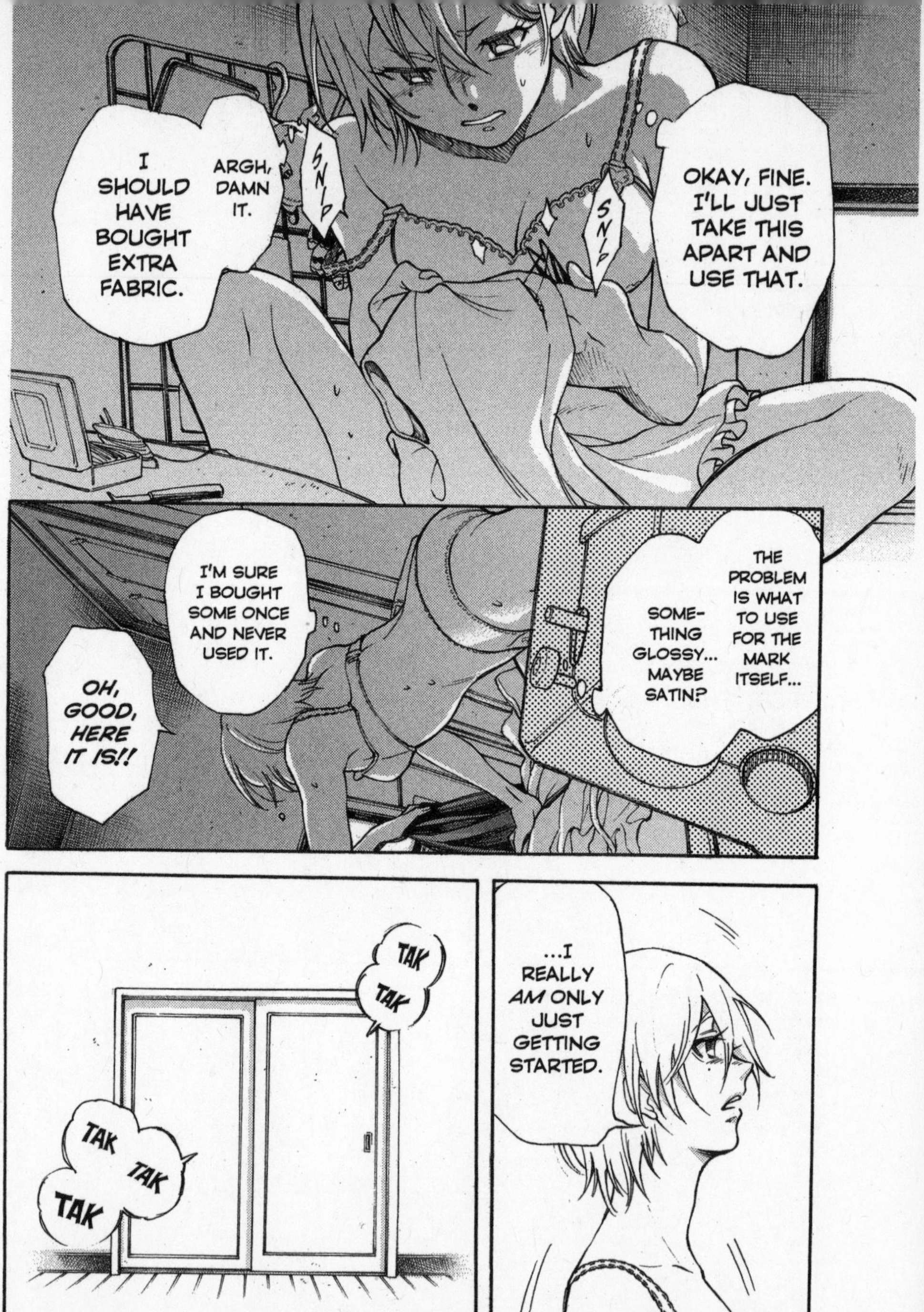
OKAY, FINE. I'LL JUST TAKE THIS APART AND USE THAT.
SNIP
SNIP
ARGH, DAMN IT.
I SHOULD HAVE BOUGHT EXTRA FABRIC.
THE PROBLEM IS WHAT TO USE FOR THE MARK ITSELF...
SOME-THING GLOSSY... MAYBE SATIN?
I'M SURE I BOUGHT SOME ONCE AND NEVER USED IT.
OH, GOOD, HERE IT IS!!
...I REALLY *AM* ONLY JUST GETTING STARTED.
TAK TAK
TAK TAK TAK

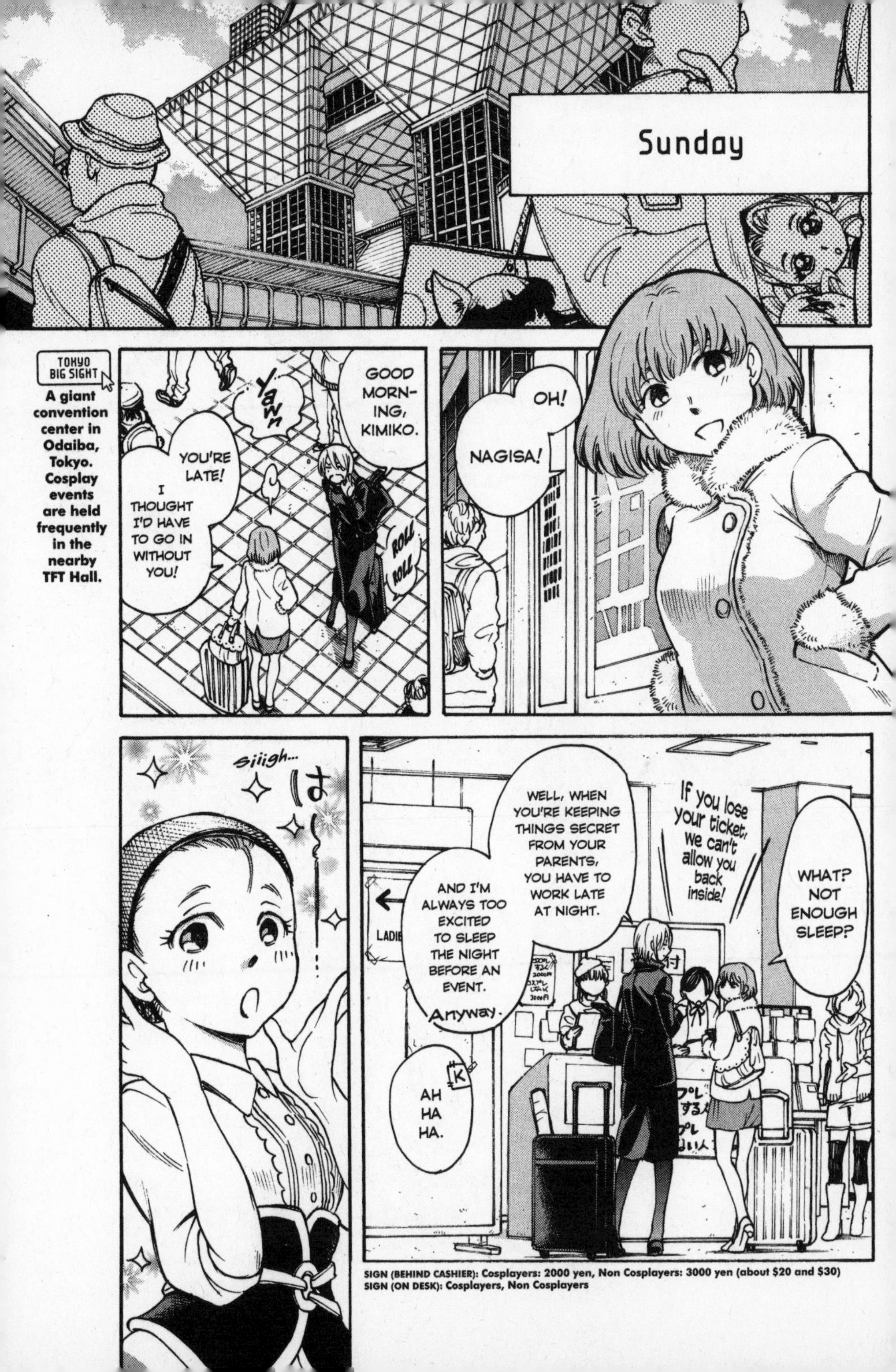
Sunday
OH!
NAGISA!
GOOD MORN-ING, KIMIKO.
Yawn
YOU'RE LATE! I THOUGHT I'D HAVE TO GO IN WITHOUT YOU!
ROLL ROLL
WHAT? NOT ENOUGH SLEEP?
If you lose your ticket, we can't allow you back inside!
WELL, WHEN YOU'RE KEEPING THINGS SECRET FROM YOUR PARENTS, YOU HAVE TO WORK LATE AT NIGHT.
AND I'M ALWAYS TOO EXCITED TO SLEEP THE NIGHT BEFORE AN EVENT.
Anyway.
AH HA HA.
K
LADIE
siiigh...
はー

TOKYO BIG SIGHT
A giant convention center in Odaiba, Tokyo. Cosplay events are held frequently in the nearby TFT Hall.

SIGN (BEHIND CASHIER): Cosplayers: 2000 yen, Non Cosplayers: 3000 yen (about $20 and $30)
SIGN (ON DESK): Cosplayers, Non Cosplayers

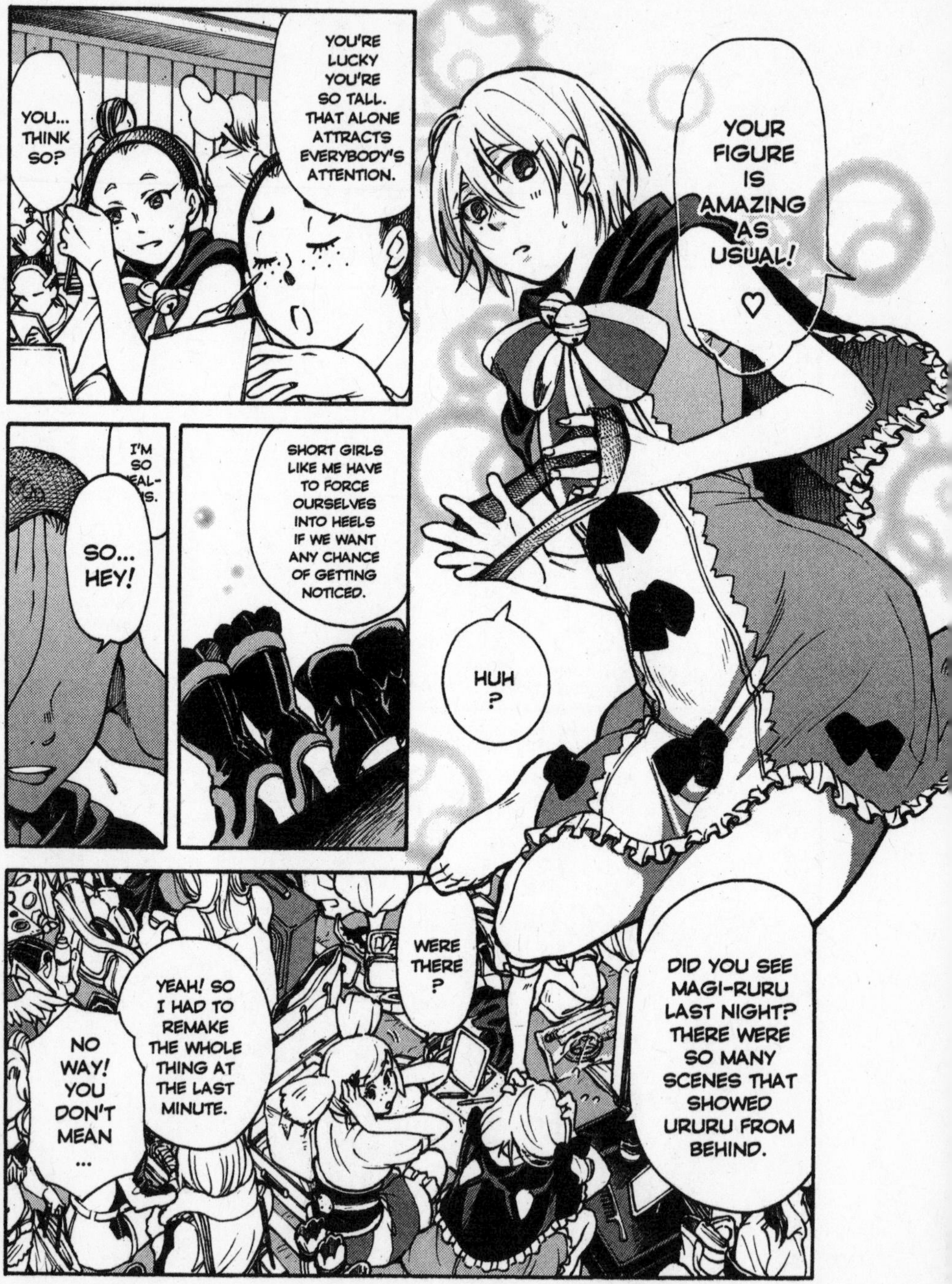
YOUR FIGURE IS AMAZING AS USUAL! ♡
HUH?
YOU'RE LUCKY YOU'RE SO TALL. THAT ALONE ATTRACTS EVERYBODY'S ATTENTION.
YOU... THINK SO?
SHORT GIRLS LIKE ME HAVE TO FORCE OURSELVES INTO HEELS IF WE WANT ANY CHANCE OF GETTING NOTICED.
I'M SO
SO... HEY!
DID YOU SEE MAGI-RURU LAST NIGHT? THERE WERE SO MANY SCENES THAT SHOWED URURU FROM BEHIND.
WERE THERE?
YEAH! SO I HAD TO REMAKE THE WHOLE THING AT THE LAST MINUTE.
NO WAY! YOU DON'T MEAN ...

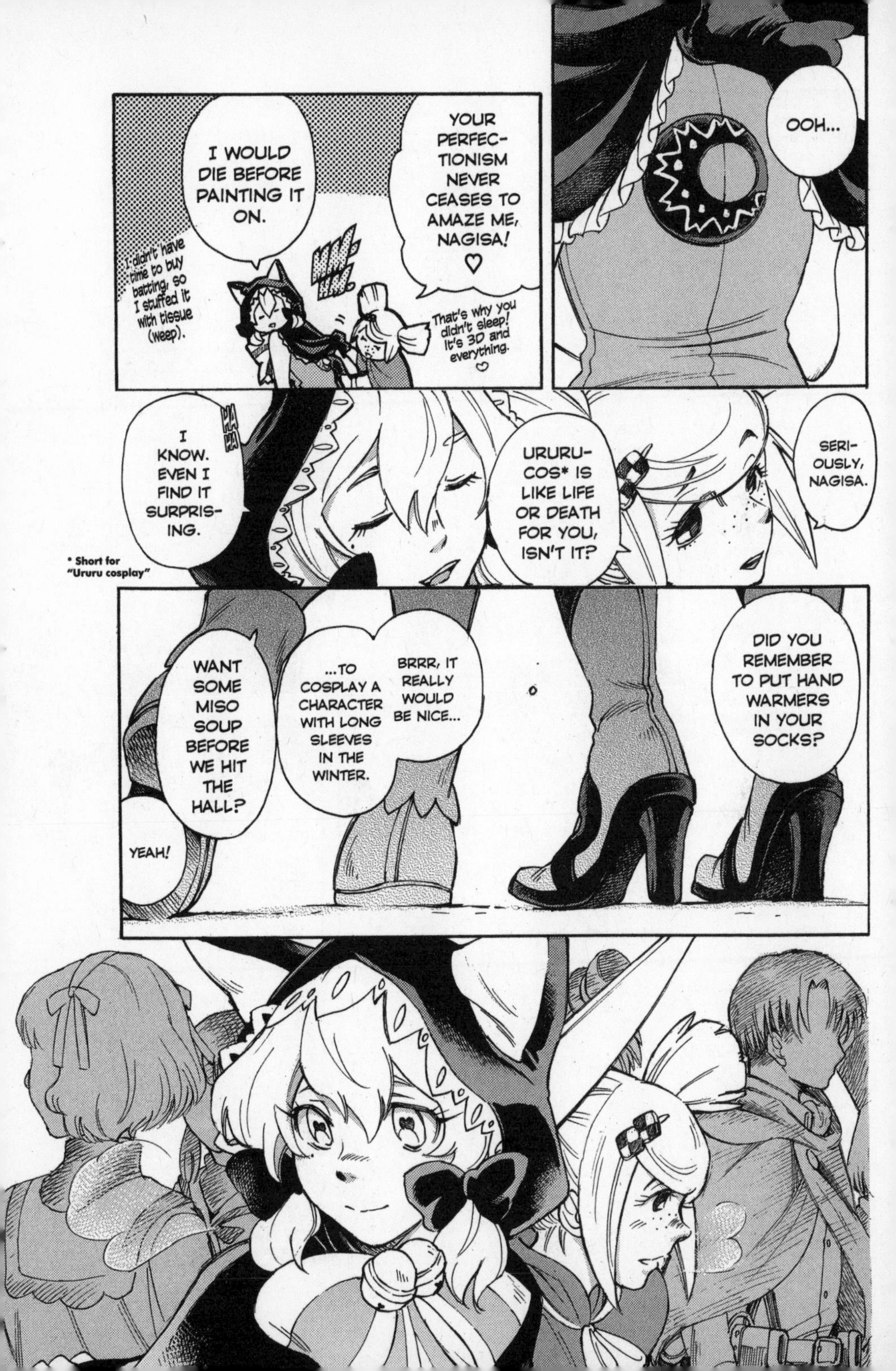
OOH...
YOUR PERFECTIONISM NEVER CEASES TO AMAZE ME, NAGISA! ♡
I WOULD DIE BEFORE PAINTING IT ON.
I didn't have time to buy batting, so I stuffed it with tissue (weep).
That's why you didn't sleep! It's 3D and everything. ♡
SERIOUSLY, NAGISA.
URURUCOS* IS LIKE LIFE OR DEATH FOR YOU, ISN'T IT?
HA HA
I KNOW. EVEN I FIND IT SURPRISING.
* Short for "Ururu cosplay"
DID YOU REMEMBER TO PUT HAND WARMERS IN YOUR SOCKS?
BRRR, IT REALLY WOULD BE NICE...
...TO COSPLAY A CHARACTER WITH LONG SLEEVES IN THE WINTER.
WANT SOME MISO SOUP BEFORE WE HIT THE HALL?
YEAH!

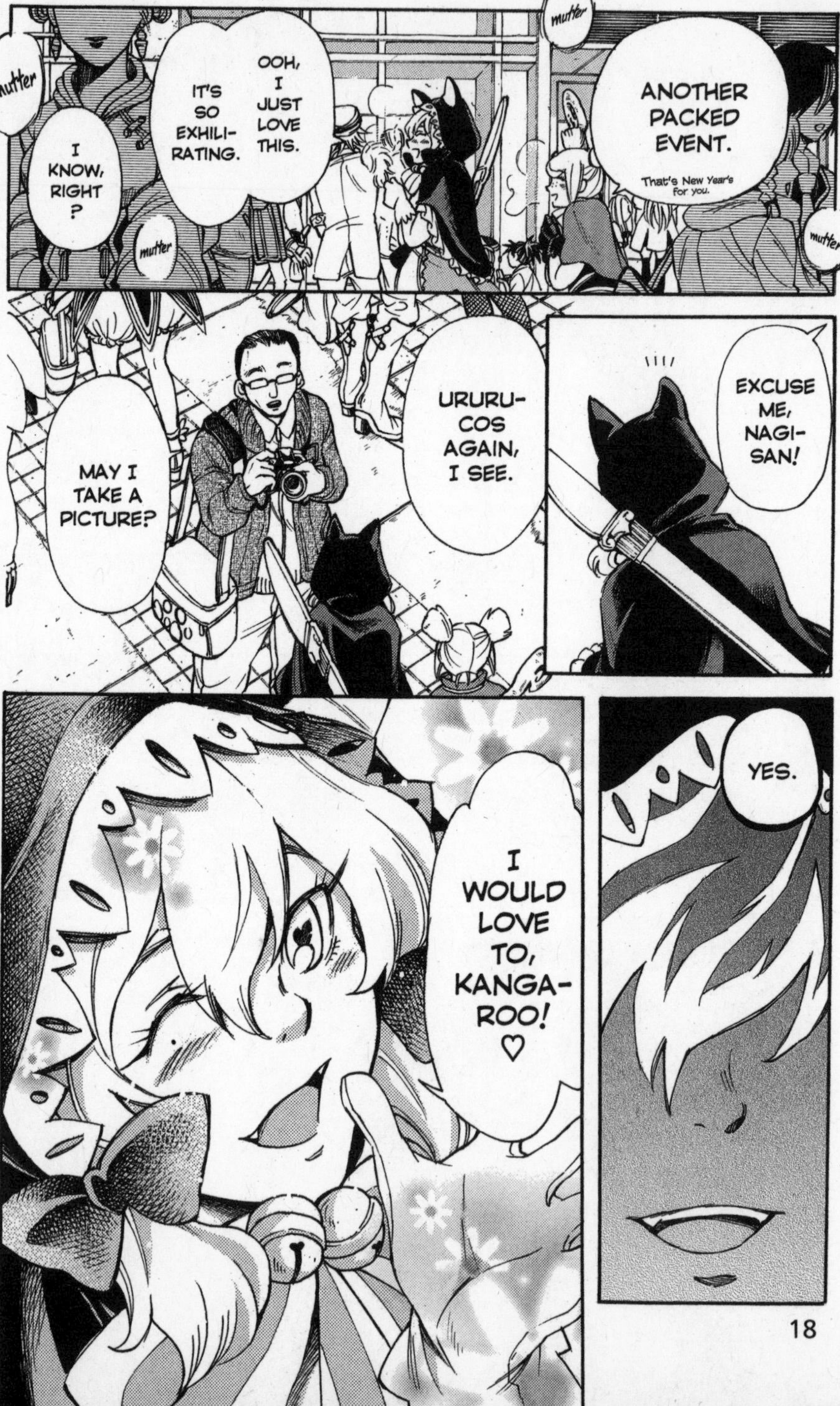
mutter
ANOTHER PACKED EVENT.
That's New Year's for you.
mutter
OOH, I JUST LOVE THIS.
IT'S SO EXHILI-RATING.
mutter
I KNOW, RIGHT?
mutter
EXCUSE ME, NAGI-SAN!
URURU-COS AGAIN, I SEE.
MAY I TAKE A PICTURE?
YES.
I WOULD LOVE TO, KANGA-ROO! ♡

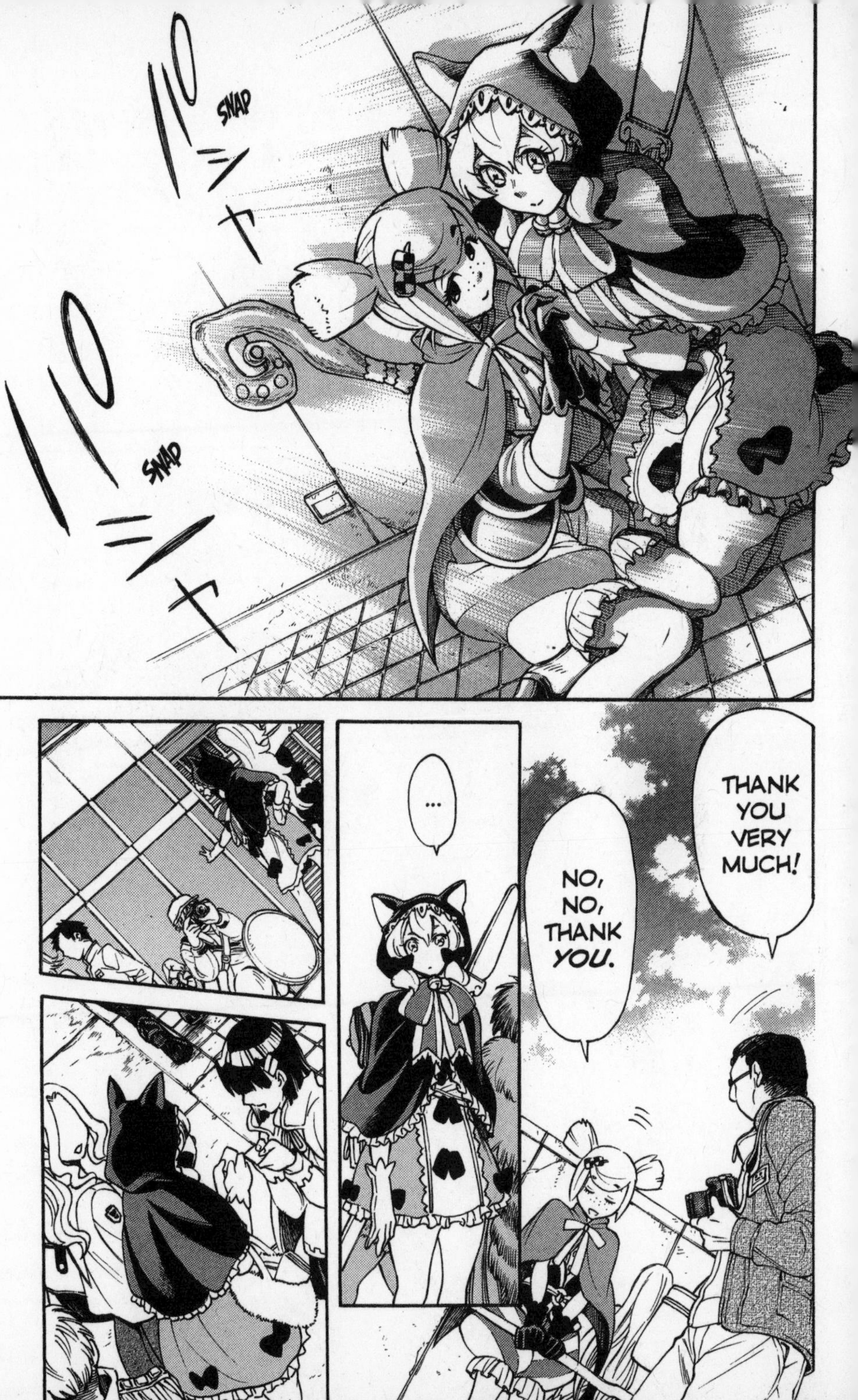
SNAP
SNAP
THANK YOU VERY MUCH!
NO, NO, THANK *YOU*.
...

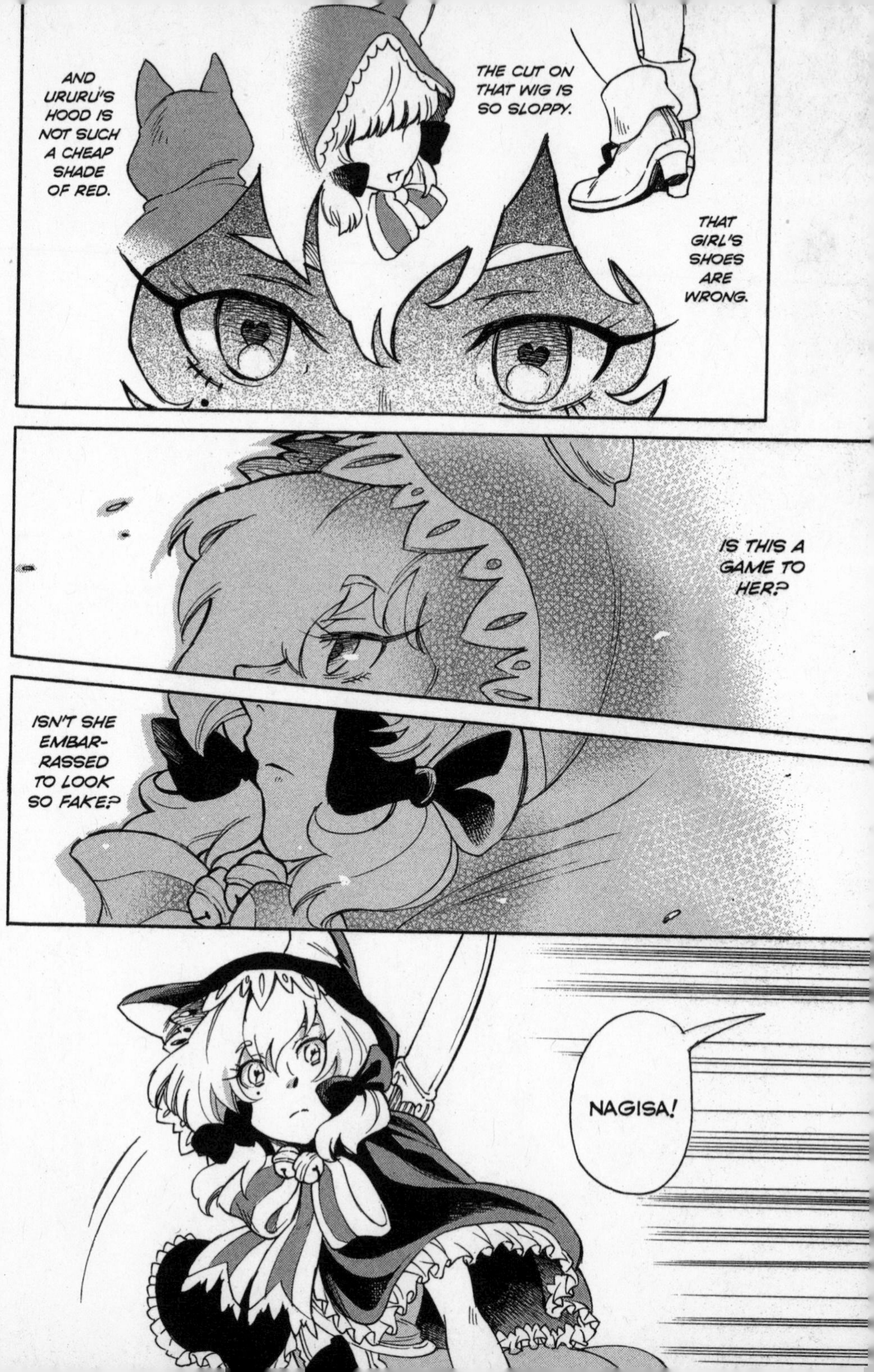
THAT GIRL'S SHOES ARE WRONG.
THE CUT ON THAT WIG IS SO SLOPPY.
AND URURU'S HOOD IS NOT SUCH A CHEAP SHADE OF RED.
IS THIS A GAME TO HER?
ISN'T SHE EMBAR-RASSED TO LOOK SO FAKE?
NAGISA!

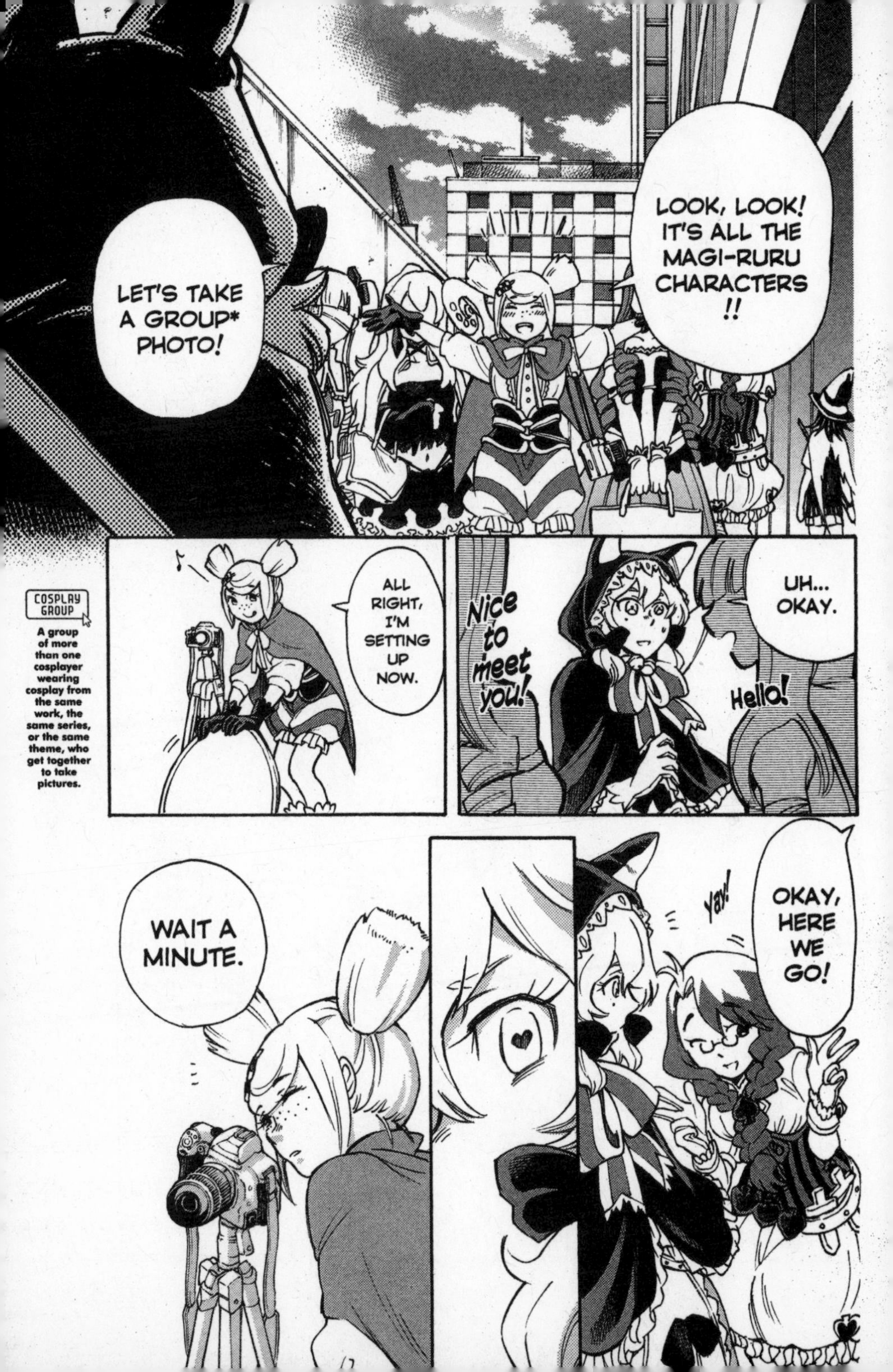
LOOK, LOOK! IT'S ALL THE MAGI-RURU CHARACTERS !!
LET'S TAKE A GROUP* PHOTO!
UH... OKAY.
Nice to meet you!
Hello!
ALL RIGHT, I'M SETTING UP NOW.
OKAY, HERE WE GO!
yay!
WAIT A MINUTE.

COSPLAY GROUP

A group of more than one cosplayer wearing cosplay from the same work, the same series, or the same theme, who get together to take pictures.

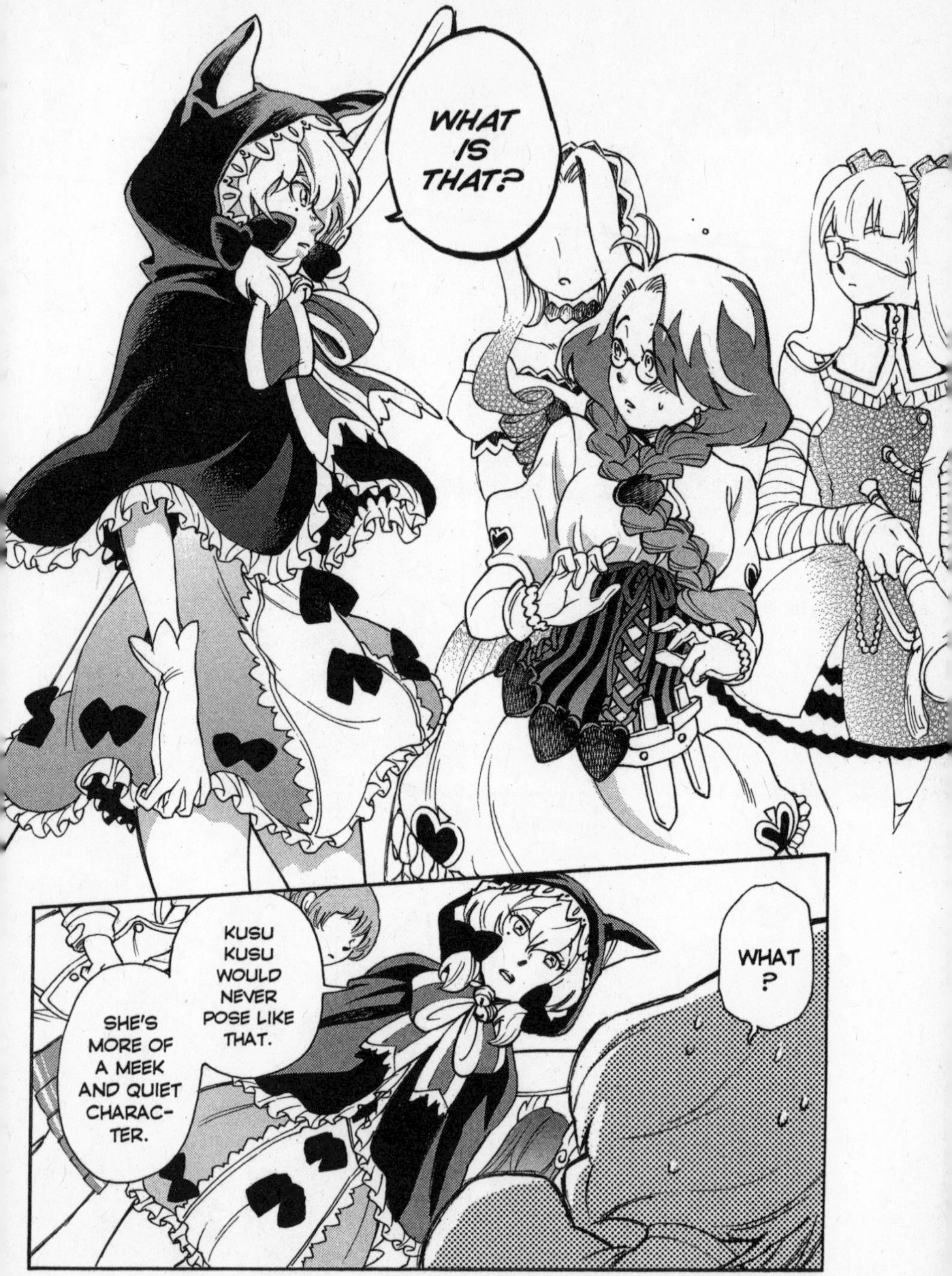
WHAT IS THAT?
WHAT ?
KUSU KUSU WOULD NEVER POSE LIKE THAT.
SHE'S MORE OF A MEEK AND QUIET CHARAC-TER.

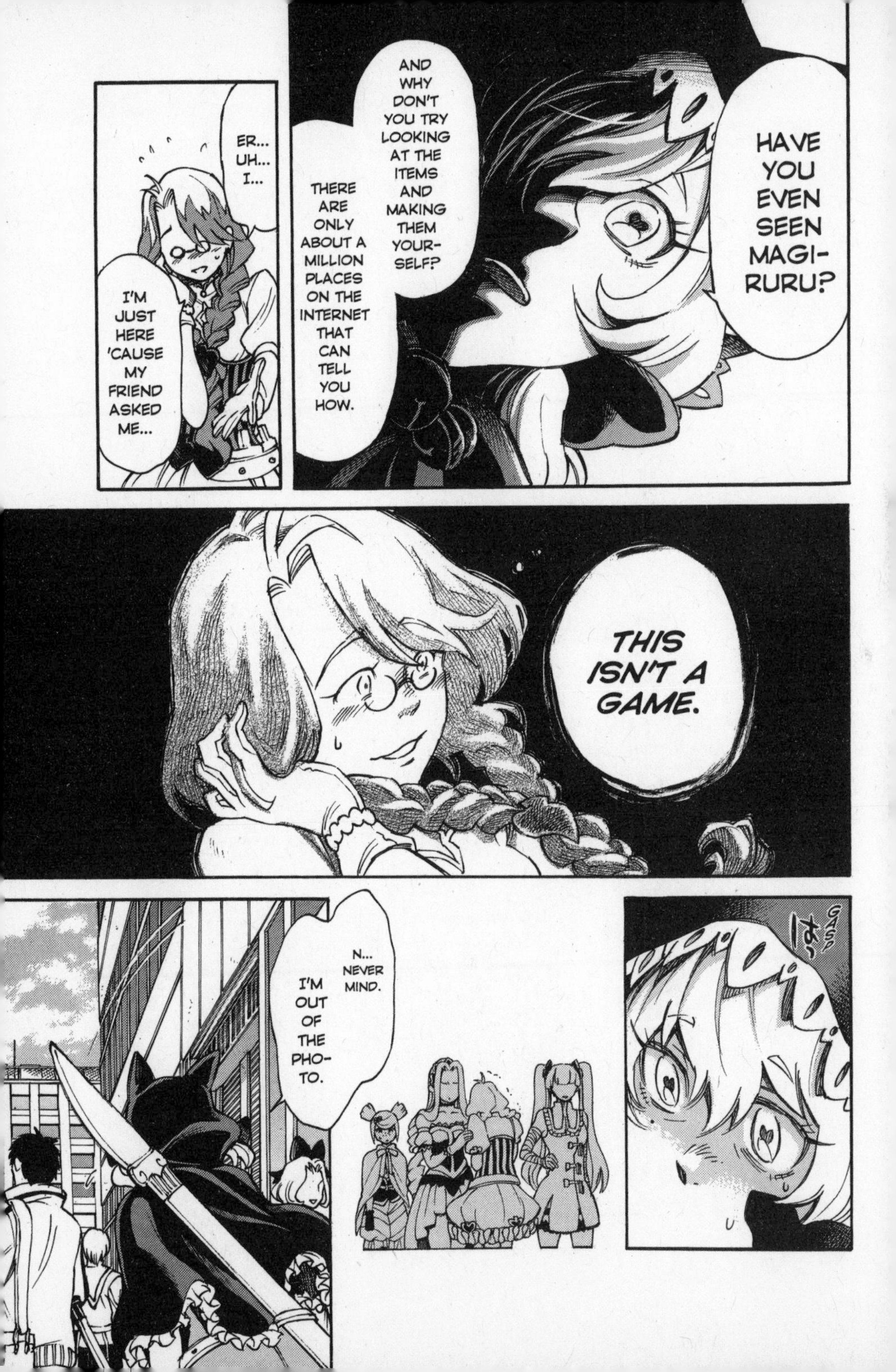
HAVE YOU EVEN SEEN MAGI-RURU?
AND WHY DON'T YOU TRY LOOKING AT THE ITEMS AND MAKING THEM YOUR-SELF?
THERE ARE ONLY ABOUT A MILLION PLACES ON THE INTERNET THAT CAN TELL YOU HOW.
ER... UH... I...
I'M JUST HERE 'CAUSE MY FRIEND ASKED ME...
THIS ISN'T A GAME.
GASP
N... NEVER MIND.
I'M OUT OF THE PHO-TO.

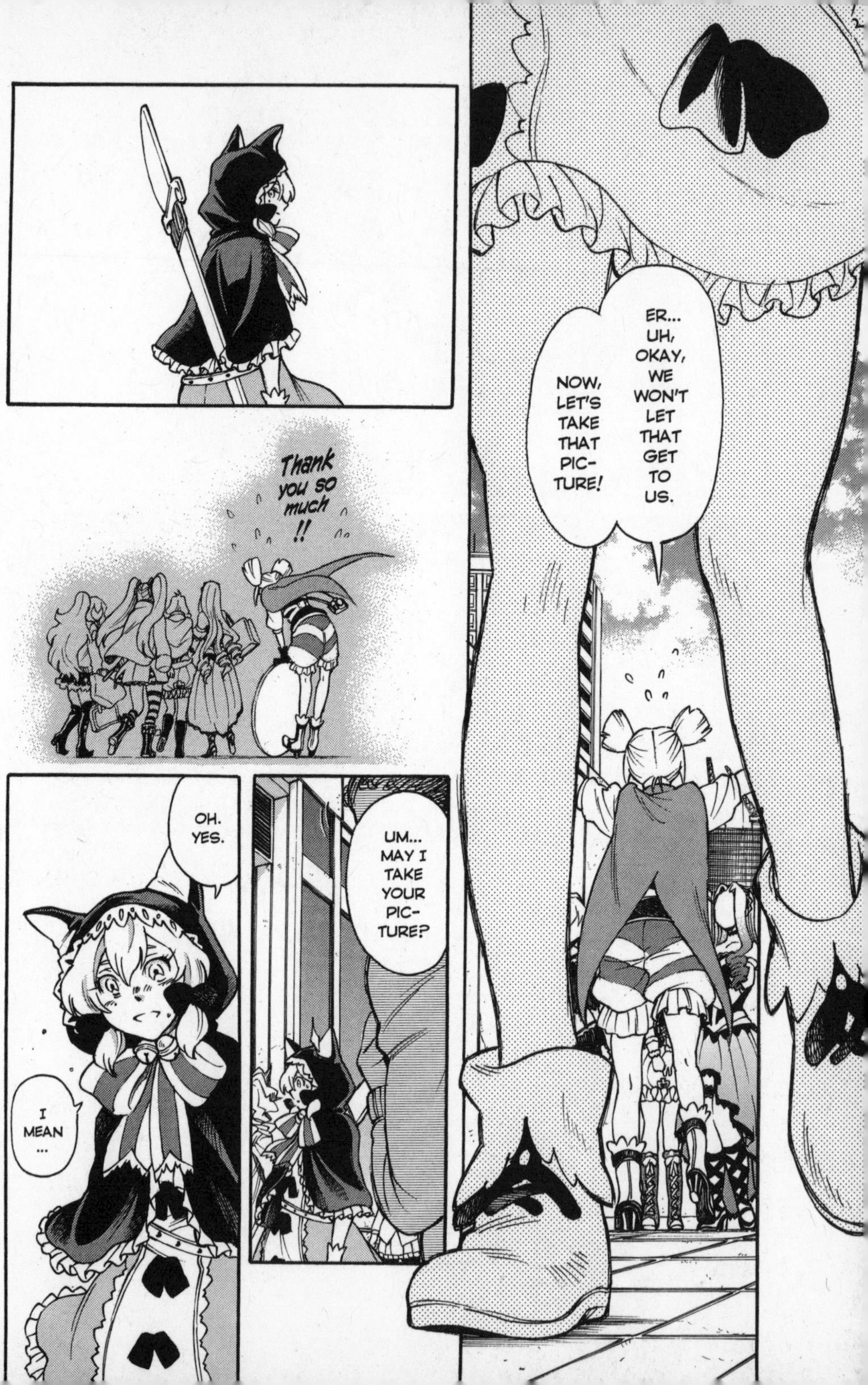

ER... UH, OKAY, WE WON'T LET THAT GET TO US.
NOW, LET'S TAKE THAT PIC-TURE!
Thank you so much !!
UM... MAY I TAKE YOUR PIC-TURE?
OH. YES.
I MEAN ...

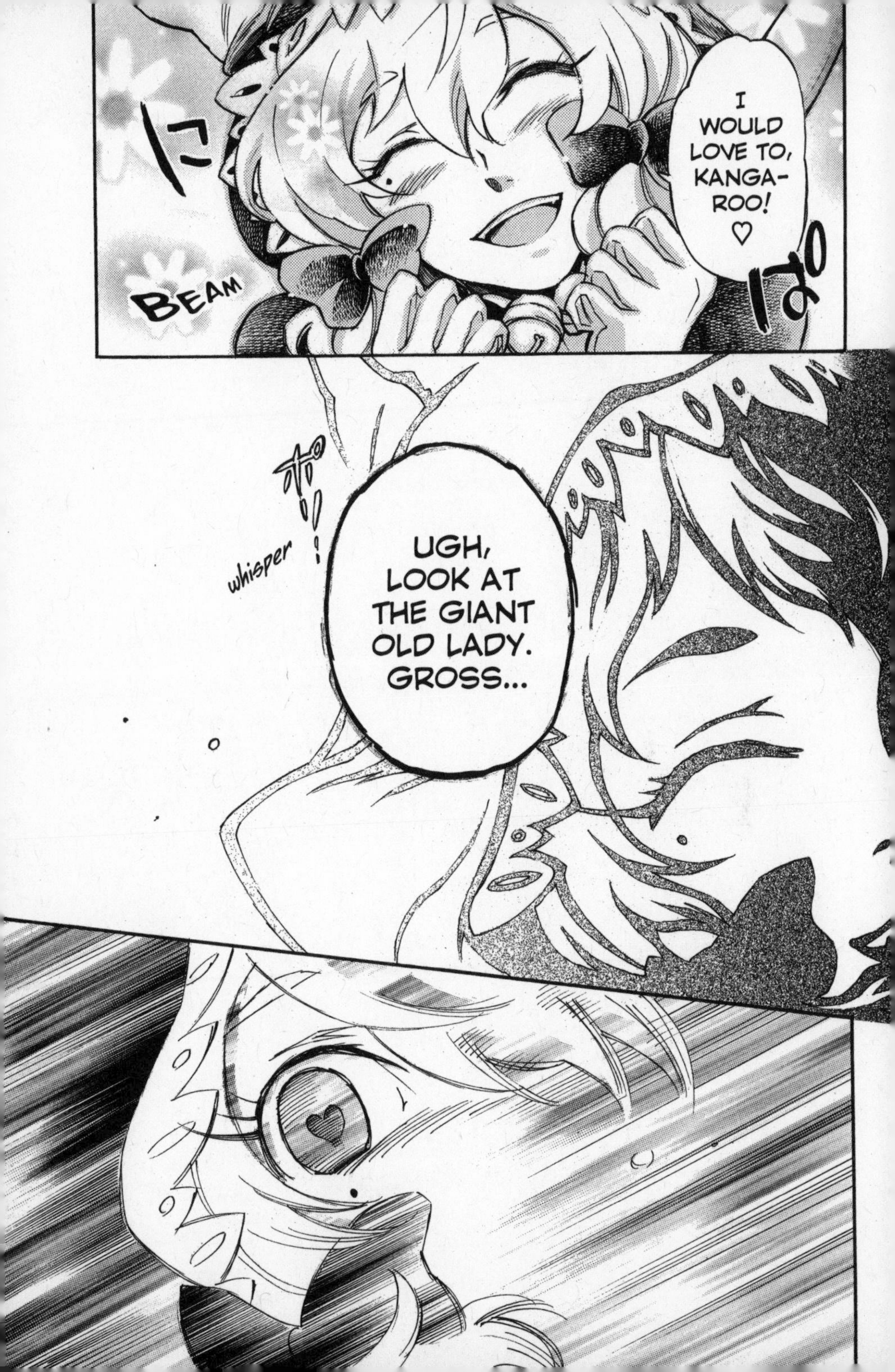
I WOULD LOVE TO, KANGA-ROO! ♡
BEAM
UGH, LOOK AT THE GIANT OLD LADY. GROSS...
whisper

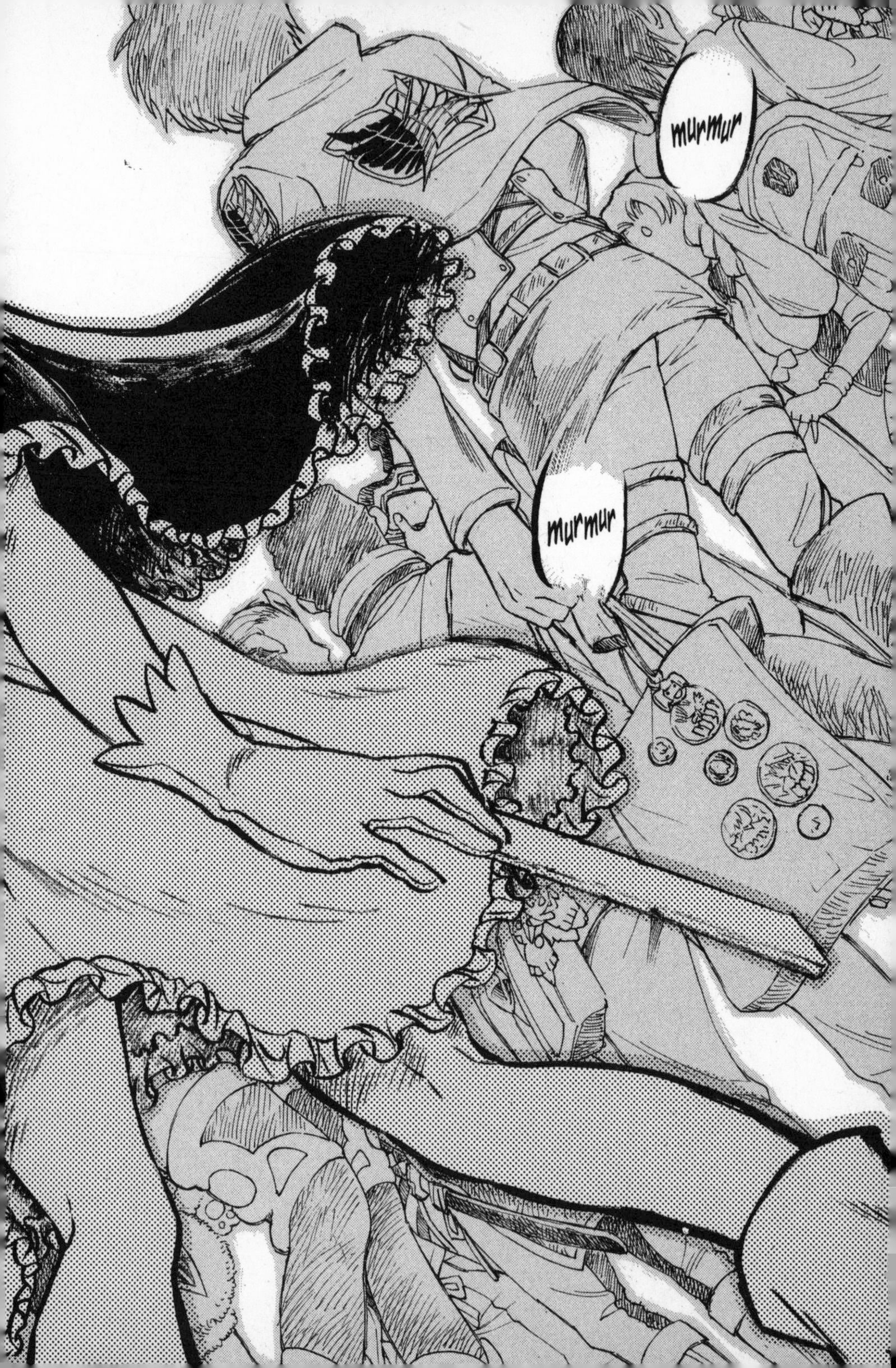
murmur
murmur

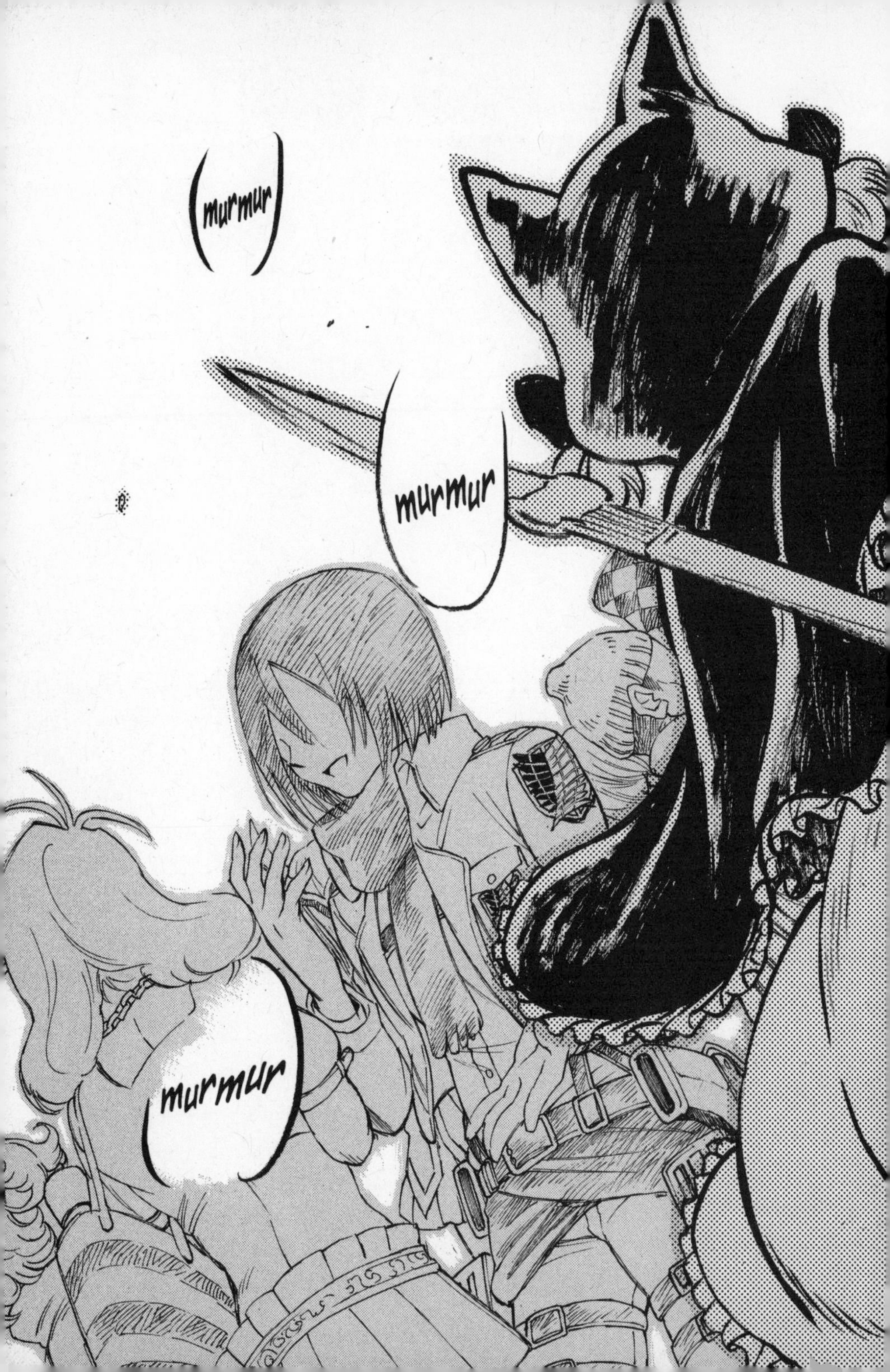
murmur
murmur
murmur

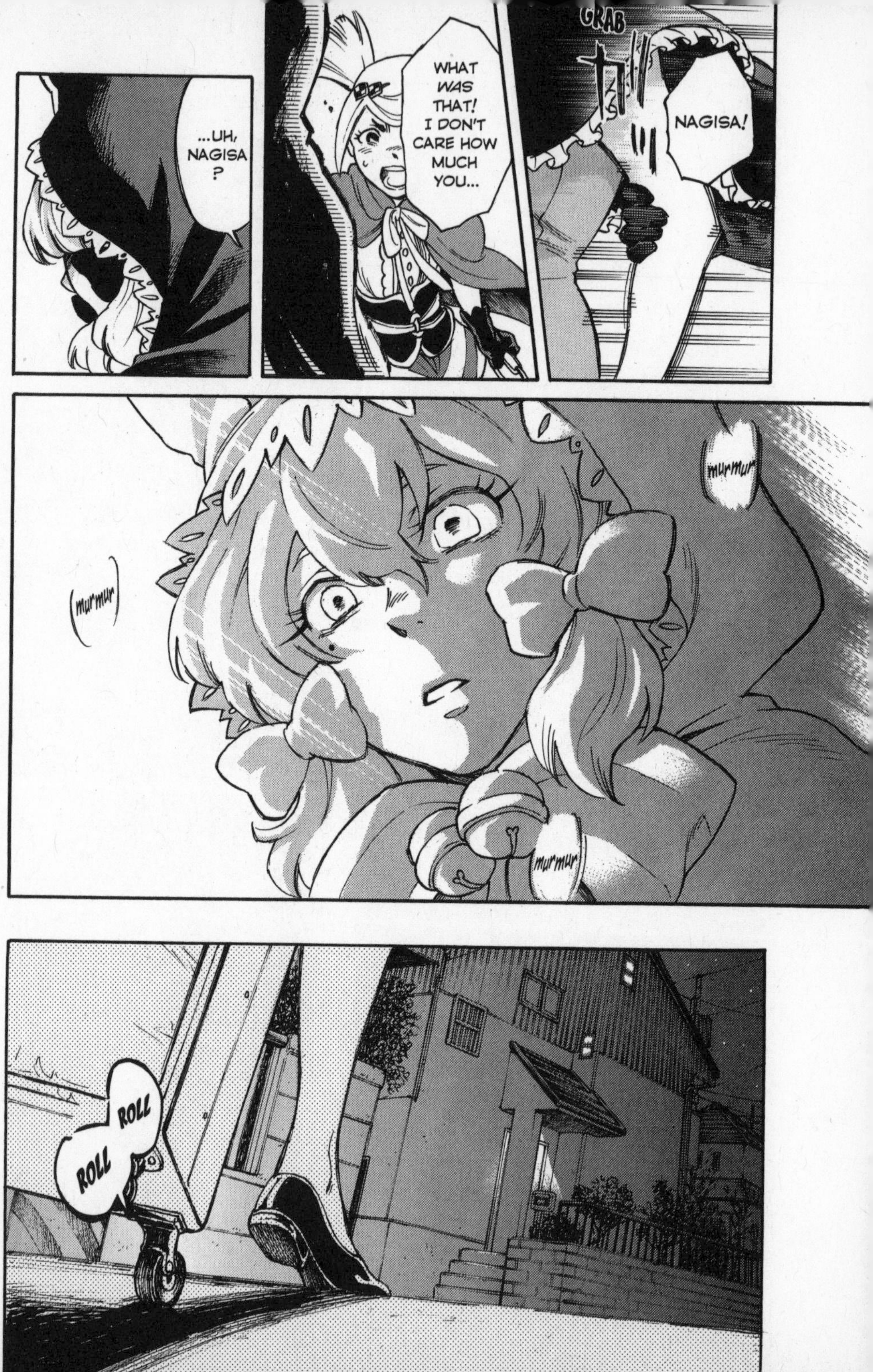
GRAB
NAGISA!
WHAT WAS THAT! I DON'T CARE HOW MUCH YOU...
...UH, NAGISA?
murmur
murmur
murmur
ROLL ROLL

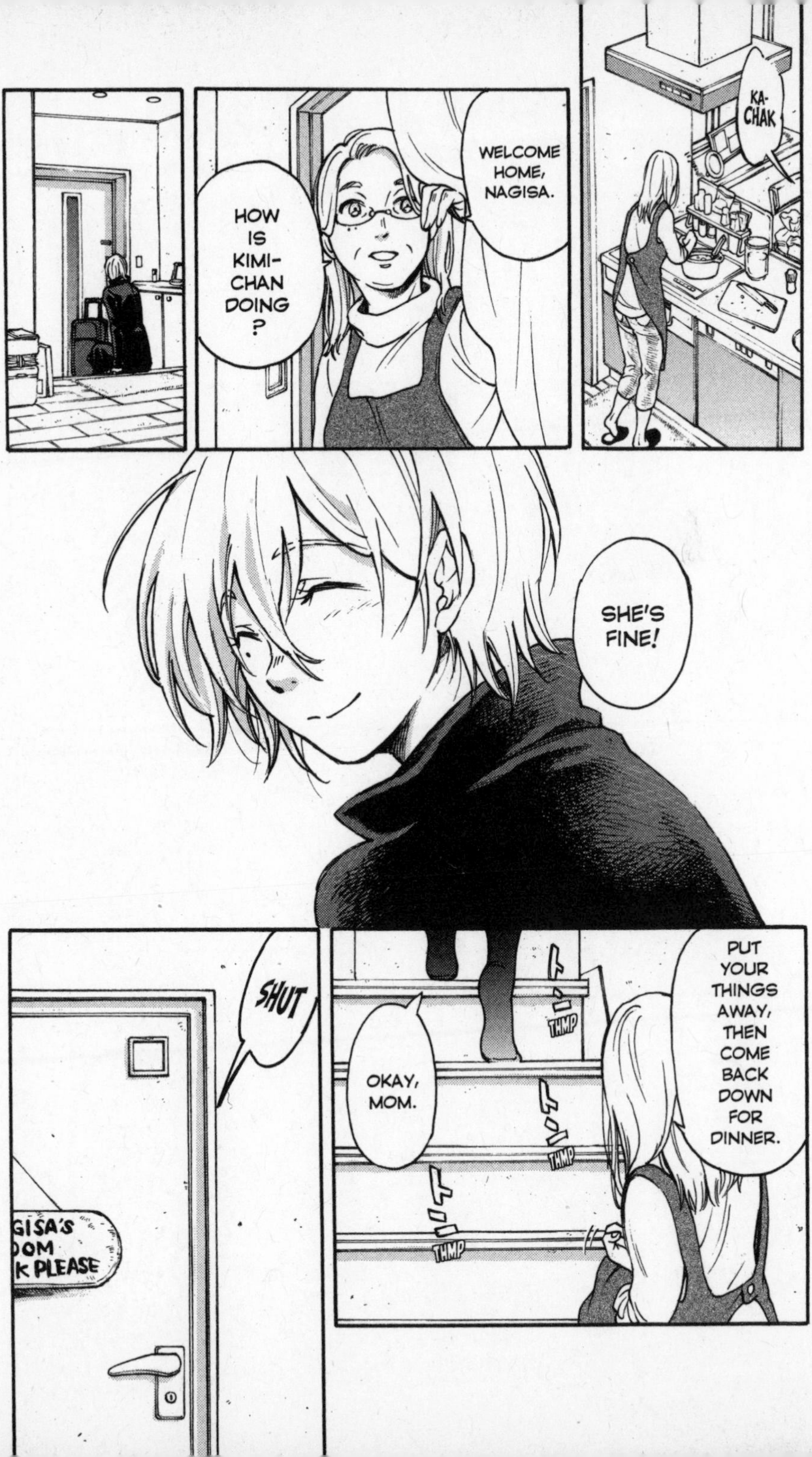
KA-CHAK
WELCOME HOME, NAGISA.
HOW IS KIMI-CHAN DOING?
SHE'S FINE!
PUT YOUR THINGS AWAY, THEN COME BACK DOWN FOR DINNER.
THMP
OKAY, MOM.
THMP
THMP
SHUT
GISA'S
OOM
K PLEASE

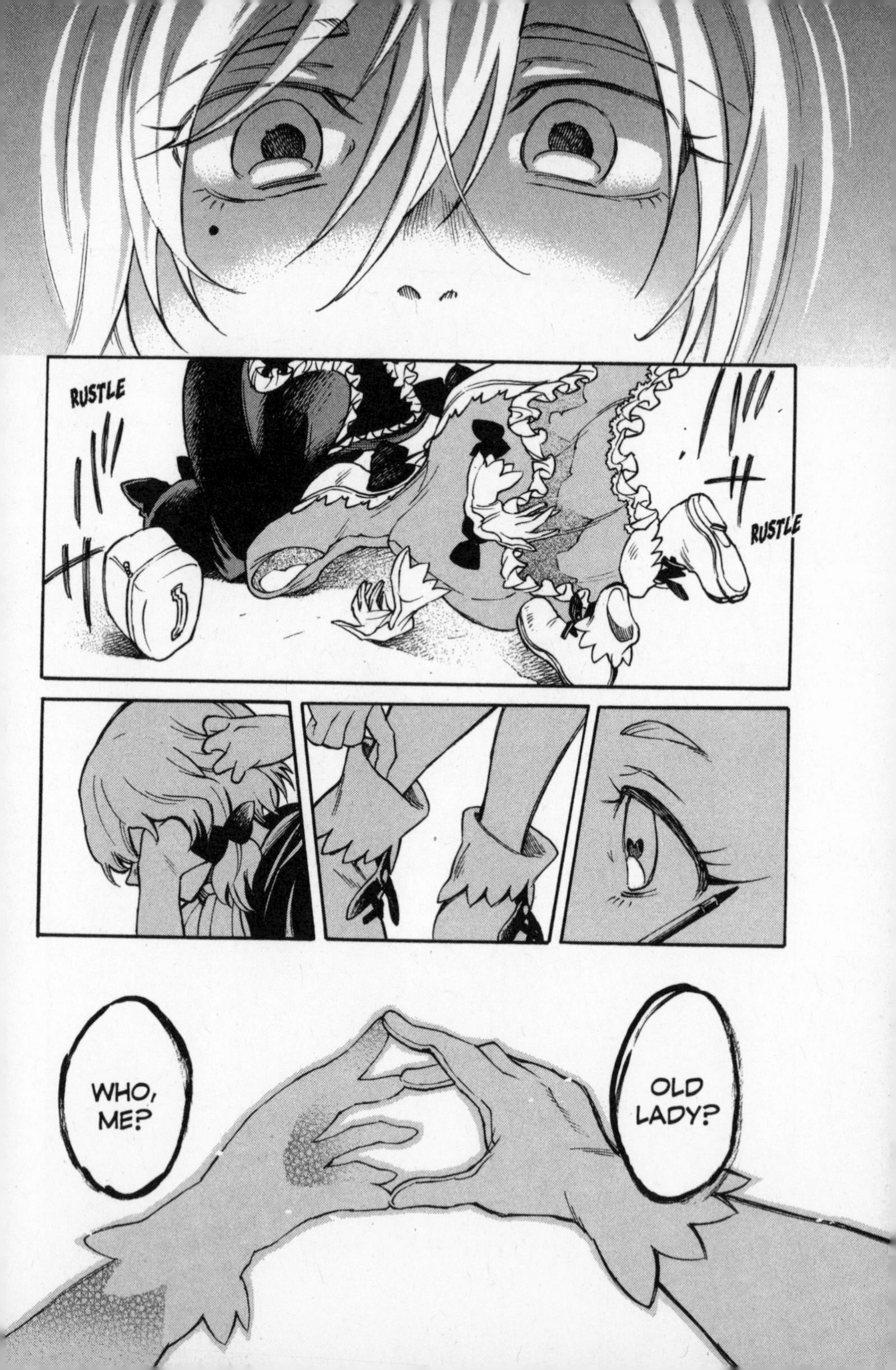
RUSTLE
RUSTLE
OLD LADY?
WHO, ME?

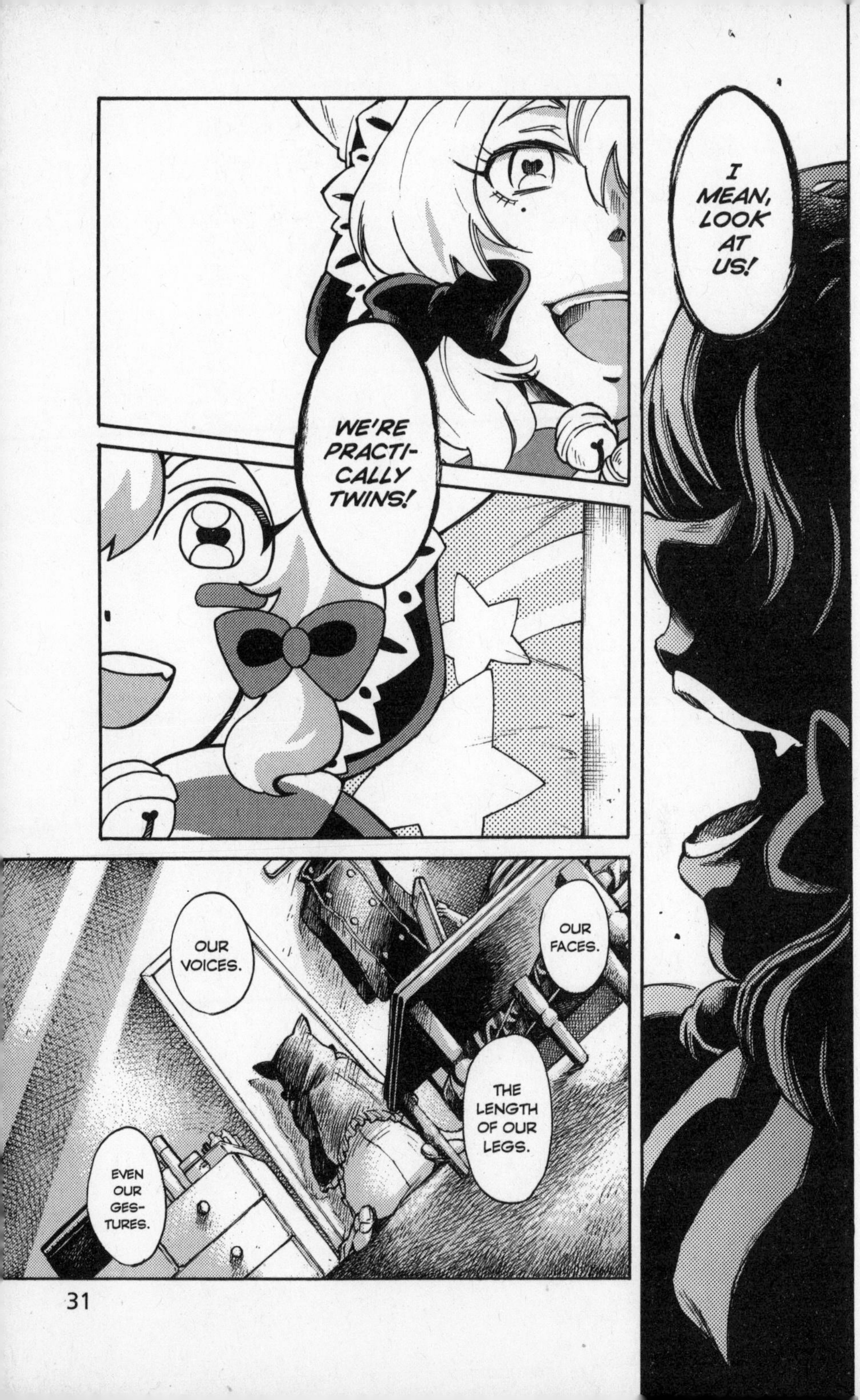
I MEAN, LOOK AT US!
WE'RE PRACTI-CALLY TWINS!
OUR FACES.
OUR VOICES.
THE LENGTH OF OUR LEGS.
EVEN OUR GES-TURES.

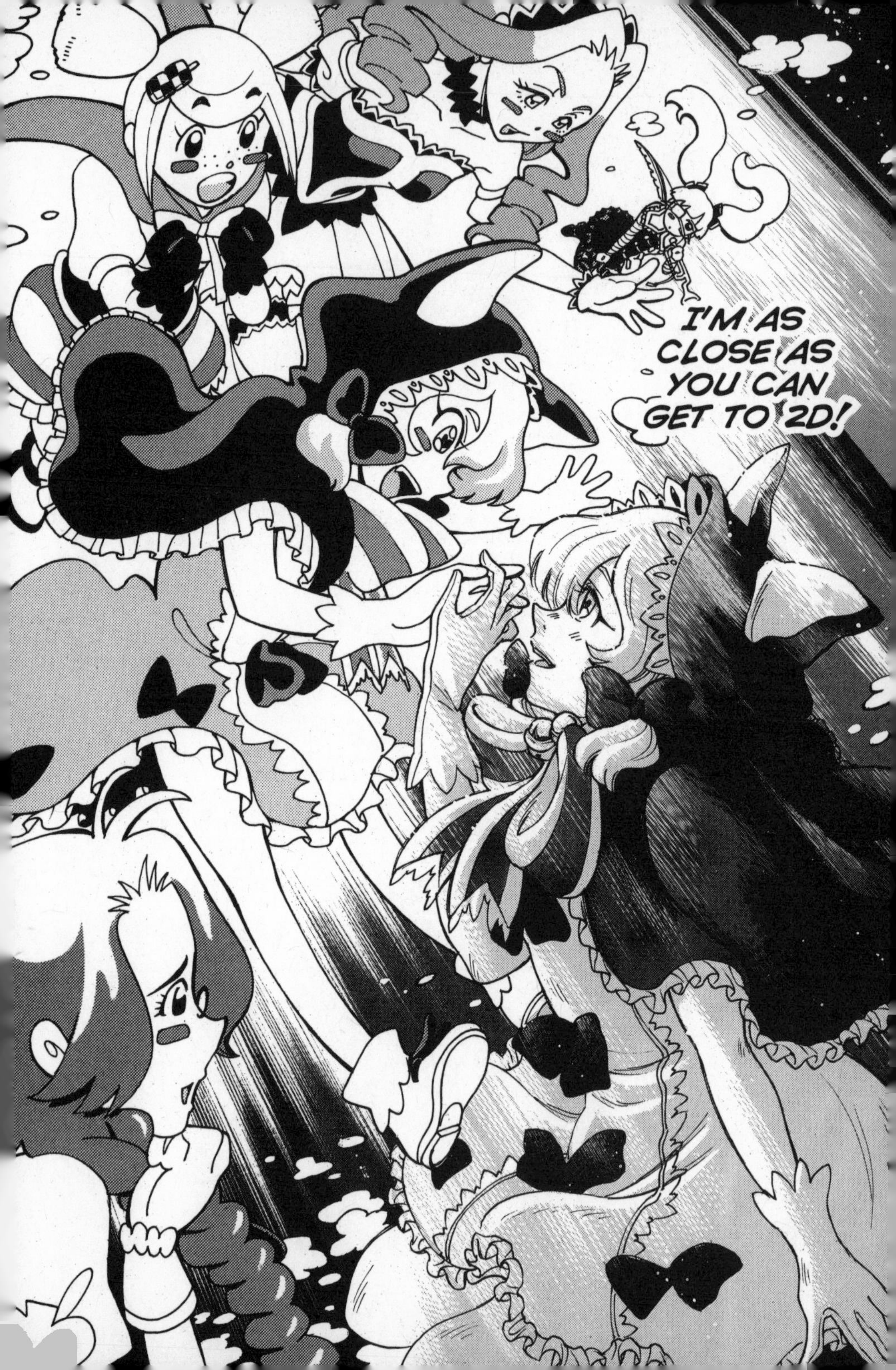
I'M AS CLOSE AS YOU CAN GET TO 2D!

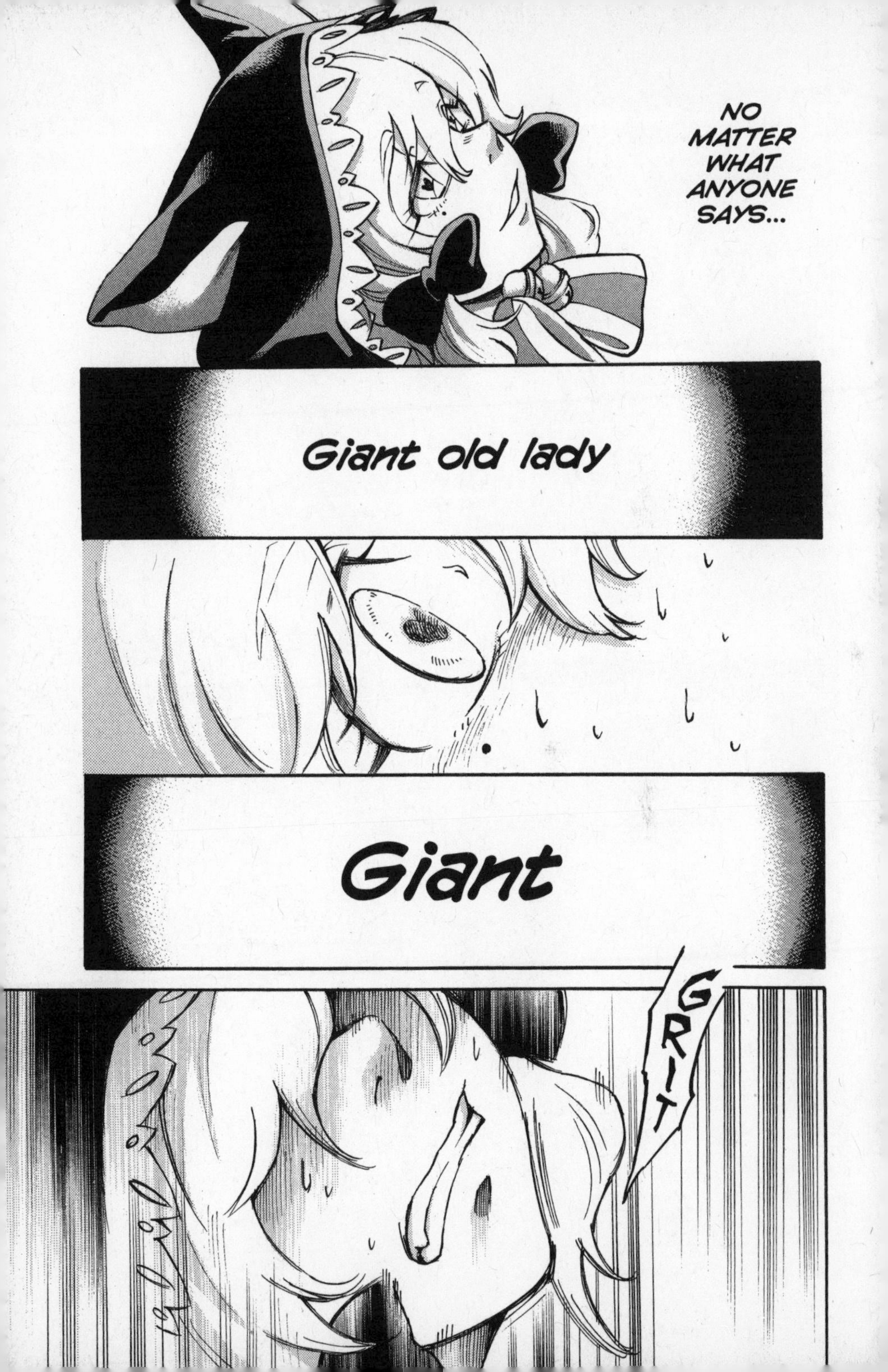
NO MATTER WHAT ANYONE SAYS...
Giant old lady
Giant
GRIT

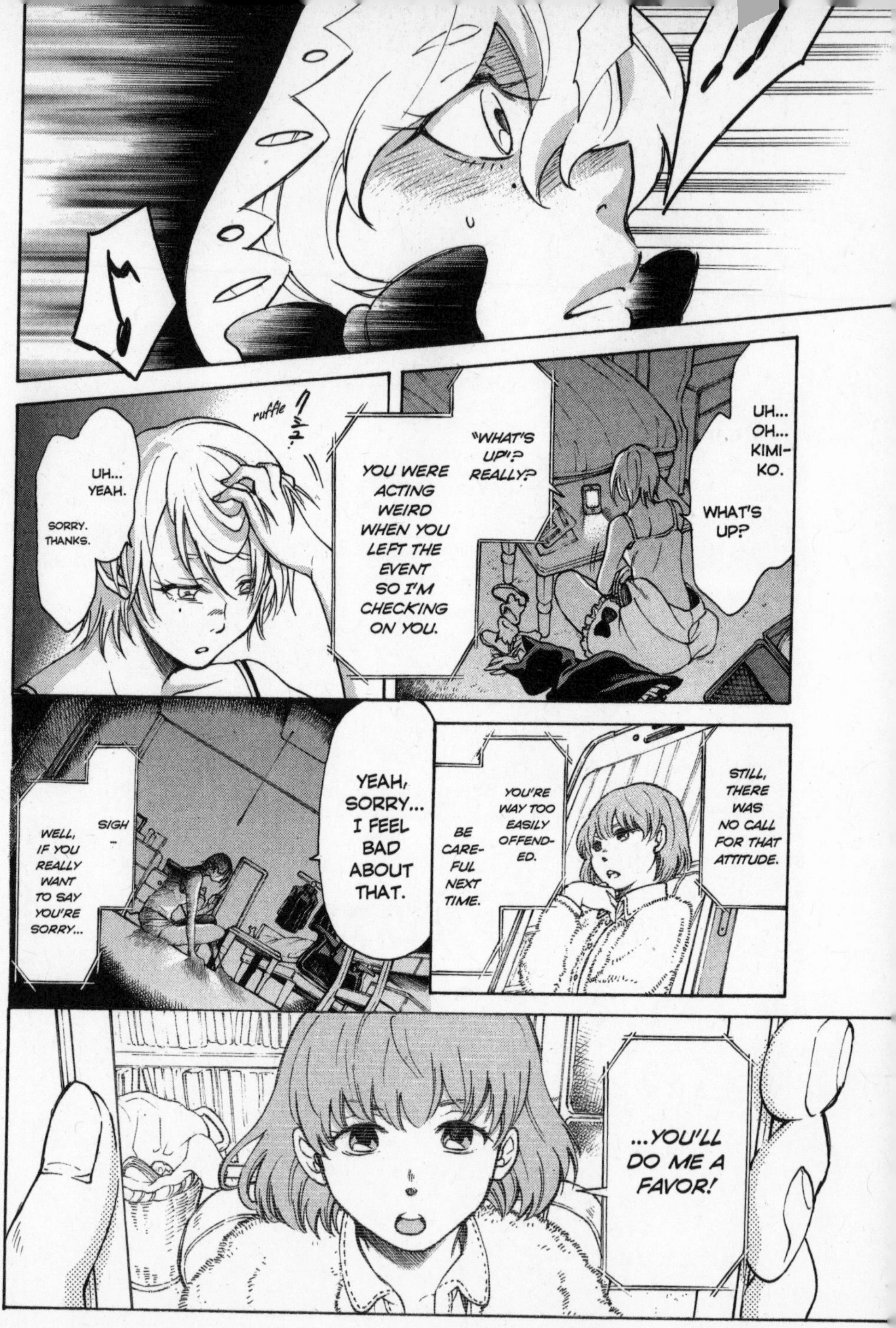
UH... OH... KIMI-KO.
WHAT'S UP?
"WHAT'S UP"? REALLY?
YOU WERE ACTING WEIRD WHEN YOU LEFT THE EVENT SO I'M CHECKING ON YOU.
ruffle
UH... YEAH.
SORRY. THANKS.
STILL, THERE WAS NO CALL FOR THAT ATTITUDE.
YOU'RE WAY TOO EASILY OFFEND-ED.
BE CARE-FUL NEXT TIME.
YEAH, SORRY... I FEEL BAD ABOUT THAT.
SIGH
WELL, IF YOU REALLY WANT TO SAY YOU'RE SORRY...
...YOU'LL DO ME A FAVOR!

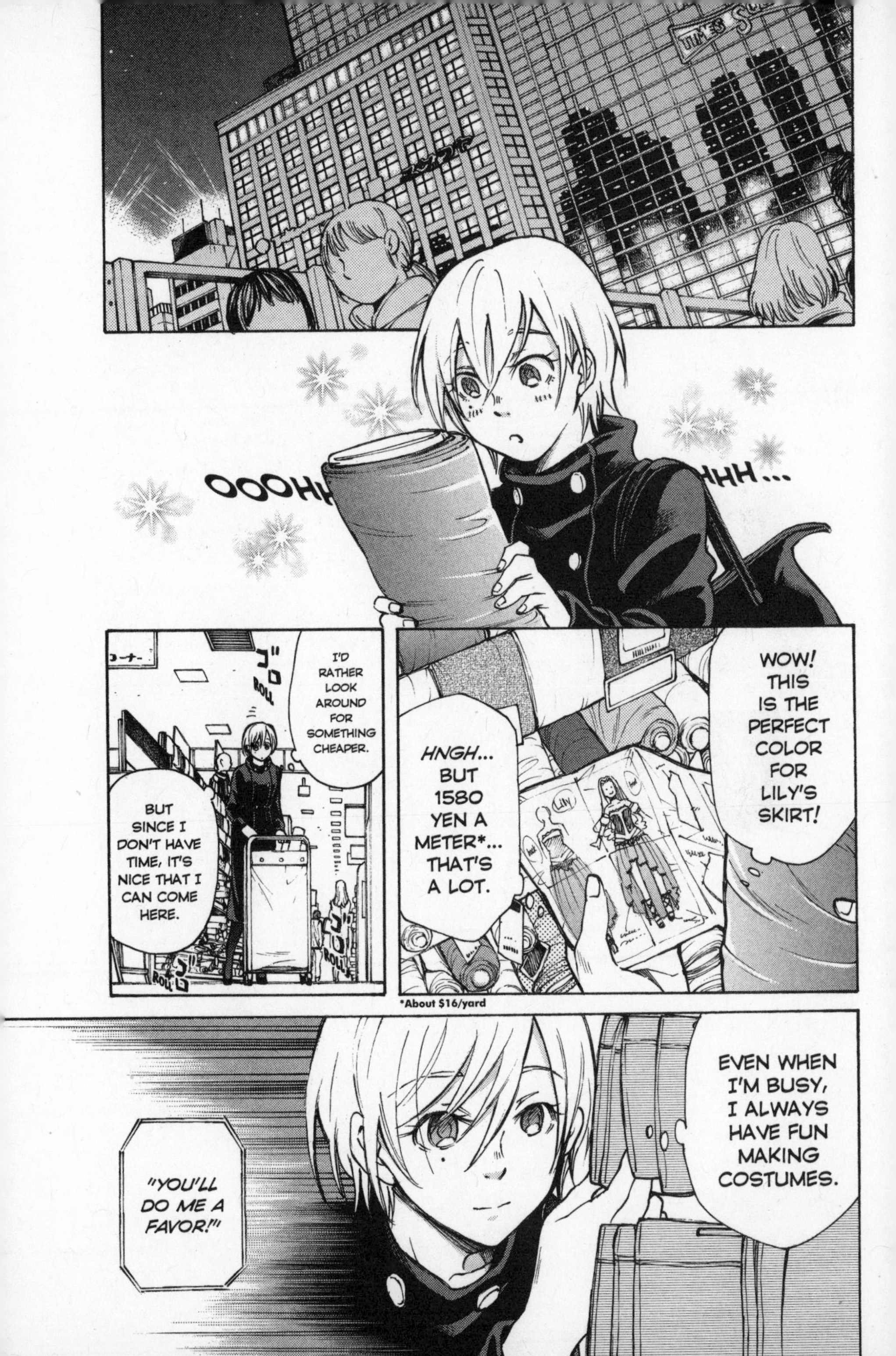
OOOHH HHH...
WOW! THIS IS THE PERFECT COLOR FOR LILY'S SKIRT!
HNGH... BUT 1580 YEN A METER*... THAT'S A LOT.
I'D RATHER LOOK AROUND FOR SOMETHING CHEAPER.
BUT SINCE I DON'T HAVE TIME, IT'S NICE THAT I CAN COME HERE.
ROLL
ROLL
ROLL
EVEN WHEN I'M BUSY, I ALWAYS HAVE FUN MAKING COSTUMES.
"YOU'LL DO ME A FAVOR!"
*About $16/yard

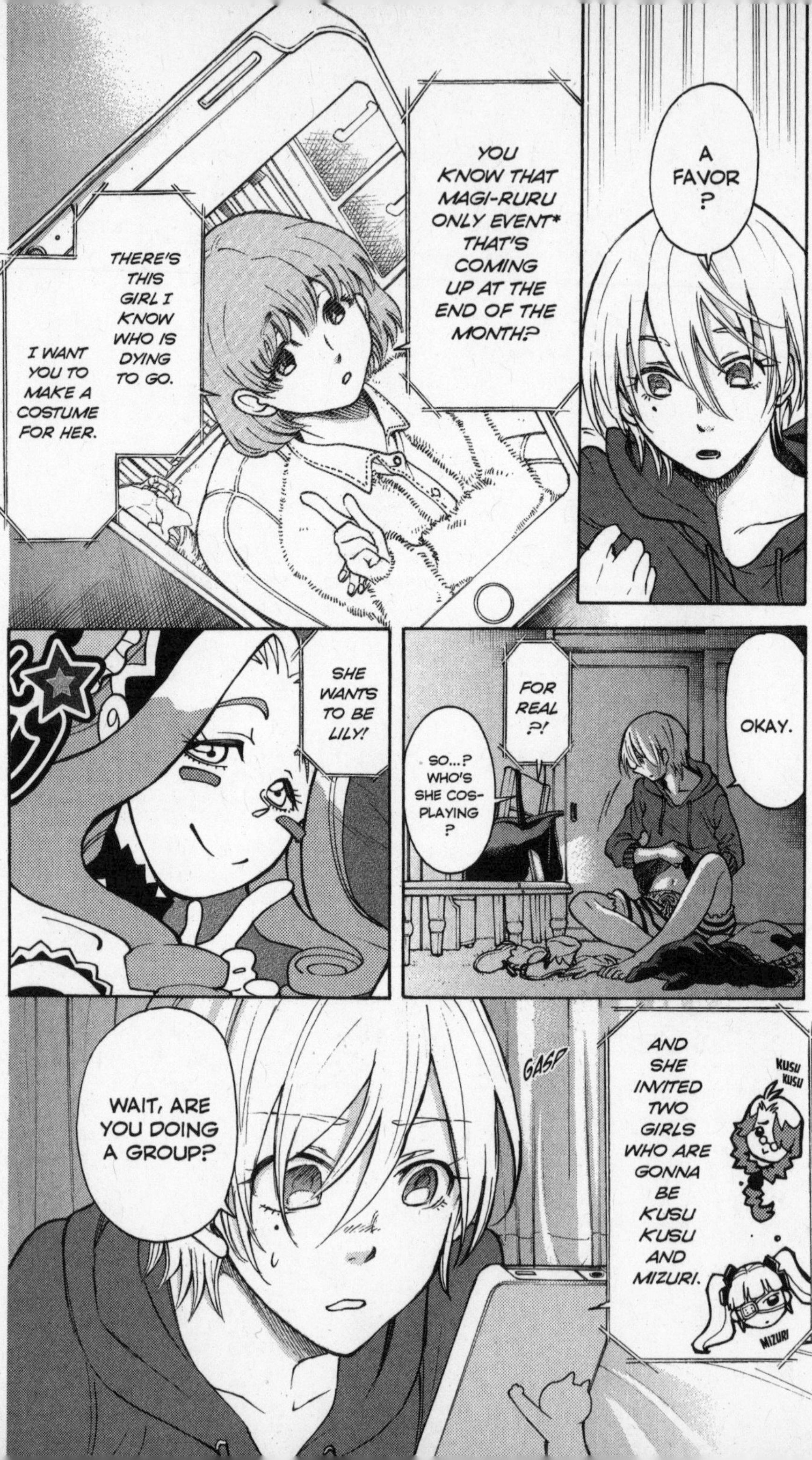

A FAVOR?
YOU KNOW THAT MAGI-RURU ONLY EVENT* THAT'S COMING UP AT THE END OF THE MONTH?
THERE'S THIS GIRL I KNOW WHO IS DYING TO GO.
I WANT YOU TO MAKE A COSTUME FOR HER.
OKAY.
FOR REAL?!
SO...? WHO'S SHE COSPLAYING?
SHE WANTS TO BE LILY!
AND SHE INVITED TWO GIRLS WHO ARE GONNA BE KUSU KUSU AND MIZURI.
KUSU KUSU
MIZURI
GASP
WAIT, ARE YOU DOING A GROUP?

ONLY EVENT

An event open only to cosplay of a specific work, genre, or theme.

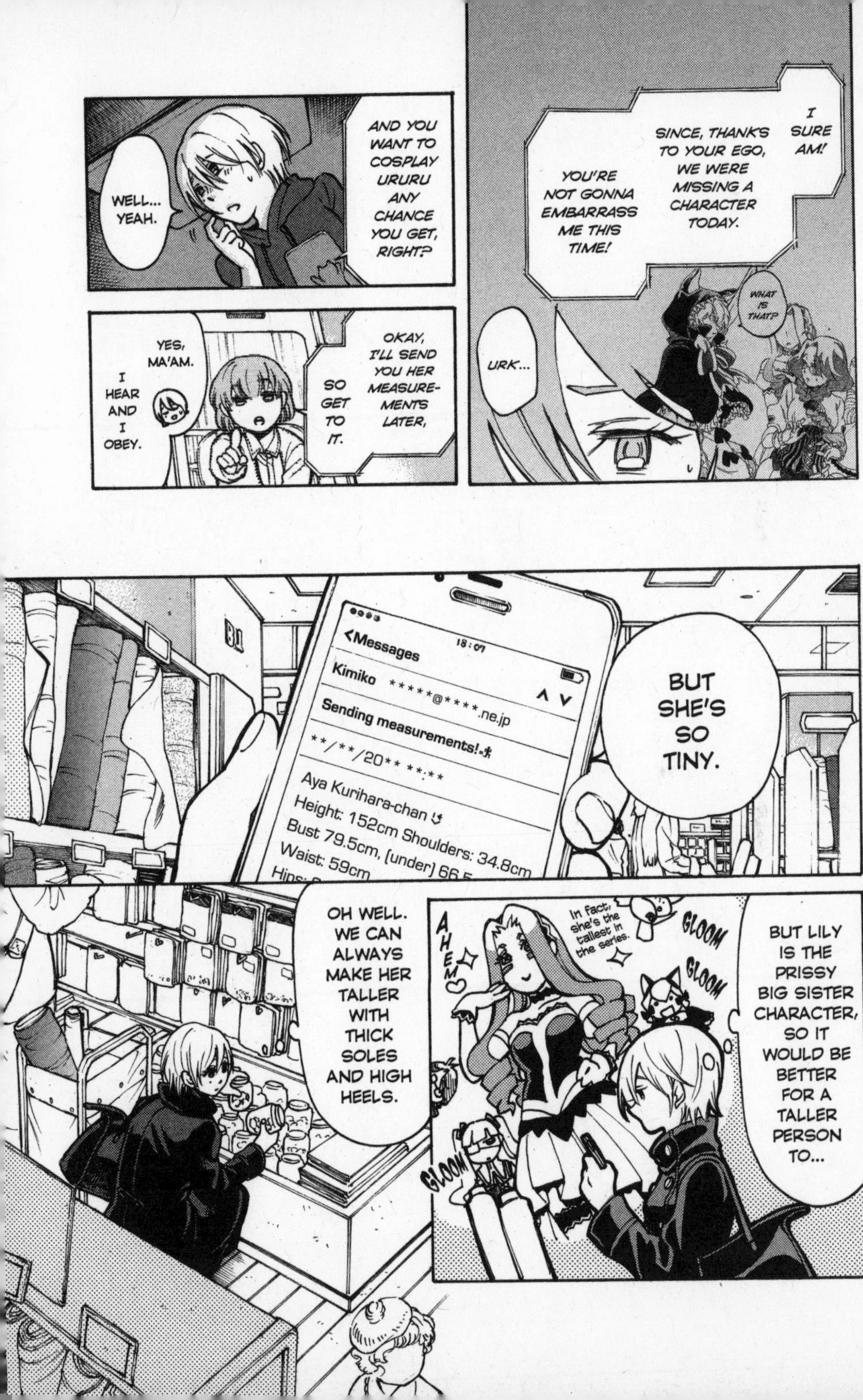
I SURE AM!
SINCE, THANKS TO YOUR EGO, WE WERE MISSING A CHARACTER TODAY.
YOU'RE NOT GONNA EMBARRASS ME THIS TIME!
WHAT IS THAT?
URK...
AND YOU WANT TO COSPLAY URURU ANY CHANCE YOU GET, RIGHT?
WELL... YEAH.
OKAY, I'LL SEND YOU HER MEASUREMENTS LATER,
SO GET TO IT.
YES, MA'AM.
I HEAR AND I OBEY.
BUT SHE'S SO TINY.
<Messages
18:07
Kimiko *****@****.ne.jp
Sending measurements!
//20** **:**
Aya Kurihara-chan
Height: 152cm Shoulders: 34.8cm
Bust 79.5cm, (under) 66.5
Waist: 59cm
BUT LILY IS THE PRISSY BIG SISTER CHARACTER, SO IT WOULD BE BETTER FOR A TALLER PERSON TO...
GLOOM
GLOOM
In fact, she's the tallest in the series.
AHEM
GLOOM
OH WELL. WE CAN ALWAYS MAKE HER TALLER WITH THICK SOLES AND HIGH HEELS.

MEASUREMENTS: Height: 5'0", Shoulders: 13.7in., Bust: 31.3in., (under) 26.2in., Waist: 23.2in.

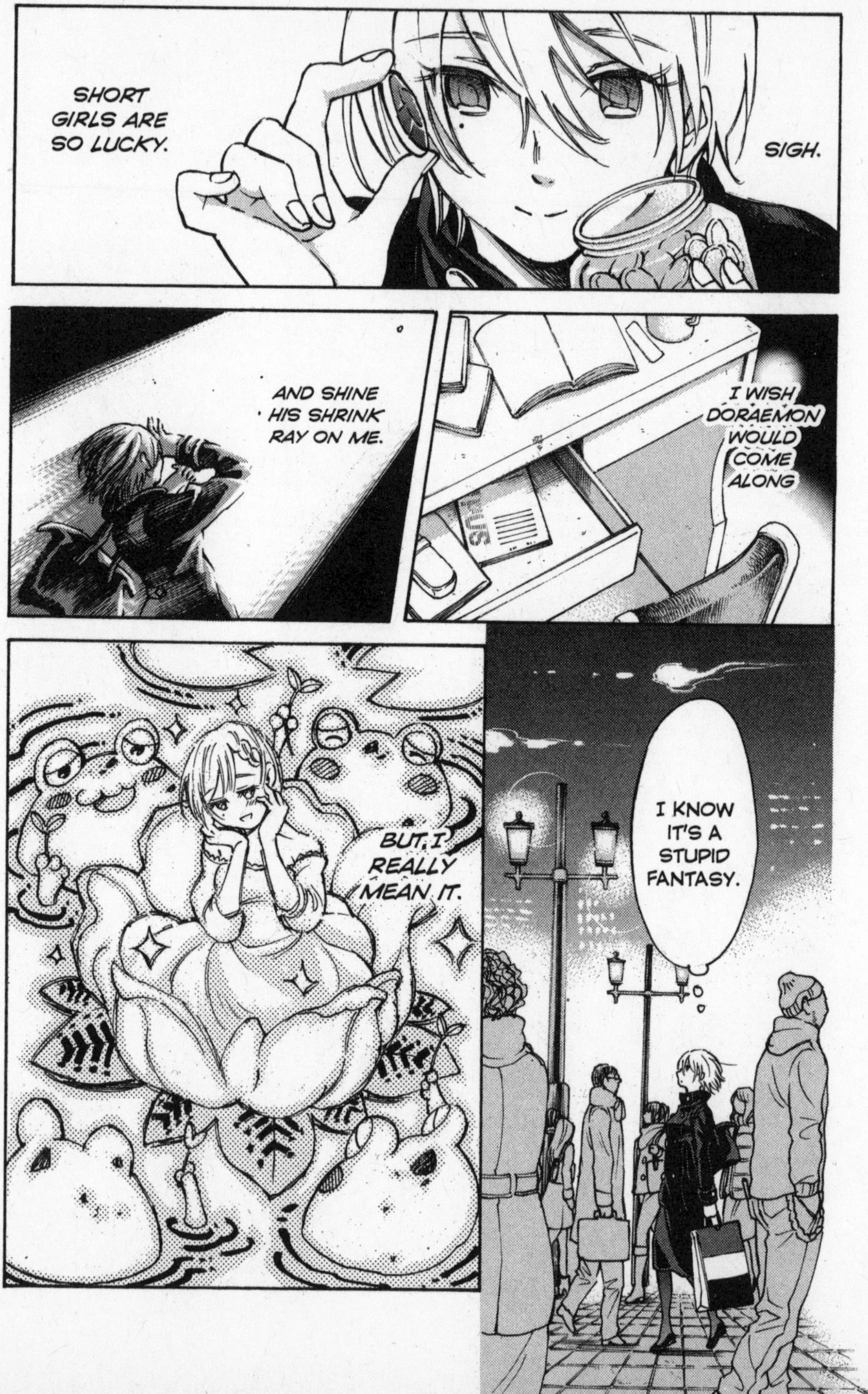
SIGH.
SHORT GIRLS ARE SO LUCKY.
I WISH DORAEMON WOULD COME ALONG
AND SHINE HIS SHRINK RAY ON ME.
I KNOW IT'S A STUPID FANTASY.
BUT I REALLY MEAN IT.

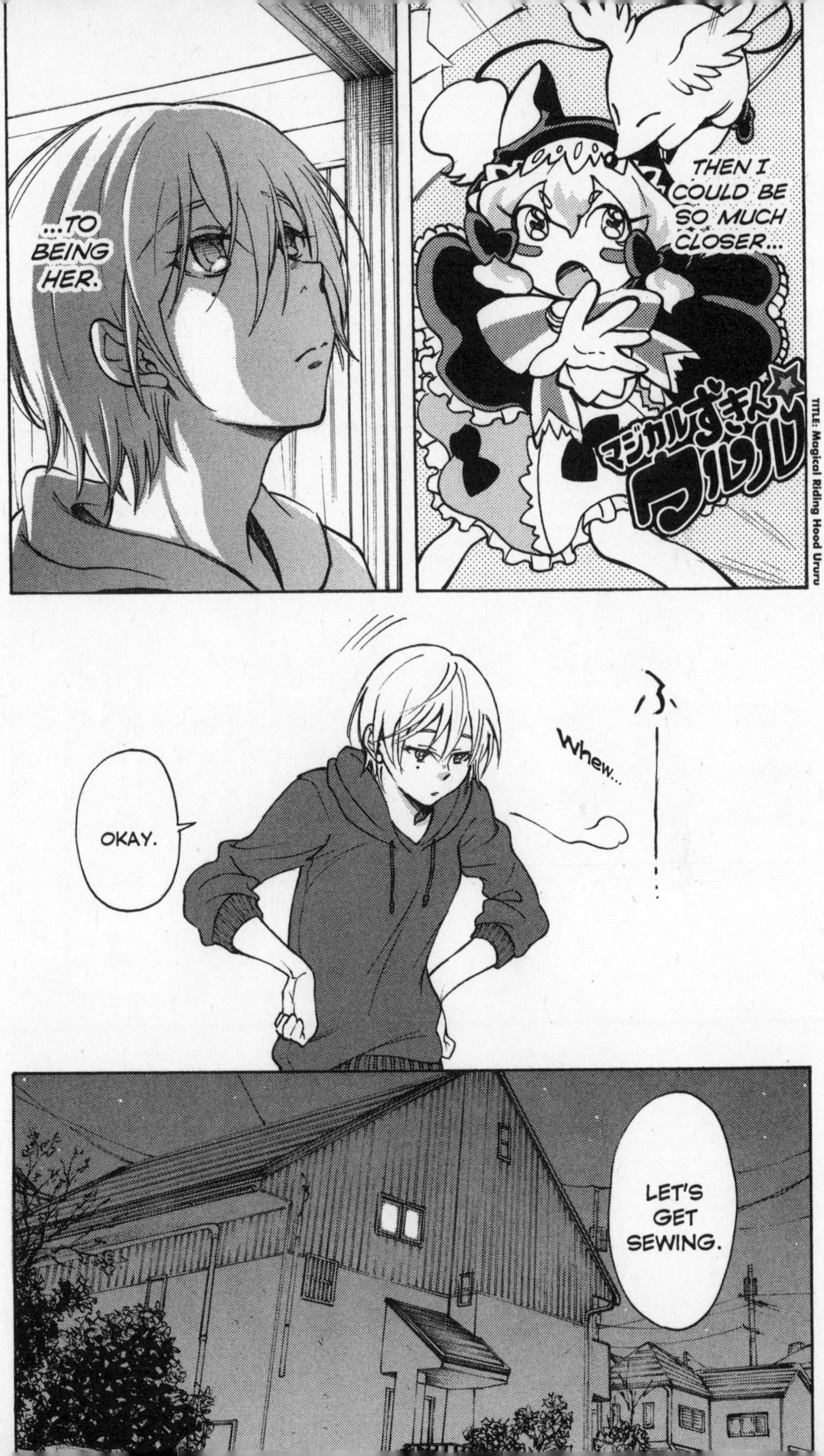
THEN I COULD BE SO MUCH CLOSER...
マジカルずきん☆ウルウル
TITLE: Magical Riding Hood Ururu
...TO BEING HER.
ふ
Whew...
OKAY.
LET'S GET SEWING.

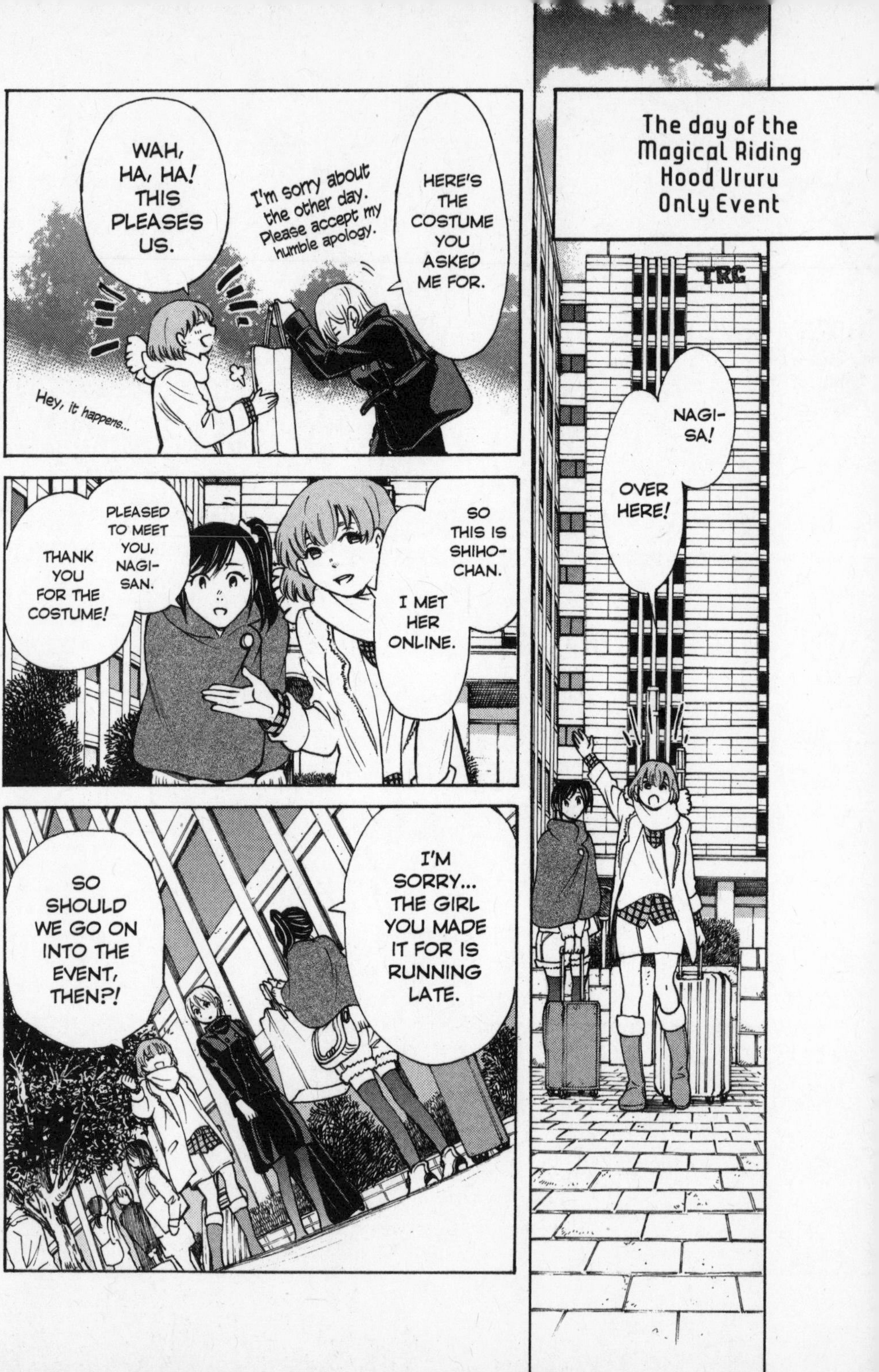
The day of the Magical Riding Hood Ururu Only Event
TRC
NAGI-SA!
OVER HERE!
HERE'S THE COSTUME YOU ASKED ME FOR.
I'm sorry about the other day. Please accept my humble apology.
WAH, HA, HA! THIS PLEASES US.
Hey, it happens...
SO THIS IS SHIHO-CHAN.
I MET HER ONLINE.
PLEASED TO MEET YOU, NAGI-SAN.
THANK YOU FOR THE COSTUME!
I'M SORRY... THE GIRL YOU MADE IT FOR IS RUNNING LATE.
SO SHOULD WE GO ON INTO THE EVENT, THEN?!

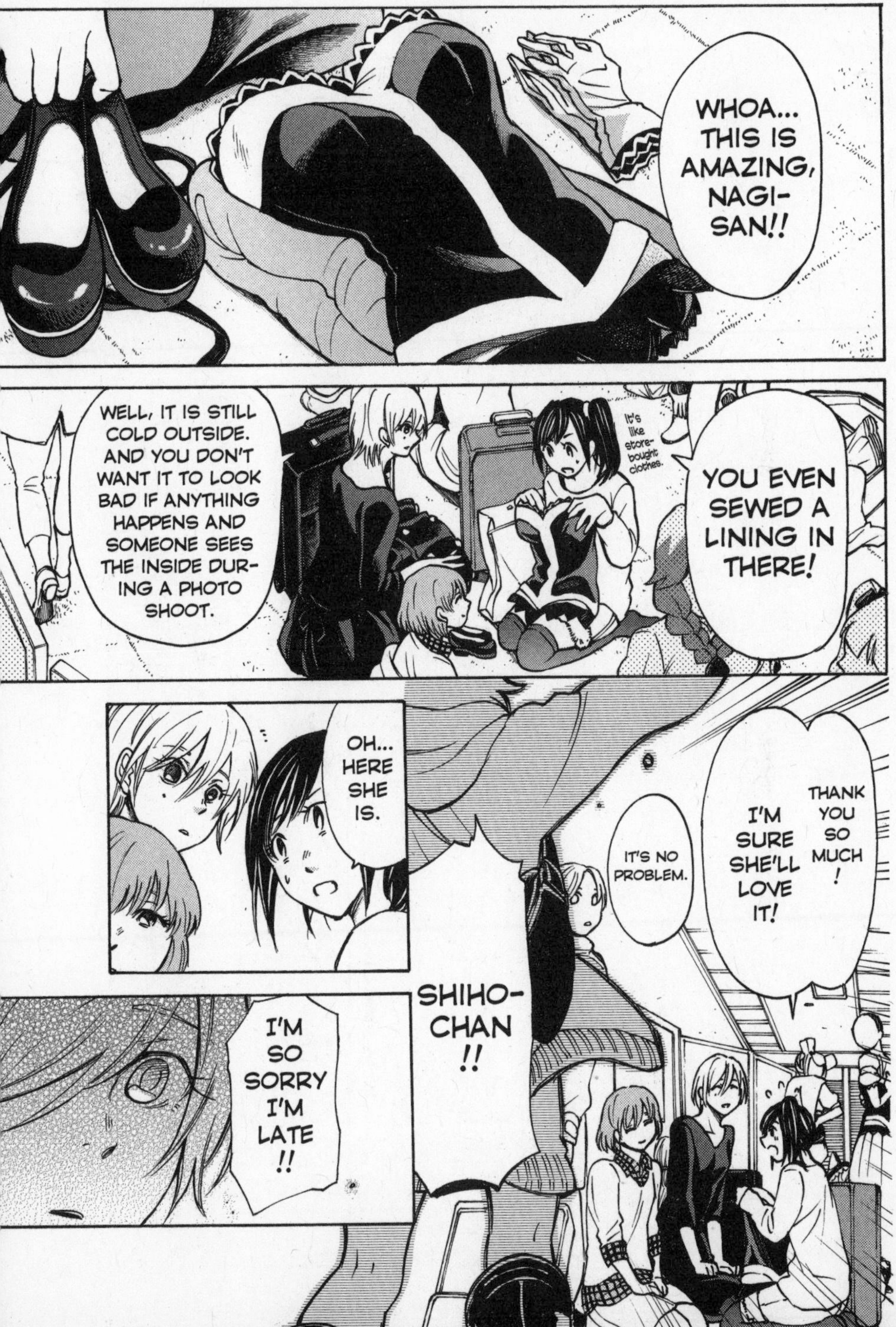
WHOA... THIS IS AMAZING, NAGI-SAN!!
YOU EVEN SEWED A LINING IN THERE!
It's like store-bought clothes.
WELL, IT IS STILL COLD OUTSIDE. AND YOU DON'T WANT IT TO LOOK BAD IF ANYTHING HAPPENS AND SOMEONE SEES THE INSIDE DURING A PHOTO SHOOT.
THANK YOU SO MUCH!
I'M SURE SHE'LL LOVE IT!
IT'S NO PROBLEM.
SHIHO-CHAN!!
OH... HERE SHE IS.
I'M SO SORRY I'M LATE!!

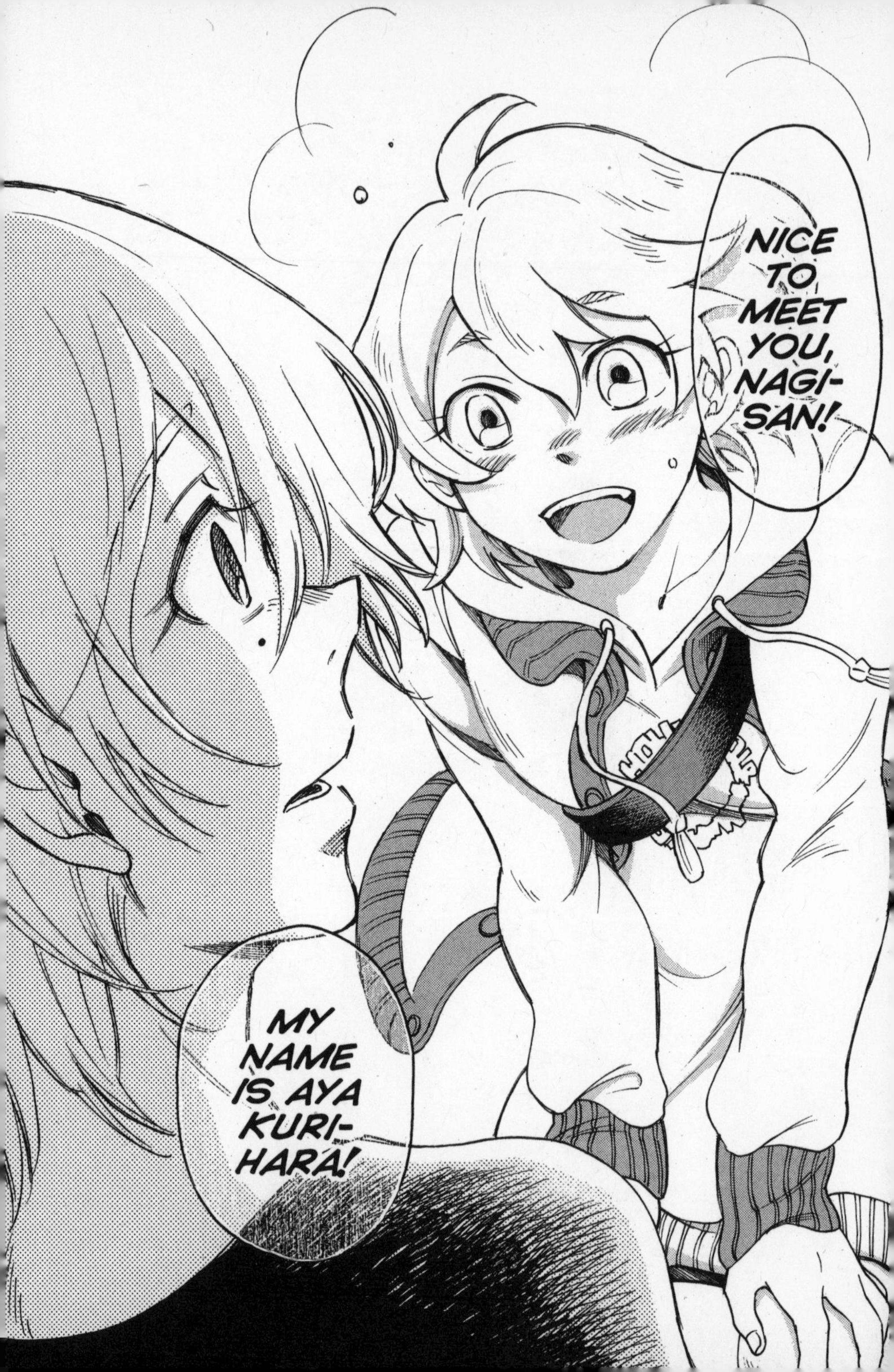
NICE TO MEET YOU, NAGI-SAN!
MY NAME IS AYA KURI-HARA!

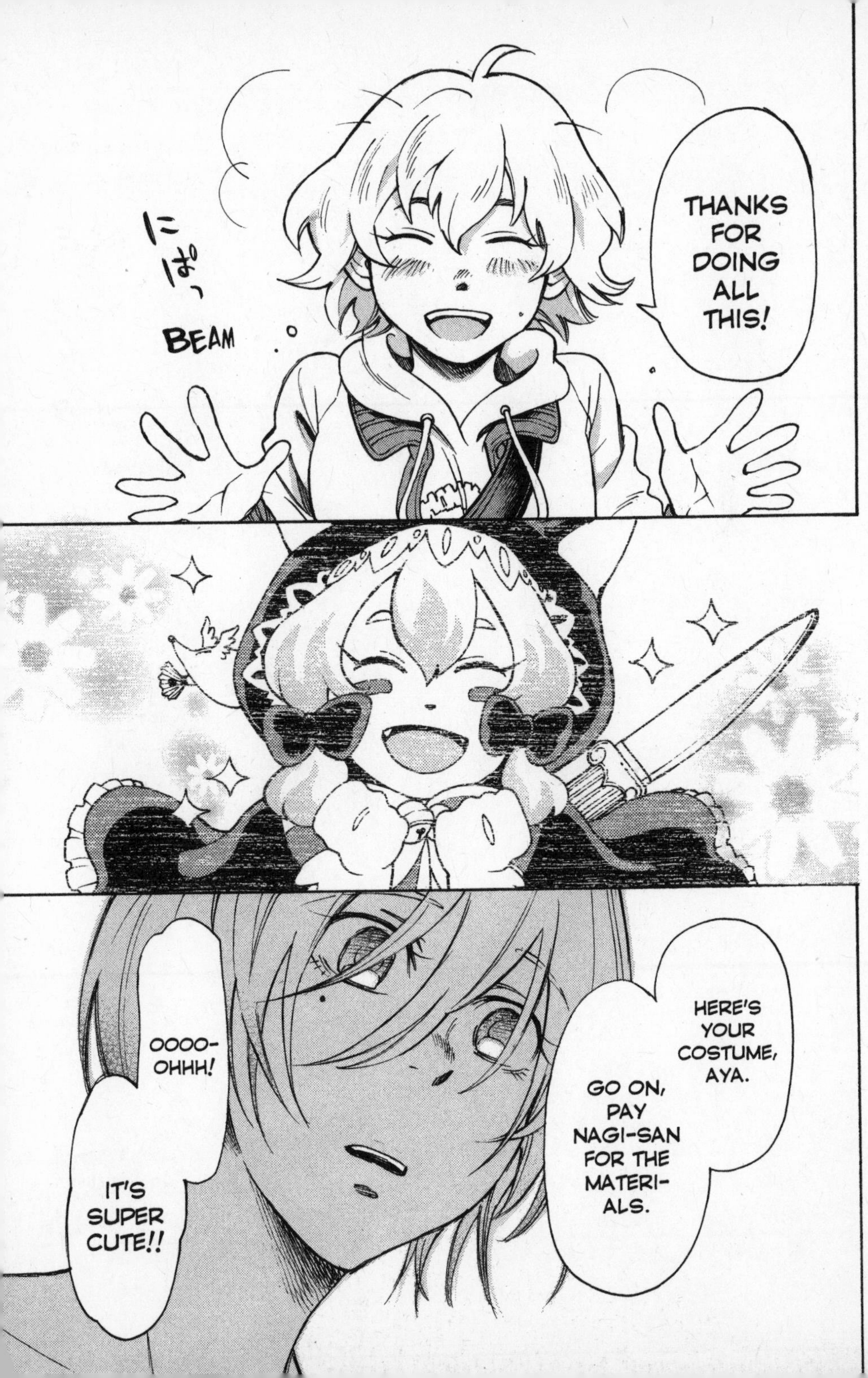
THANKS FOR DOING ALL THIS!
にぱ、
BEAM
HERE'S YOUR COSTUME, AYA.
GO ON, PAY NAGI-SAN FOR THE MATERI-ALS.
OOOO-OHHH!
IT'S SUPER CUTE!!

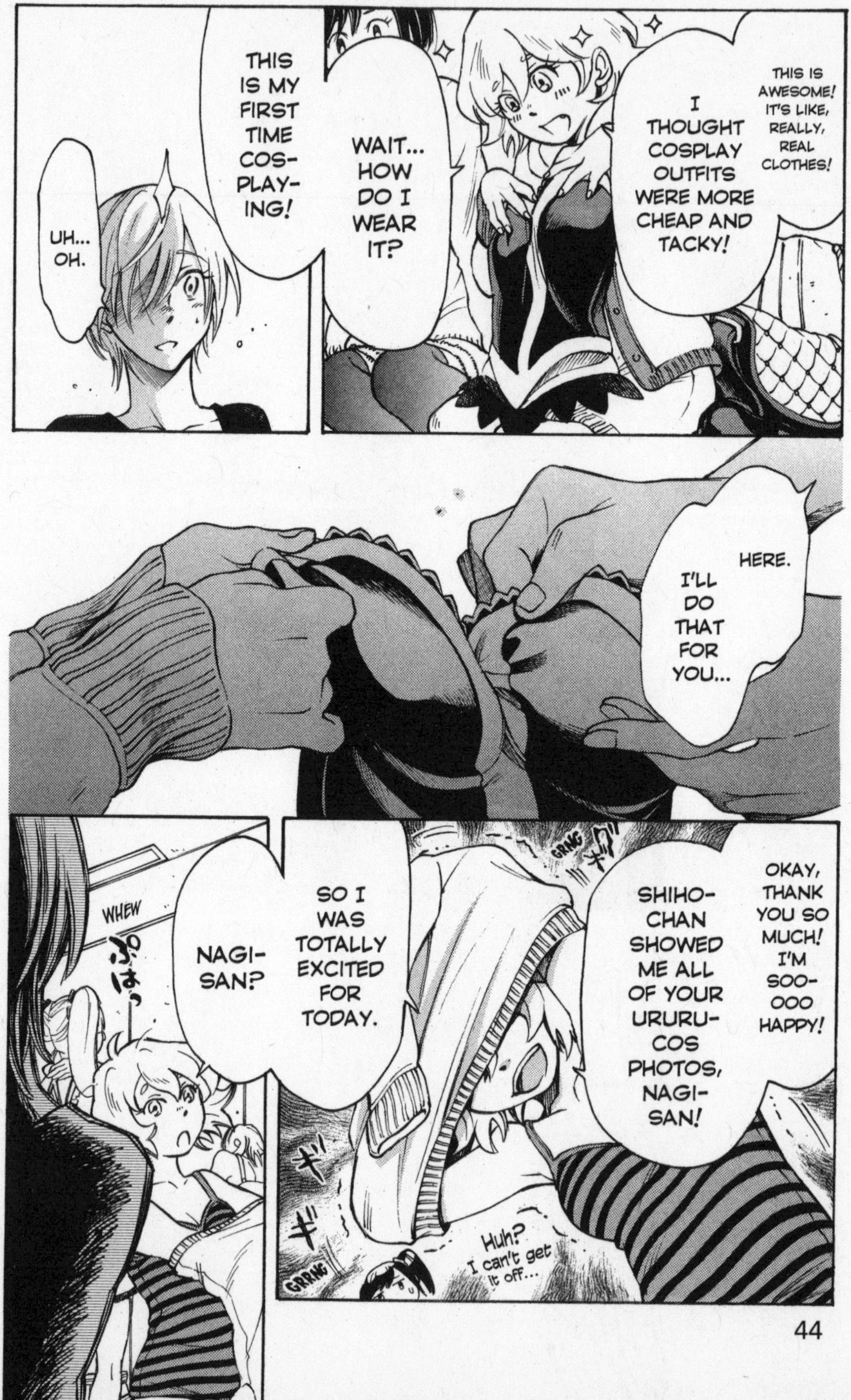
THIS IS AWESOME! IT'S LIKE, REALLY, REAL CLOTHES!
I THOUGHT COSPLAY OUTFITS WERE MORE CHEAP AND TACKY!
WAIT... HOW DO I WEAR IT?
THIS IS MY FIRST TIME COS-PLAY-ING!
UH... OH.
HERE. I'LL DO THAT FOR YOU...
OKAY, THANK YOU SO MUCH! I'M SOO-OOO HAPPY!
SHIHO-CHAN SHOWED ME ALL OF YOUR URURU-COS PHOTOS, NAGI-SAN!
GRNG
SO I WAS TOTALLY EXCITED FOR TODAY.
GRRNG
Huh? I can't get it off...
NAGI-SAN?
WHEW

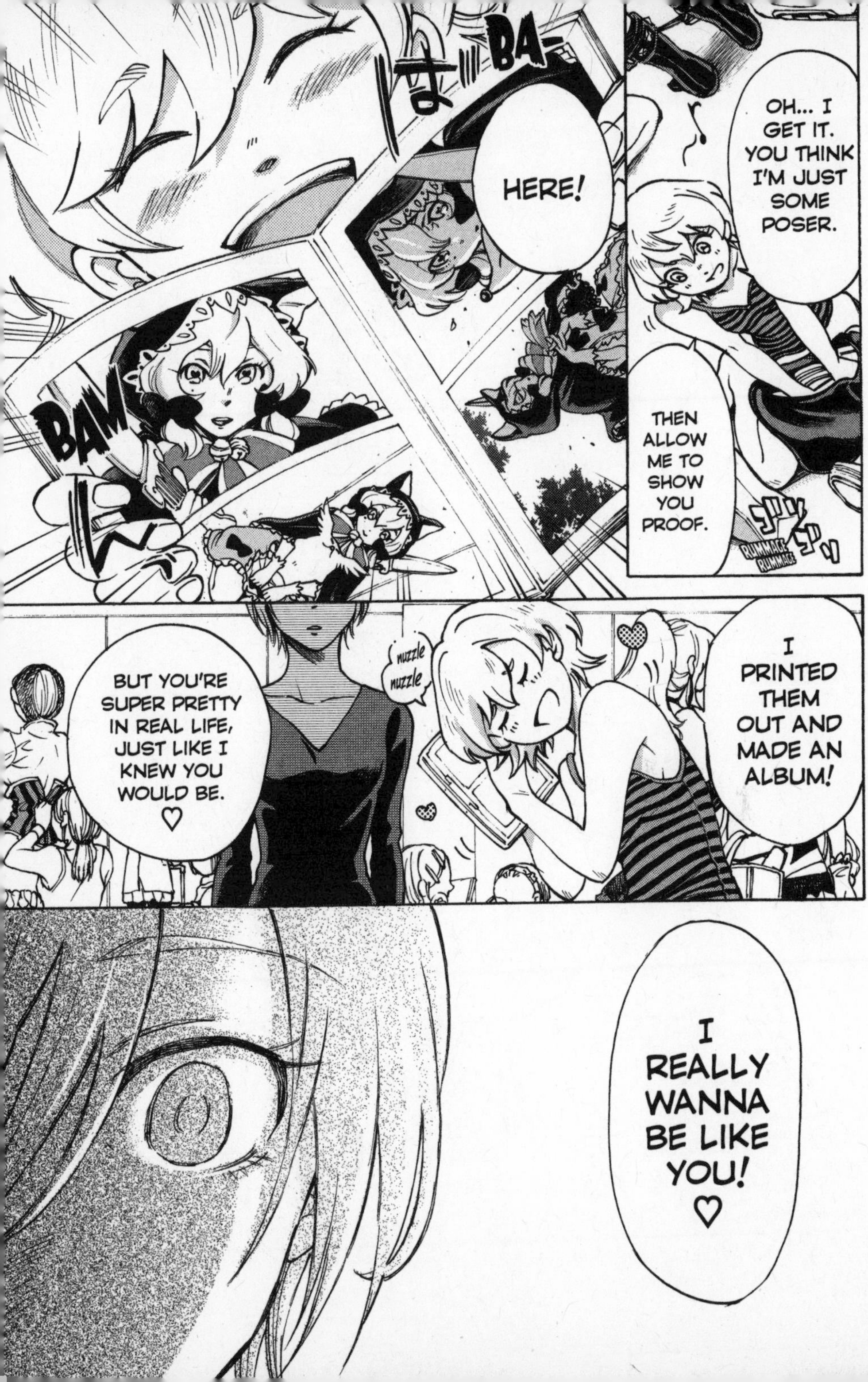
OH... I GET IT. YOU THINK I'M JUST SOME POSER.
THEN ALLOW ME TO SHOW YOU PROOF.
RUMMAGE RUMMAGE
BA-
HERE!
BAM
I PRINTED THEM OUT AND MADE AN ALBUM!
muzzle muzzle
BUT YOU'RE SUPER PRETTY IN REAL LIFE, JUST LIKE I KNEW YOU WOULD BE. ♡
I REALLY WANNA BE LIKE YOU! ♡

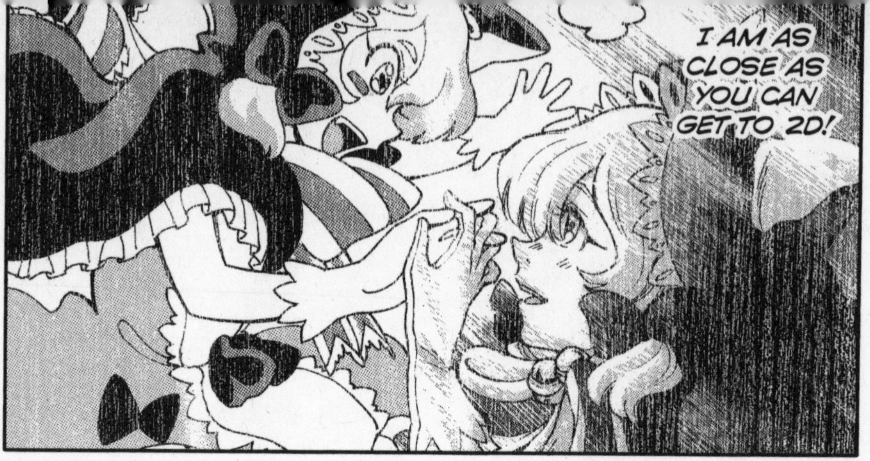
I AM AS CLOSE AS YOU CAN GET TO 2D!
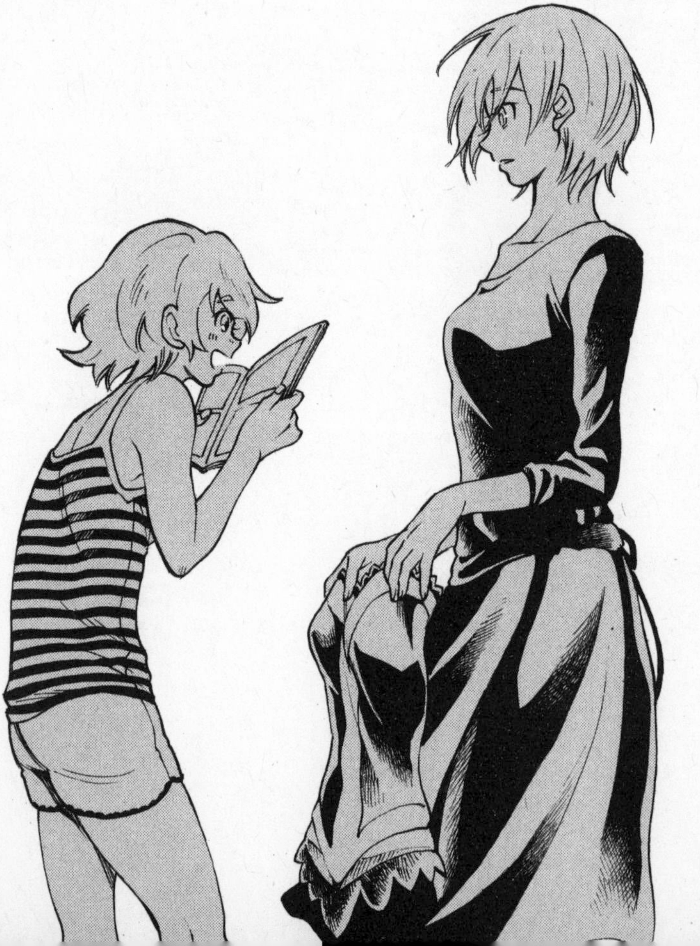

Complex Age ①

Thank you very much for buying this.

No, really. I mean it.

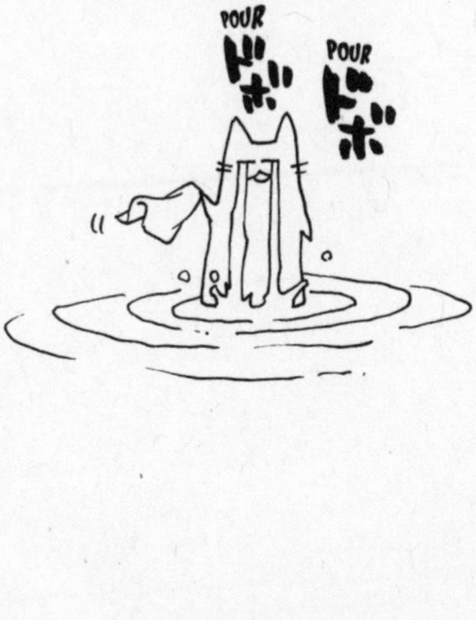

POUR
ドボ
POUR
ドボ

Kimiko-san Has an Idea

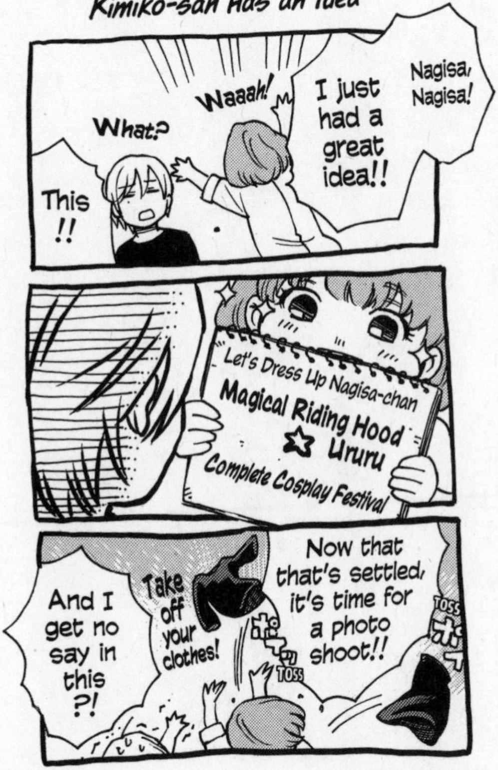

Nagisa, Nagisa!
I just had a great idea!!
Waaah!
What?
This!!
Let's Dress Up Nagisa-chan
Magical Riding Hood ☆ Ururu
Complete Cosplay Festival
Now that that's settled, it's time for a photo shoot!!
TOSS
Take off your clothes!
TOSS
And I get no say in this?!

Magical Riding Hood Ururu Complete Cosplay Festival! 1

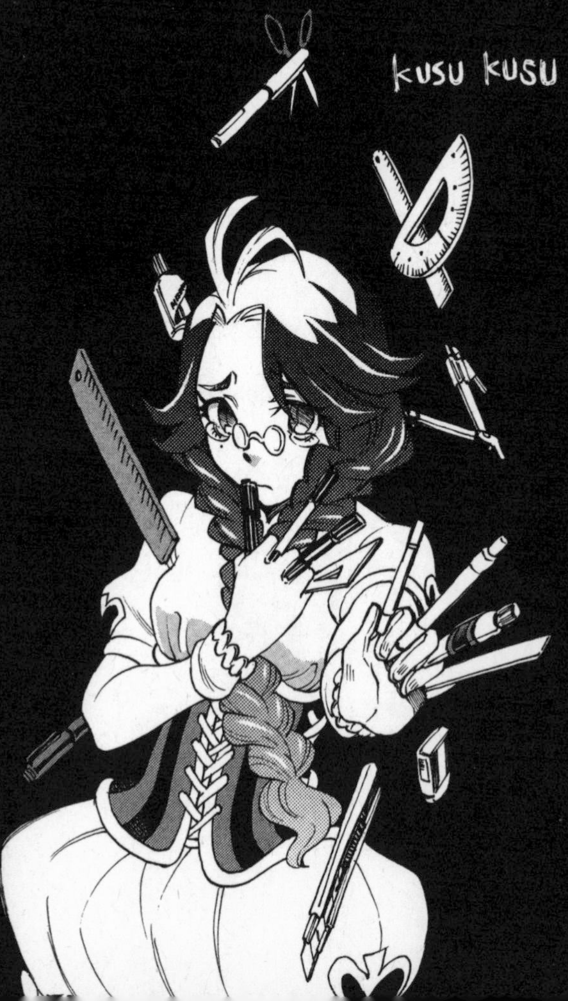
kusu kusu

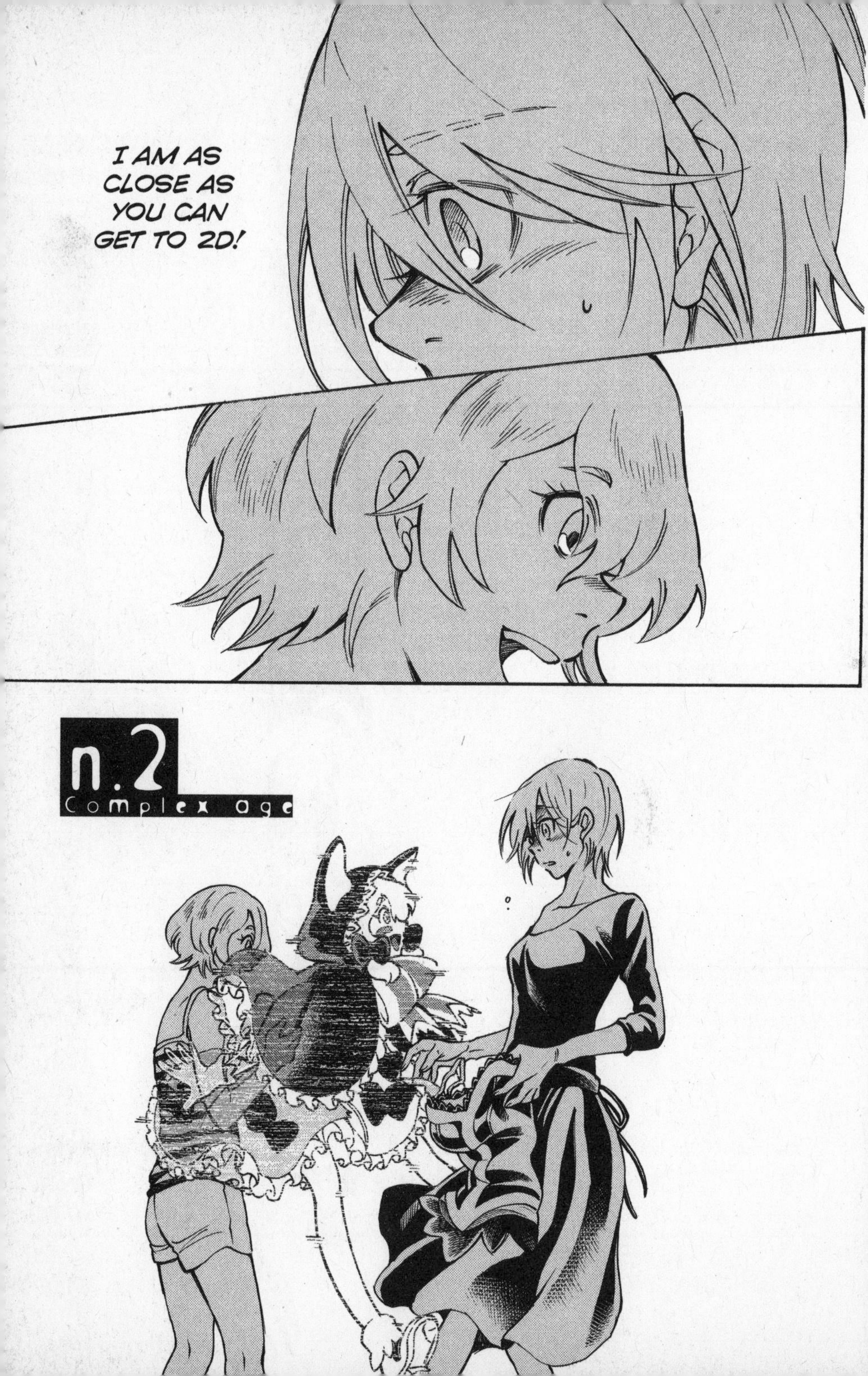
I AM AS CLOSE AS YOU CAN GET TO 2D!
n.2
Complex age

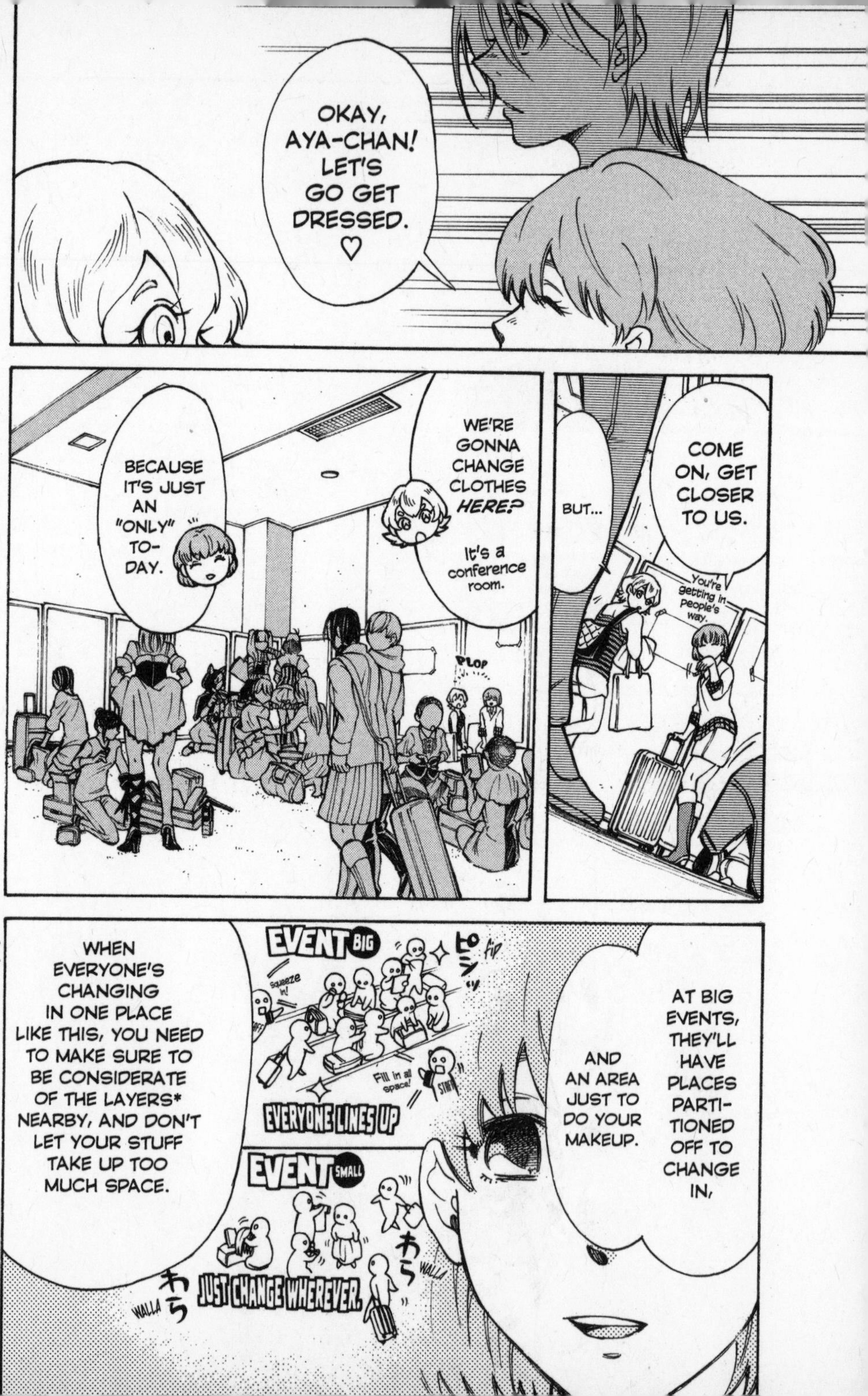
OKAY, AYA-CHAN! LET'S GO GET DRESSED. ♡
COME ON, GET CLOSER TO US.
You're getting in people's way.
BUT...
WE'RE GONNA CHANGE CLOTHES HERE?
It's a conference room.
BECAUSE IT'S JUST AN "ONLY" TO-DAY.
PLOP
AT BIG EVENTS, THEY'LL HAVE PLACES PARTITIONED OFF TO CHANGE IN,
AND AN AREA JUST TO DO YOUR MAKEUP.
EVENT BIG
Squeeze in!
Fill in all space!
EVERYONE LINES UP
EVENT SMALL
わら
WALLA
わら
WALLA
JUST CHANGE WHEREVER.
WHEN EVERYONE'S CHANGING IN ONE PLACE LIKE THIS, YOU NEED TO MAKE SURE TO BE CONSIDERATE OF THE LAYERS* NEARBY, AND DON'T LET YOUR STUFF TAKE UP TOO MUCH SPACE.

*Short for "cosplayer"

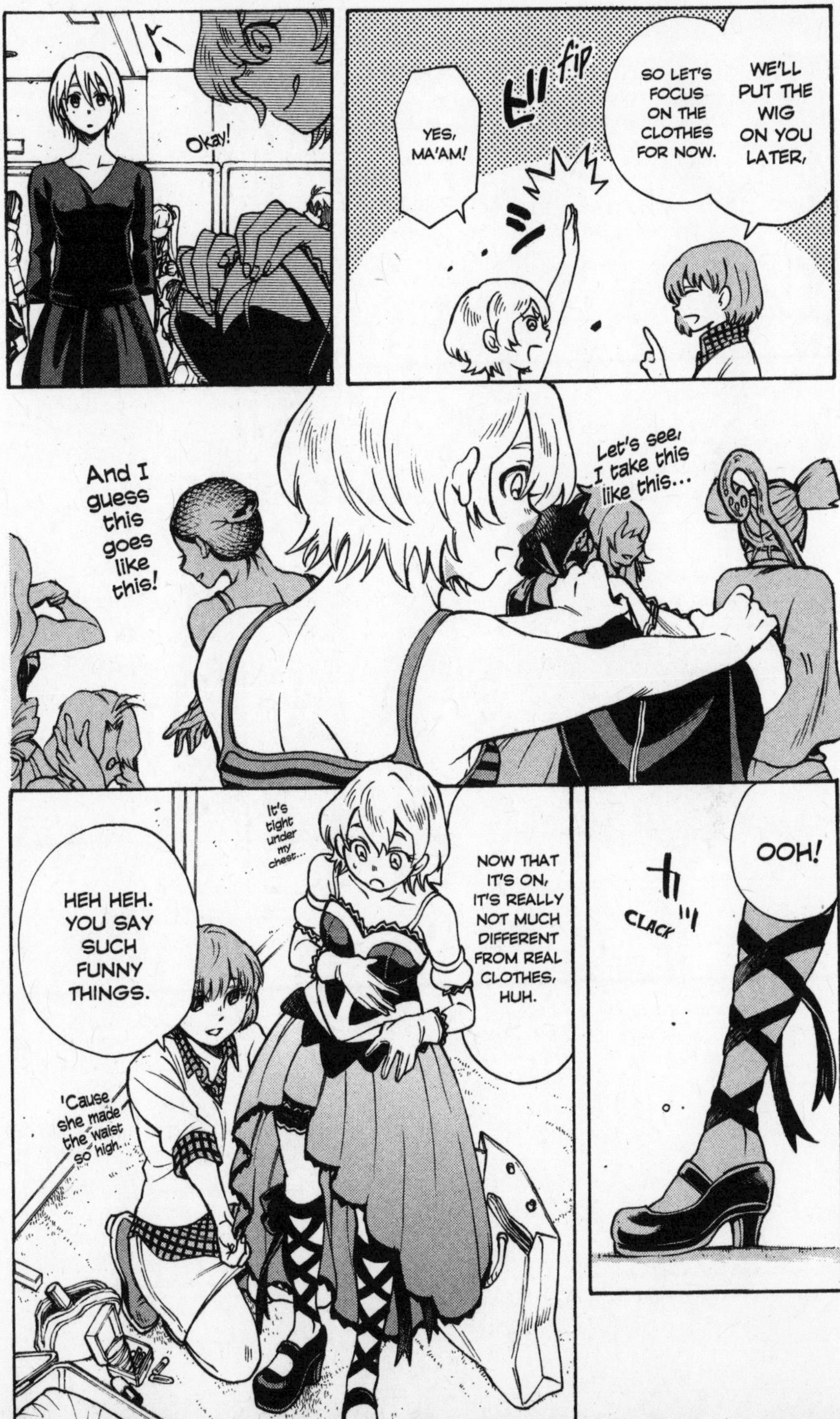
WE'LL PUT THE WIG ON YOU LATER,
SO LET'S FOCUS ON THE CLOTHES FOR NOW.
fip
YES, MA'AM!
Okay!
Let's see, I take this like this...
And I guess this goes like this!
OOH!
CLACK
NOW THAT IT'S ON, IT'S REALLY NOT MUCH DIFFERENT FROM REAL CLOTHES, HUH.
It's tight under my chest...
HEH HEH. YOU SAY SUCH FUNNY THINGS.
'Cause she made the waist so high.

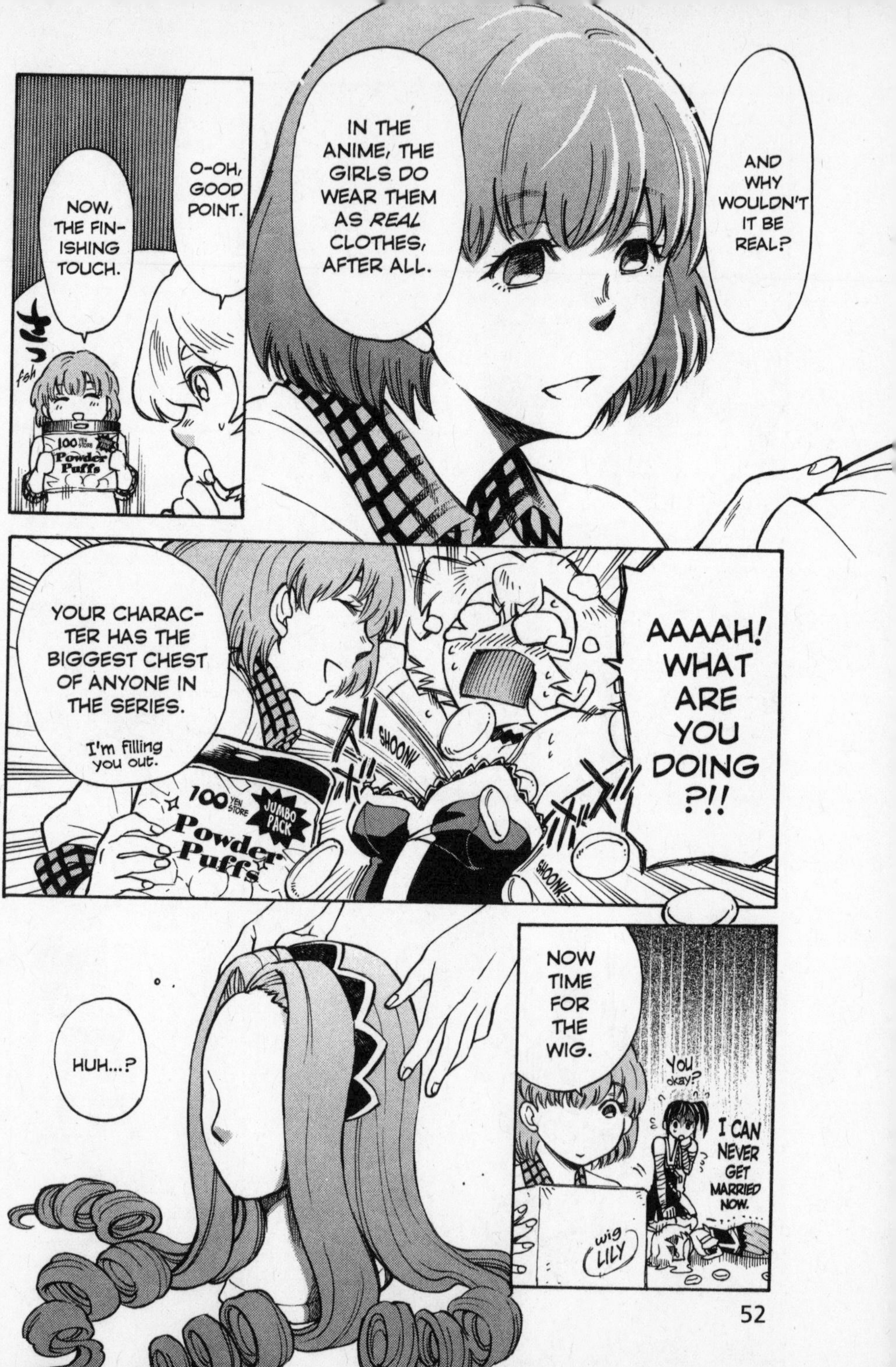
AND WHY WOULDN'T IT BE REAL?
IN THE ANIME, THE GIRLS DO WEAR THEM AS REAL CLOTHES, AFTER ALL.
O-OH, GOOD POINT.
NOW, THE FIN-ISHING TOUCH.
fsh
100 YEN STORE Powder Puffs
AAAAH! WHAT ARE YOU DOING?!!
YOUR CHARAC-TER HAS THE BIGGEST CHEST OF ANYONE IN THE SERIES.
I'm filling you out.
SHOONK
SHOONK
100 YEN STORE JUMBO PACK Powder Puffs
NOW TIME FOR THE WIG.
You okay?
I CAN NEVER GET MARRIED NOW.
wig LILY
HUH...?

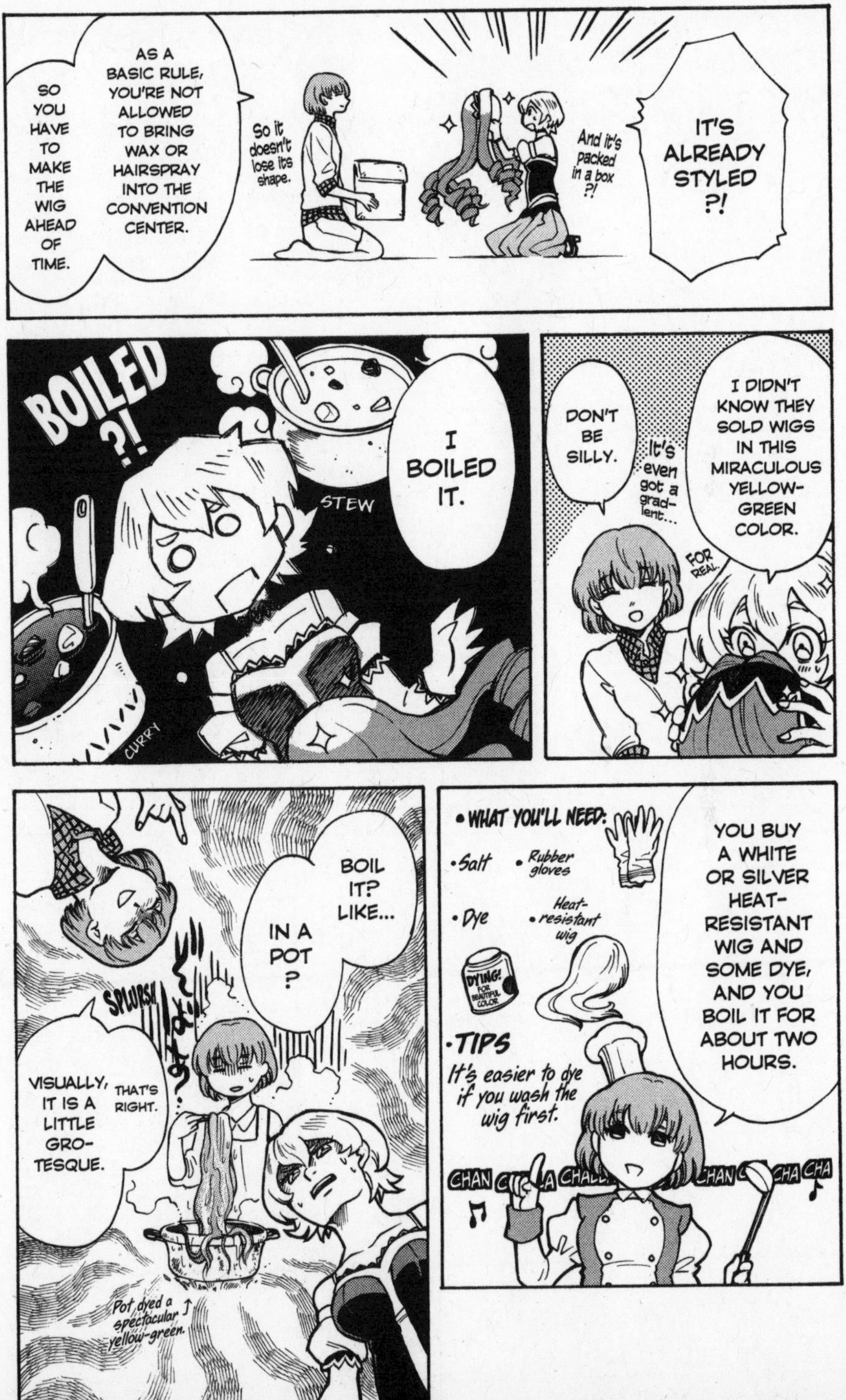
IT'S ALREADY STYLED ?!
And it's packed in a box ?!
So it doesn't lose its shape.
AS A BASIC RULE, YOU'RE NOT ALLOWED TO BRING WAX OR HAIRSPRAY INTO THE CONVENTION CENTER.
SO YOU HAVE TO MAKE THE WIG AHEAD OF TIME.
I DIDN'T KNOW THEY SOLD WIGS IN THIS MIRACULOUS YELLOW-GREEN COLOR.
FOR REAL.
It's even got a grad-ient...
DON'T BE SILLY.
I BOILED IT.
STEW
BOILED ?!
CURRY
YOU BUY A WHITE OR SILVER HEAT-RESISTANT WIG AND SOME DYE, AND YOU BOIL IT FOR ABOUT TWO HOURS.
• WHAT YOU'LL NEED:
• Salt
• Rubber gloves
• Dye
• Heat-resistant wig
DYING! FOR BEAUTIFUL COLOR
• TIPS
It's easier to dye if you wash the wig first.
CHAN
CHAN
CHA
CHA
BOIL IT? LIKE...
IN A POT ?
SPLURSH
THAT'S RIGHT.
VISUALLY, IT IS A LITTLE GRO-TESQUE.
Pot dyed a spectacular yellow-green.

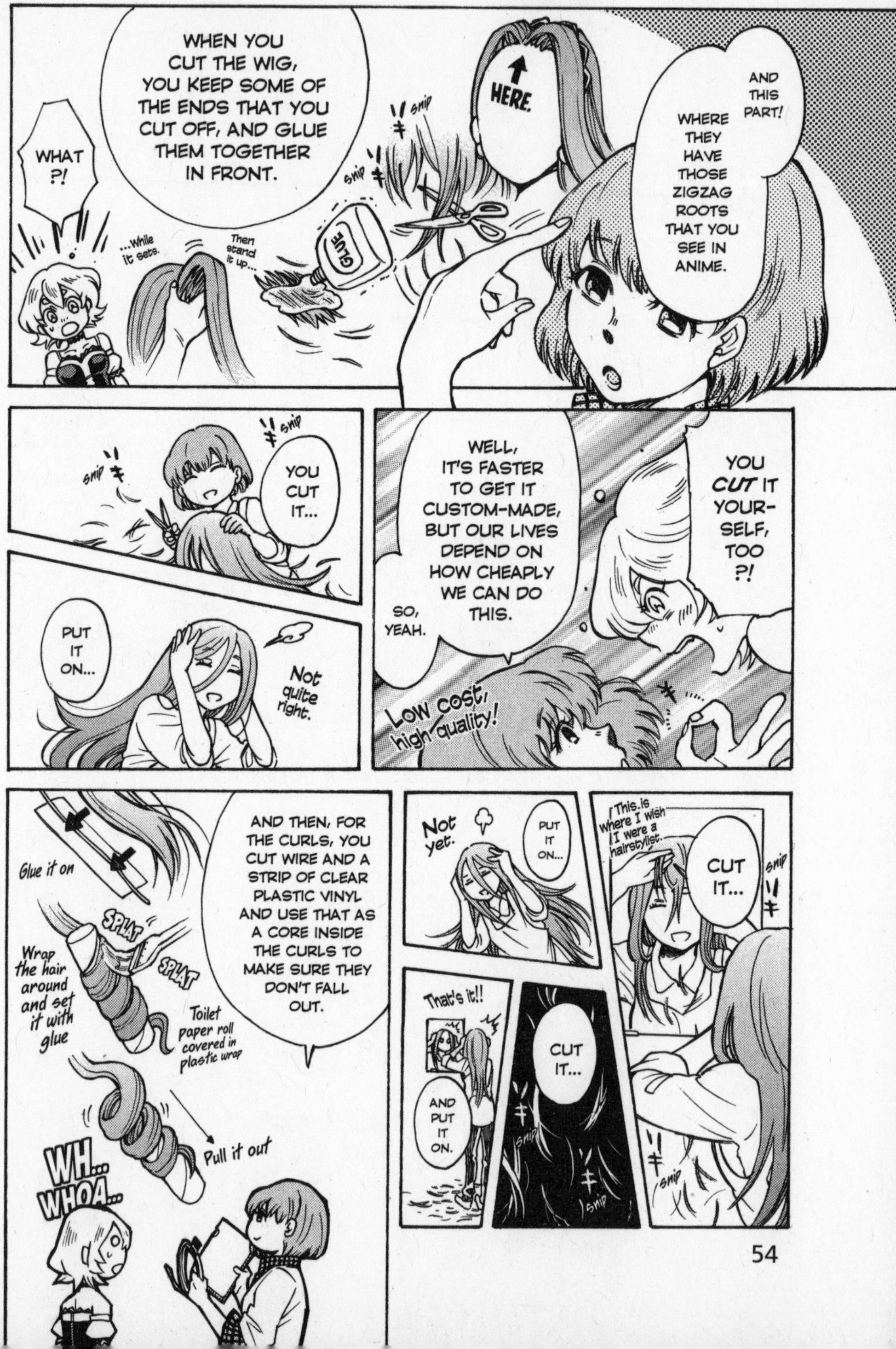
AND THIS PART!
WHERE THEY HAVE THOSE ZIGZAG ROOTS THAT YOU SEE IN ANIME.
HERE.
snip
snip
WHEN YOU CUT THE WIG, YOU KEEP SOME OF THE ENDS THAT YOU CUT OFF, AND GLUE THEM TOGETHER IN FRONT.
GLUE
Then stand it up...
...While it sets.
WHAT?!
YOU CUT IT YOURSELF, TOO?!
WELL, IT'S FASTER TO GET IT CUSTOM-MADE, BUT OUR LIVES DEPEND ON HOW CHEAPLY WE CAN DO THIS.
SO, YEAH.
Low cost, high quality!
snip
YOU CUT IT...
snip
PUT IT ON...
Not quite right.
This is where I wish I were a hairstylist.
CUT IT...
snip
PUT IT ON...
Not yet.
CUT IT...
snip
snip
snip
That's it!!
AND PUT IT ON.
AND THEN, FOR THE CURLS, YOU CUT WIRE AND A STRIP OF CLEAR PLASTIC VINYL AND USE THAT AS A CORE INSIDE THE CURLS TO MAKE SURE THEY DON'T FALL OUT.
Glue it on
SPLAT
SPLAT
Wrap the hair around and set it with glue
Toilet paper roll covered in plastic wrap
Pull it out
WH... WHOA...

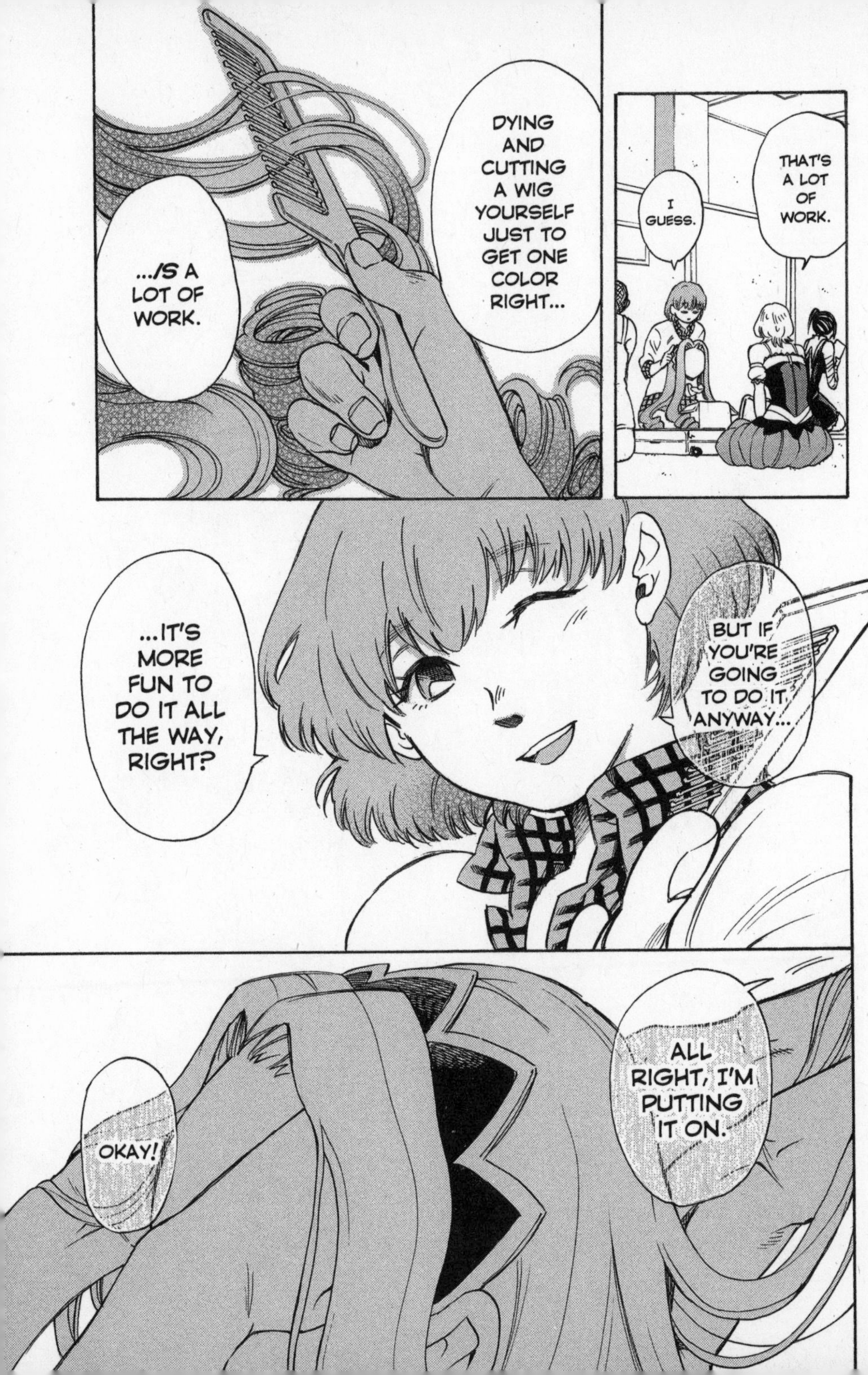
THAT'S A LOT OF WORK.
I GUESS.
DYING AND CUTTING A WIG YOURSELF JUST TO GET ONE COLOR RIGHT...
...IS A LOT OF WORK.
BUT IF YOU'RE GOING TO DO IT ANYWAY...
...IT'S MORE FUN TO DO IT ALL THE WAY, RIGHT?
ALL RIGHT, I'M PUTTING IT ON.
OKAY!

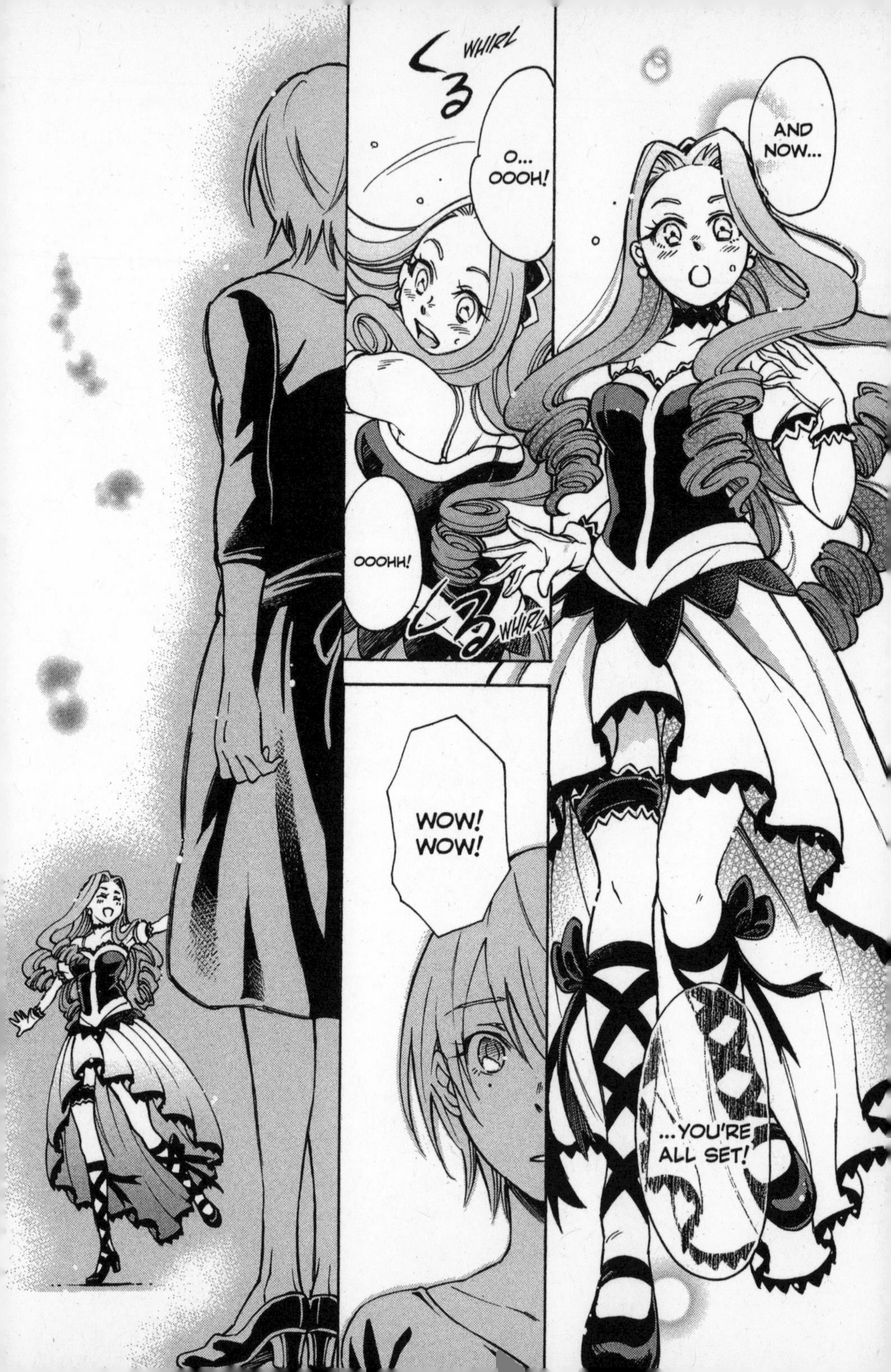
AND NOW...
...YOU'RE ALL SET!
くる WHIRL
O... OOOH!
OOOHH!
くる WHIRL
WOW! WOW!

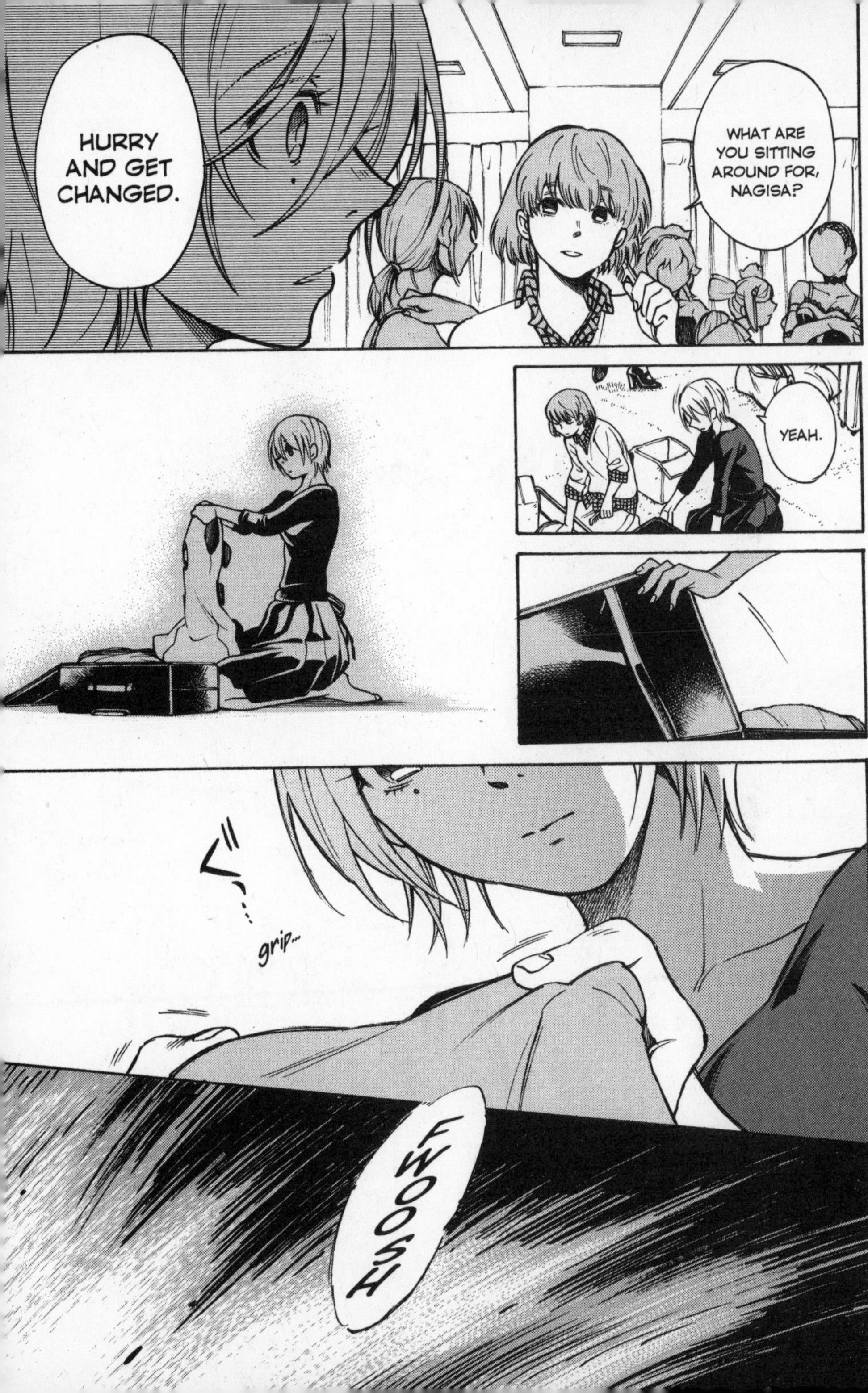
WHAT ARE YOU SITTING AROUND FOR, NAGISA?
HURRY AND GET CHANGED.
YEAH.
grip...
FWOOSH

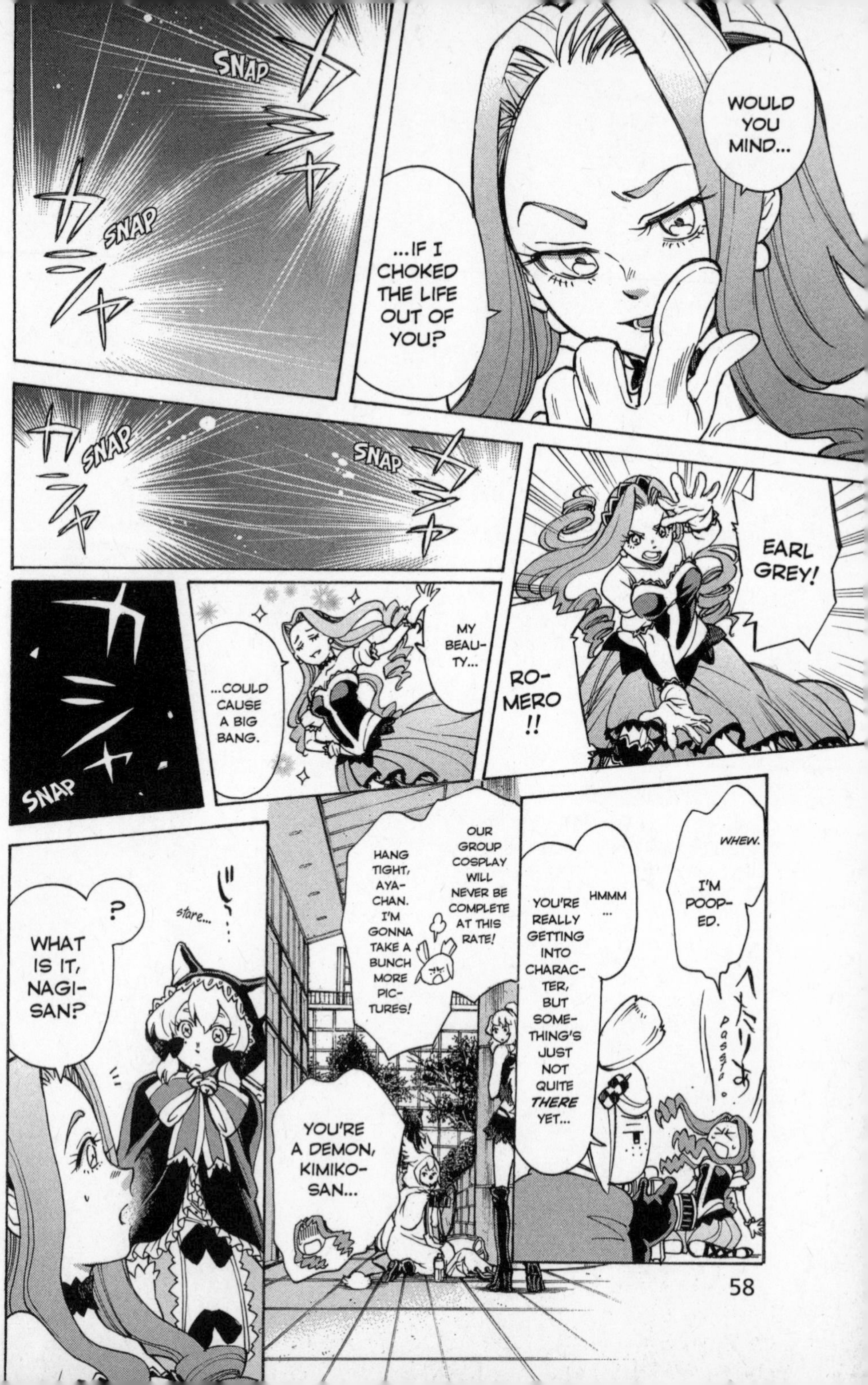
WOULD YOU MIND...
...IF I CHOKED THE LIFE OUT OF YOU?
SNAP
SNAP
EARL GREY!
RO-MERO!!
SNAP
SNAP
MY BEAU-TY...
...COULD CAUSE A BIG BANG.
SNAP
WHEW.
I'M POOP-ED.
HMMM...
YOU'RE REALLY GETTING INTO CHARAC-TER, BUT SOME-THING'S JUST NOT QUITE *THERE* YET...
OUR GROUP COSPLAY WILL NEVER BE COMPLETE AT THIS RATE!
HANG TIGHT, AYA-CHAN. I'M GONNA TAKE A BUNCH MORE PIC-TURES!
YOU'RE A DEMON, KIMIKO-SAN...
stare...
?
WHAT IS IT, NAGI-SAN?

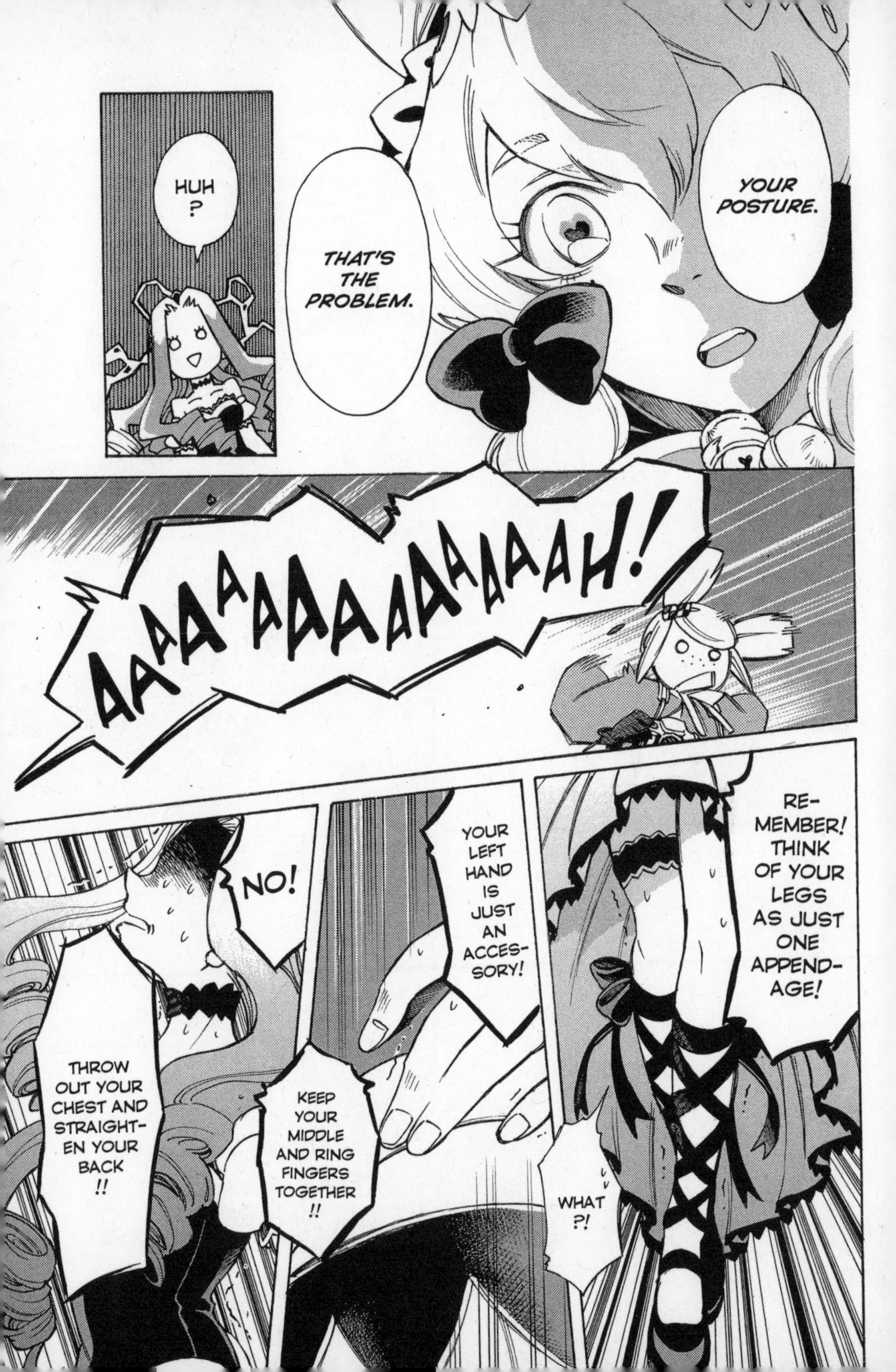
YOUR POSTURE.
THAT'S THE PROBLEM.
HUH ?
AAAAAAAAAAAAH!
REMEMBER! THINK OF YOUR LEGS AS JUST ONE APPENDAGE!
WHAT ?!
YOUR LEFT HAND IS JUST AN ACCESSORY!
KEEP YOUR MIDDLE AND RING FINGERS TOGETHER !!
NO!
THROW OUT YOUR CHEST AND STRAIGHTEN YOUR BACK !!

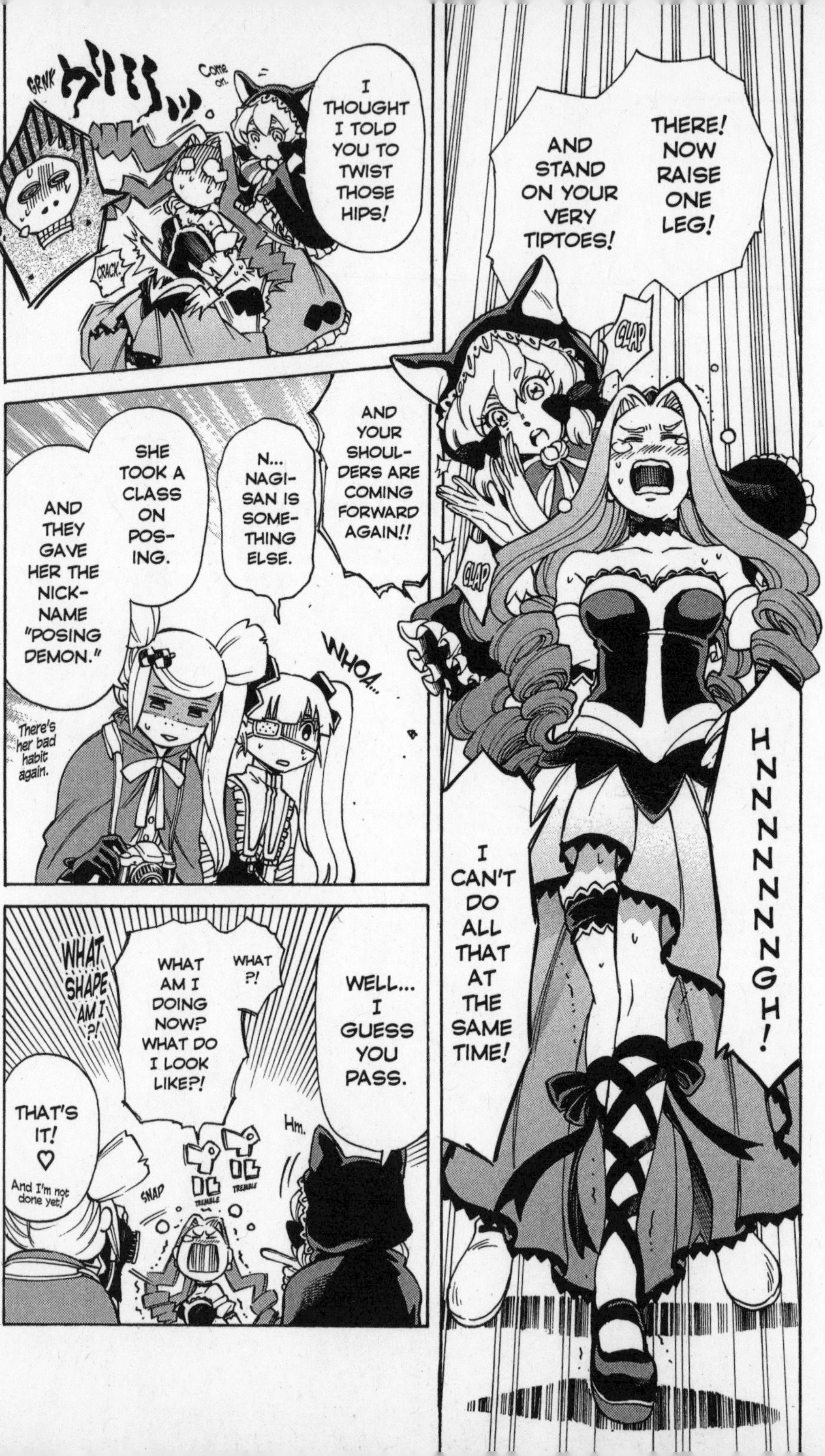
THERE! NOW RAISE ONE LEG!
AND STAND ON YOUR VERY TIPTOES!
CLAP
CLAP
HNNNNNNGH!
I CAN'T DO ALL THAT AT THE SAME TIME!
I THOUGHT I TOLD YOU TO TWIST THOSE HIPS!
Come on.
GRNK
CRACK
AND YOUR SHOULDERS ARE COMING FORWARD AGAIN!!
N... NAGI-SAN IS SOMETHING ELSE.
SHE TOOK A CLASS ON POSING.
AND THEY GAVE HER THE NICKNAME "POSING DEMON."
WHOA...
There's her bad habit again.
WELL... I GUESS YOU PASS.
Hm.
WHAT?!
WHAT AM I DOING NOW? WHAT DO I LOOK LIKE?!
WHAT SHAPE AM I?!
TREMBLE
TREMBLE
THAT'S IT! ♡
And I'm not done yet!
SNAP

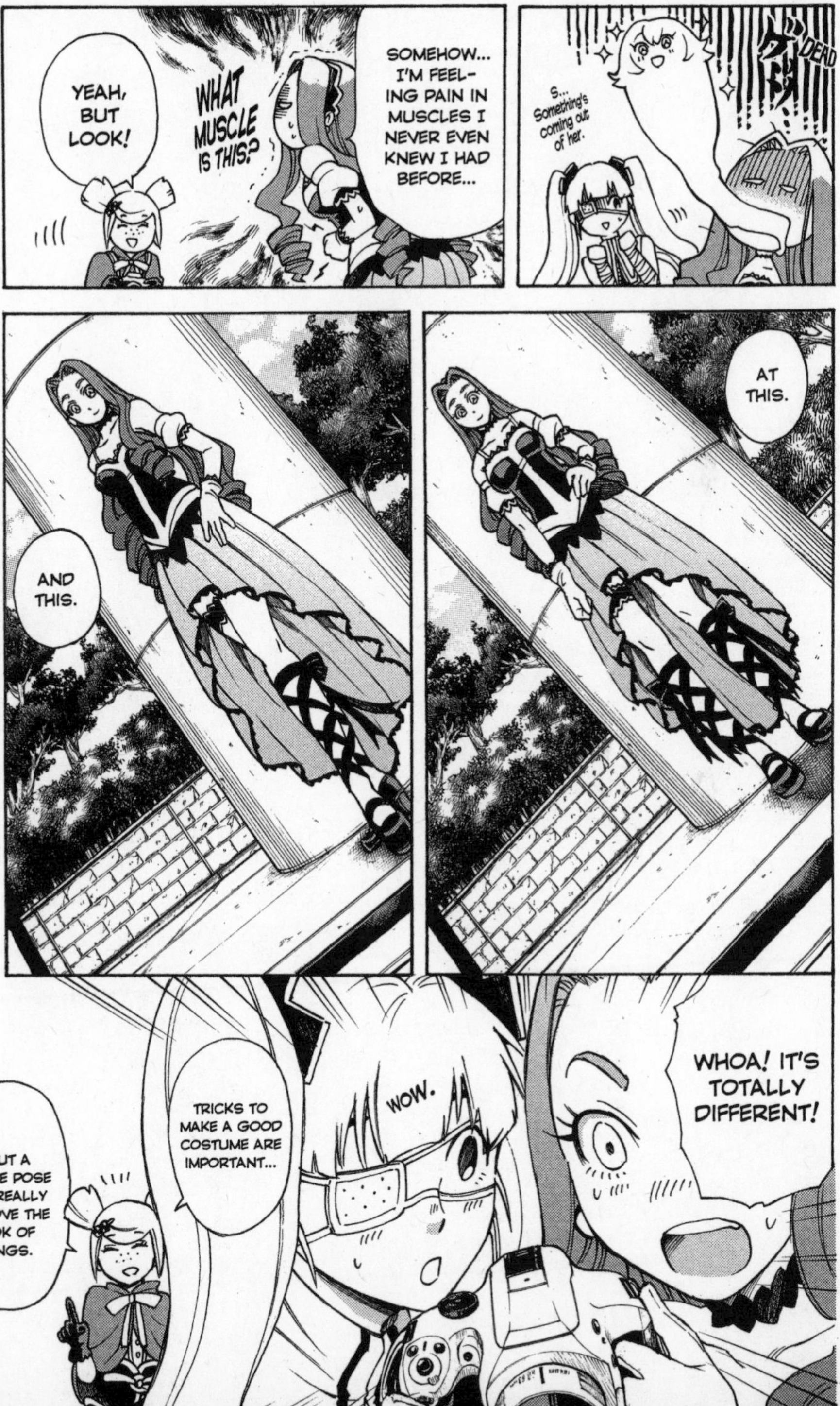
DEAD
S... Something's coming out of her.
SOMEHOW... I'M FEEL-ING PAIN IN MUSCLES I NEVER EVEN KNEW I HAD BEFORE...
WHAT MUSCLE IS THIS?
YEAH, BUT LOOK!
AT THIS.
AND THIS.
WHOA! IT'S TOTALLY DIFFERENT!
WOW.
TRICKS TO MAKE A GOOD COSTUME ARE IMPORTANT...
...BUT A SINGLE POSE CAN REALLY IMPROVE THE LOOK OF THINGS.

NAME ON CARD: Nagi

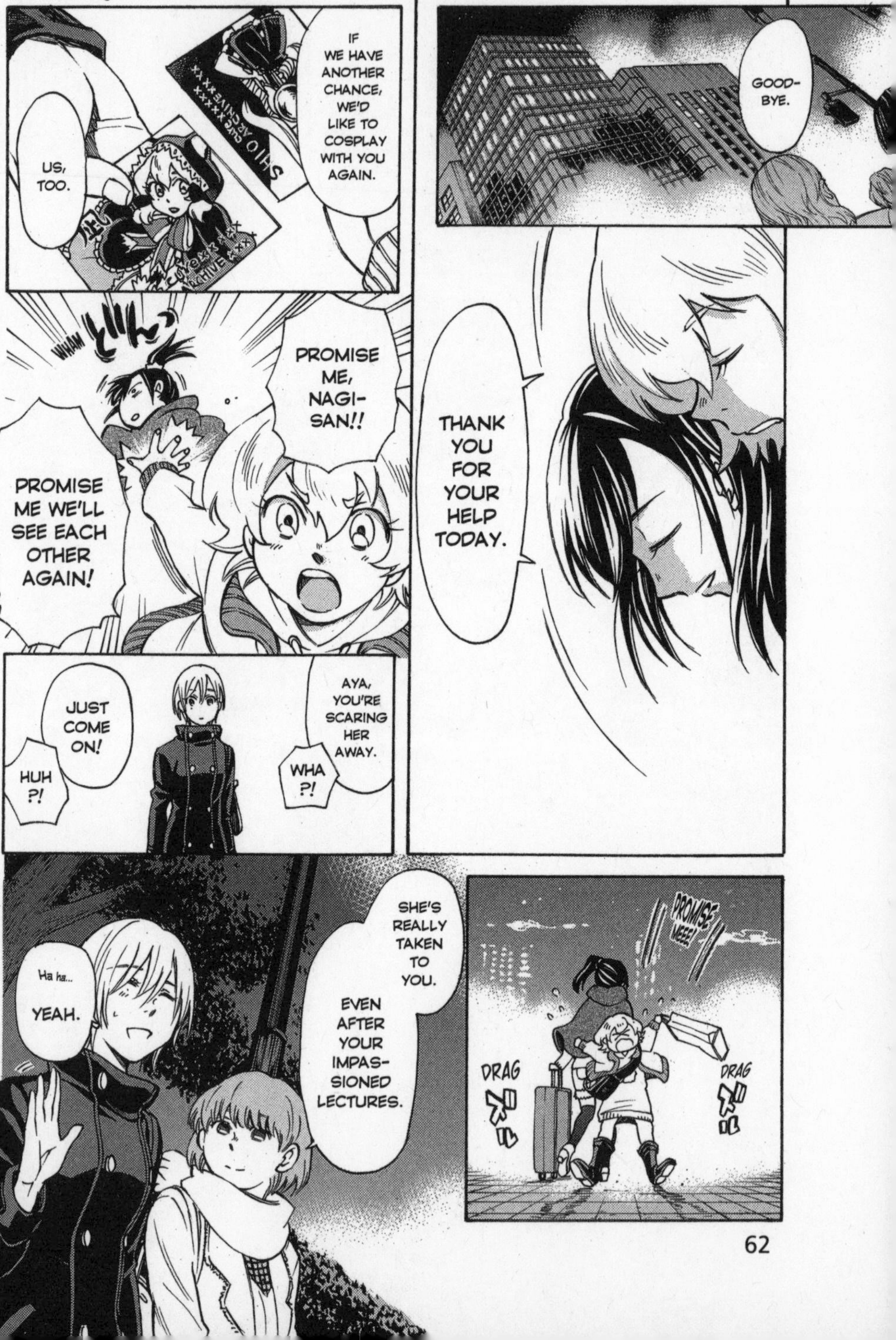

GOOD-BYE.
THANK YOU FOR YOUR HELP TODAY.
IF WE HAVE ANOTHER CHANCE, WE'D LIKE TO COSPLAY WITH YOU AGAIN.
US, TOO.
PROMISE ME, NAGI-SAN!!
WHAM
PROMISE ME WE'LL SEE EACH OTHER AGAIN!
AYA, YOU'RE SCARING HER AWAY.
WHA ?!
JUST COME ON!
HUH ?!
PROMISE MEEE!
DRAG
DRAG
SHE'S REALLY TAKEN TO YOU.
EVEN AFTER YOUR IMPASSIONED LECTURES.
Ha ha...
YEAH.

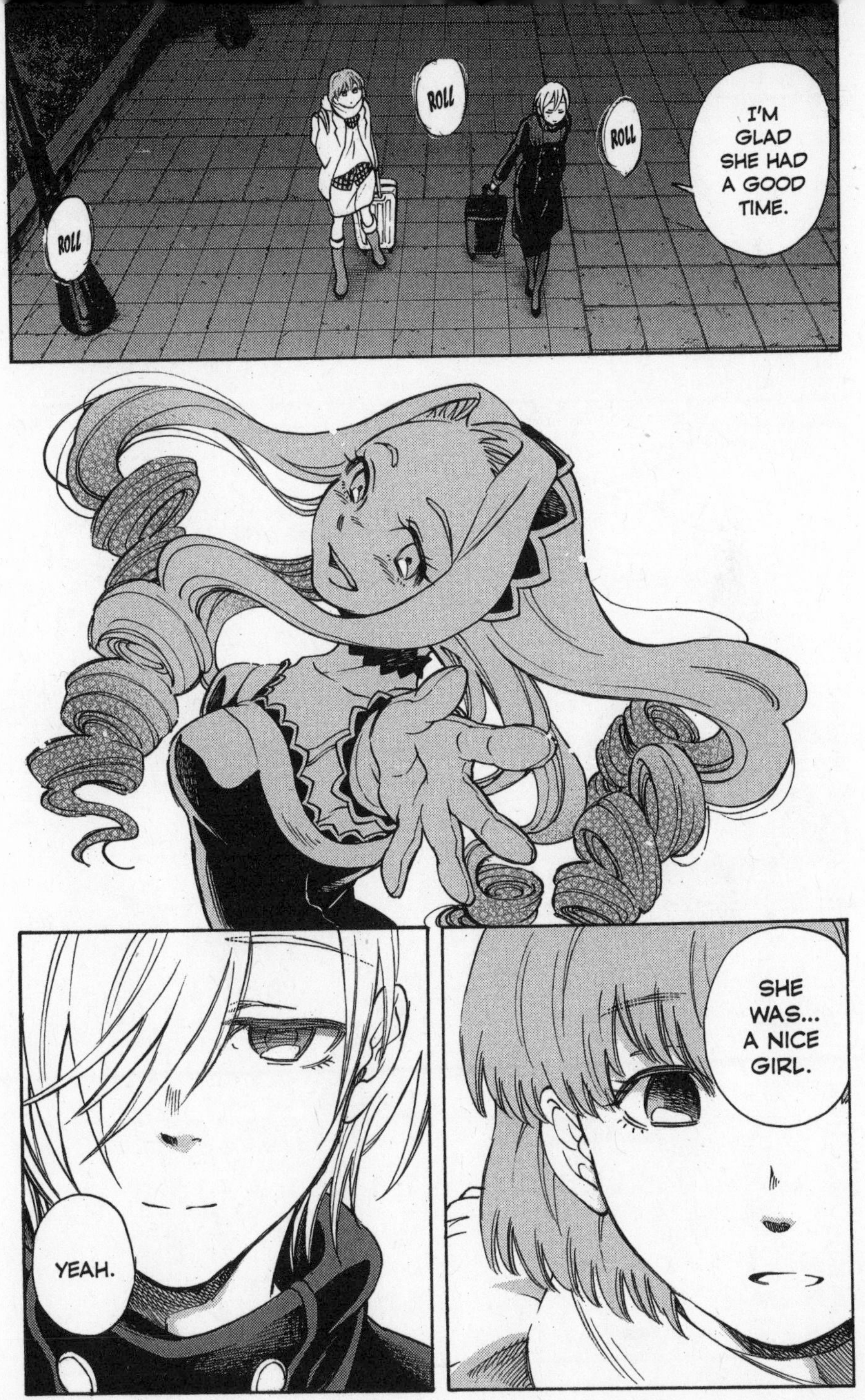
I'M GLAD SHE HAD A GOOD TIME.
ROLL
ROLL
ROLL
SHE WAS... A NICE GIRL.
YEAH.

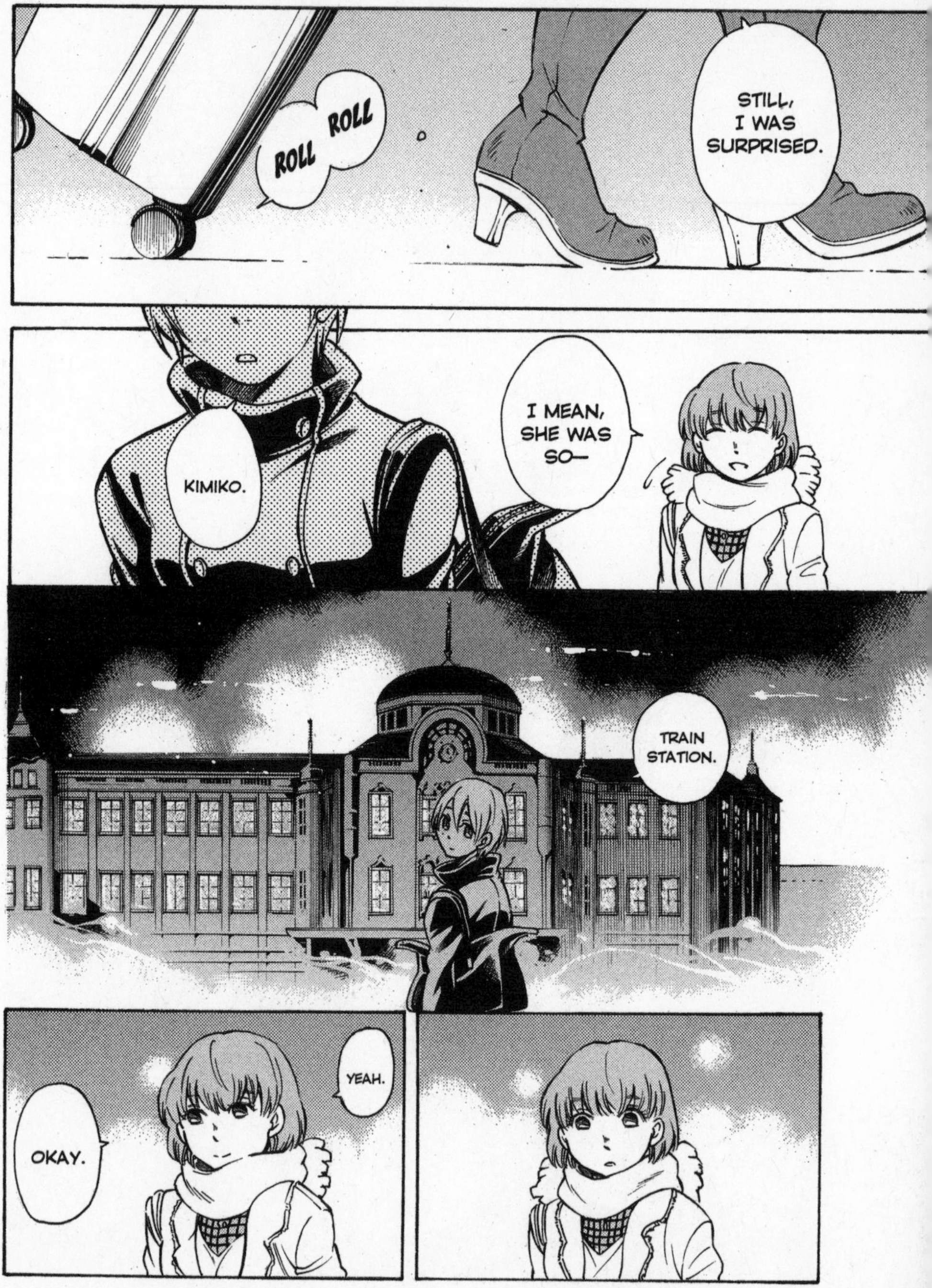
STILL, I WAS SURPRISED.
ROLL ROLL
I MEAN, SHE WAS SO—
KIMIKO.
TRAIN STATION.
YEAH.
OKAY.

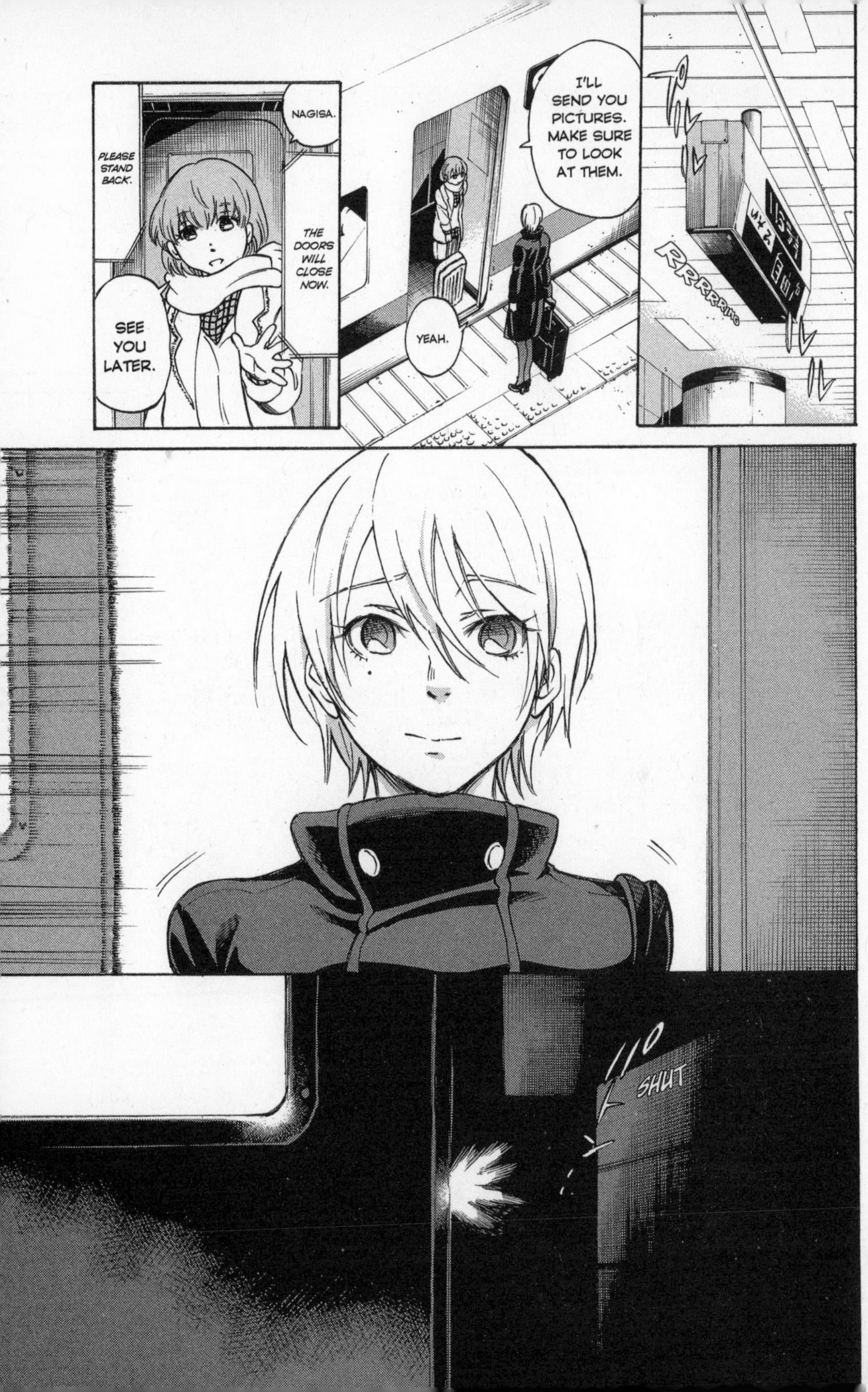
RRRRRING
I'LL SEND YOU PICTURES. MAKE SURE TO LOOK AT THEM.
YEAH.
NAGISA.
PLEASE STAND BACK.
THE DOORS WILL CLOSE NOW.
SEE YOU LATER.
SHUT

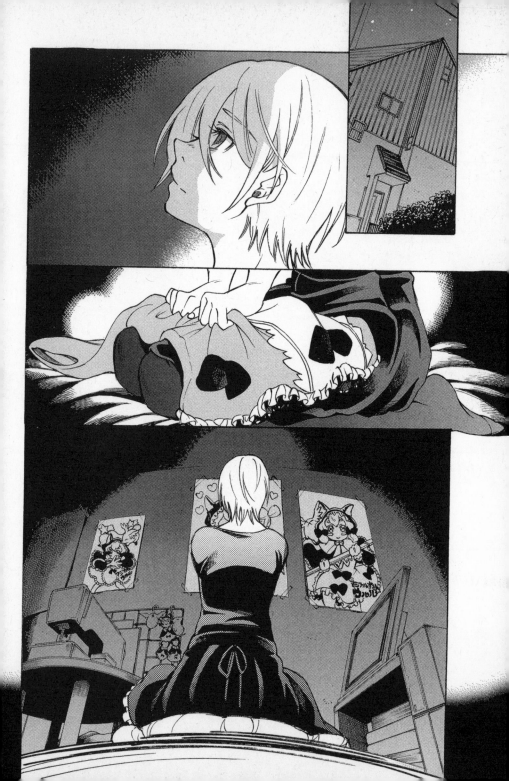

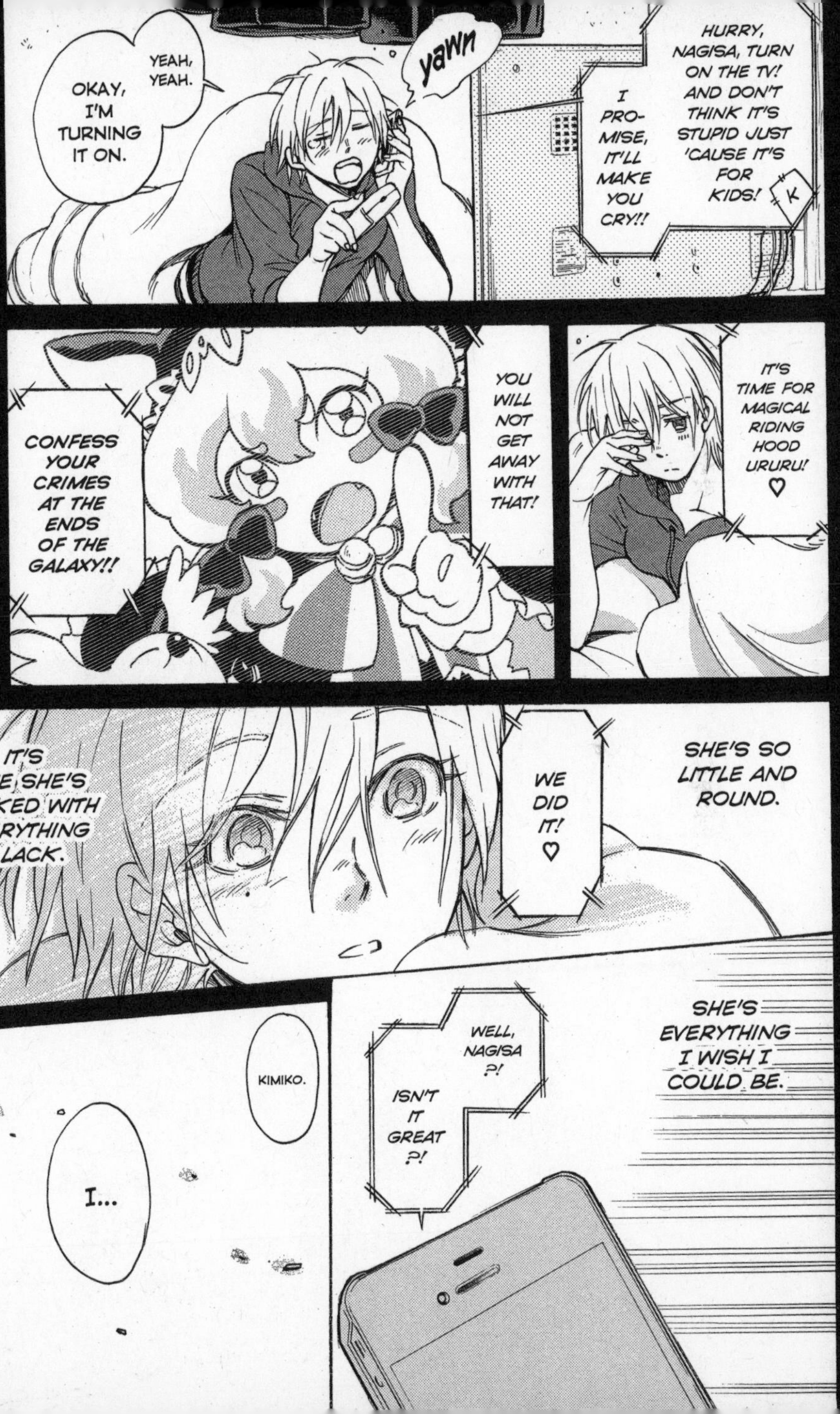
HURRY, NAGISA, TURN ON THE TV! AND DON'T THINK IT'S STUPID JUST 'CAUSE IT'S FOR KIDS!
I PRO-MISE, IT'LL MAKE YOU CRY!!
K
yawn
YEAH, YEAH.
OKAY, I'M TURNING IT ON.
IT'S TIME FOR MAGICAL RIDING HOOD URURU! ♡
YOU WILL NOT GET AWAY WITH THAT!
CONFESS YOUR CRIMES AT THE ENDS OF THE GALAXY!!
SHE'S SO LITTLE AND ROUND.
WE DID IT! ♡
IT'S LIKE SHE'S PACKED WITH EVERYTHING I LACK.
SHE'S EVERYTHING I WISH I COULD BE.
WELL, NAGISA ?!
ISN'T IT GREAT ?!
KIMIKO.
I...

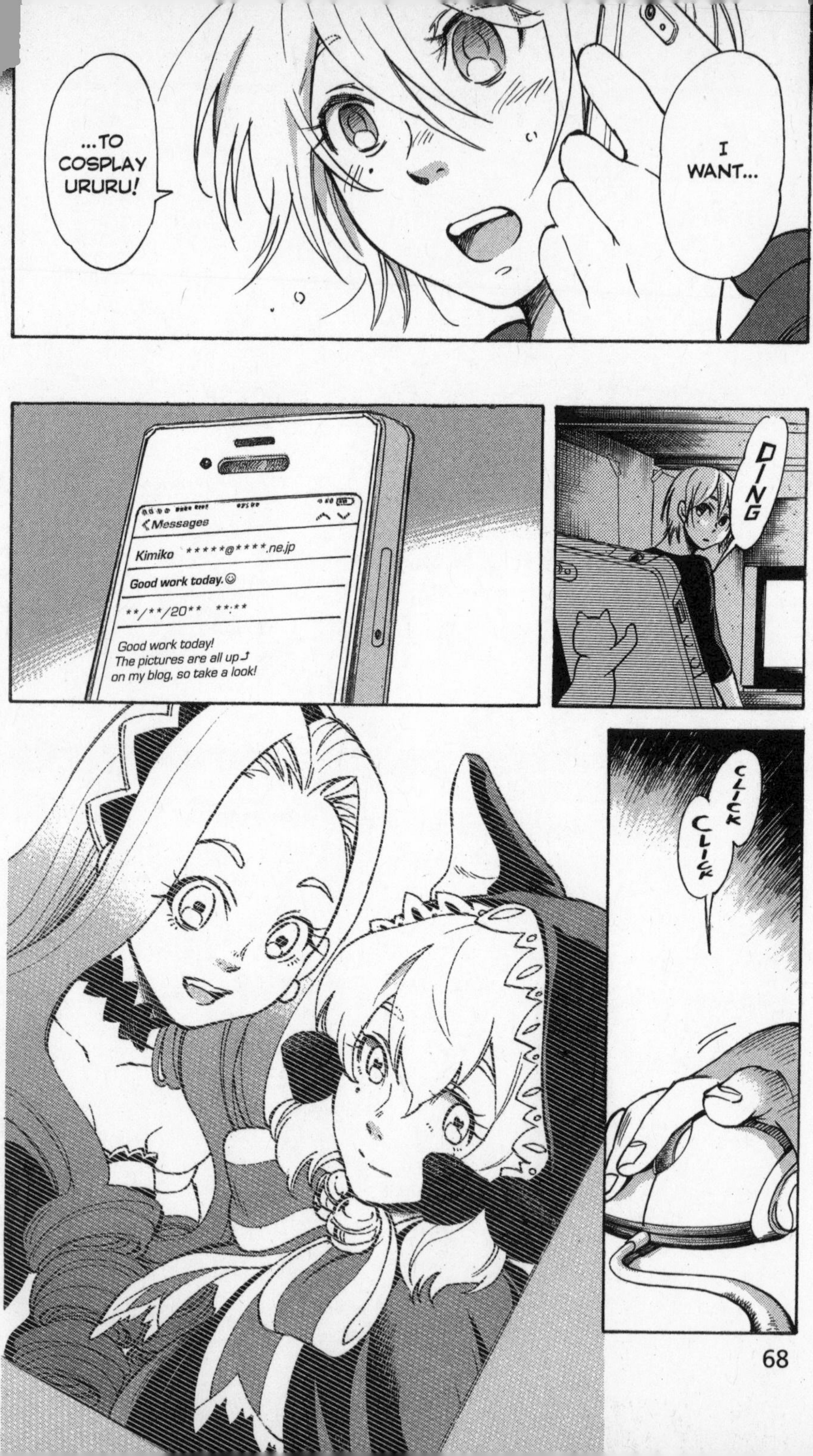

I WANT...
...TO COSPLAY URURU!
DING
Messages
Kimiko *****@****.ne.jp
Good work today.☺
//20** **:**
Good work today!
The pictures are all up
on my blog, so take a look!
CLICK
CLICK

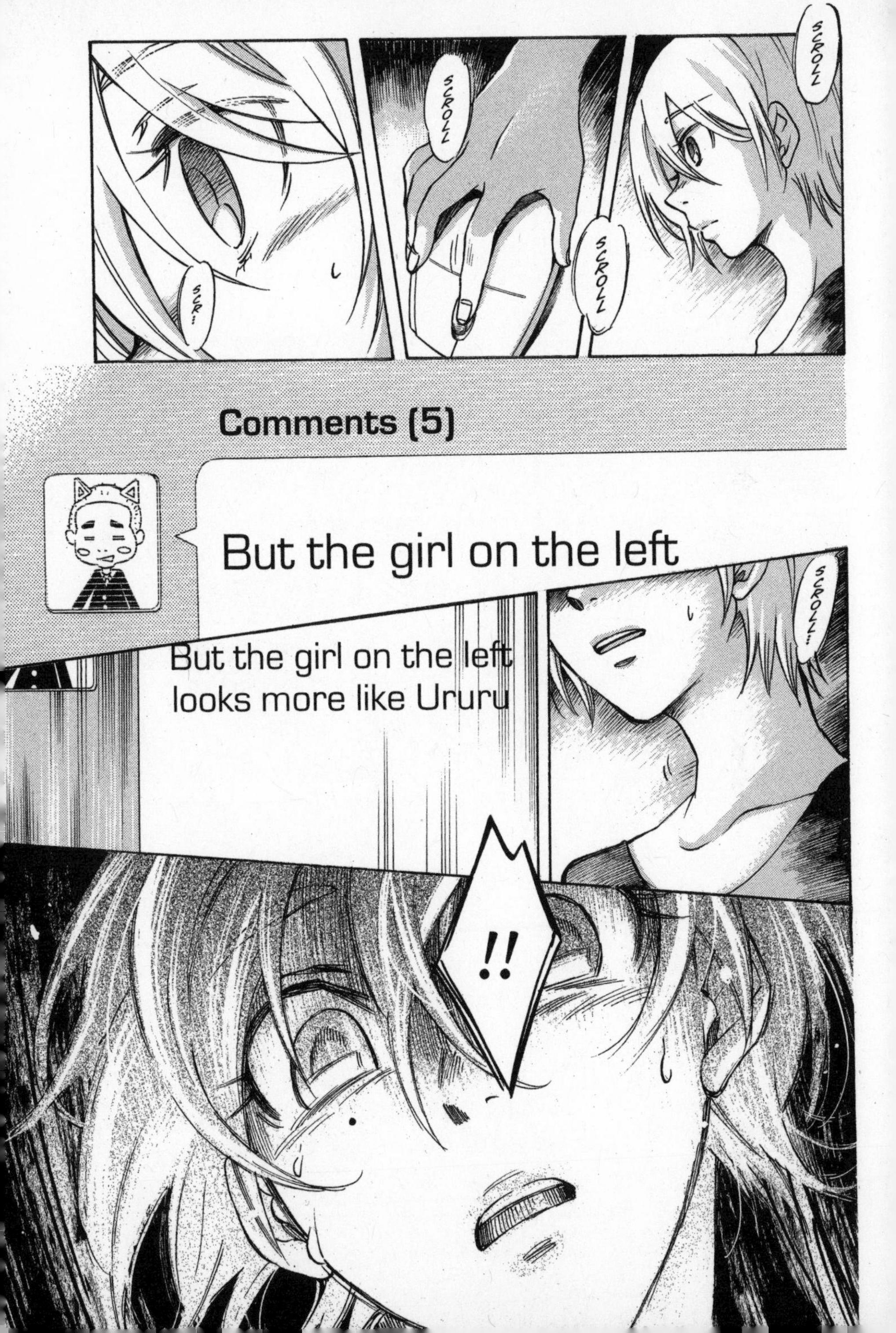
SCROLL
SCROLL
SCROLL
SCR...
Comments (5)
But the girl on the left
SCROLL...
But the girl on the left
looks more like Ururu
!!

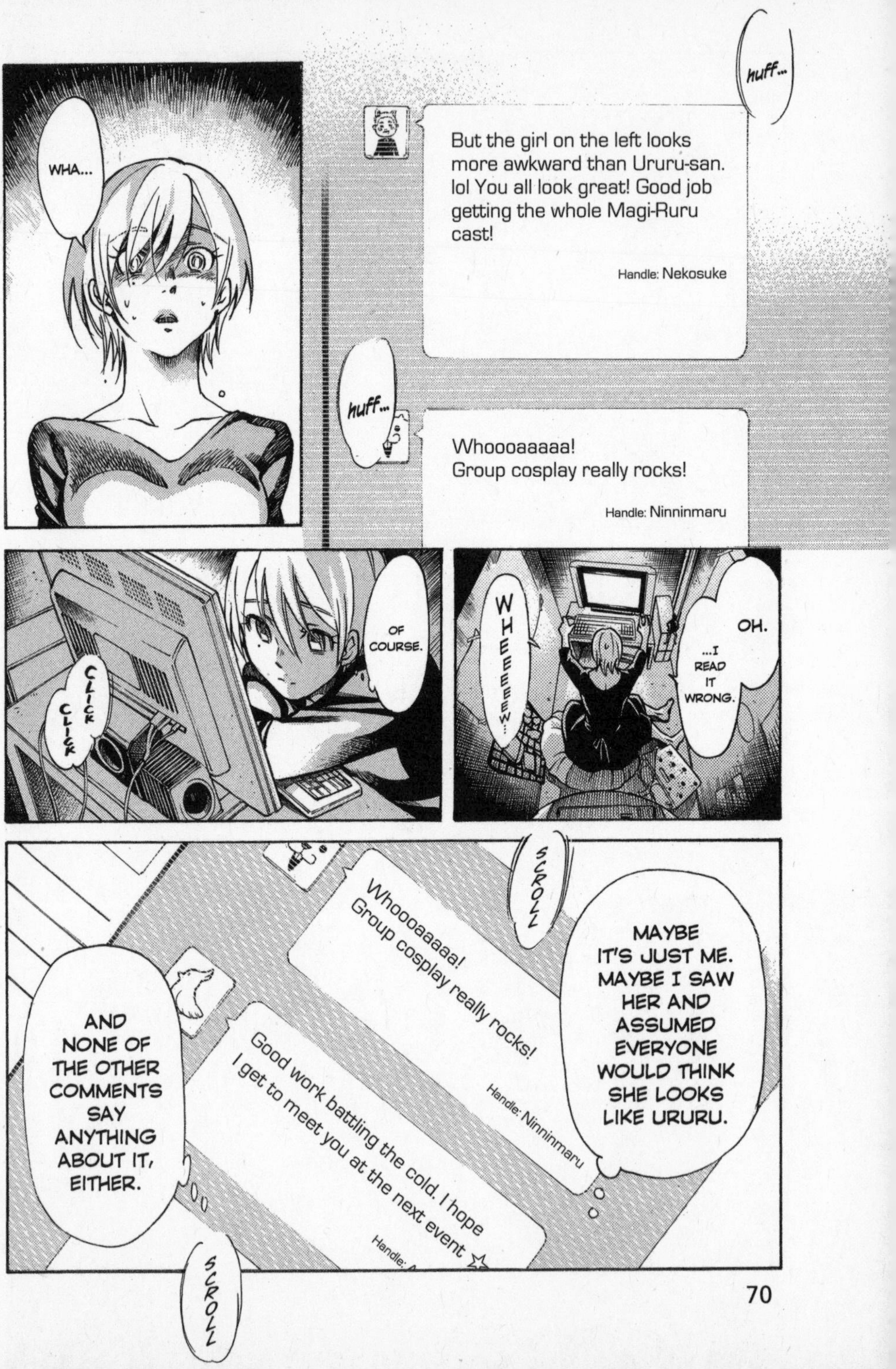
huff...
But the girl on the left looks more awkward than Ururu-san. lol You all look great! Good job getting the whole Magi-Ruru cast!
Handle: Nekosuke
huff...
Whoooaaaaa! Group cosplay really rocks!
Handle: Ninninmaru
WHA...
OH.
...I READ IT WRONG.
WHEEEEEW...
OF COURSE.
CLICK CLICK
SCROLL
MAYBE IT'S JUST ME. MAYBE I SAW HER AND ASSUMED EVERYONE WOULD THINK SHE LOOKS LIKE URURU.
Whoooaaaaa! Group cosplay really rocks!
Handle: Ninninmaru
Good work battling the cold. I hope I get to meet you at the next event ☆
AND NONE OF THE OTHER COMMENTS SAY ANYTHING ABOUT IT, EITHER.
SCROLL

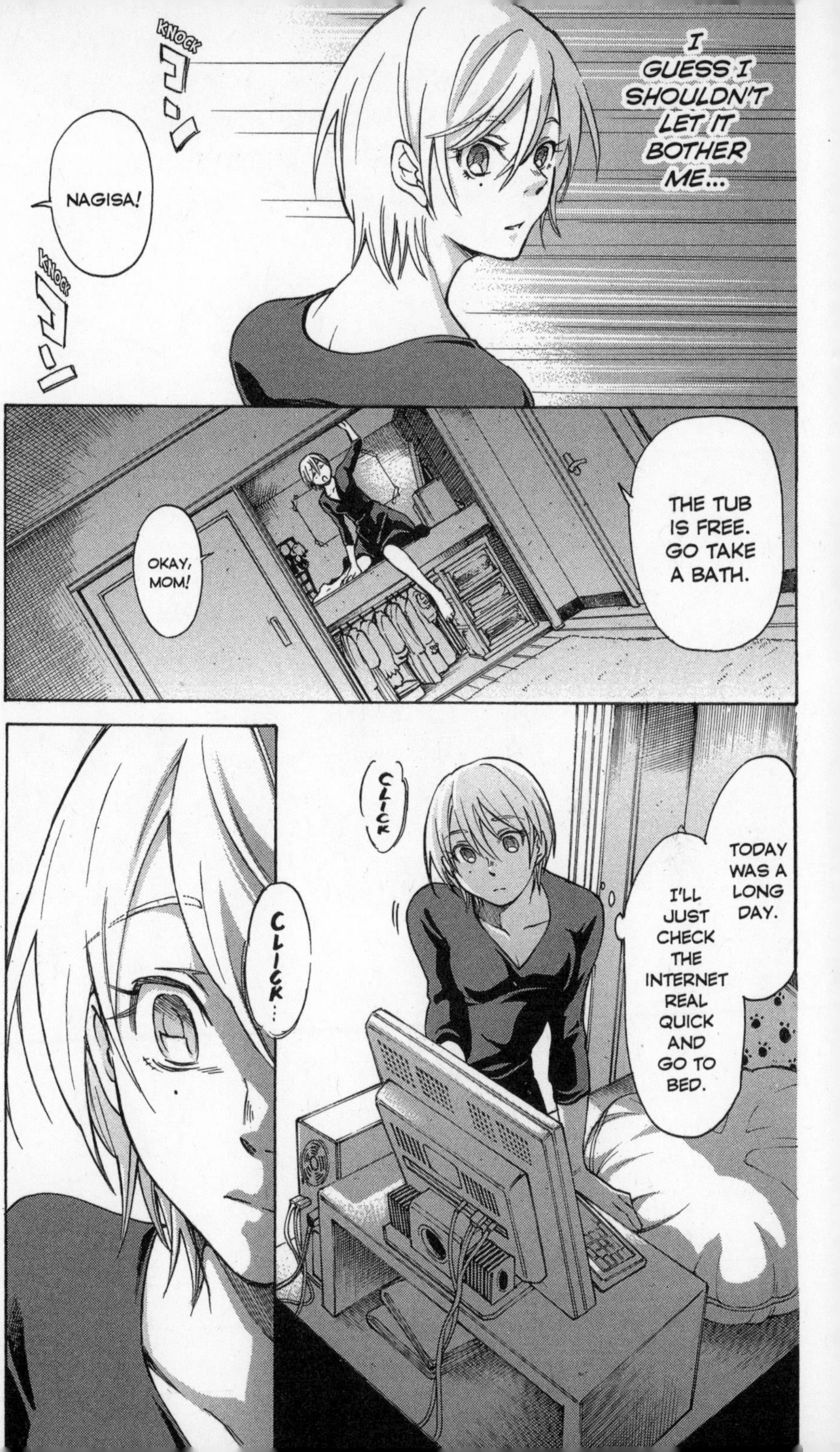
I GUESS I SHOULDN'T LET IT BOTHER ME...
KNOCK
NAGISA!
KNOCK
THE TUB IS FREE. GO TAKE A BATH.
OKAY, MOM!
TODAY WAS A LONG DAY.
I'LL JUST CHECK THE INTERNET REAL QUICK AND GO TO BED.
CLICK
CLICK...

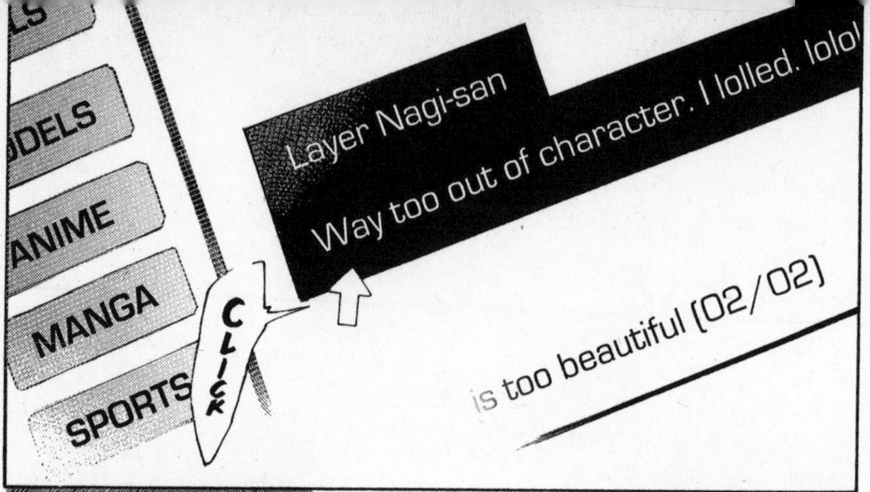
ANIME
MANGA
SPORTS
CLICK
Layer Nagi-san
Way too out of character. I lolled. lolo
is too beautiful (02/02)

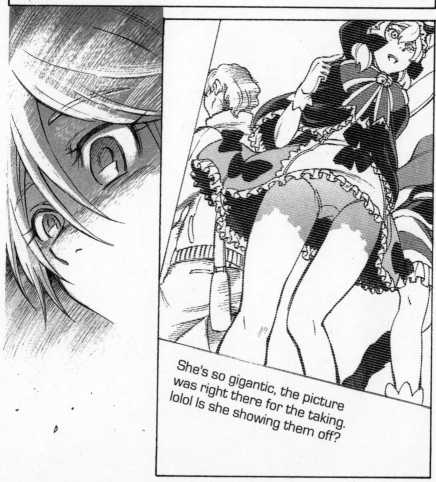

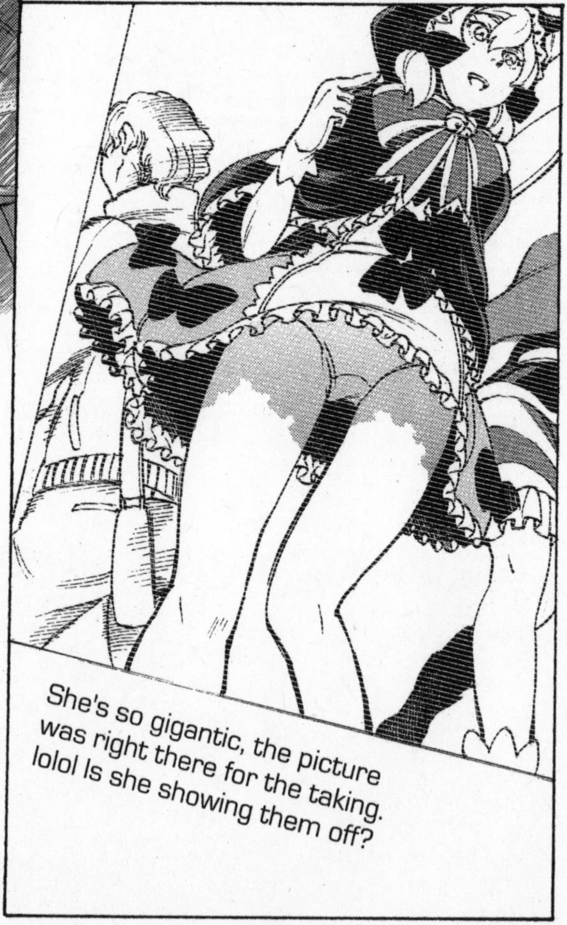
She's so gigantic, the picture was right there for the taking. lolol Is she showing them off?

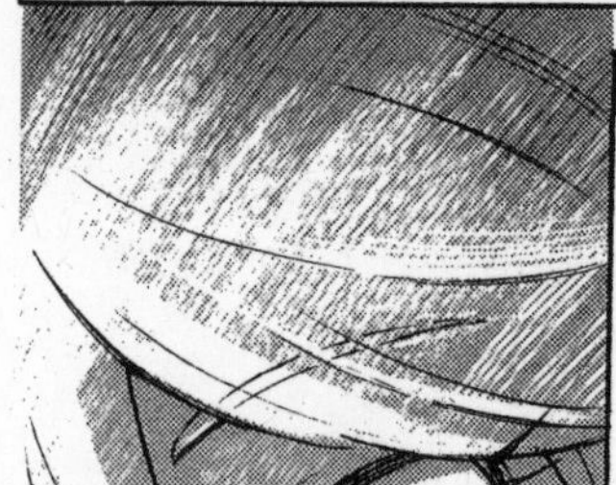

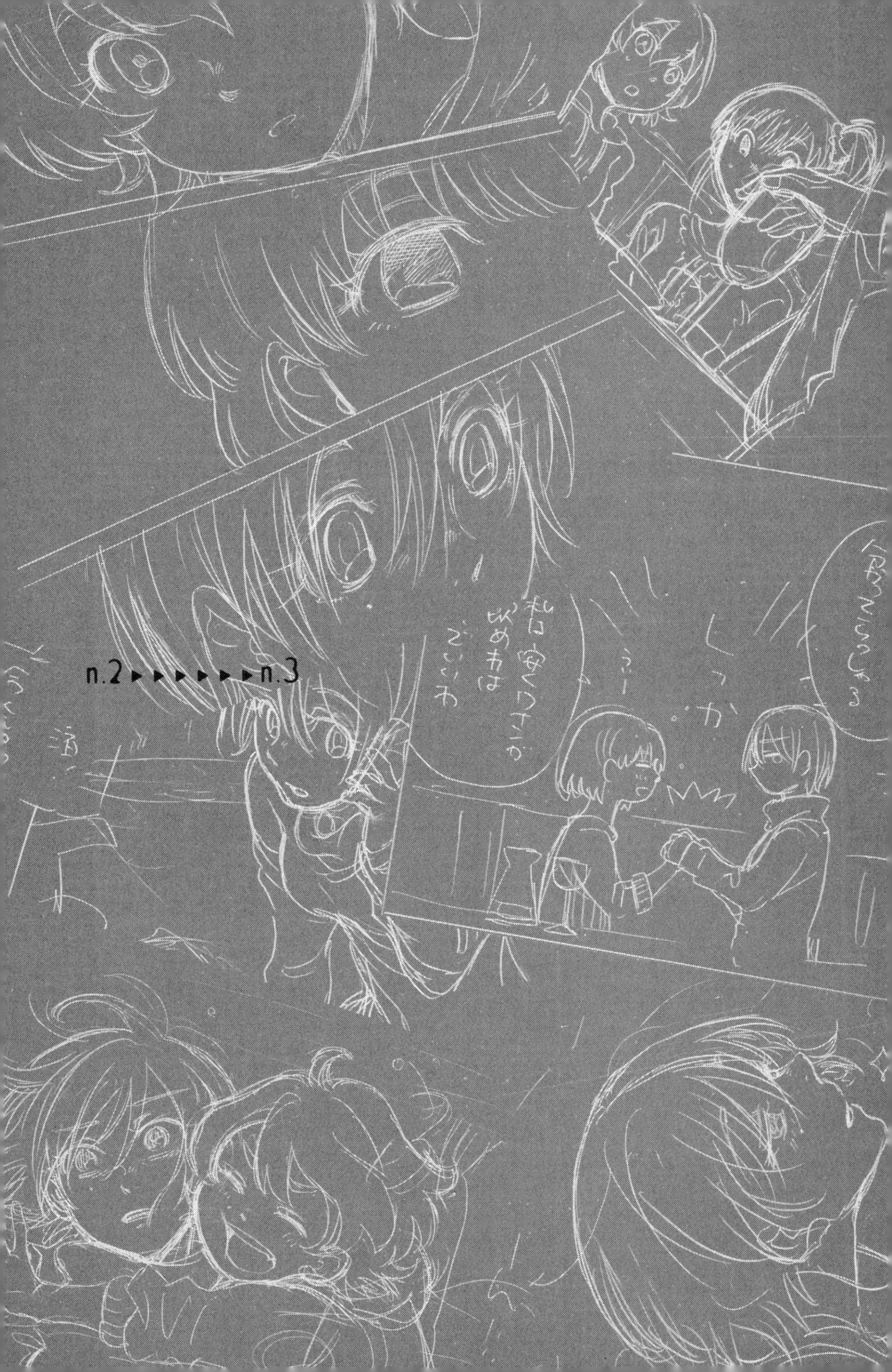
n.2▸▸▸▸▸▸▸n.3

Magical Riding Hood Ururu Complete Cosplay Festival! 2

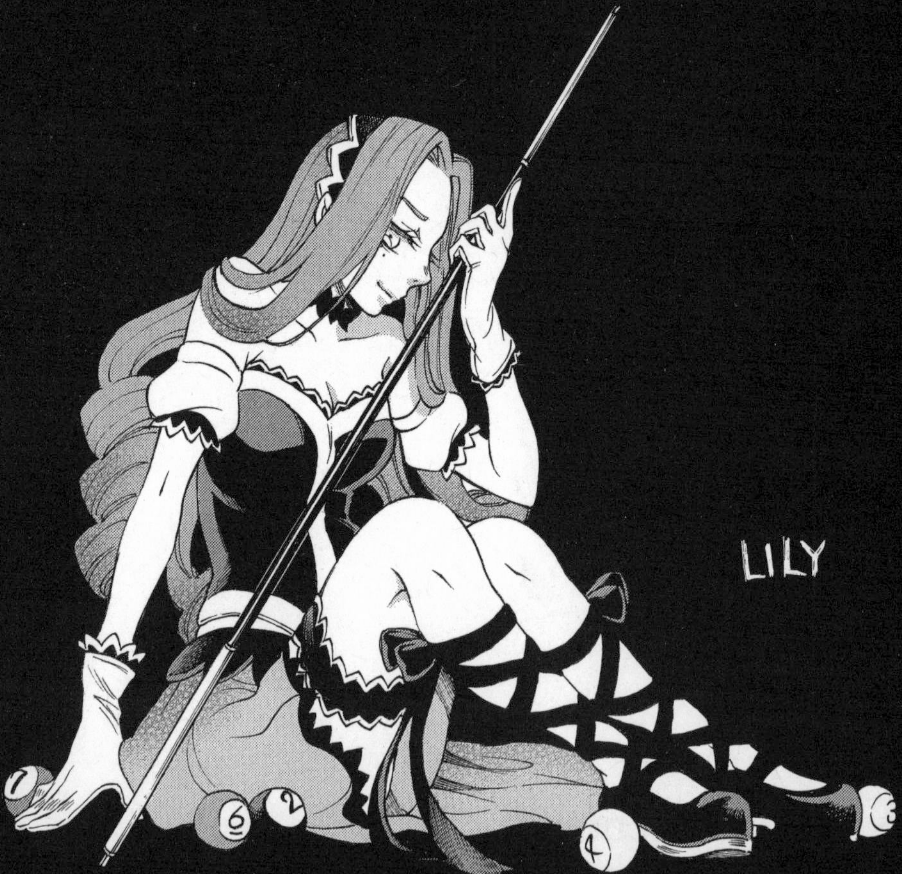
LILY

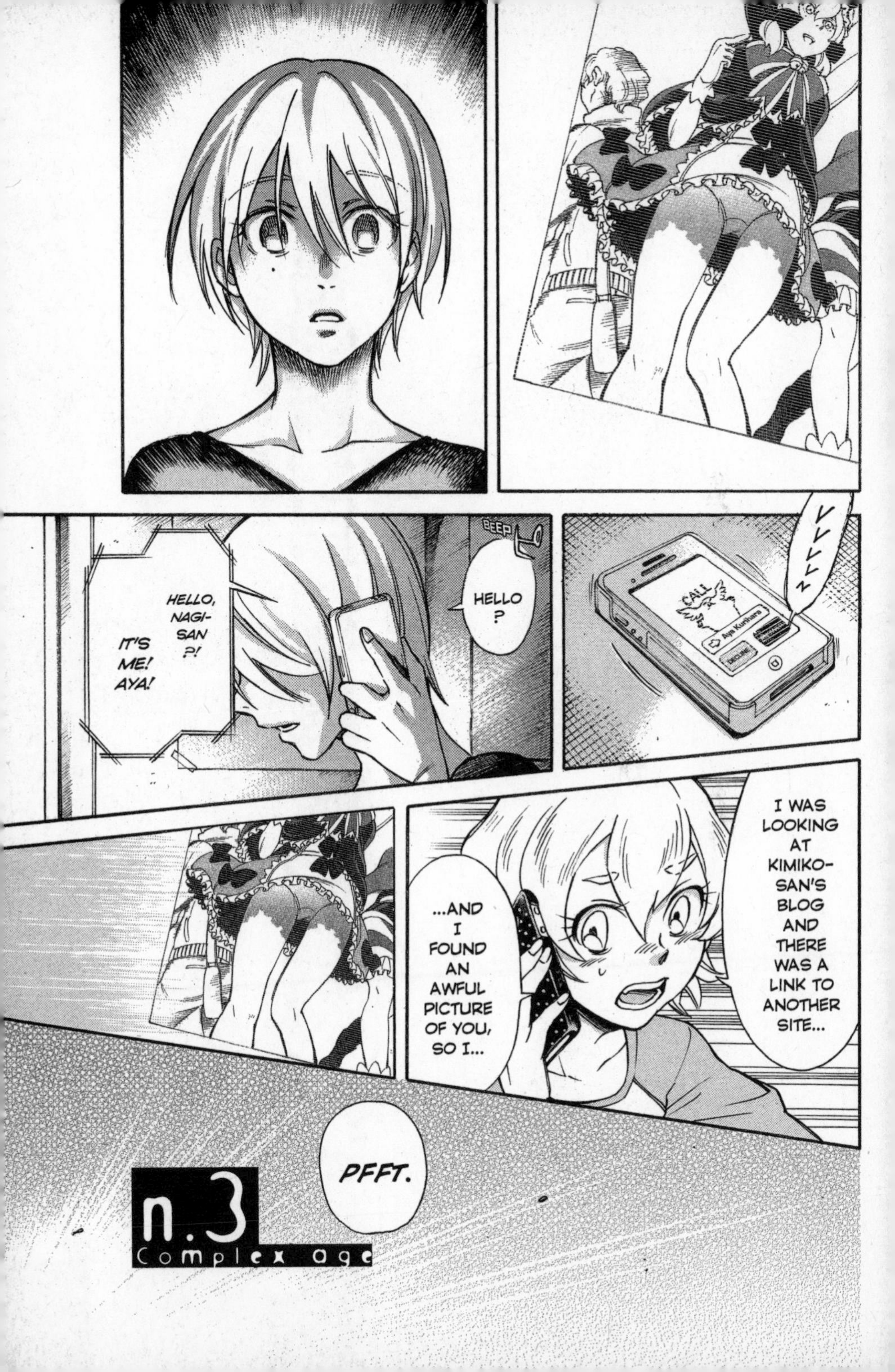
VVVVVN
CALL
Aya Kurihara
DECLINE
BEEP
HELLO?
HELLO, NAGI-SAN?!
IT'S ME! AYA!
I WAS LOOKING AT KIMIKO-SAN'S BLOG AND THERE WAS A LINK TO ANOTHER SITE...
...AND I FOUND AN AWFUL PICTURE OF YOU, SO I...
PFFT.
n.3
Complex age

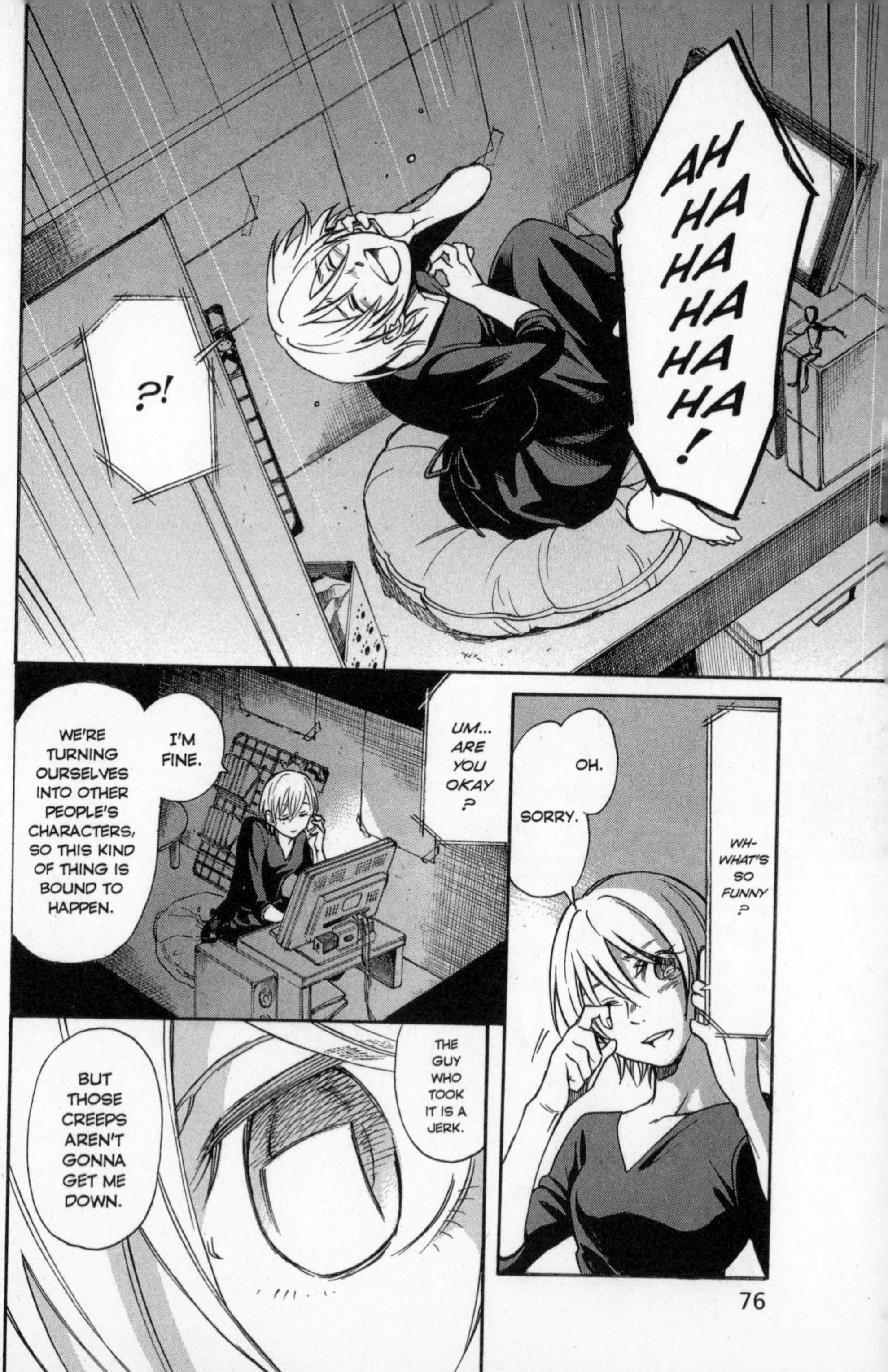
AH HAHAHAHAHA!
?!
OH. SORRY.
WH- WHAT'S SO FUNNY?
UM... ARE YOU OKAY?
I'M FINE.
WE'RE TURNING OURSELVES INTO OTHER PEOPLE'S CHARACTERS, SO THIS KIND OF THING IS BOUND TO HAPPEN.
THE GUY WHO TOOK IT IS A JERK.
BUT THOSE CREEPS AREN'T GONNA GET ME DOWN.

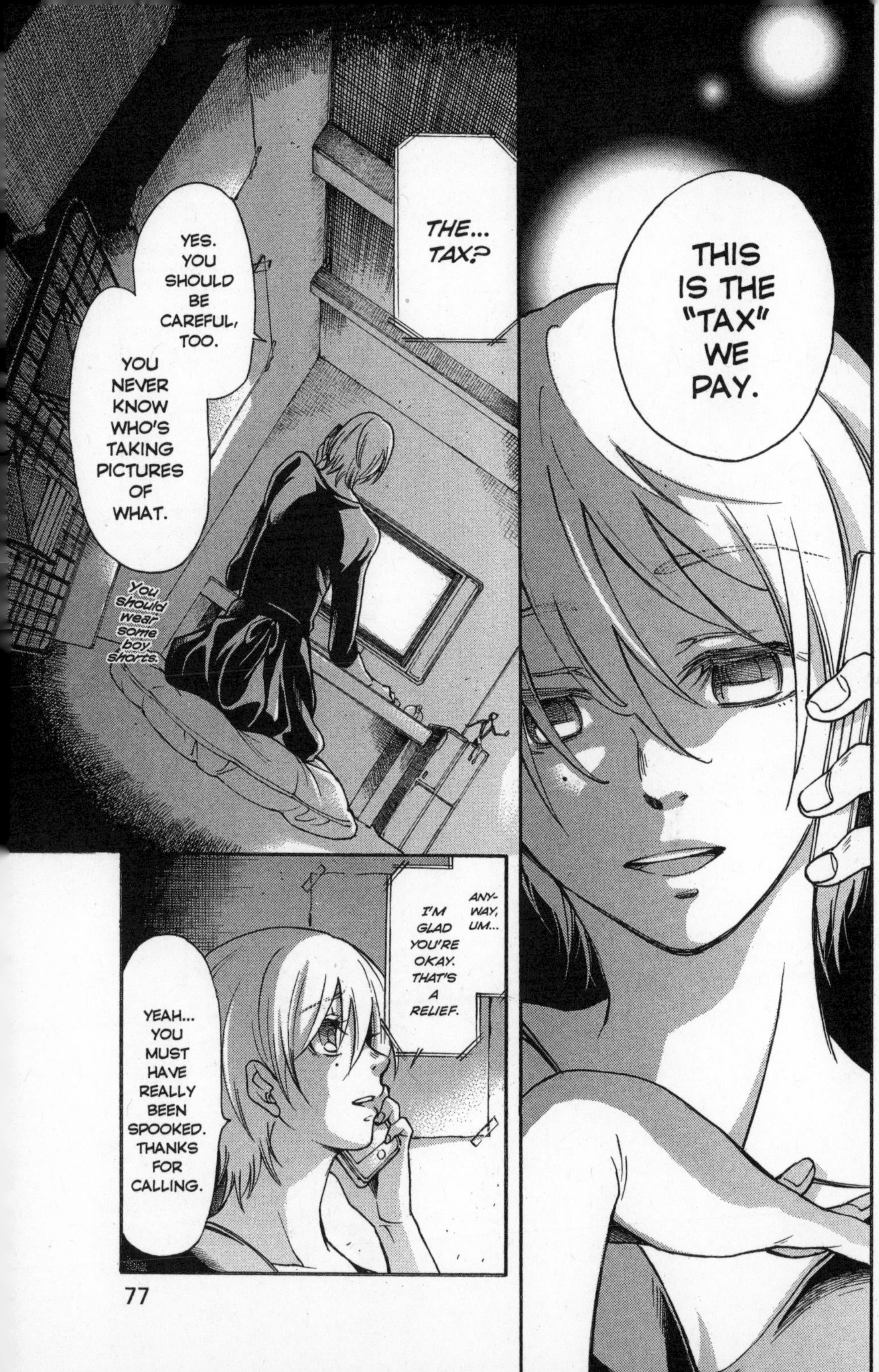
THIS IS THE "TAX" WE PAY.
THE... TAX?
YES. YOU SHOULD BE CAREFUL, TOO.
YOU NEVER KNOW WHO'S TAKING PICTURES OF WHAT.
You should wear some boy shorts.
ANY-WAY, UM...
I'M GLAD YOU'RE OKAY. THAT'S A RELIEF.
YEAH... YOU MUST HAVE REALLY BEEN SPOOKED. THANKS FOR CALLING.

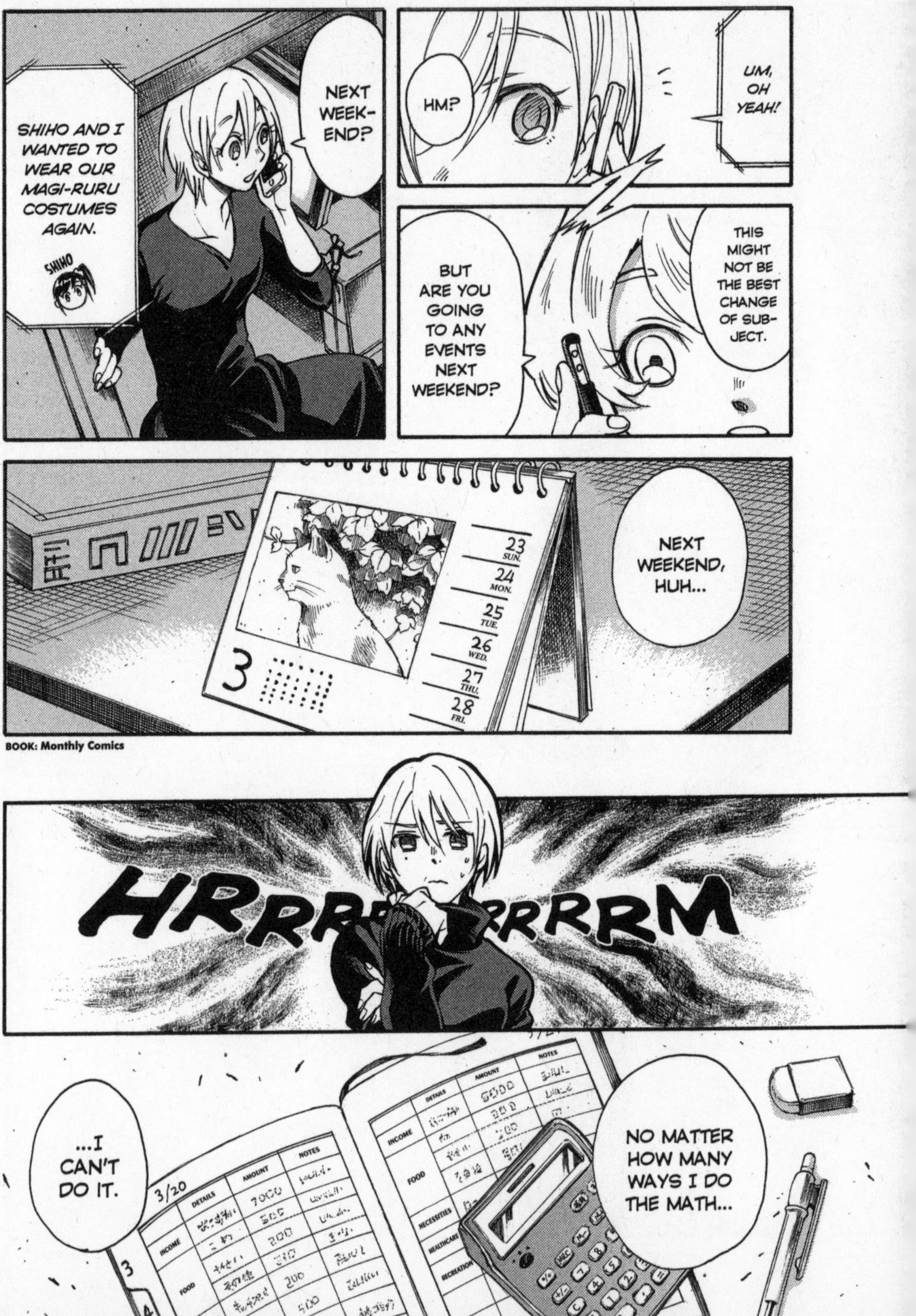
UM, OH YEAH!
HM?
THIS MIGHT NOT BE THE BEST CHANGE OF SUB-JECT.
BUT ARE YOU GOING TO ANY EVENTS NEXT WEEKEND?
NEXT WEEK-END?
SHIHO AND I WANTED TO WEAR OUR MAGI-RURU COSTUMES AGAIN.
SHIHO
NEXT WEEKEND, HUH...
23 SUN. 24 MON. 25 TUE. 26 WED. 27 THU. 28 FRI.
3
HRRRRRRRRRM
NO MATTER HOW MANY WAYS I DO THE MATH...
...I CAN'T DO IT.
3/20
DETAILS AMOUNT NOTES
INCOME FOOD NECESSITIES HEALTHCARE RECREATION TOTAL EXPENSES
BOOK: Monthly Comics

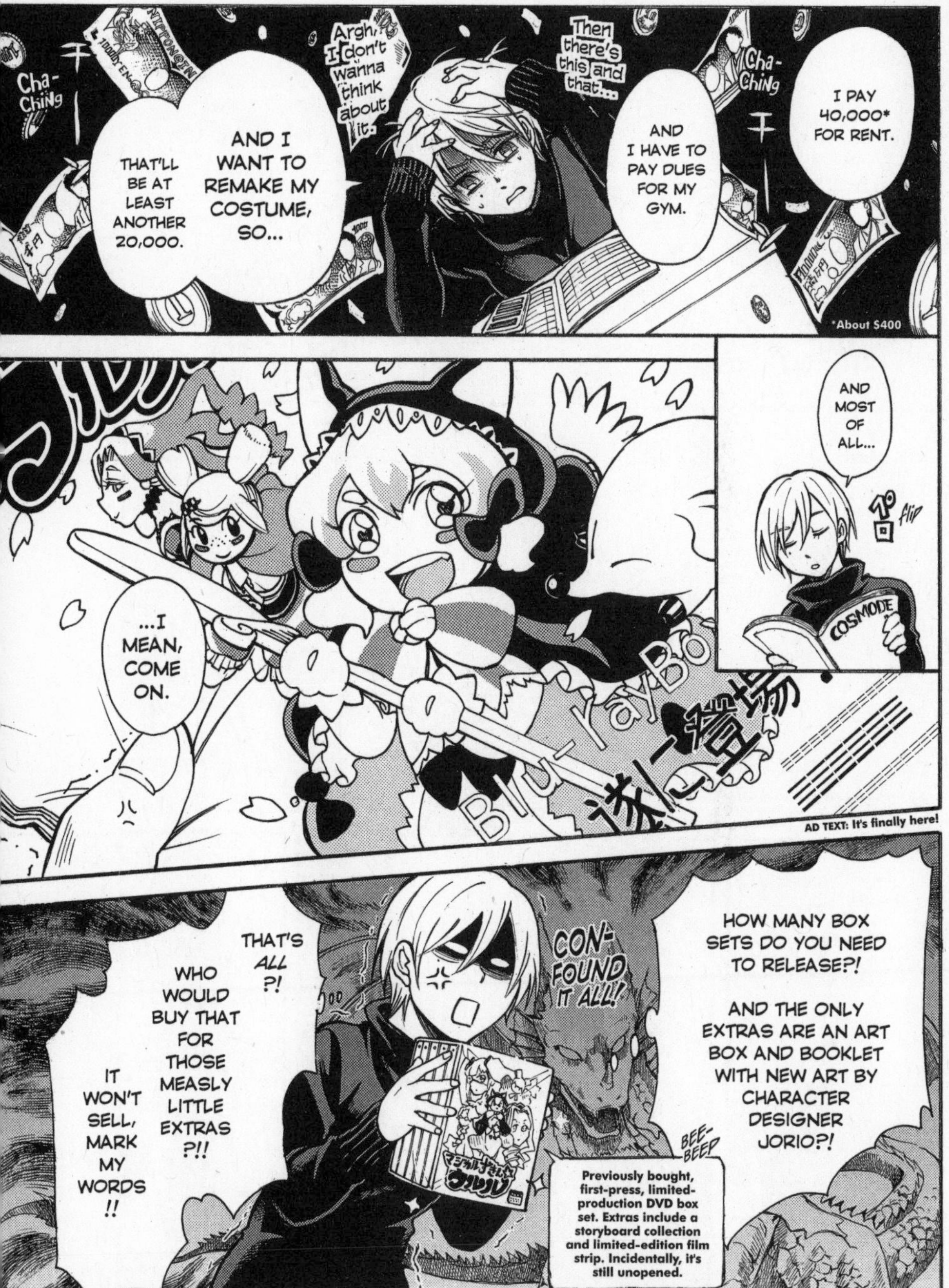
I PAY 40,000* FOR RENT.
Cha-Ching
AND I HAVE TO PAY DUES FOR MY GYM.
Then there's this and that...
Argh, I don't wanna think about it.
AND I WANT TO REMAKE MY COSTUME, SO...
THAT'LL BE AT LEAST ANOTHER 20,000.
Cha-Ching
*About $400
AND MOST OF ALL...
flip
COSMODE
...I MEAN, COME ON.
Blu-ray Box
AD TEXT: It's finally here!
HOW MANY BOX SETS DO YOU NEED TO RELEASE?!
AND THE ONLY EXTRAS ARE AN ART BOX AND BOOKLET WITH NEW ART BY CHARACTER DESIGNER JORIO?!
CON-FOUND IT ALL!
BEE-BEEP
Previously bought, first-press, limited-production DVD box set. Extras include a storyboard collection and limited-edition film strip. Incidentally, it's still unopened.
THAT'S ALL ?!
WHO WOULD BUY THAT FOR THOSE MEASLY LITTLE EXTRAS ?!!
IT WON'T SELL, MARK MY WORDS !!

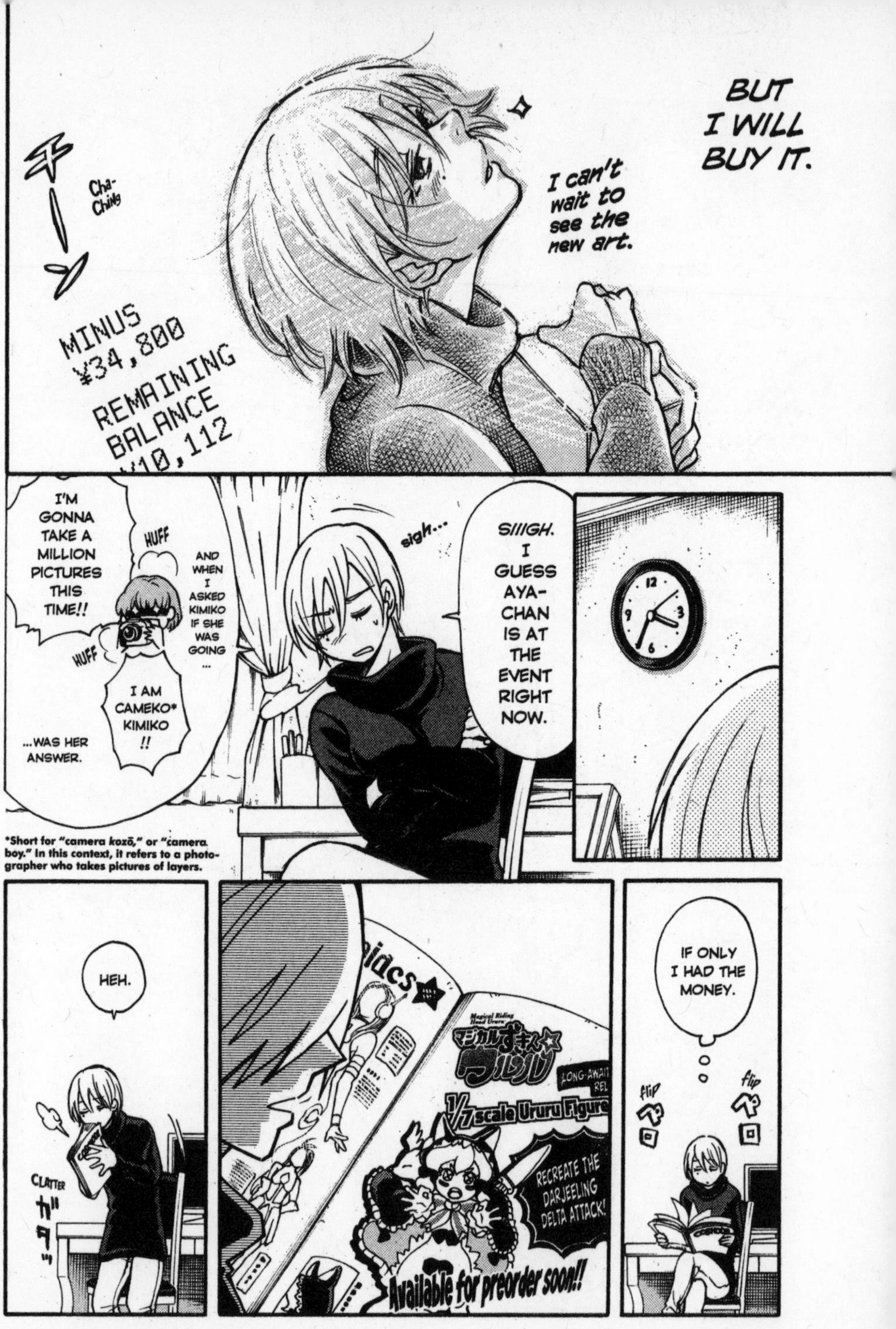
BUT I WILL BUY IT.
I can't wait to see the new art.
Cha-Ching
MINUS ¥34,800
REMAINING BALANCE ¥10,112
SIIIGH. I GUESS AYA-CHAN IS AT THE EVENT RIGHT NOW.
sigh...
I'M GONNA TAKE A MILLION PICTURES THIS TIME!!
HUFF
HUFF
AND WHEN I ASKED KIMIKO IF SHE WAS GOING ...
I AM CAMEKO* KIMIKO !!
...WAS HER ANSWER.
IF ONLY I HAD THE MONEY.
flip
flip
Magical Riding Hood Ururu
マジカルずきん☆ウルル
1/7 scale Ururu Figure
RECREATE THE DARJEELING DELTA ATTACK!
Available for preorder soon!!
HEH.
CLATTER

*Short for "camera kozō," or "camera boy." In this context, it refers to a photographer who takes pictures of layers.

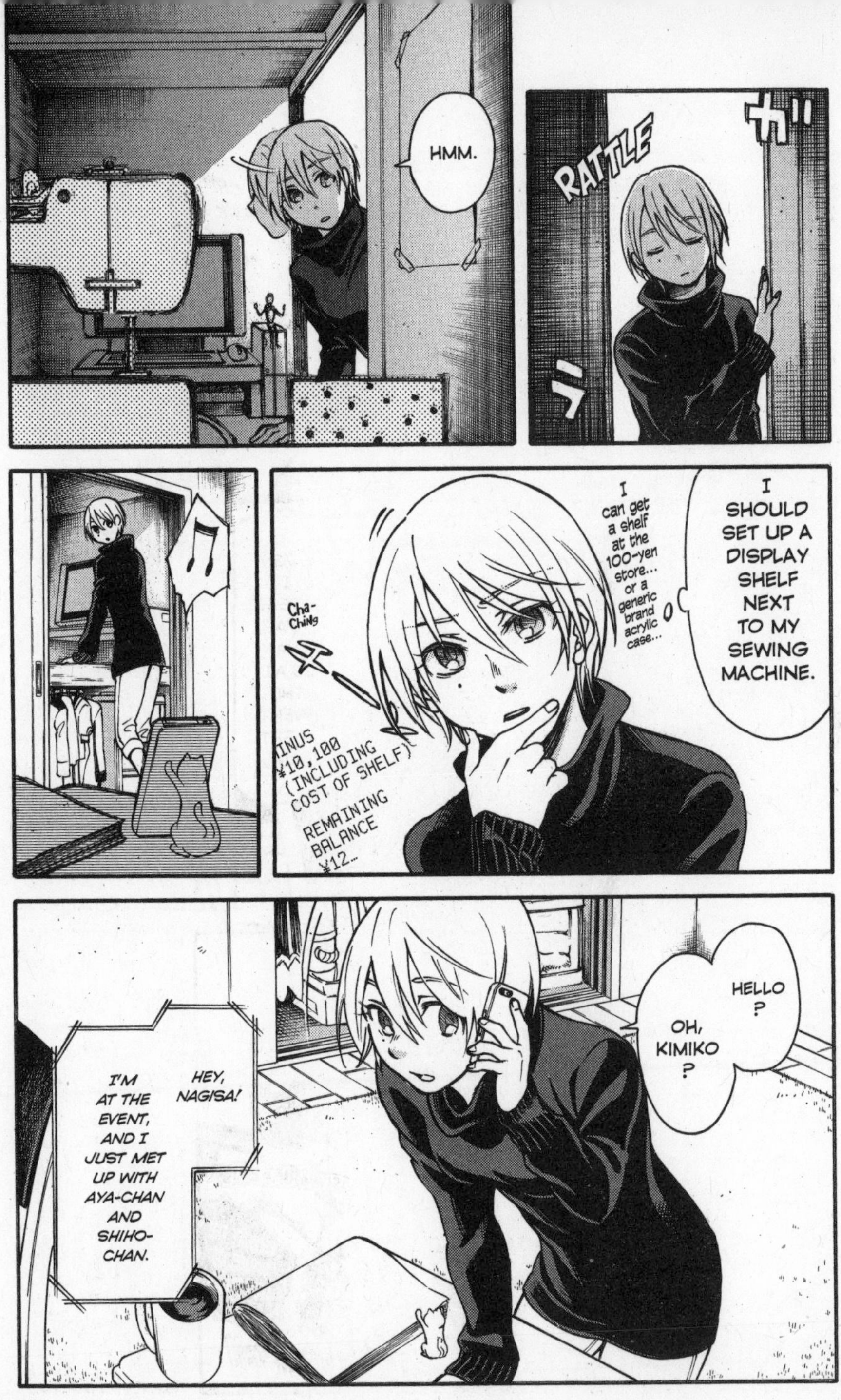

RATTLE
ガ
ラ
HMM.
I SHOULD SET UP A DISPLAY SHELF NEXT TO MY SEWING MACHINE.
I can get a shelf at the 100-yen store... or a generic brand acrylic case...
Cha-Ching
INUS ¥10,100 (INCLUDING COST OF SHELF)
REMAINING BALANCE ¥12...
HELLO?
OH, KIMIKO?
HEY, NAGISA!
I'M AT THE EVENT, AND I JUST MET UP WITH AYA-CHAN AND SHIHO-CHAN.

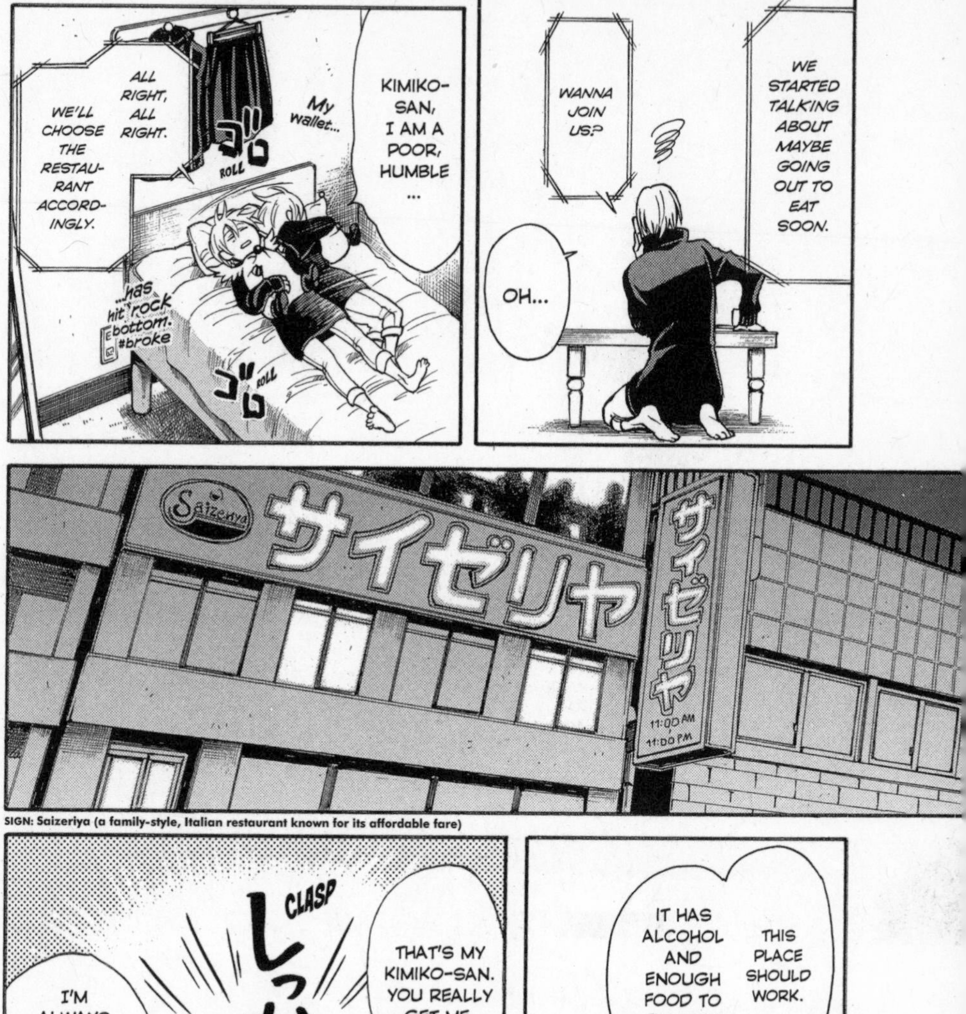
WE STARTED TALKING ABOUT MAYBE GOING OUT TO EAT SOON.
WANNA JOIN US?
OH...
KIMIKO-SAN, I AM A POOR, HUMBLE ...
My wallet...
...has hit rock bottom. #broke
ゴロ
ROLL
ゴロ
ROLL
ALL RIGHT, ALL RIGHT.
WE'LL CHOOSE THE RESTAU-RANT ACCORD-INGLY.
Saizeriya
サイゼリヤ
サイゼリヤ
11:00 AM
11:00 PM

SIGN: Saizeriya (a family-style, Italian restaurant known for its affordable fare)

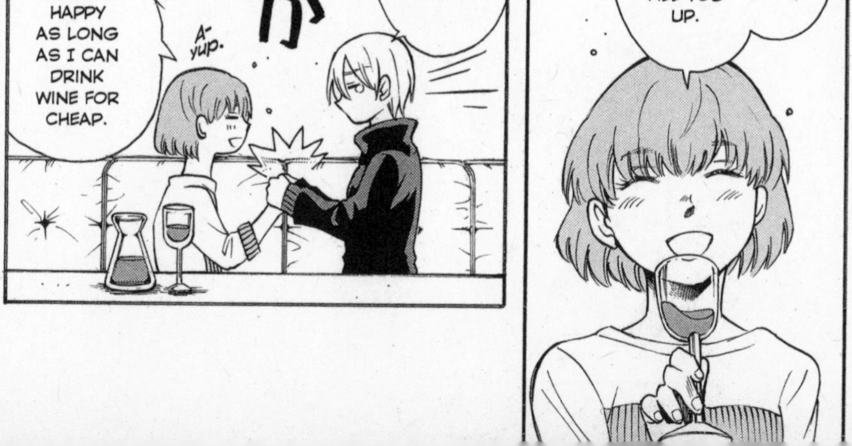
THIS PLACE SHOULD WORK.
IT HAS ALCOHOL AND ENOUGH FOOD TO FILL YOU UP.
THAT'S MY KIMIKO-SAN. YOU REALLY GET ME.
しっか
CLASP
A-yup.
I'M ALWAYS HAPPY AS LONG AS I CAN DRINK WINE FOR CHEAP.

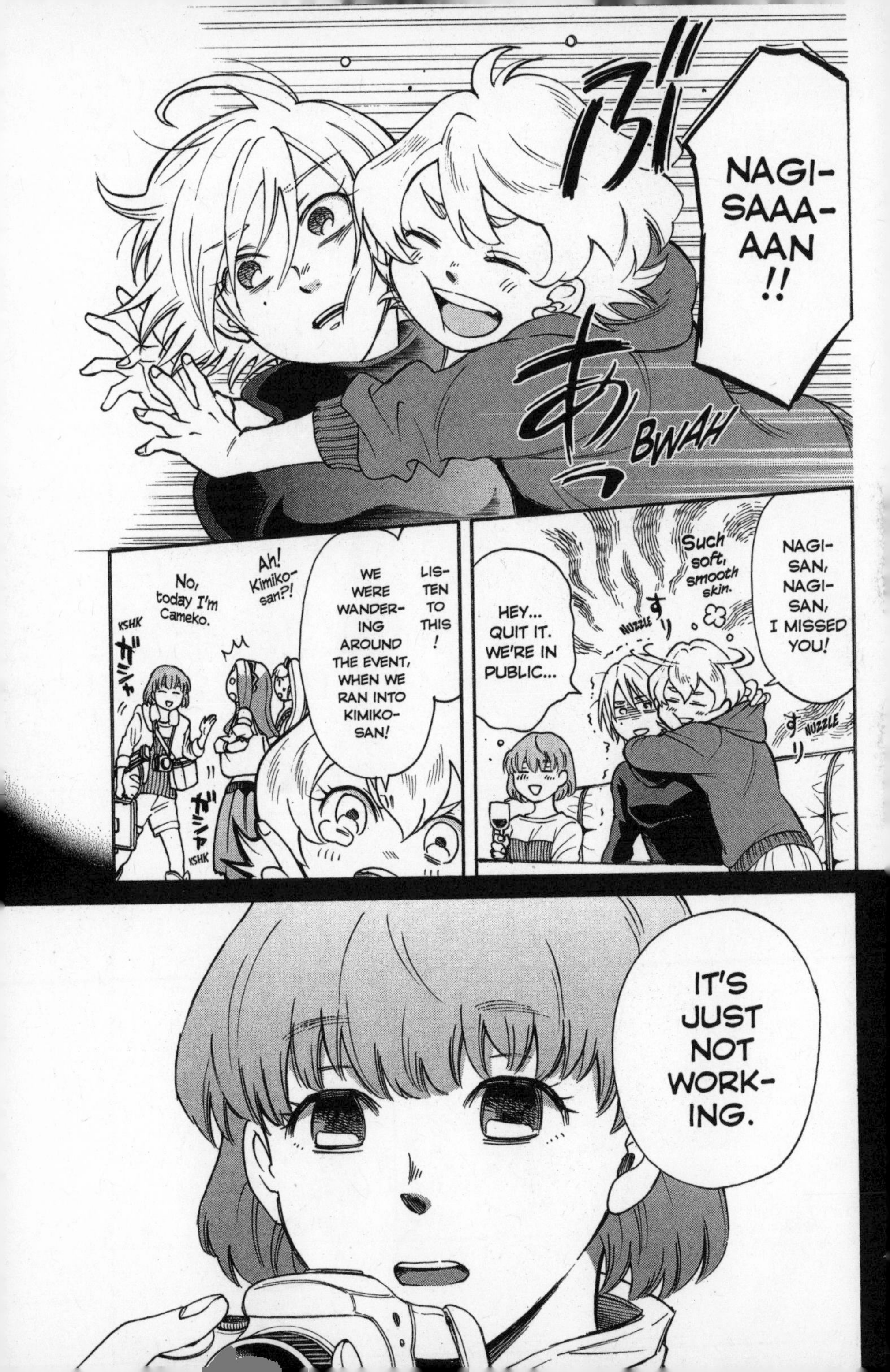
NAGI-SAAAA-AAN!!
BWAH
NAGI-SAN, NAGI-SAN, I MISSED YOU!
Such soft, smooth skin.
NUZZLE
NUZZLE
HEY... QUIT IT. WE'RE IN PUBLIC...
LISTEN TO THIS!
WE WERE WANDERING AROUND THE EVENT, WHEN WE RAN INTO KIMIKO-SAN!
Ah! Kimiko-san?!
No, today I'm Cameko.
KSHK
KSHK
IT'S JUST NOT WORKING.

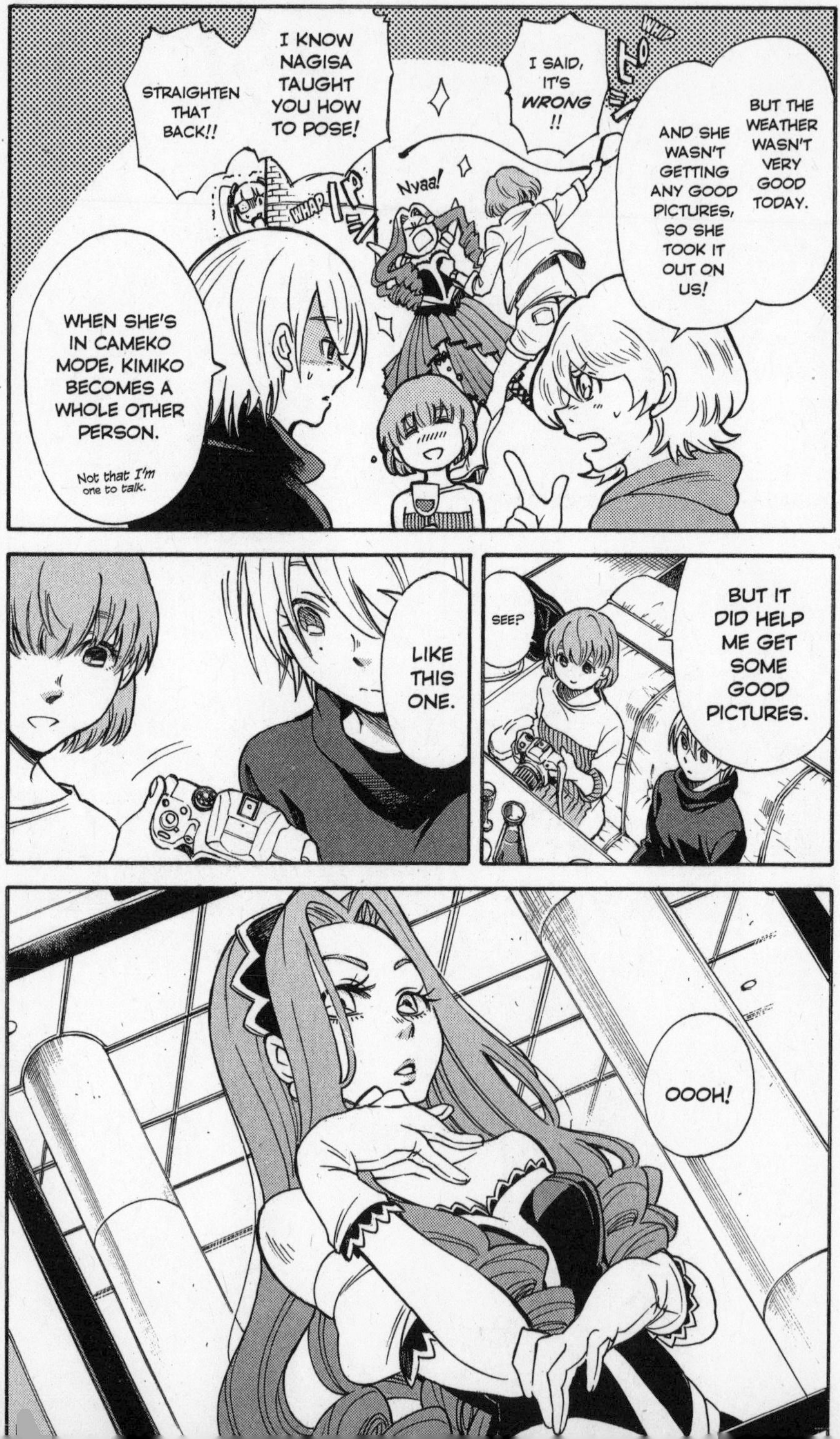
BUT THE WEATHER WASN'T VERY GOOD TODAY.
AND SHE WASN'T GETTING ANY GOOD PICTURES, SO SHE TOOK IT OUT ON US!
WHIP
I SAID, IT'S *WRONG*!!
I KNOW NAGISA TAUGHT YOU HOW TO POSE!
STRAIGHTEN THAT BACK!!
Nyaa!
WHAP
WHEN SHE'S IN CAMEKO MODE, KIMIKO BECOMES A WHOLE OTHER PERSON.
Not that *I'm* one to talk.
BUT IT DID HELP ME GET SOME GOOD PICTURES.
SEE?
LIKE THIS ONE.
OOOH!

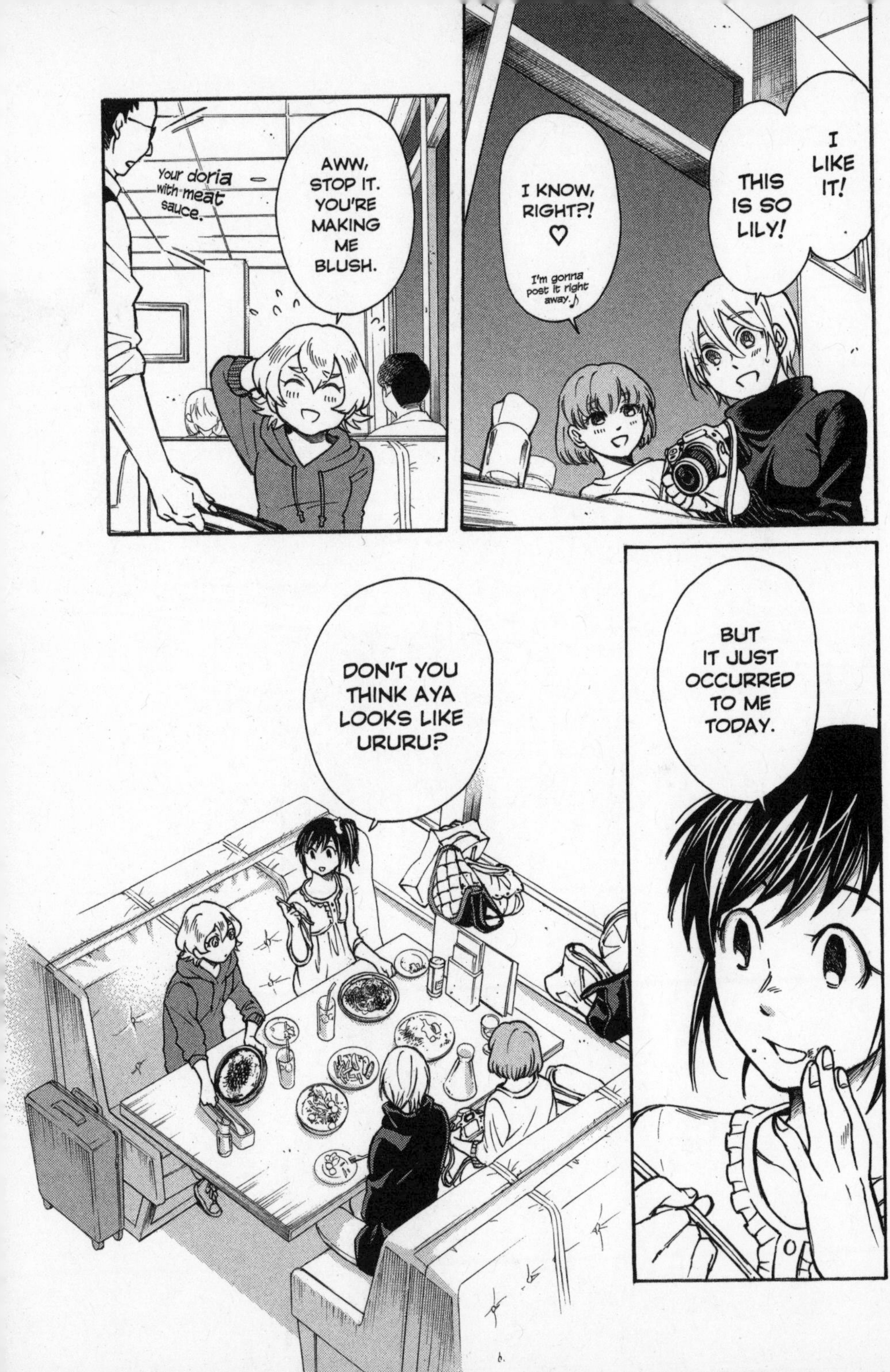
I LIKE IT!
THIS IS SO LILY!
I KNOW, RIGHT?! ♡
I'm gonna post it right away.♪
AWW, STOP IT. YOU'RE MAKING ME BLUSH.
Your doria with meat sauce.
BUT IT JUST OCCURRED TO ME TODAY.
DON'T YOU THINK AYA LOOKS LIKE URURU?

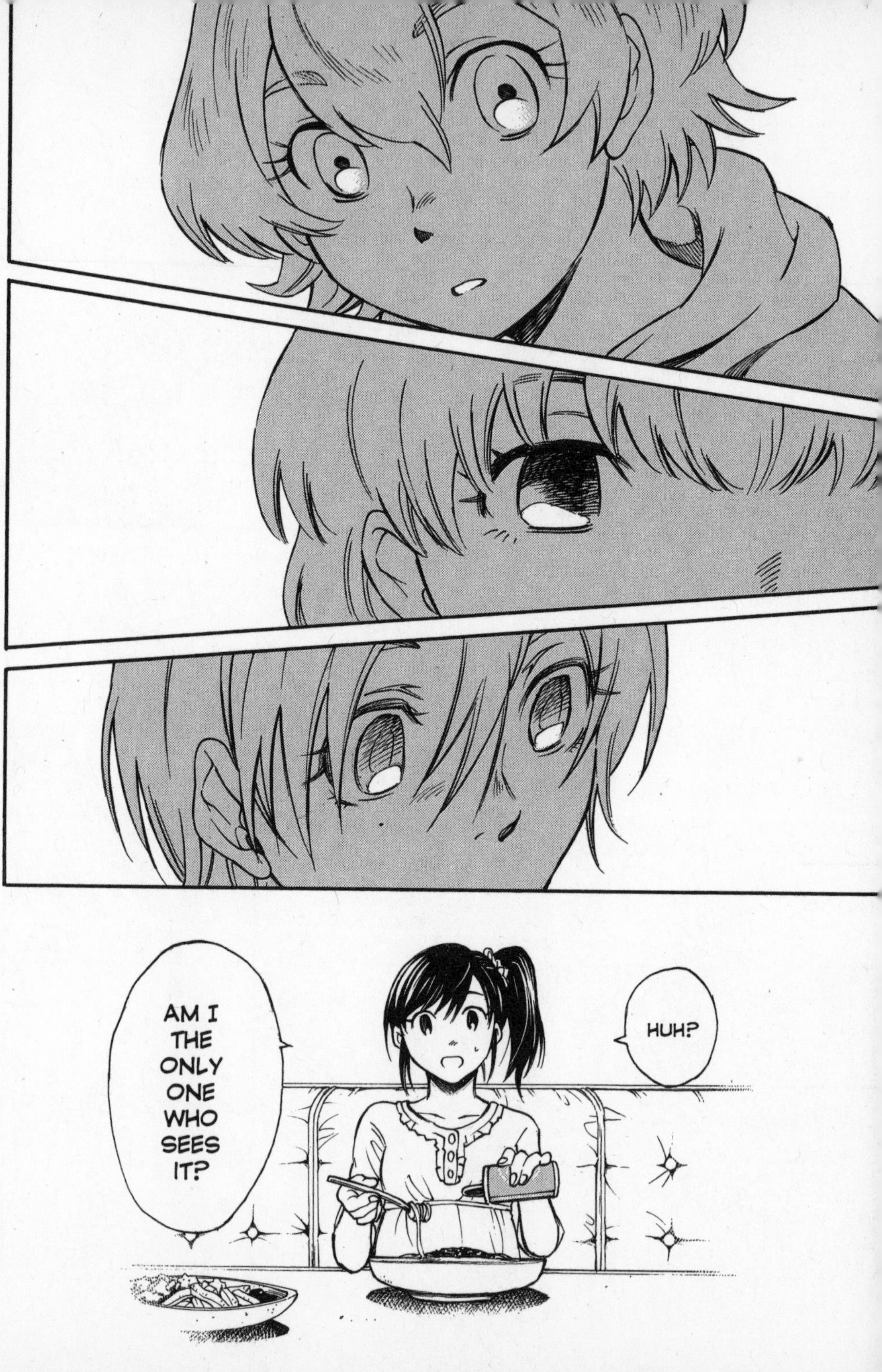
HUH?
AM I THE ONLY ONE WHO SEES IT?

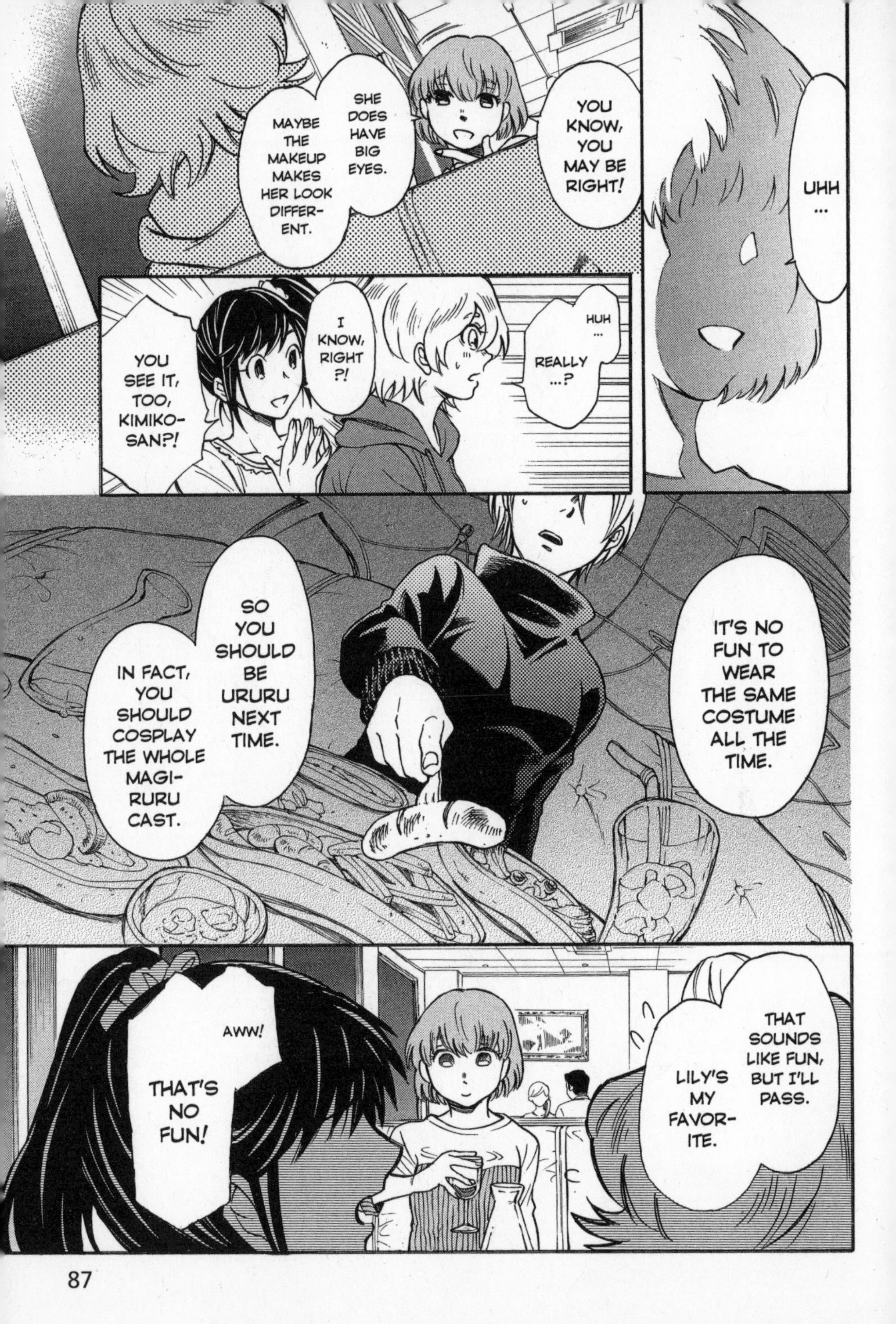
UHH...
YOU KNOW, YOU MAY BE RIGHT!
SHE DOES HAVE BIG EYES.
MAYBE THE MAKEUP MAKES HER LOOK DIFFER-ENT.
HUH... REALLY...?
I KNOW, RIGHT?!
YOU SEE IT, TOO, KIMIKO-SAN?!
IT'S NO FUN TO WEAR THE SAME COSTUME ALL THE TIME.
SO YOU SHOULD BE URURU NEXT TIME.
IN FACT, YOU SHOULD COSPLAY THE WHOLE MAGI-RURU CAST.
THAT SOUNDS LIKE FUN, BUT I'LL PASS.
LILY'S MY FAVOR-ITE.
AWW!
THAT'S NO FUN!

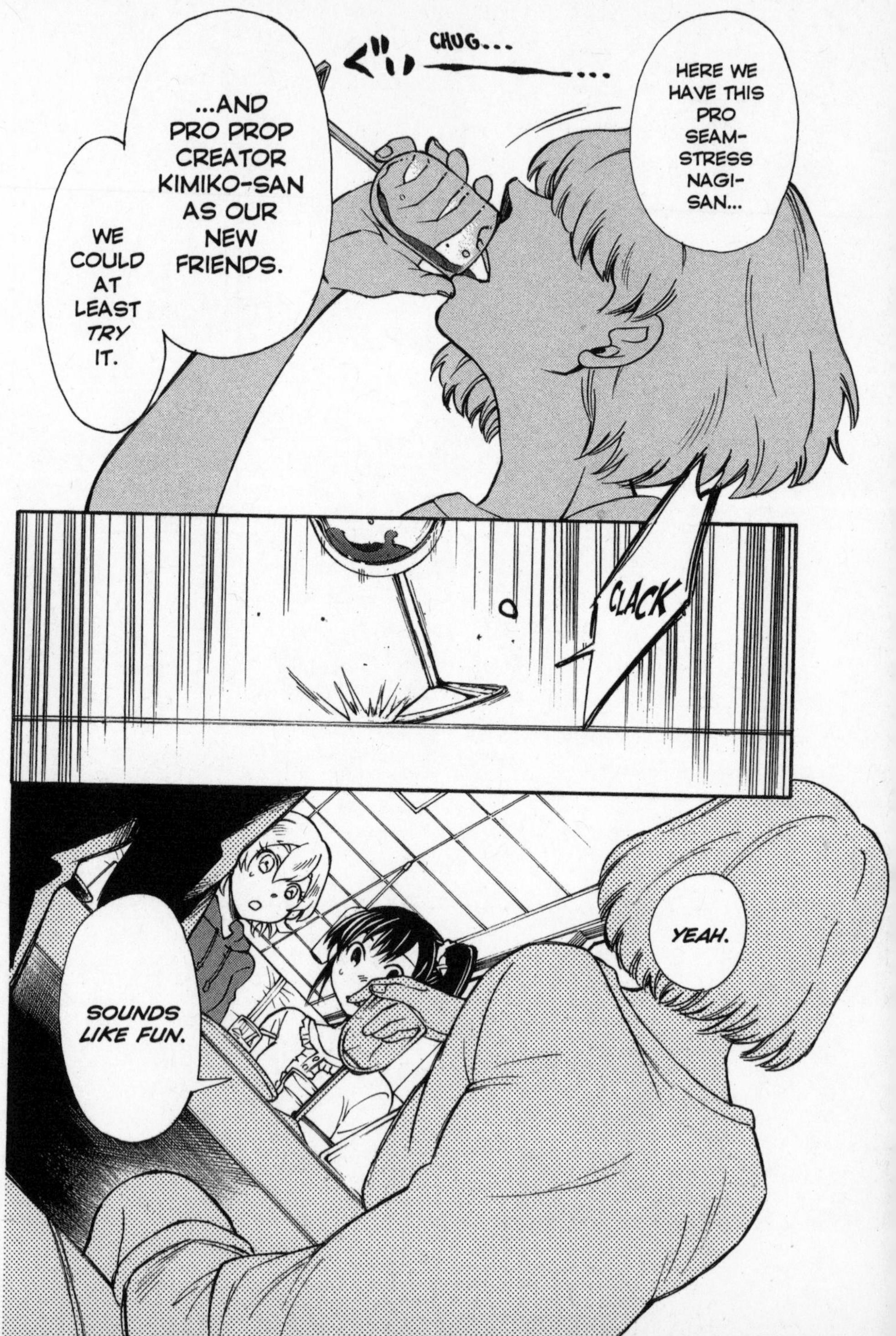

HERE WE HAVE THIS PRO SEAM-STRESS NAGI-SAN...
CHUG...
...AND PRO PROP CREATOR KIMIKO-SAN AS OUR NEW FRIENDS.
WE COULD AT LEAST *TRY* IT.
CLACK
YEAH.
SOUNDS LIKE FUN.

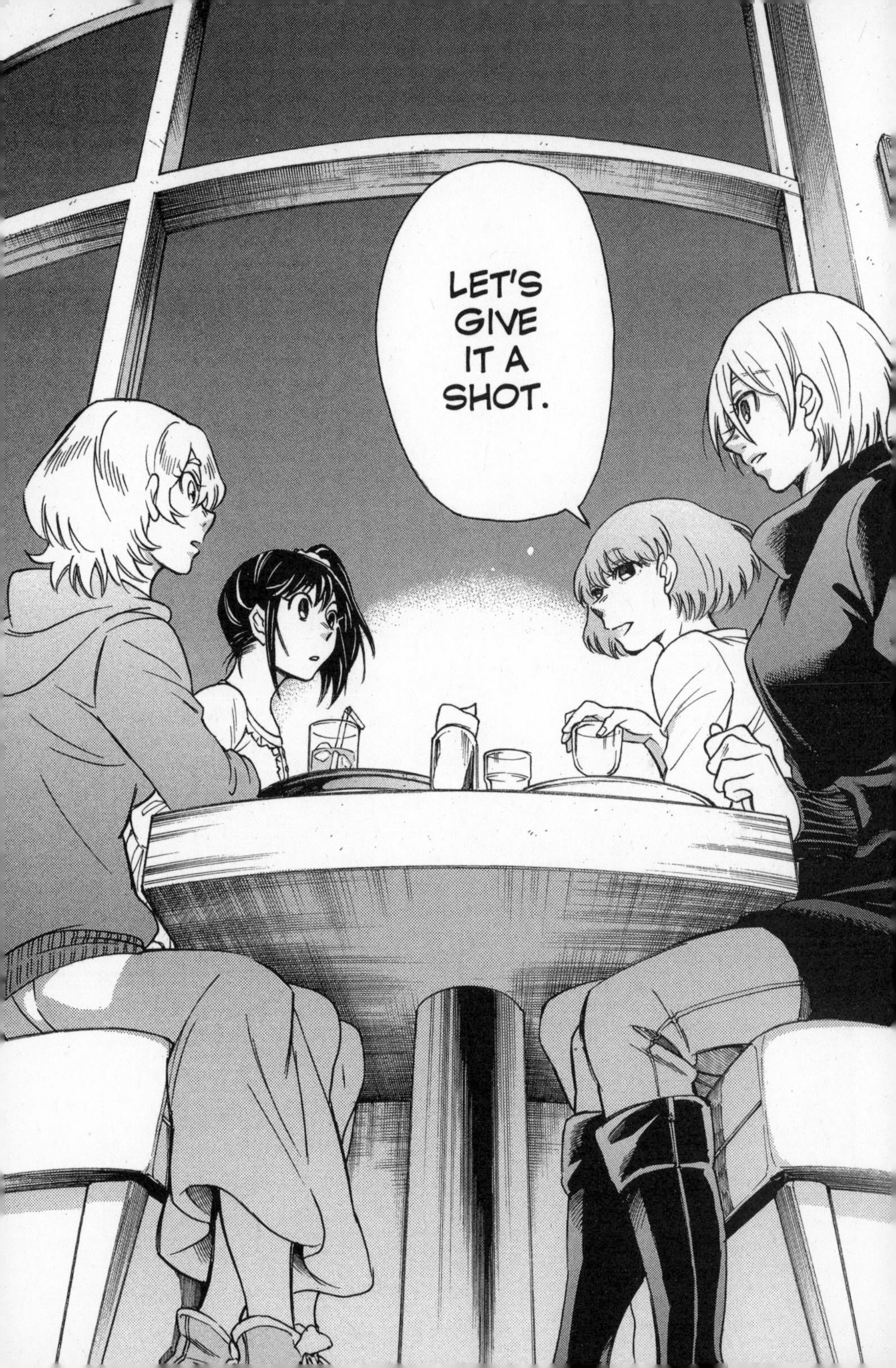
LET'S GIVE IT A SHOT.

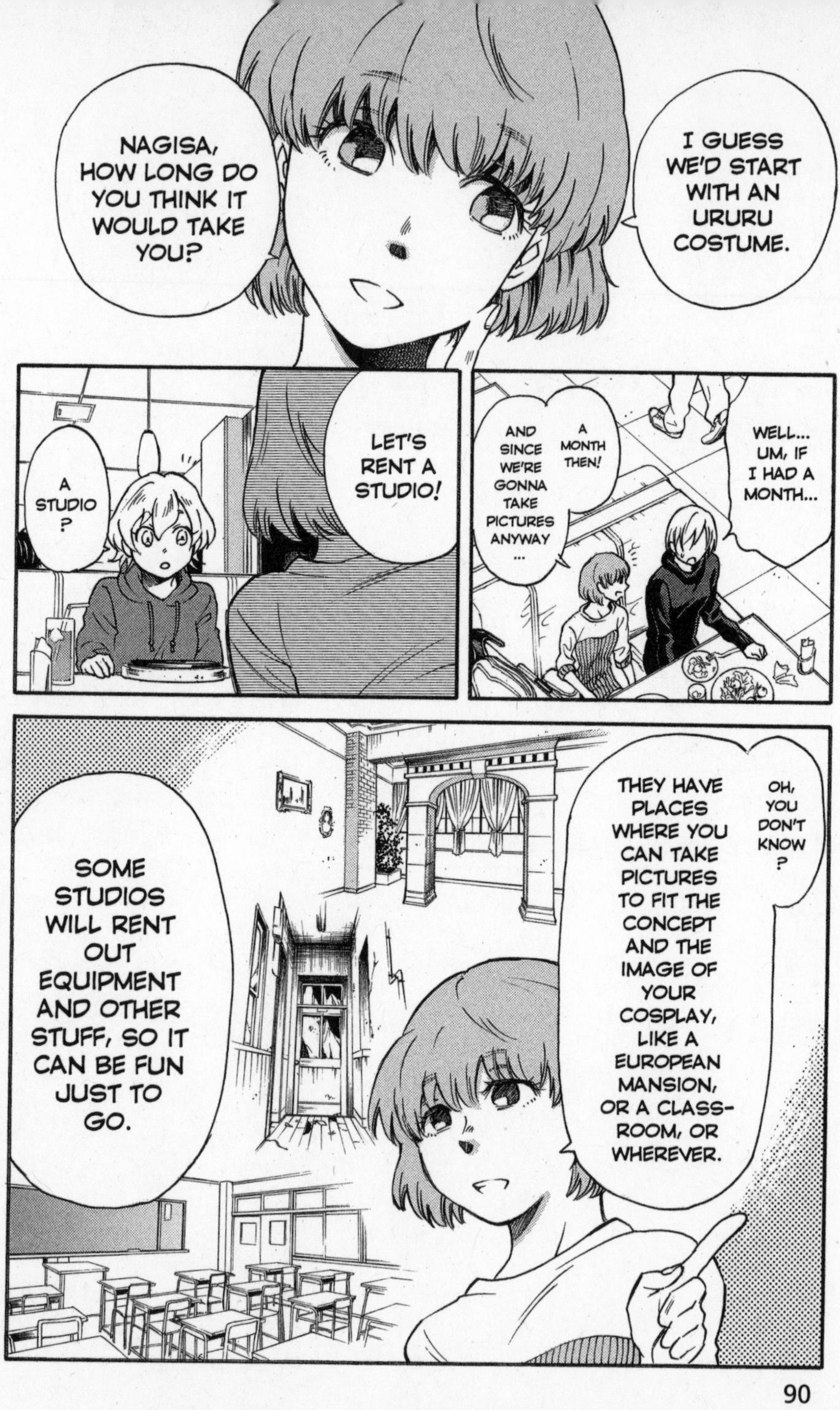
I GUESS WE'D START WITH AN URURU COSTUME.
NAGISA, HOW LONG DO YOU THINK IT WOULD TAKE YOU?
WELL... UM, IF I HAD A MONTH...
A MONTH THEN!
AND SINCE WE'RE GONNA TAKE PICTURES ANYWAY ...
LET'S RENT A STUDIO!
A STUDIO ?
OH, YOU DON'T KNOW ?
THEY HAVE PLACES WHERE YOU CAN TAKE PICTURES TO FIT THE CONCEPT AND THE IMAGE OF YOUR COSPLAY, LIKE A EUROPEAN MANSION, OR A CLASS-ROOM, OR WHEREVER.
SOME STUDIOS WILL RENT OUT EQUIPMENT AND OTHER STUFF, SO IT CAN BE FUN JUST TO GO.

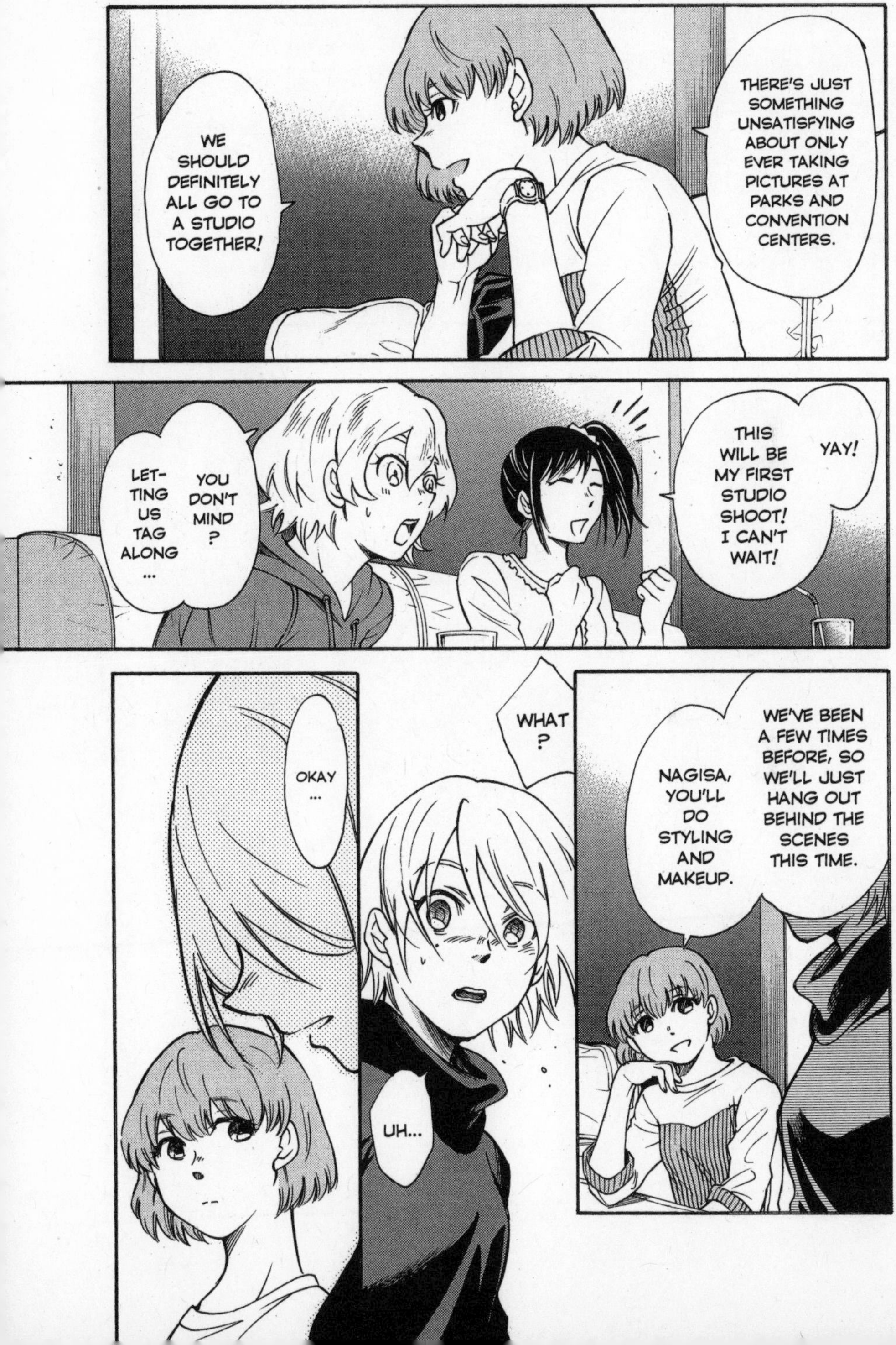
THERE'S JUST SOMETHING UNSATISFYING ABOUT ONLY EVER TAKING PICTURES AT PARKS AND CONVENTION CENTERS.
WE SHOULD DEFINITELY ALL GO TO A STUDIO TOGETHER!
THIS WILL BE MY FIRST STUDIO SHOOT! I CAN'T WAIT!
YAY!
YOU DON'T MIND? LETTING US TAG ALONG...
WE'VE BEEN A FEW TIMES BEFORE, SO WE'LL JUST HANG OUT BEHIND THE SCENES THIS TIME.
NAGISA, YOU'LL DO STYLING AND MAKEUP.
WHAT?
OKAY...
UH...

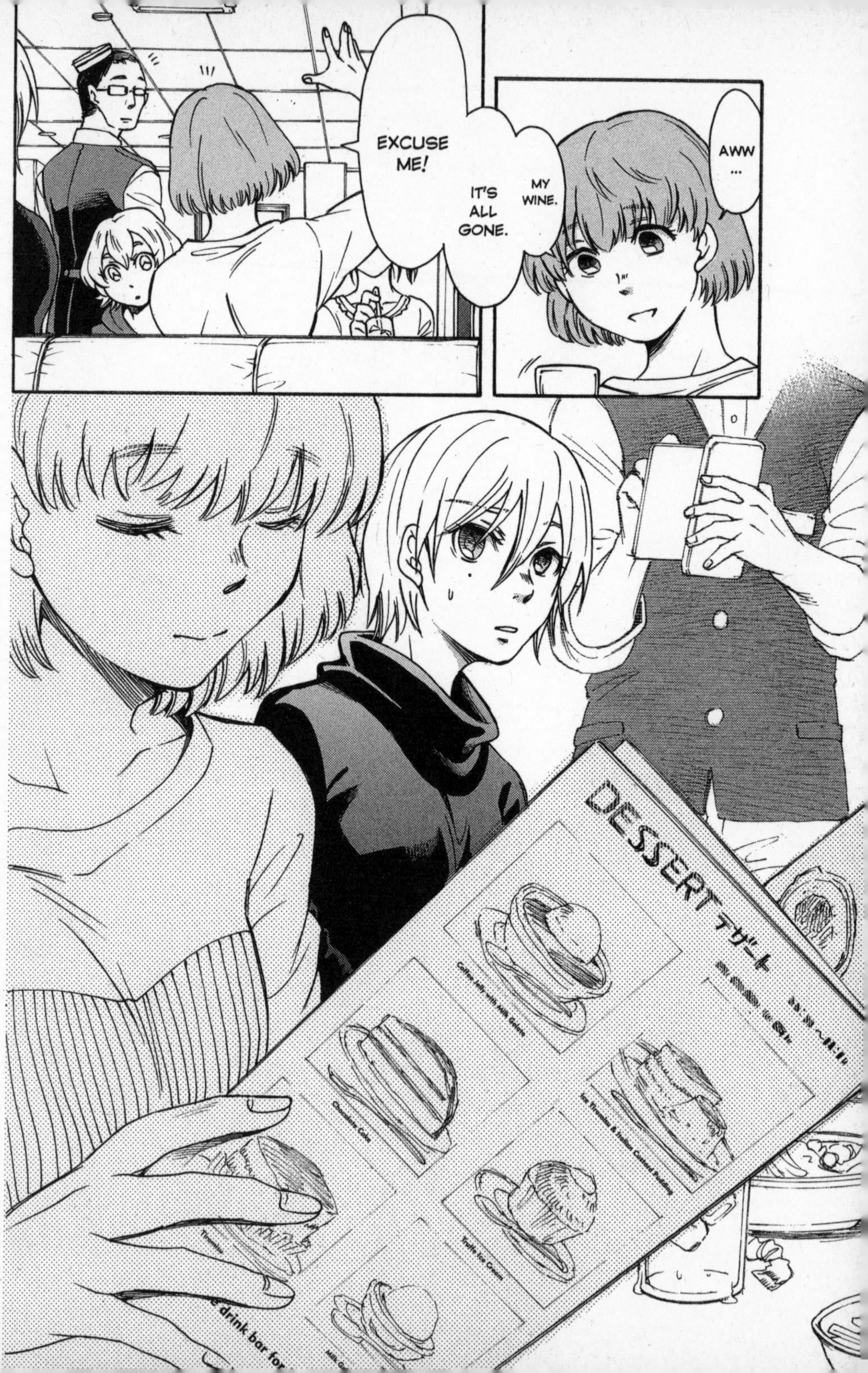
AWW ...
MY WINE.
IT'S ALL GONE.
EXCUSE ME!
DESSERT デザート

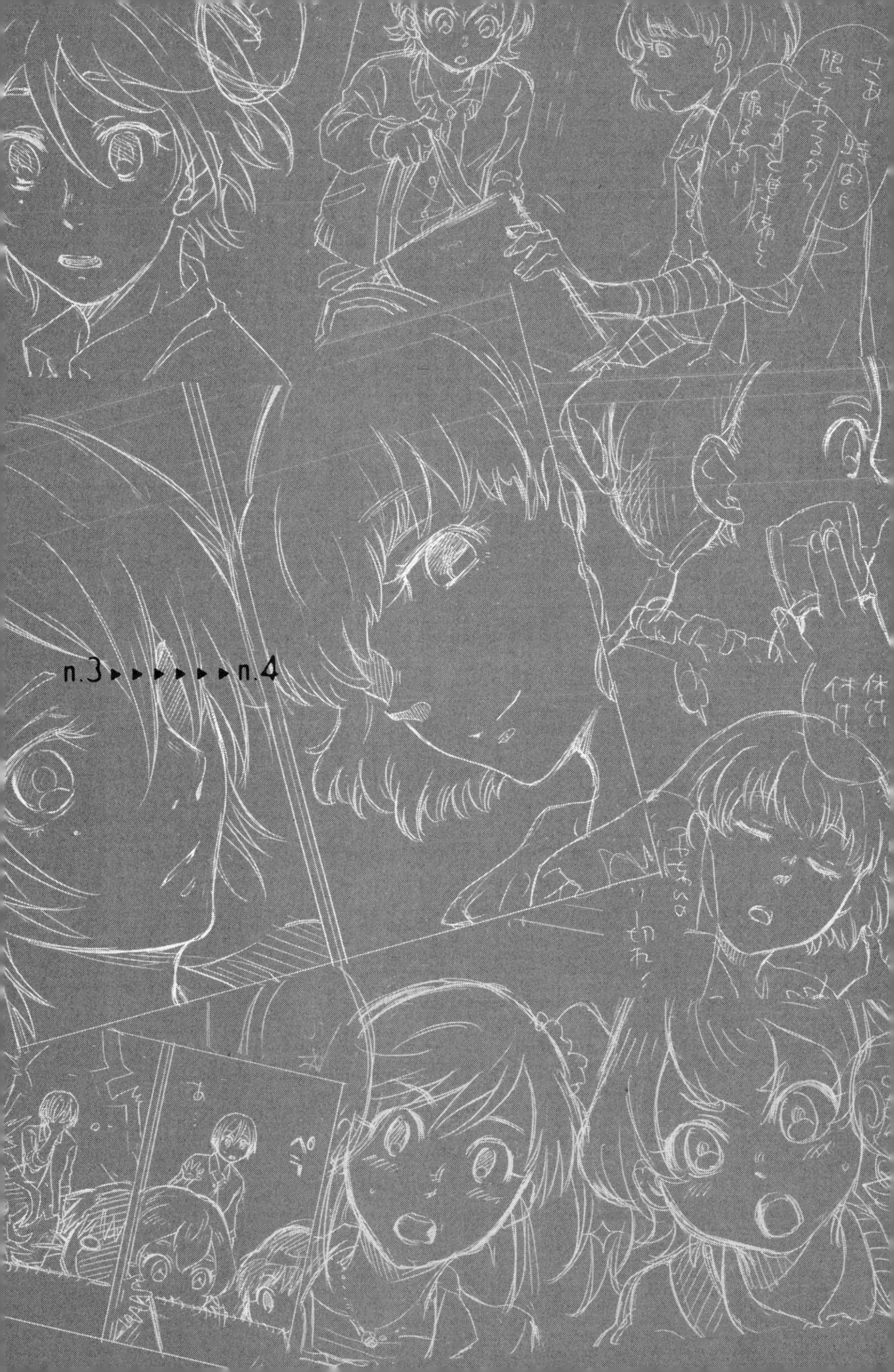
n.3▸▸▸▸▸▸▸▸n.4

Magical Riding Hood Ururu Complete Cosplay Festival! 3

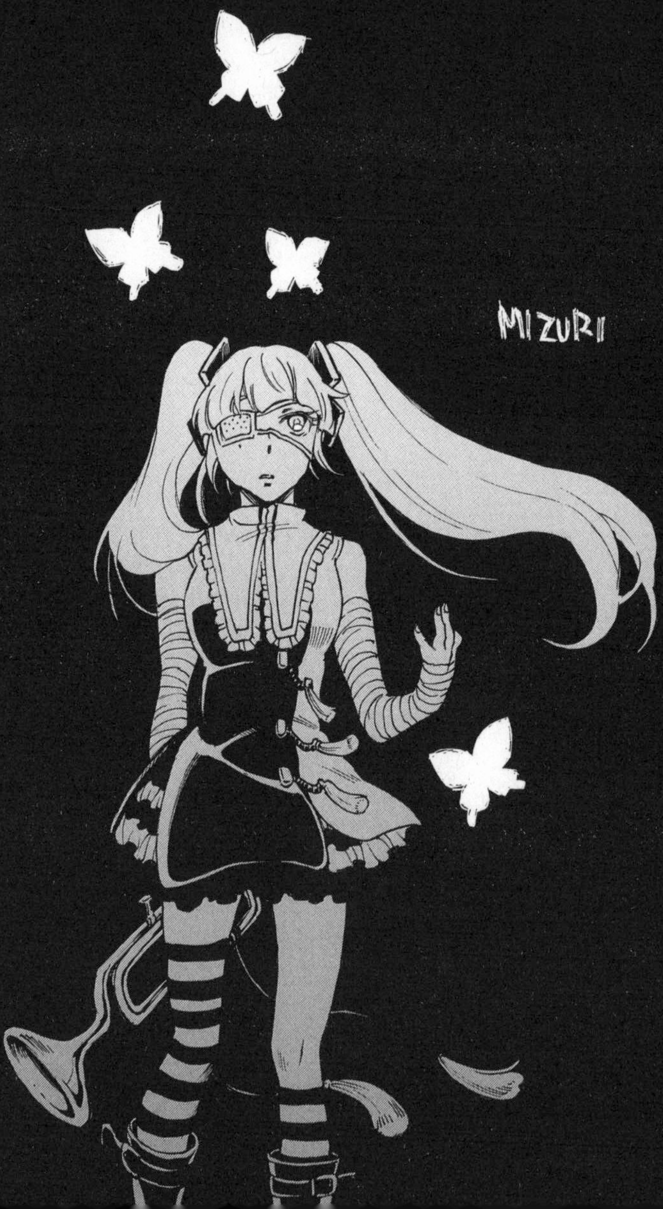
MIZURI

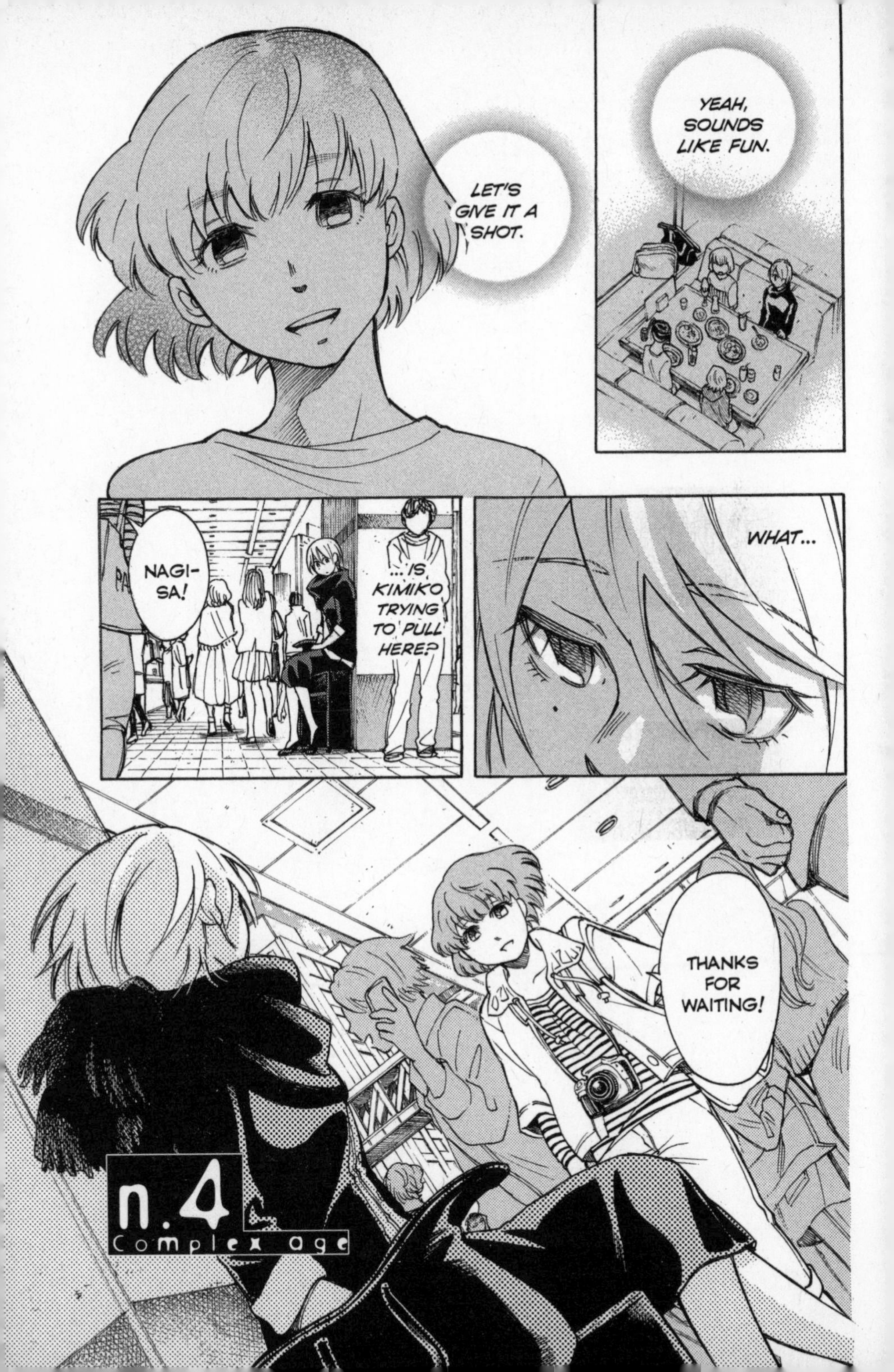
YEAH, SOUNDS LIKE FUN.
LET'S GIVE IT A SHOT.
WHAT...
...IS KIMIKO TRYING TO PULL HERE?
NAGI-SA!
THANKS FOR WAITING!
n.4
Complex age

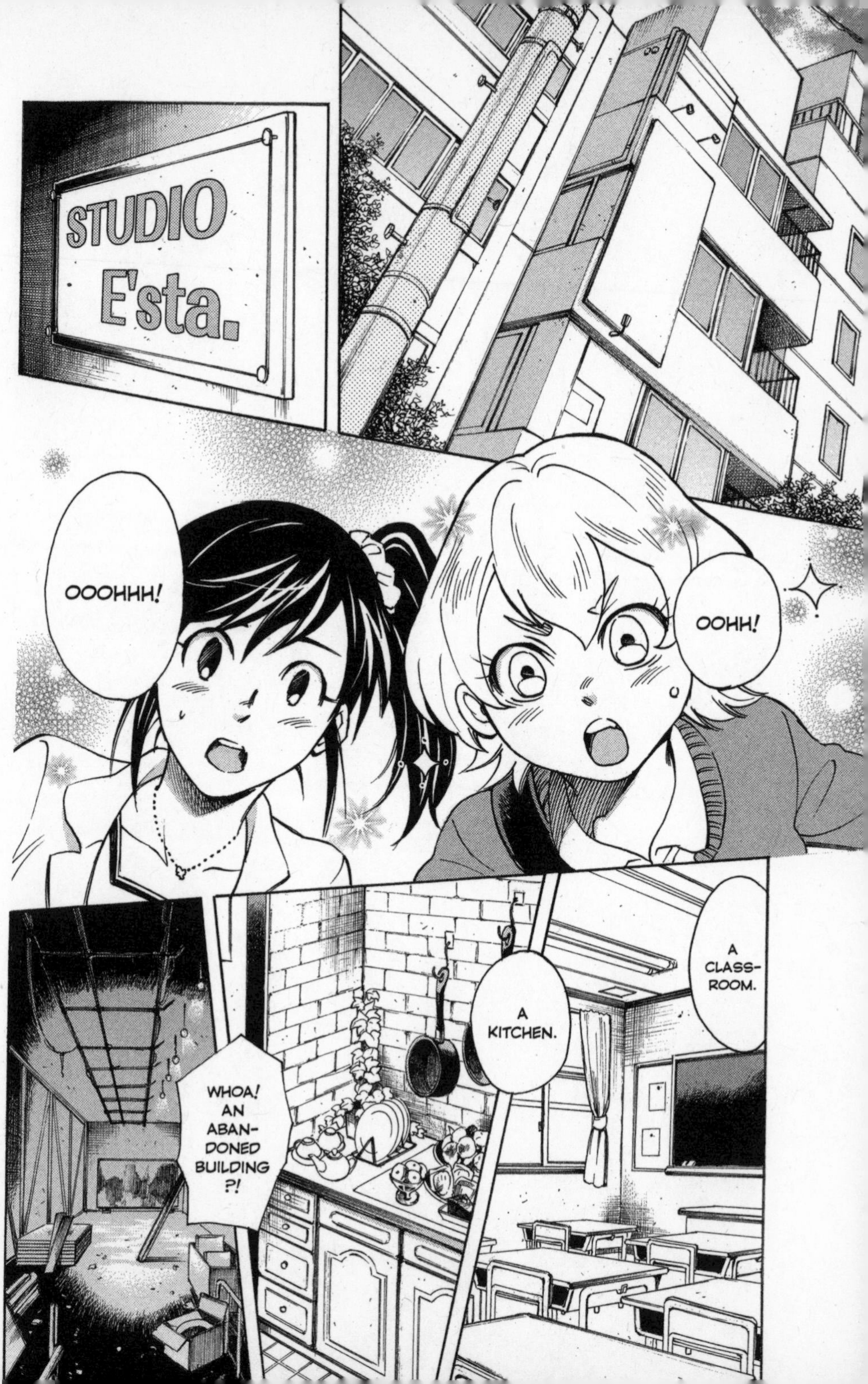
STUDIO E'sta.
OOHH!
OOOHHH!
A CLASS-ROOM.
A KITCHEN.
WHOA! AN ABAN-DONED BUILDING?!

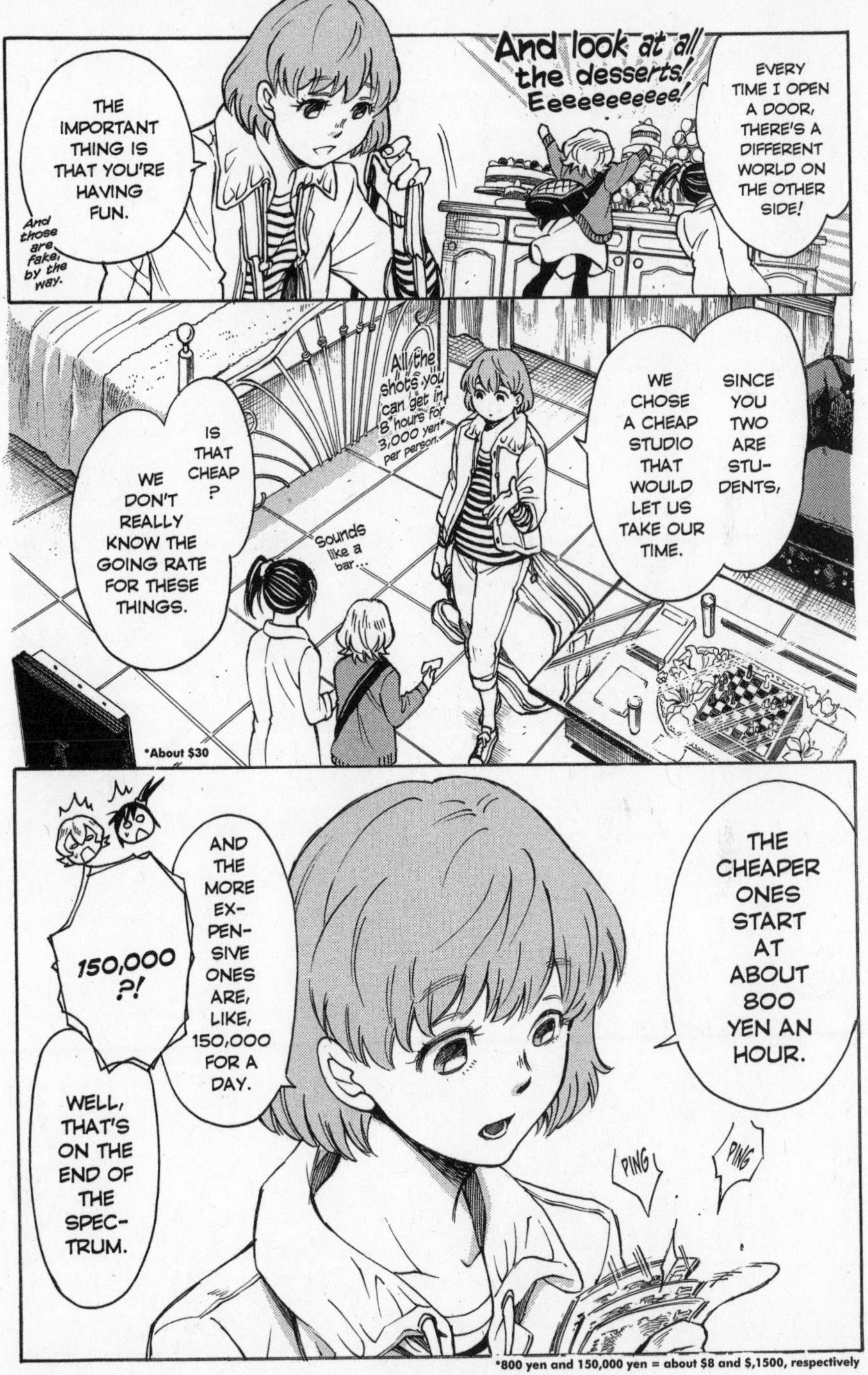
EVERY TIME I OPEN A DOOR, THERE'S A DIFFERENT WORLD ON THE OTHER SIDE!
And look at all the desserts! Eeeeeeeeee!
THE IMPORTANT THING IS THAT YOU'RE HAVING FUN.
And those are fake, by the way.
SINCE YOU TWO ARE STU-DENTS,
WE CHOSE A CHEAP STUDIO THAT WOULD LET US TAKE OUR TIME.
All the shots you can get in 8 hours for 3,000 yen* per person.
IS THAT CHEAP?
WE DON'T REALLY KNOW THE GOING RATE FOR THESE THINGS.
Sounds like a bar...
*About $30
THE CHEAPER ONES START AT ABOUT 800 YEN AN HOUR.
AND THE MORE EX-PEN-SIVE ONES ARE, LIKE, 150,000 FOR A DAY.
150,000?!
WELL, THAT'S ON THE END OF THE SPEC-TRUM.
PING
PING

*800 yen and 150,000 yen = about $8 and $,1500, respectively

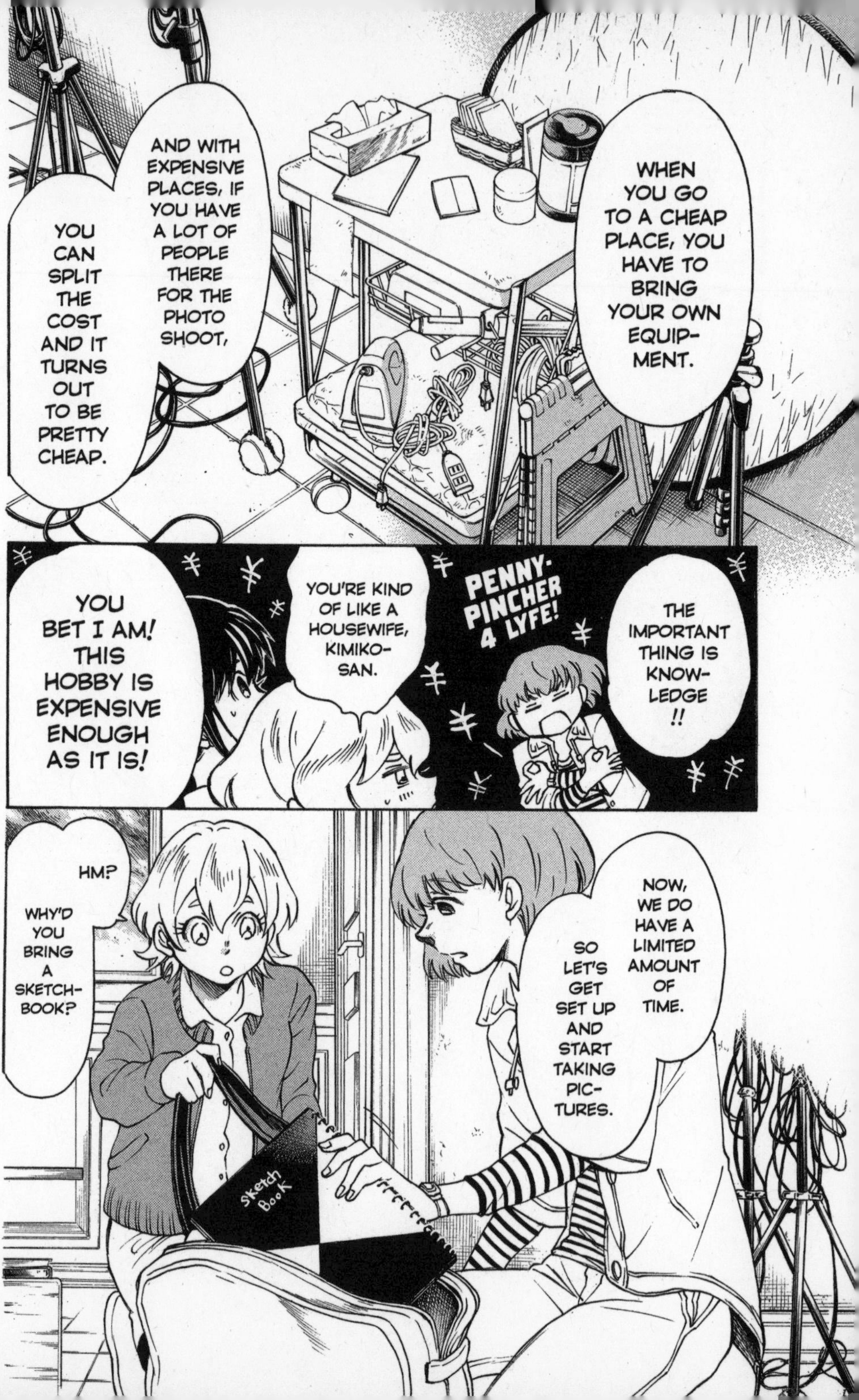
WHEN YOU GO TO A CHEAP PLACE, YOU HAVE TO BRING YOUR OWN EQUIP-MENT.
AND WITH EXPENSIVE PLACES, IF YOU HAVE A LOT OF PEOPLE THERE FOR THE PHOTO SHOOT,
YOU CAN SPLIT THE COST AND IT TURNS OUT TO BE PRETTY CHEAP.
THE IMPORTANT THING IS KNOW-LEDGE !!
PENNY-PINCHER 4 LYFE!
YOU'RE KIND OF LIKE A HOUSEWIFE, KIMIKO-SAN.
YOU BET I AM! THIS HOBBY IS EXPENSIVE ENOUGH AS IT IS!
NOW, WE DO HAVE A LIMITED AMOUNT OF TIME.
SO LET'S GET SET UP AND START TAKING PIC-TURES.
HM?
WHY'D YOU BRING A SKETCH-BOOK?
Sketch Book

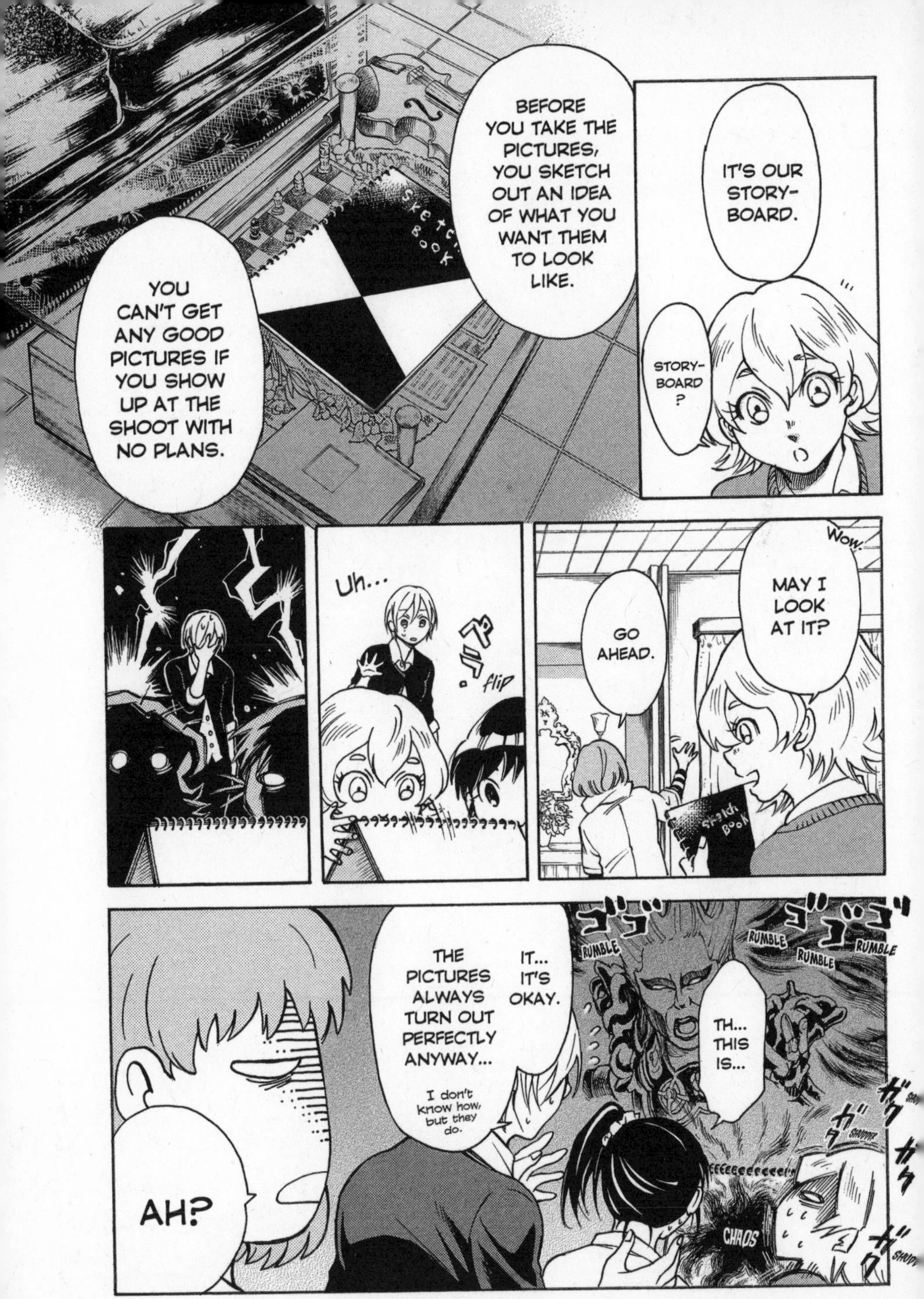
IT'S OUR STORY-BOARD.
STORY-BOARD?
BEFORE YOU TAKE THE PICTURES, YOU SKETCH OUT AN IDEA OF WHAT YOU WANT THEM TO LOOK LIKE.
YOU CAN'T GET ANY GOOD PICTURES IF YOU SHOW UP AT THE SHOOT WITH NO PLANS.
SKETCH BOOK
Wow!
MAY I LOOK AT IT?
GO AHEAD.
SKETCH BOOK
Uh...
flip
RUMBLE
RUMBLE
RUMBLE
RUMBLE
TH... THIS IS...
IT... IT'S OKAY.
THE PICTURES ALWAYS TURN OUT PERFECTLY ANYWAY...
I don't know how, but they do.
CHAOS
AH?

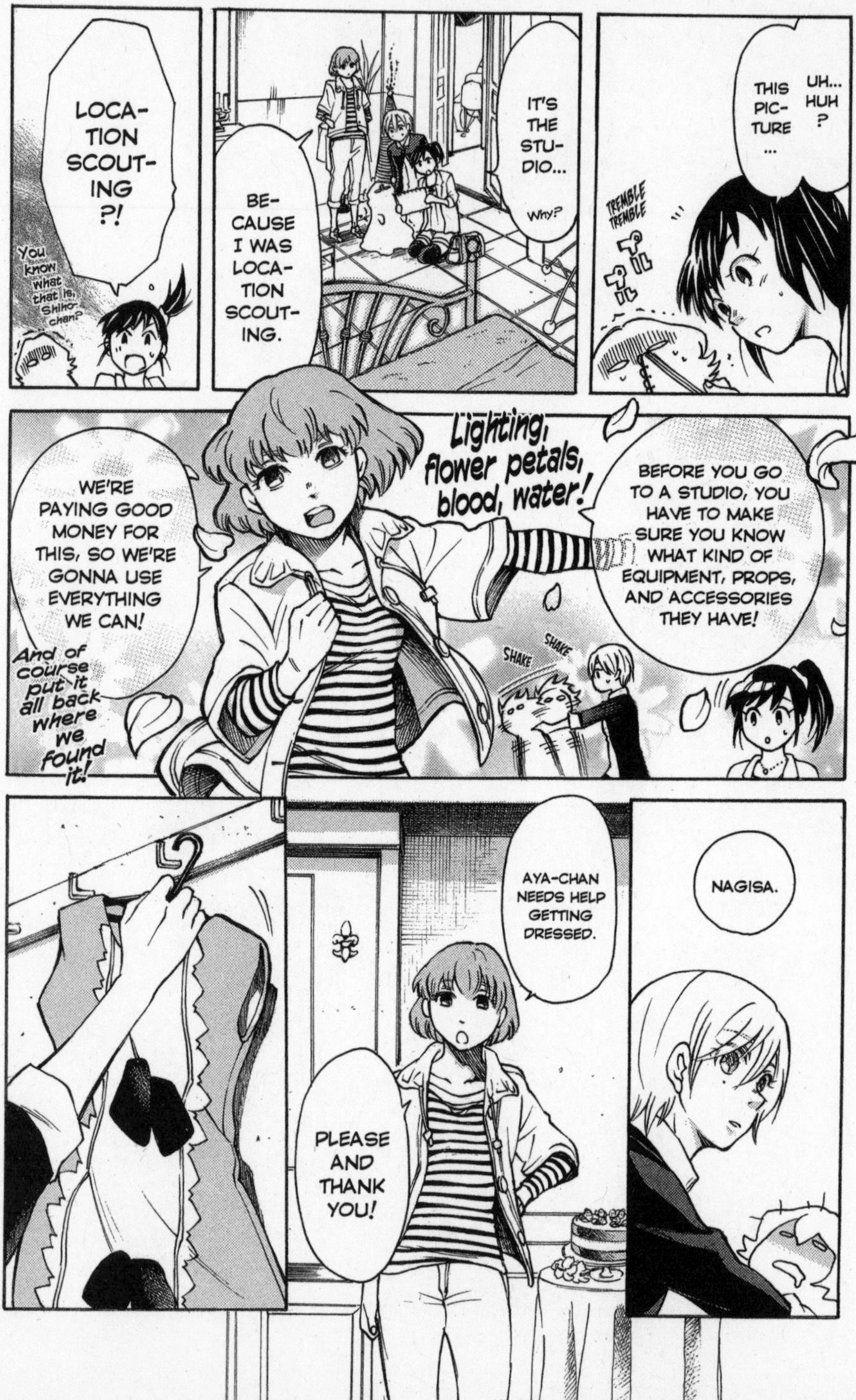
UH... HUH?
THIS PICTURE...
TREMBLE TREMBLE
IT'S THE STUDIO...
Why?
BECAUSE I WAS LOCATION SCOUTING.
LOCATION SCOUTING?!
You know what that is, Shiho-chan?
BEFORE YOU GO TO A STUDIO, YOU HAVE TO MAKE SURE YOU KNOW WHAT KIND OF EQUIPMENT, PROPS, AND ACCESSORIES THEY HAVE!
Lighting, flower petals, blood, water!
SHAKE SHAKE
WE'RE PAYING GOOD MONEY FOR THIS, SO WE'RE GONNA USE EVERYTHING WE CAN!
And of course put it all back where we found it!
NAGISA.
AYA-CHAN NEEDS HELP GETTING DRESSED.
PLEASE AND THANK YOU!

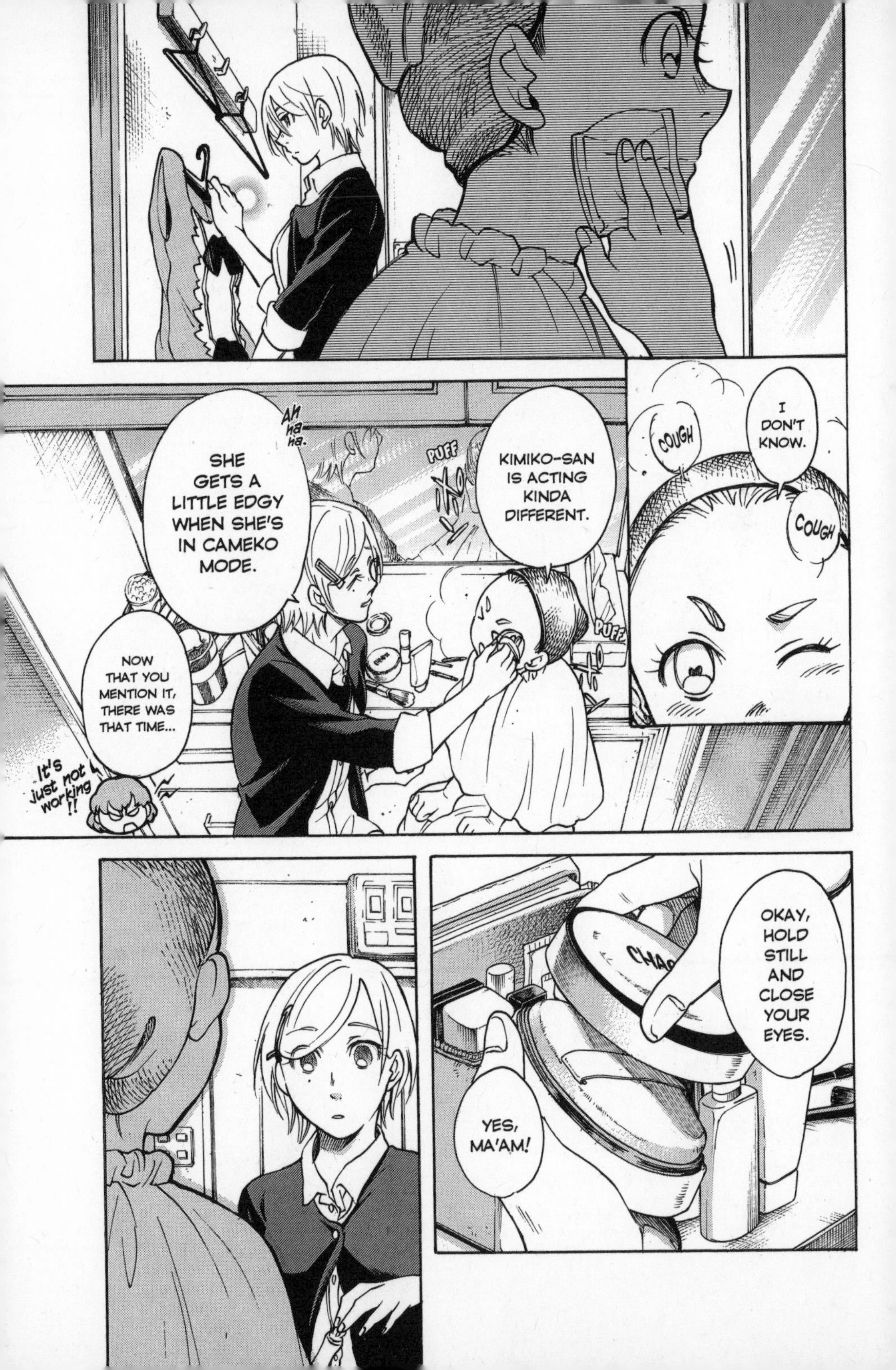
I DON'T KNOW.
COUGH
COUGH
KIMIKO-SAN IS ACTING KINDA DIFFERENT.
PUFF
AH HA HA.
SHE GETS A LITTLE EDGY WHEN SHE'S IN CAMEKO MODE.
PUFF
NOW THAT YOU MENTION IT, THERE WAS THAT TIME...
It's just not working!!
OKAY, HOLD STILL AND CLOSE YOUR EYES.
YES, MA'AM!

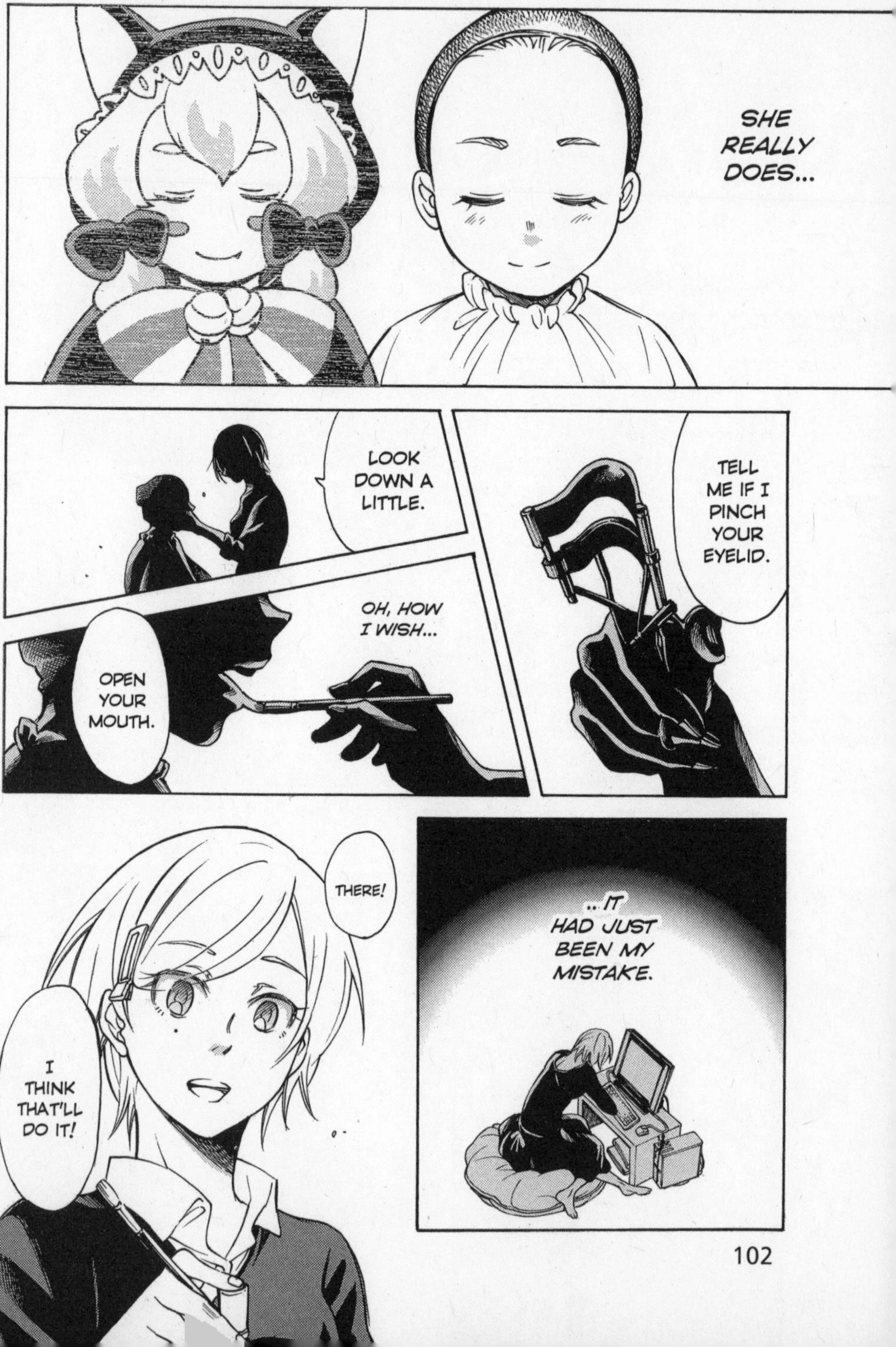
SHE REALLY DOES...
TELL ME IF I PINCH YOUR EYELID.
LOOK DOWN A LITTLE.
OH, HOW I WISH...
OPEN YOUR MOUTH.
...IT HAD JUST BEEN MY MISTAKE.
THERE!
I THINK THAT'LL DO IT!

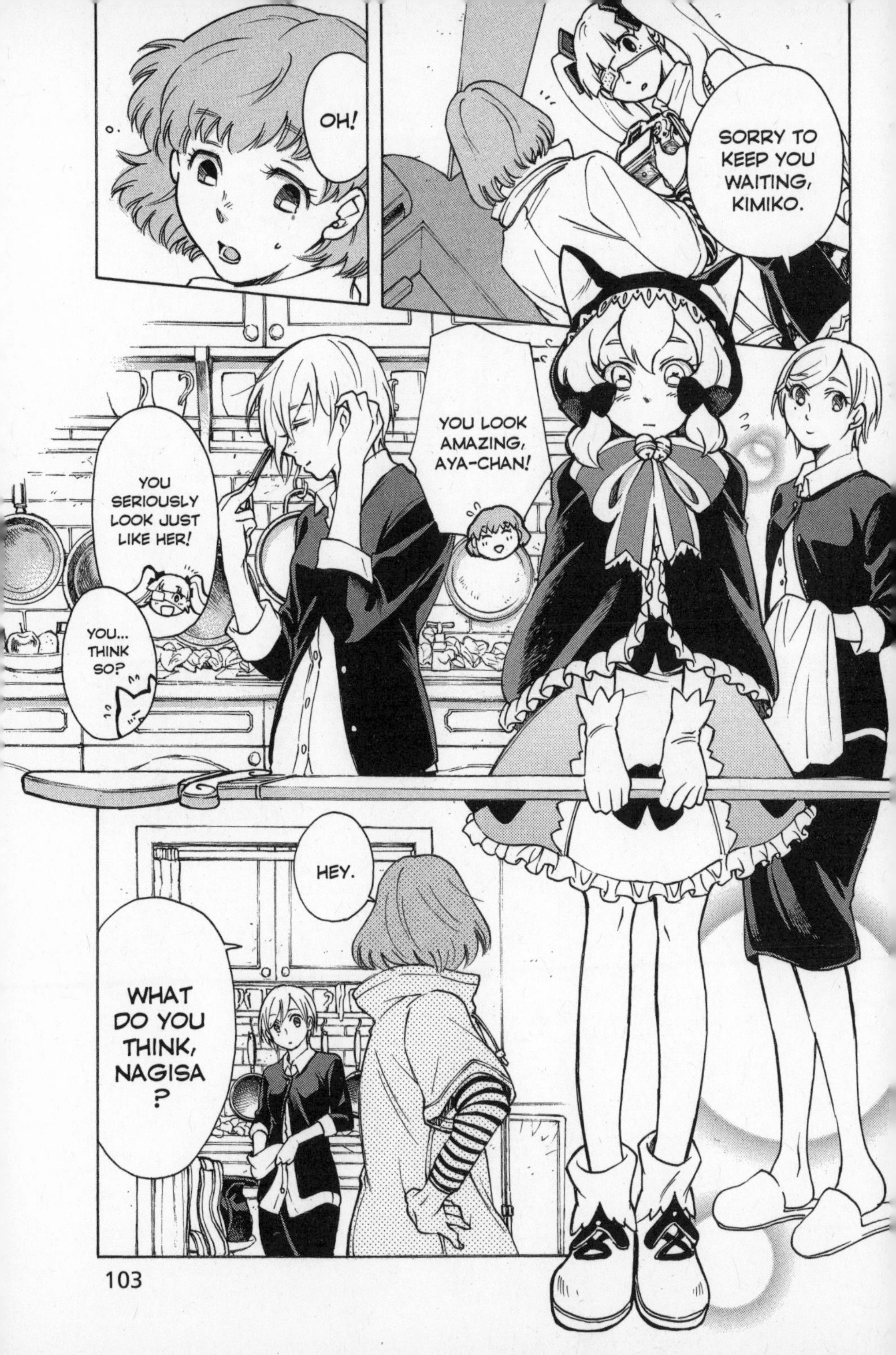
SORRY TO KEEP YOU WAITING, KIMIKO.
OH!
YOU LOOK AMAZING, AYA-CHAN!
YOU SERIOUSLY LOOK JUST LIKE HER!
YOU... THINK SO?
HEY.
WHAT DO YOU THINK, NAGISA?

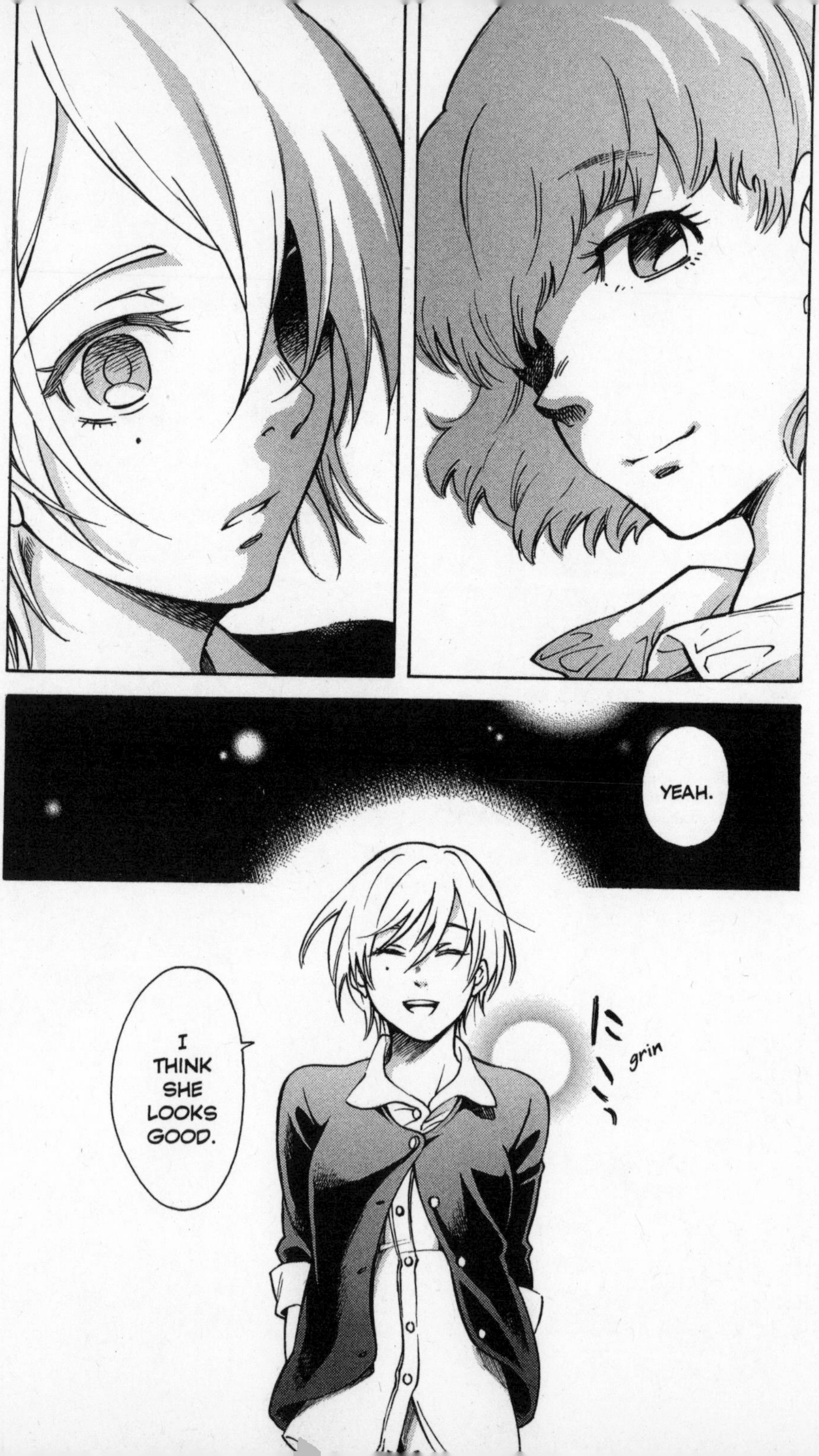
YEAH.
grin
I THINK SHE LOOKS GOOD.

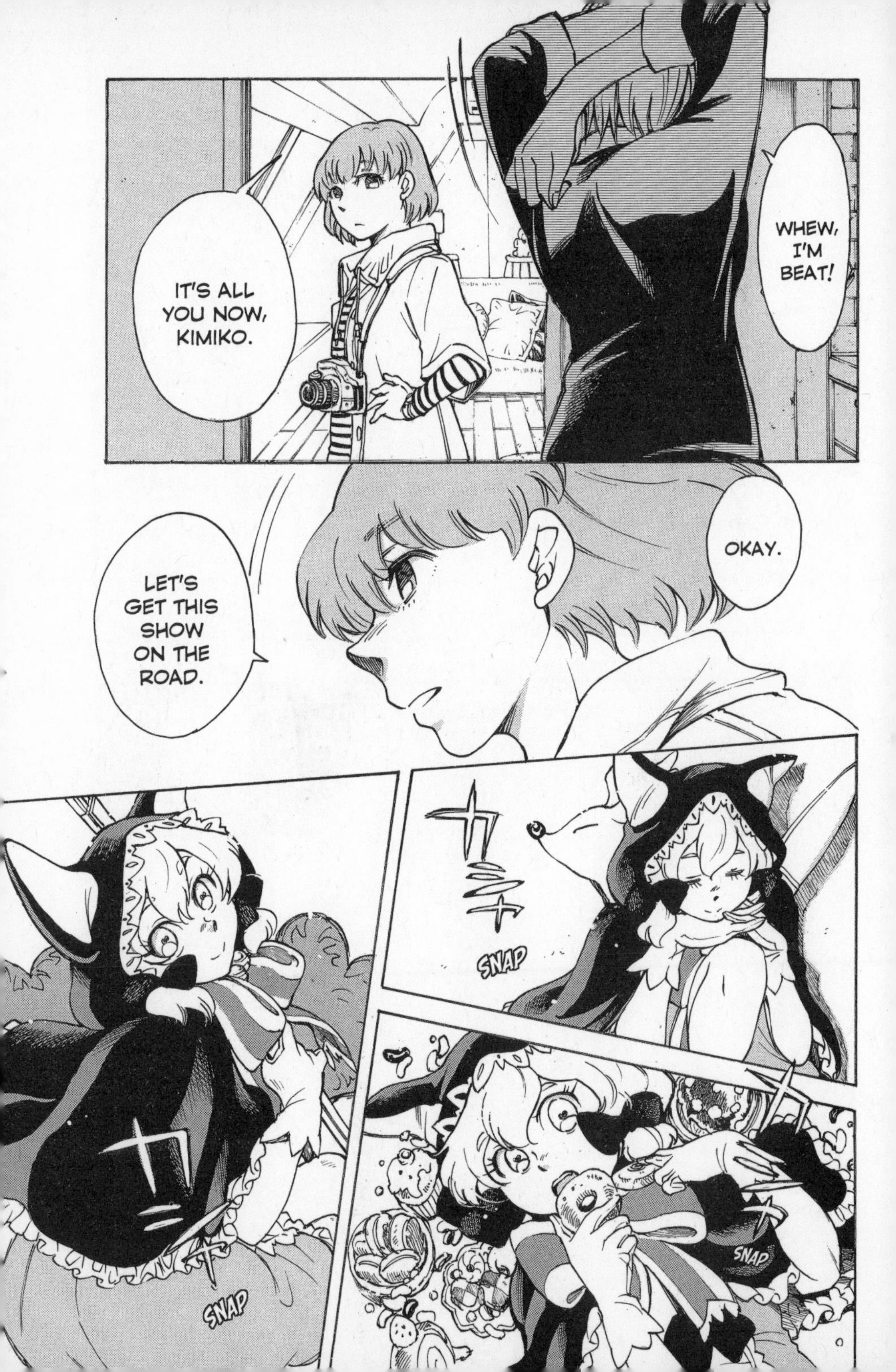
WHEW, I'M BEAT!
IT'S ALL YOU NOW, KIMIKO.
OKAY.
LET'S GET THIS SHOW ON THE ROAD.
SNAP
SNAP
SNAP

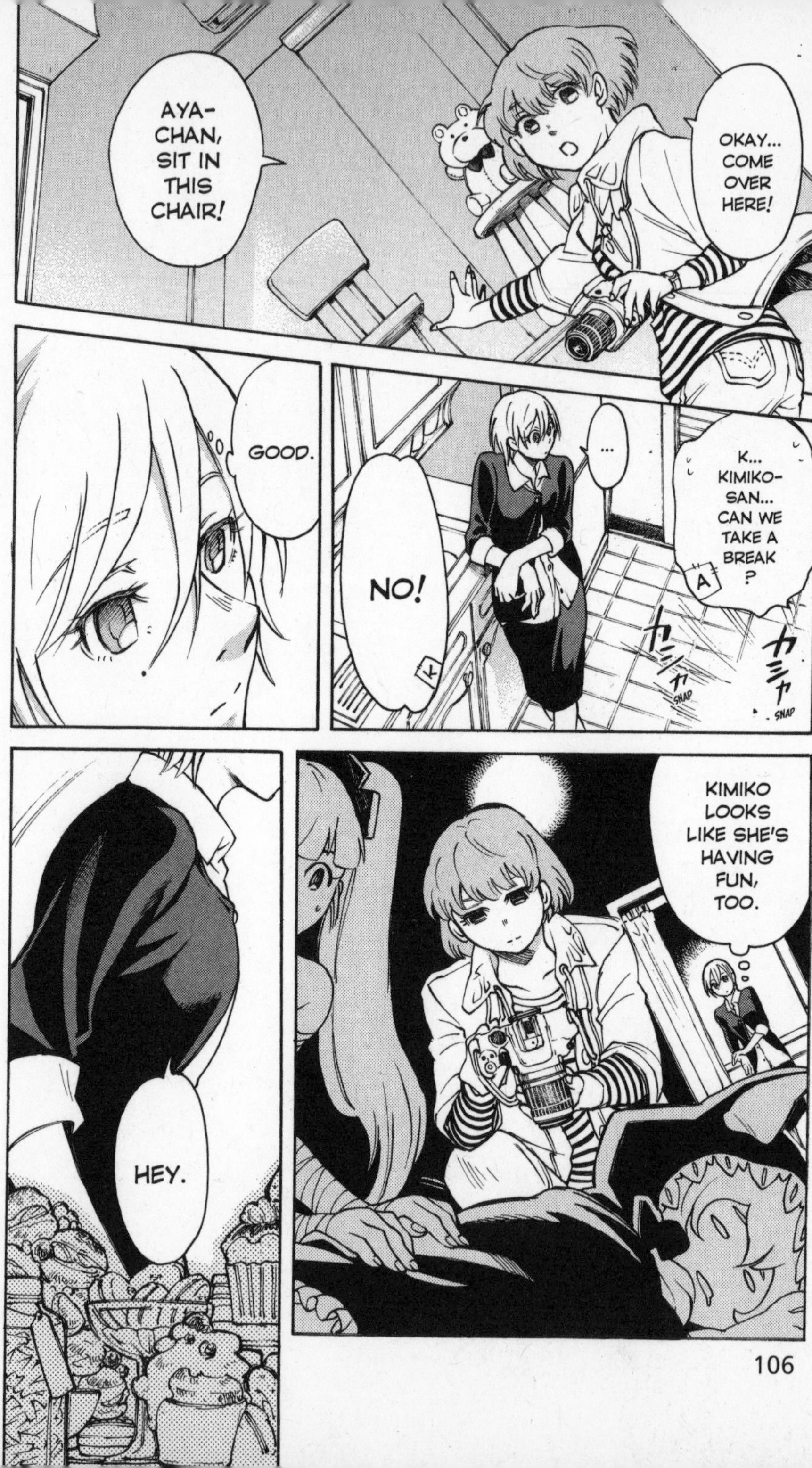
OKAY... COME OVER HERE!
AYA-CHAN, SIT IN THIS CHAIR!
K... KIMIKO-SAN... CAN WE TAKE A BREAK?
SNAP
SNAP
...
NO!
GOOD.
KIMIKO LOOKS LIKE SHE'S HAVING FUN, TOO.
HEY.

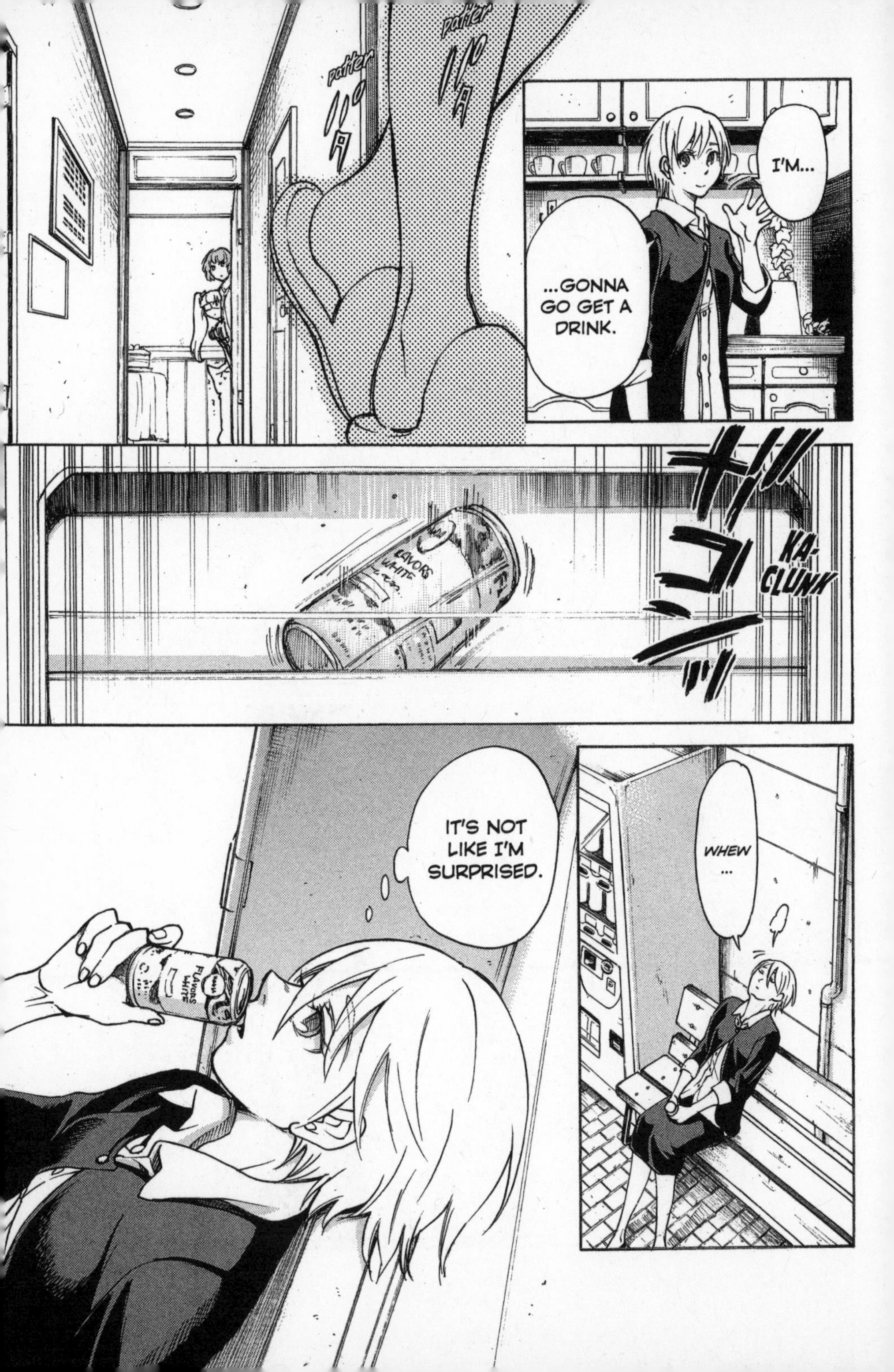
I'M...
...GONNA GO GET A DRINK.
patter
patter
KA-CLUNK
FLAVORS WHITE
WHEW ...
IT'S NOT LIKE I'M SURPRISED.

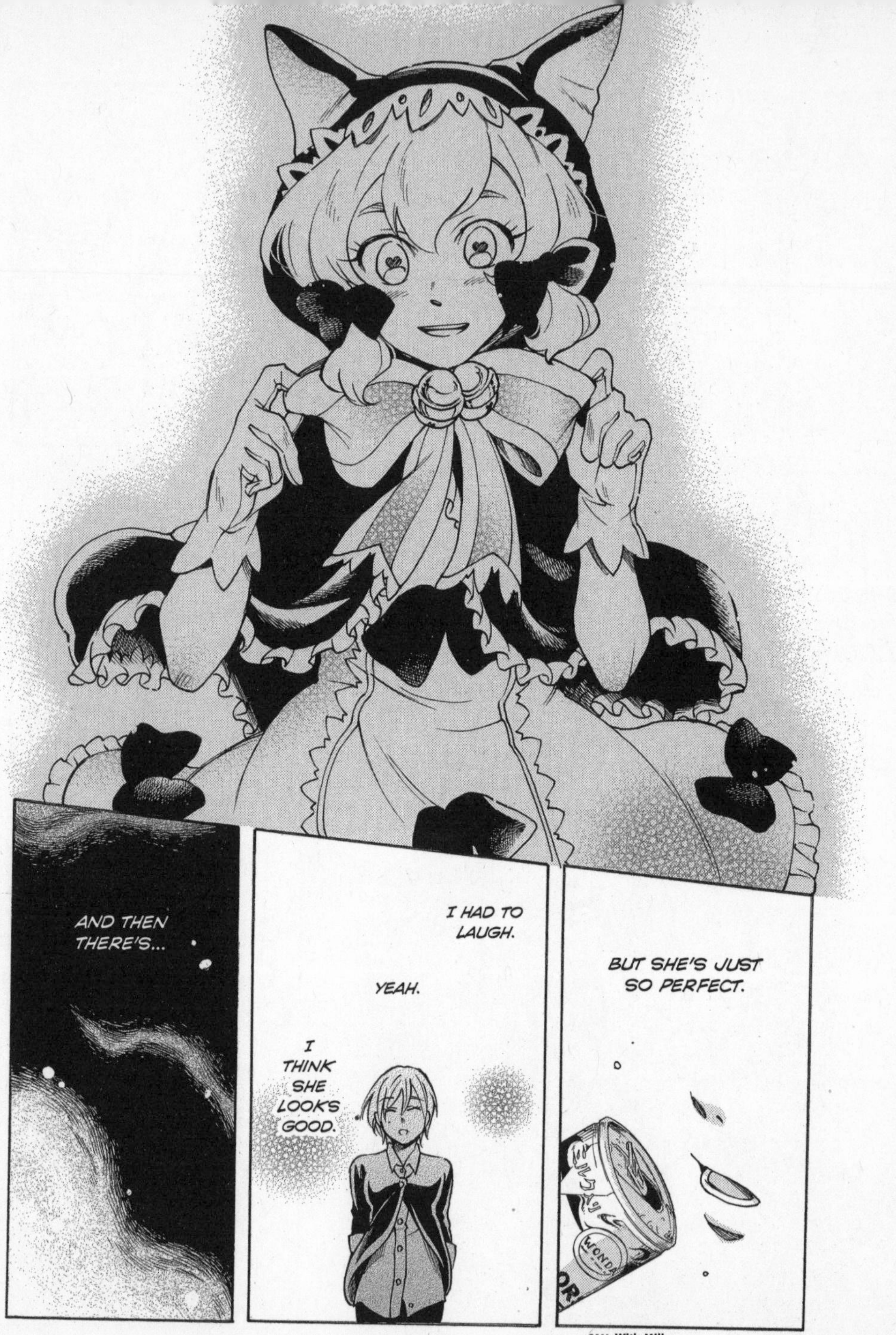
BUT SHE'S JUST SO PERFECT.
I HAD TO LAUGH.
YEAH.
I THINK SHE LOOKS GOOD.
AND THEN THERE'S...

CAN: With Milk

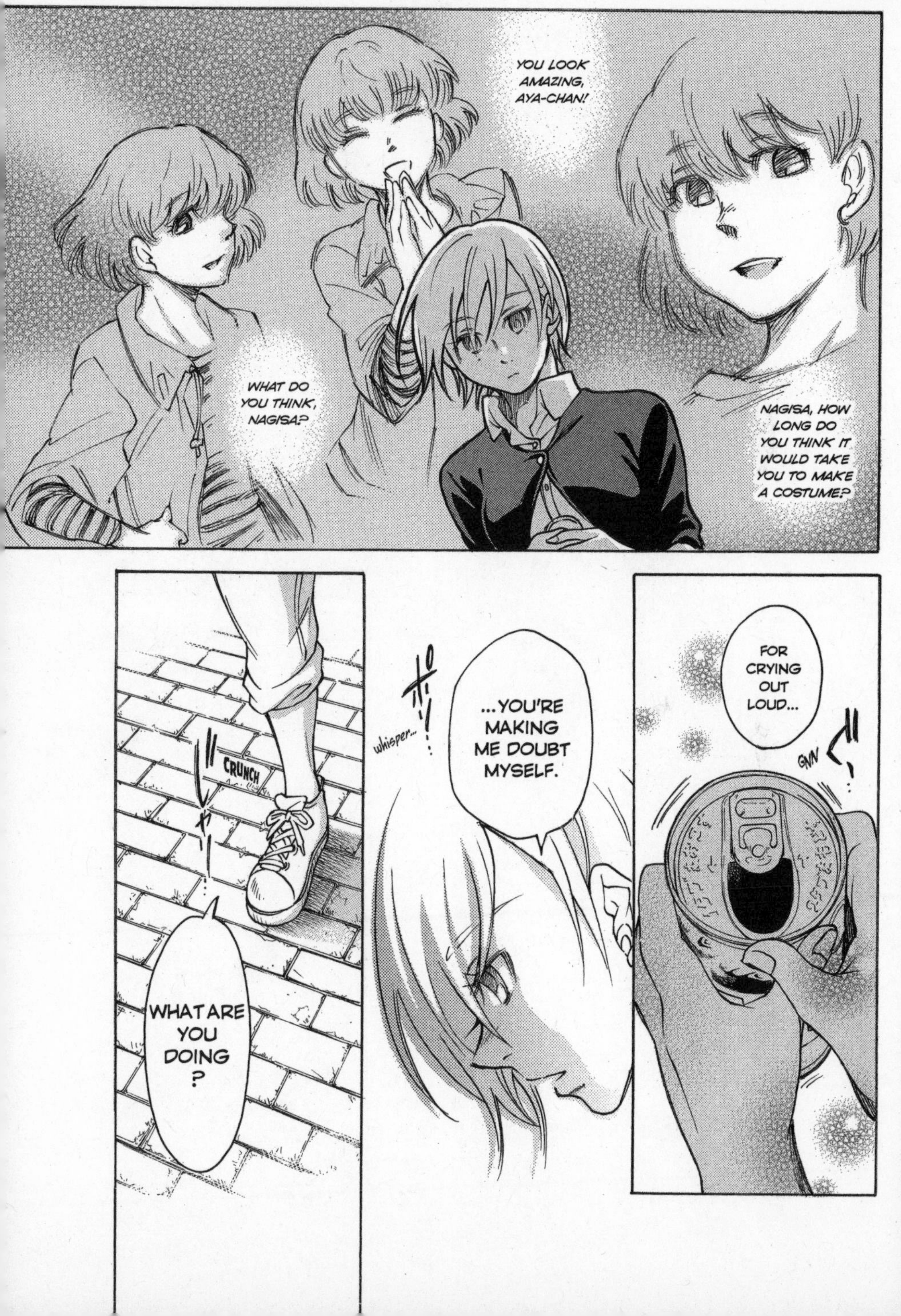
YOU LOOK AMAZING, AYA-CHAN!
NAGISA, HOW LONG DO YOU THINK IT WOULD TAKE YOU TO MAKE A COSTUME?
WHAT DO YOU THINK, NAGISA?
FOR CRYING OUT LOUD...
GNN
whisper...
...YOU'RE MAKING ME DOUBT MYSELF.
CRUNCH
WHAT ARE YOU DOING?

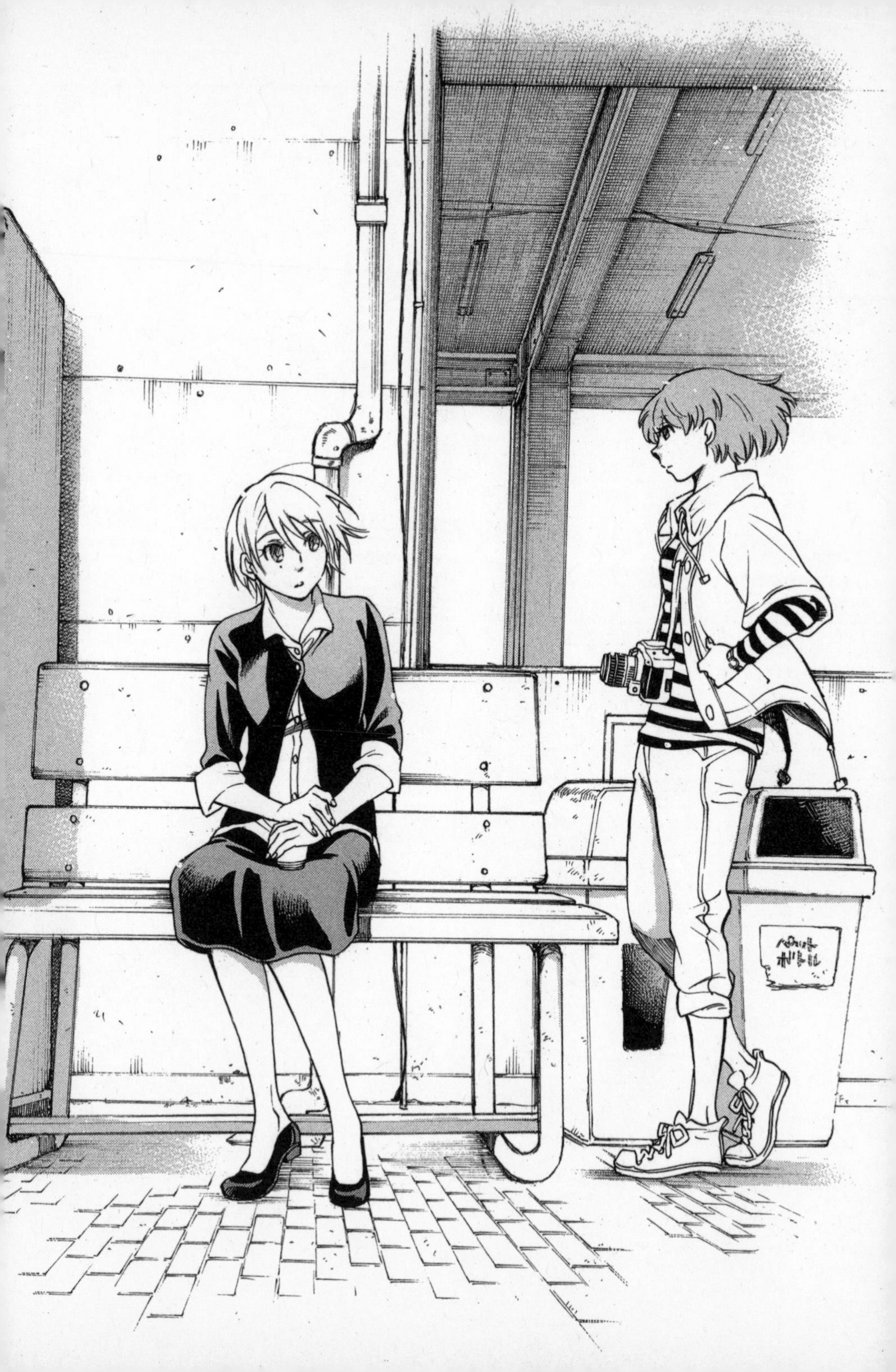
ペット
ボトル

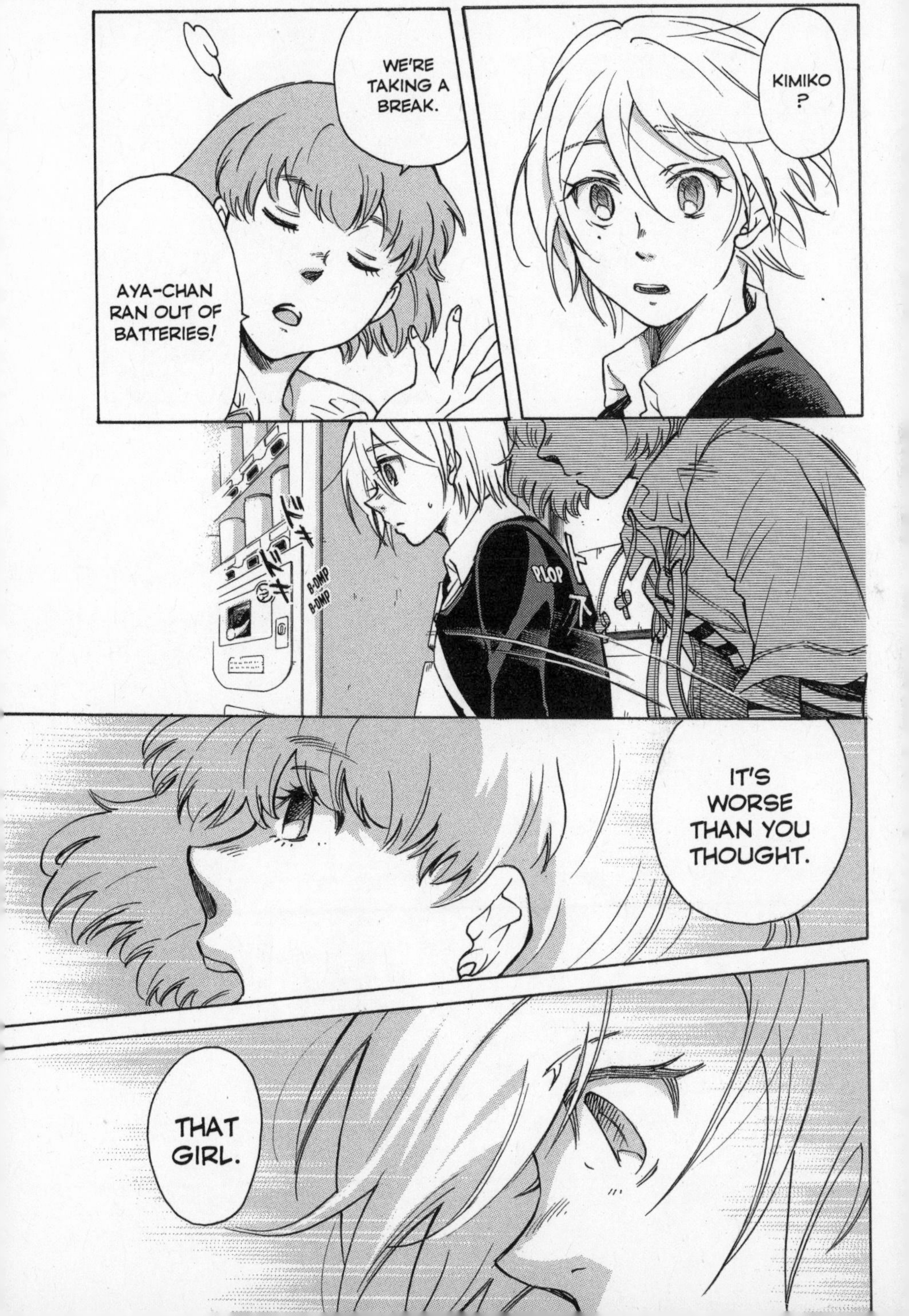
KIMIKO ?
WE'RE TAKING A BREAK.
AYA-CHAN RAN OUT OF BATTERIES!
PLOP
B-DMP B-DMP
IT'S WORSE THAN YOU THOUGHT.
THAT GIRL.

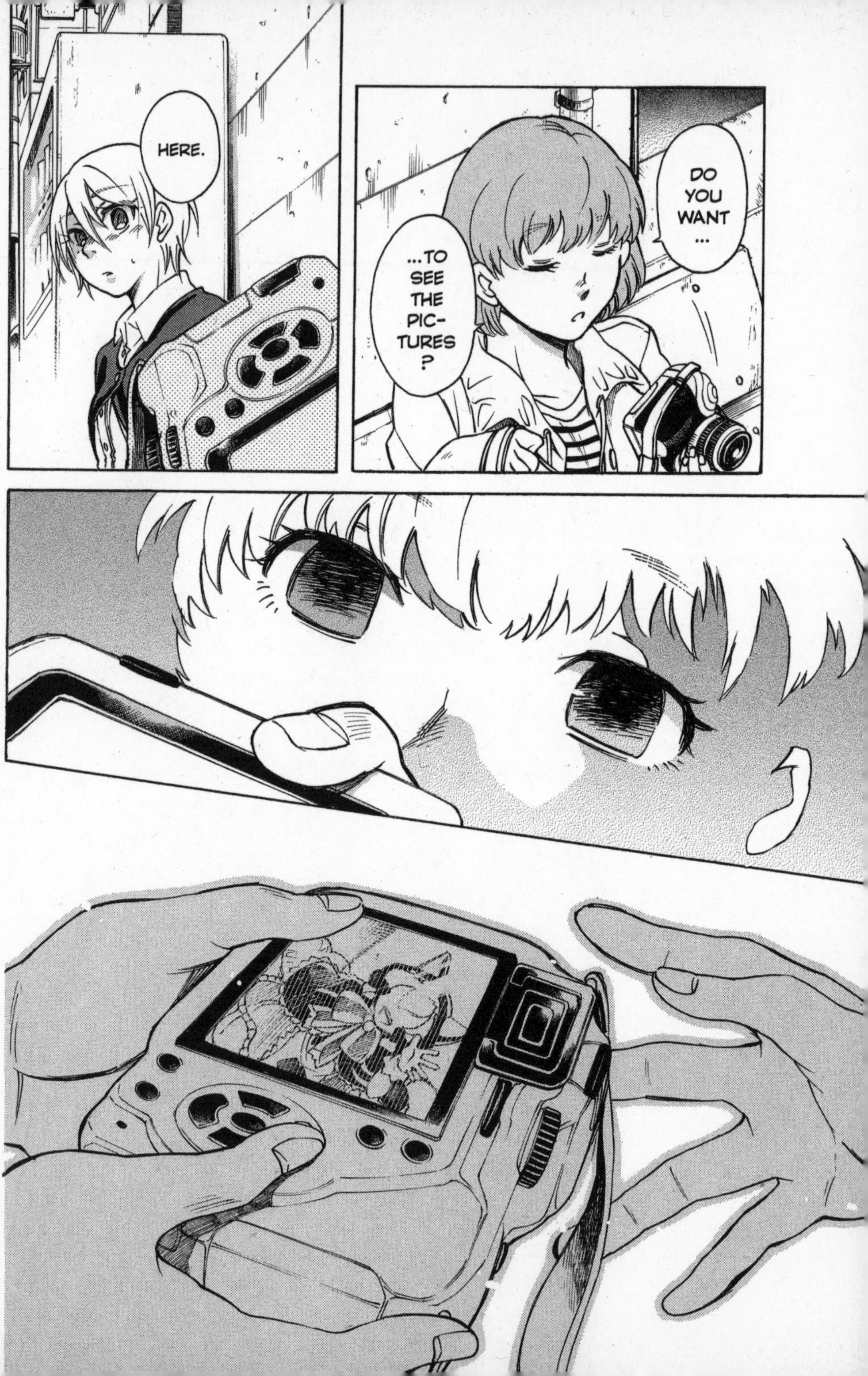
DO YOU WANT ...
...TO SEE THE PIC-TURES?
HERE.

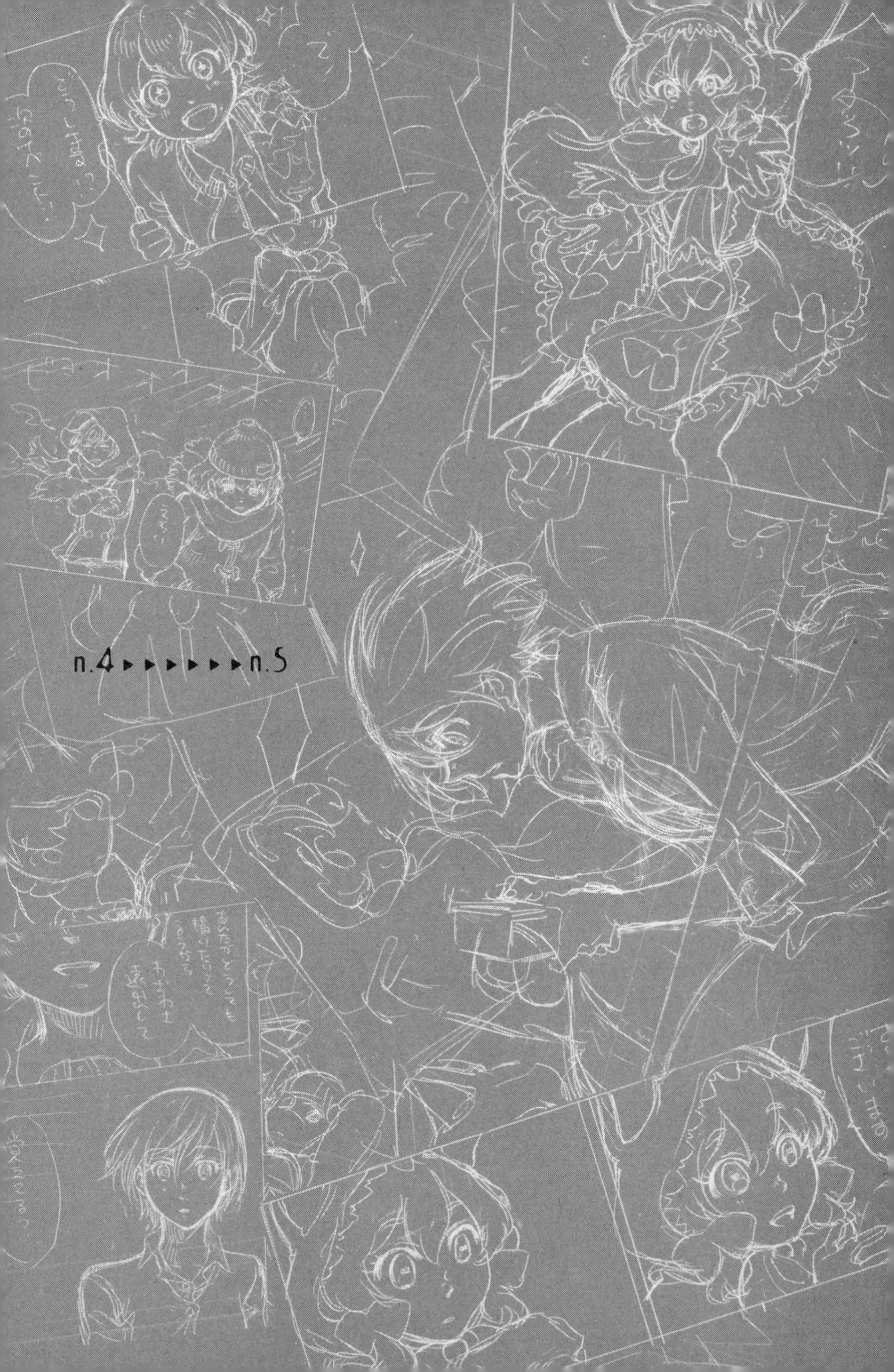
n.4▸▸▸▸▸▸▸▸n.5

Magical Riding Hood Ururu Complete Cosplay Festival! ④

KOKEMOMO

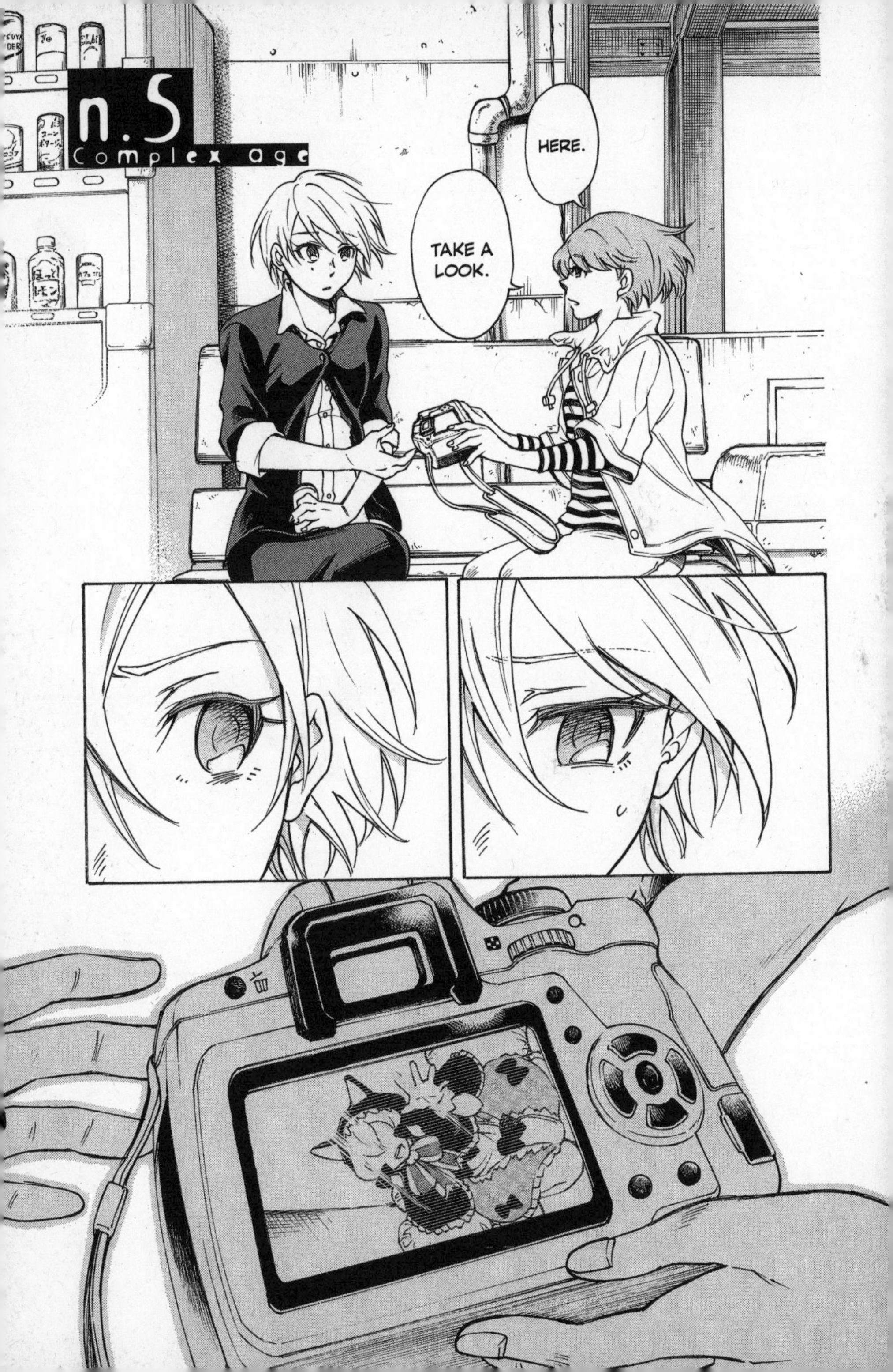
n.5
Complex age
HERE.
TAKE A LOOK.

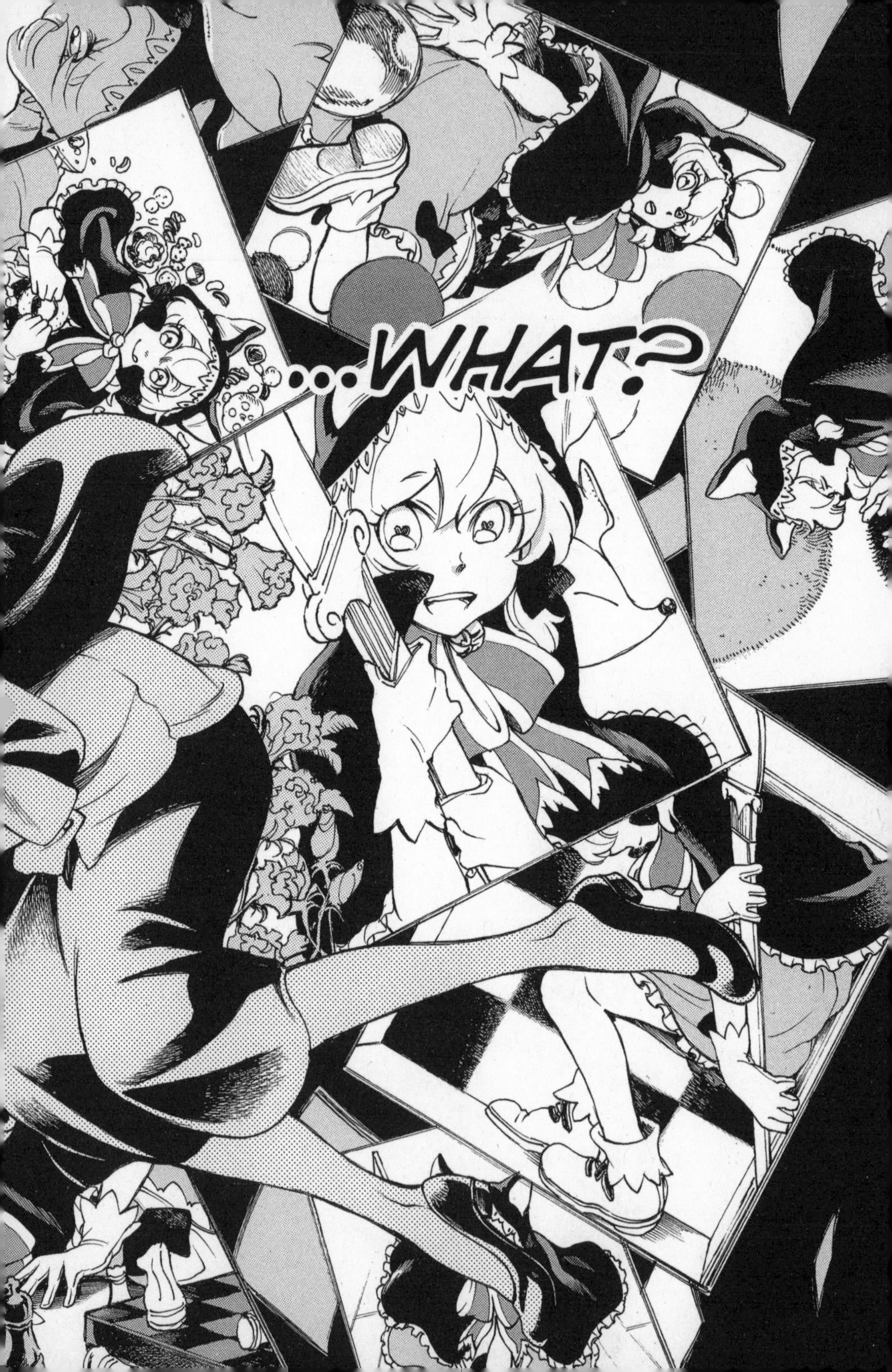
...WHAT?

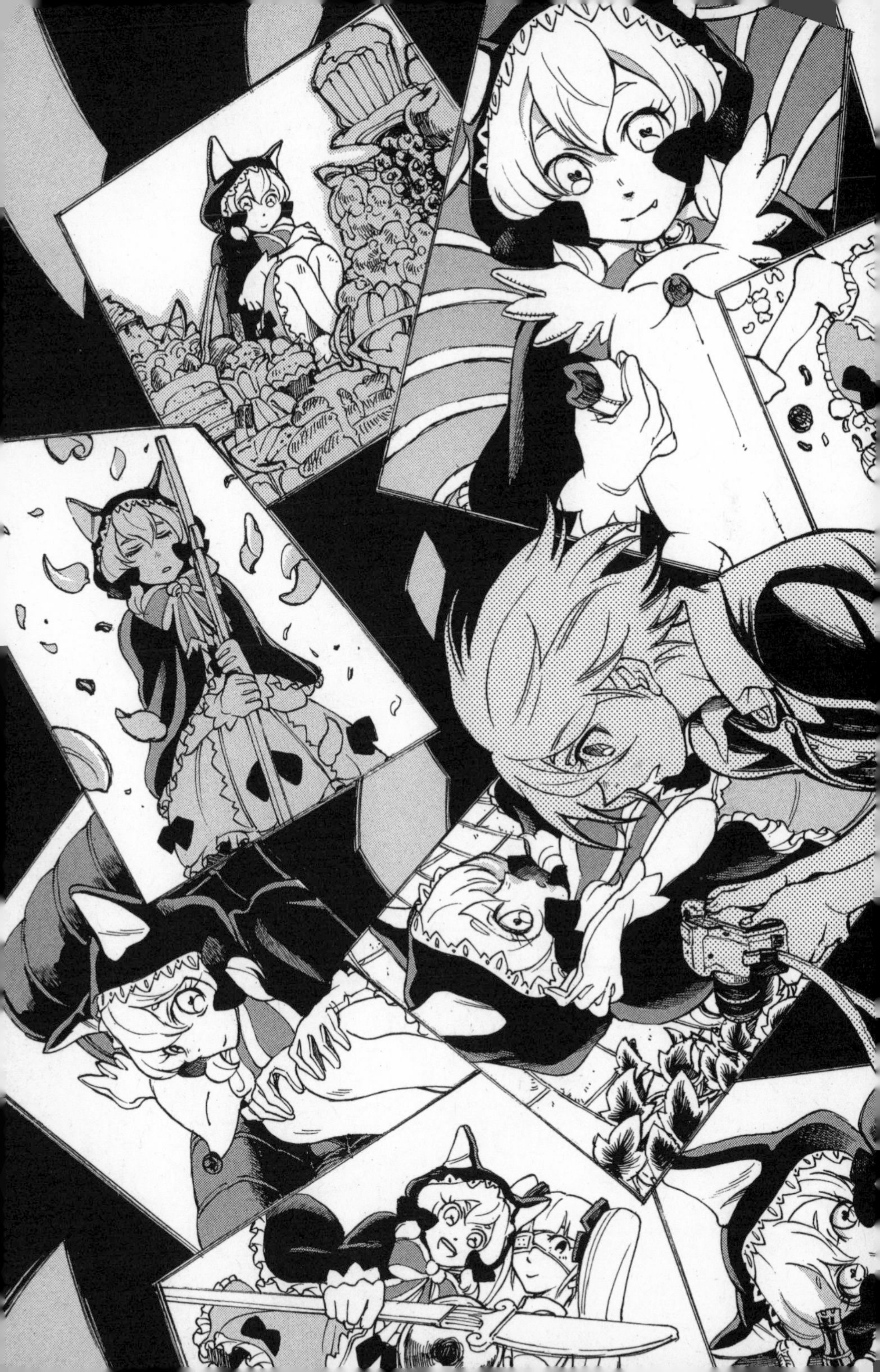

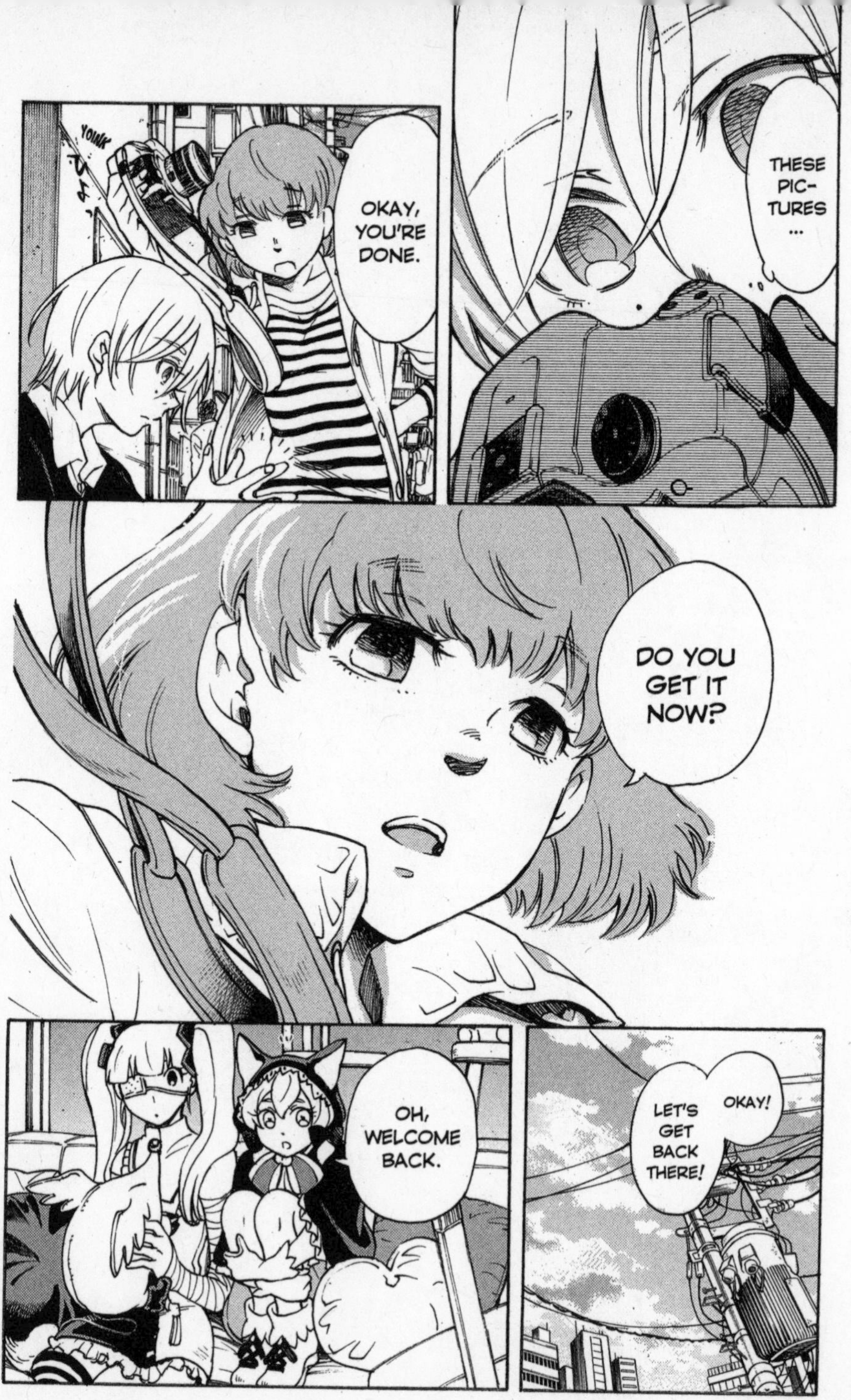
THESE PIC- TURES ...
OKAY, YOU'RE DONE.
YOINK
DO YOU GET IT NOW?
LET'S GET BACK THERE!
OKAY!
OH, WELCOME BACK.

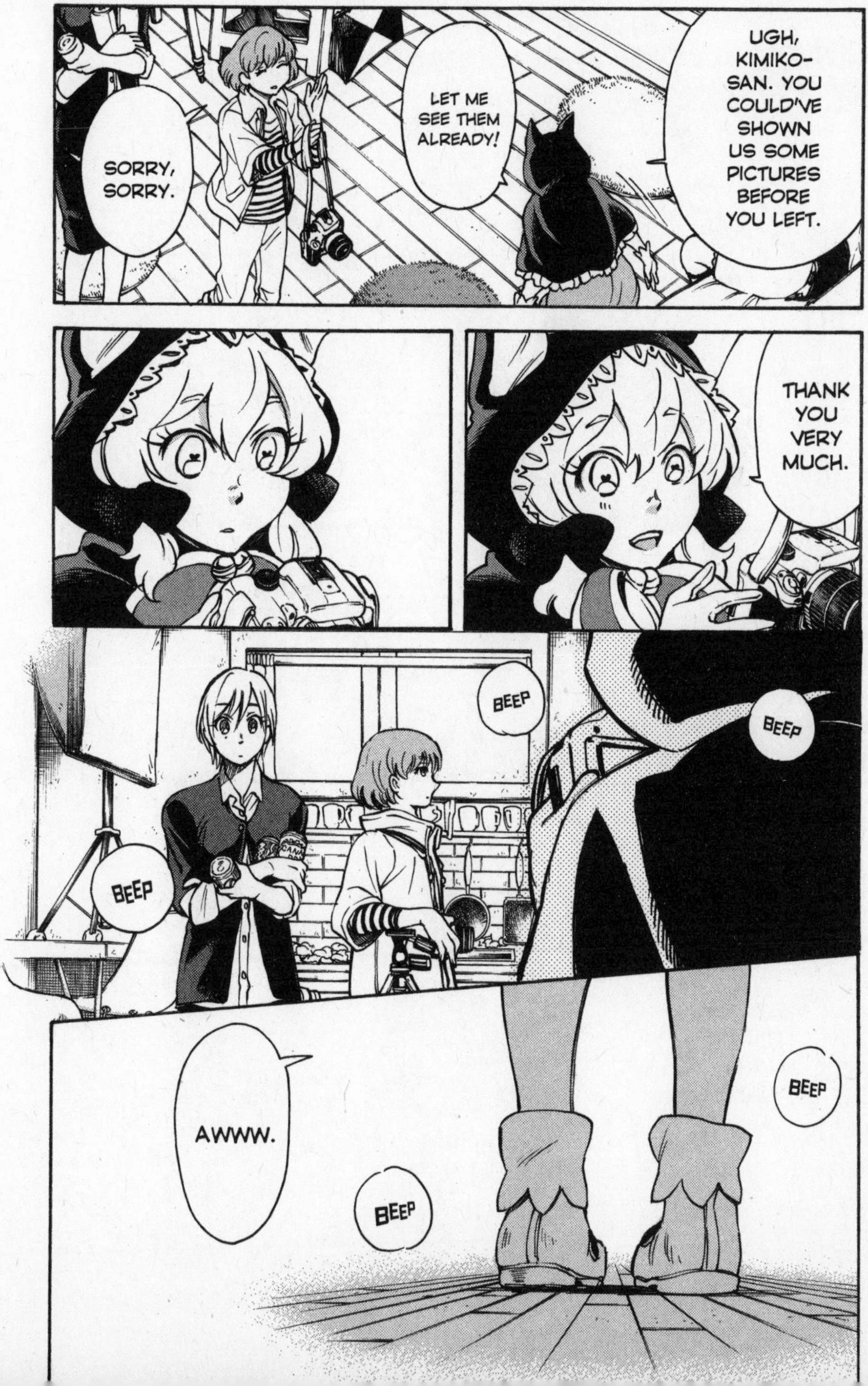
UGH, KIMIKO-SAN. YOU COULD'VE SHOWN US SOME PICTURES BEFORE YOU LEFT.
LET ME SEE THEM ALREADY!
SORRY, SORRY.
THANK YOU VERY MUCH.
BEEP
BEEP
BEEP
BEEP
AWWW.
BEEP

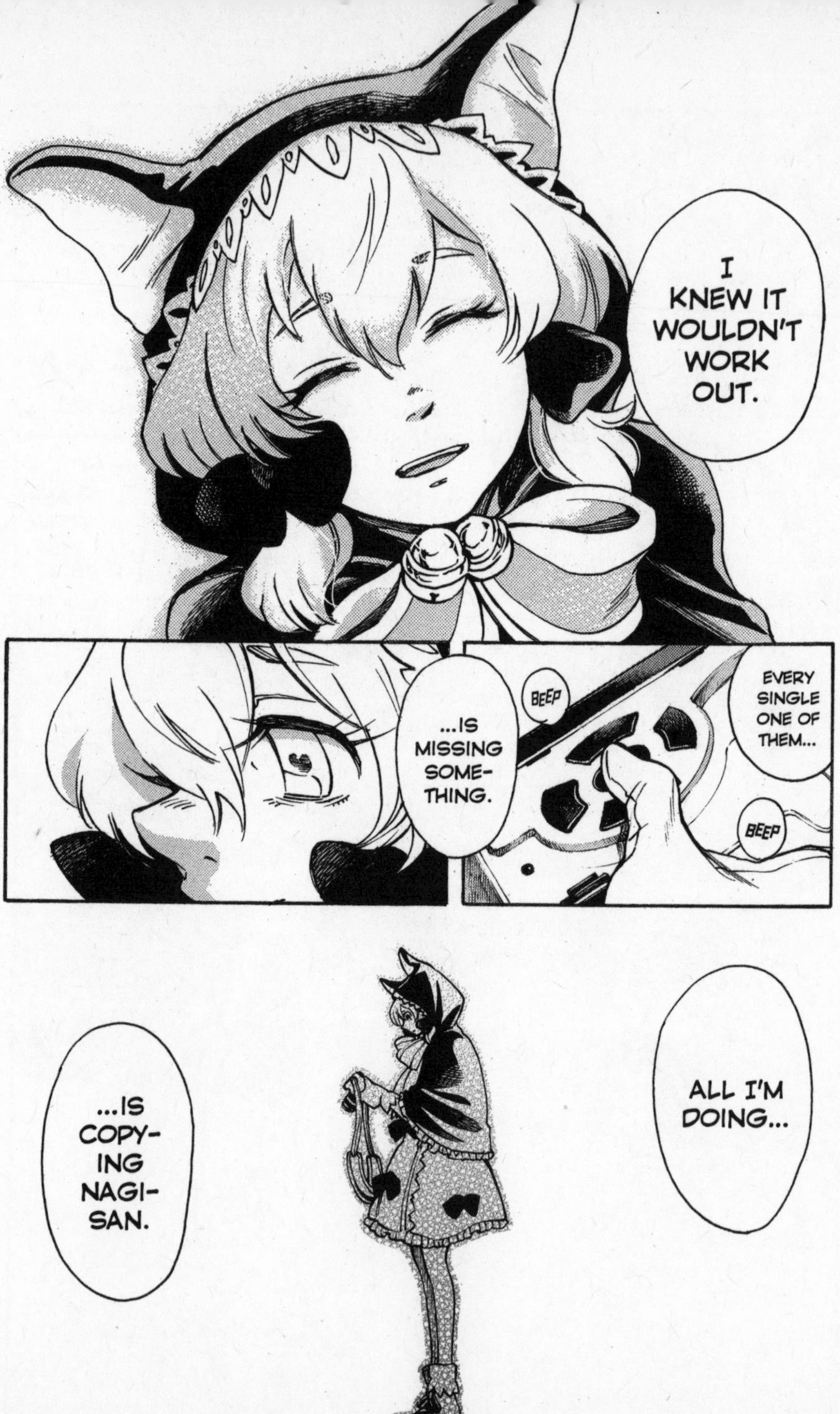
I KNEW IT WOULDN'T WORK OUT.
EVERY SINGLE ONE OF THEM...
BEEP
BEEP
...IS MISSING SOME-THING.
ALL I'M DOING...
...IS COPY-ING NAGI-SAN.

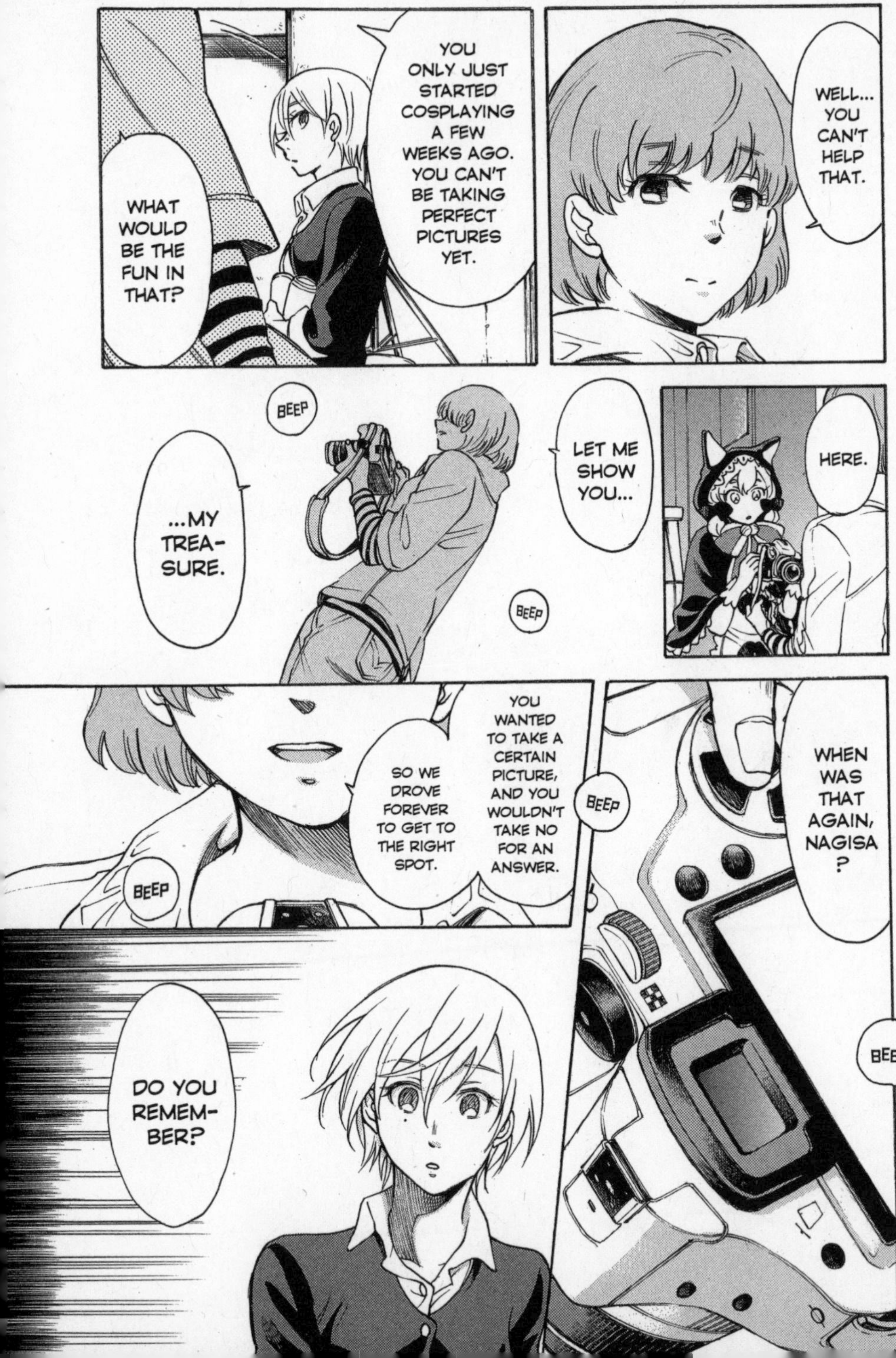
WELL... YOU CAN'T HELP THAT.
YOU ONLY JUST STARTED COSPLAYING A FEW WEEKS AGO. YOU CAN'T BE TAKING PERFECT PICTURES YET.
WHAT WOULD BE THE FUN IN THAT?
HERE.
LET ME SHOW YOU...
BEEP
...MY TREASURE.
BEEP
WHEN WAS THAT AGAIN, NAGISA?
BEEP
YOU WANTED TO TAKE A CERTAIN PICTURE, AND YOU WOULDN'T TAKE NO FOR AN ANSWER.
BEEP
SO WE DROVE FOREVER TO GET TO THE RIGHT SPOT.
BEEP
DO YOU REMEMBER?

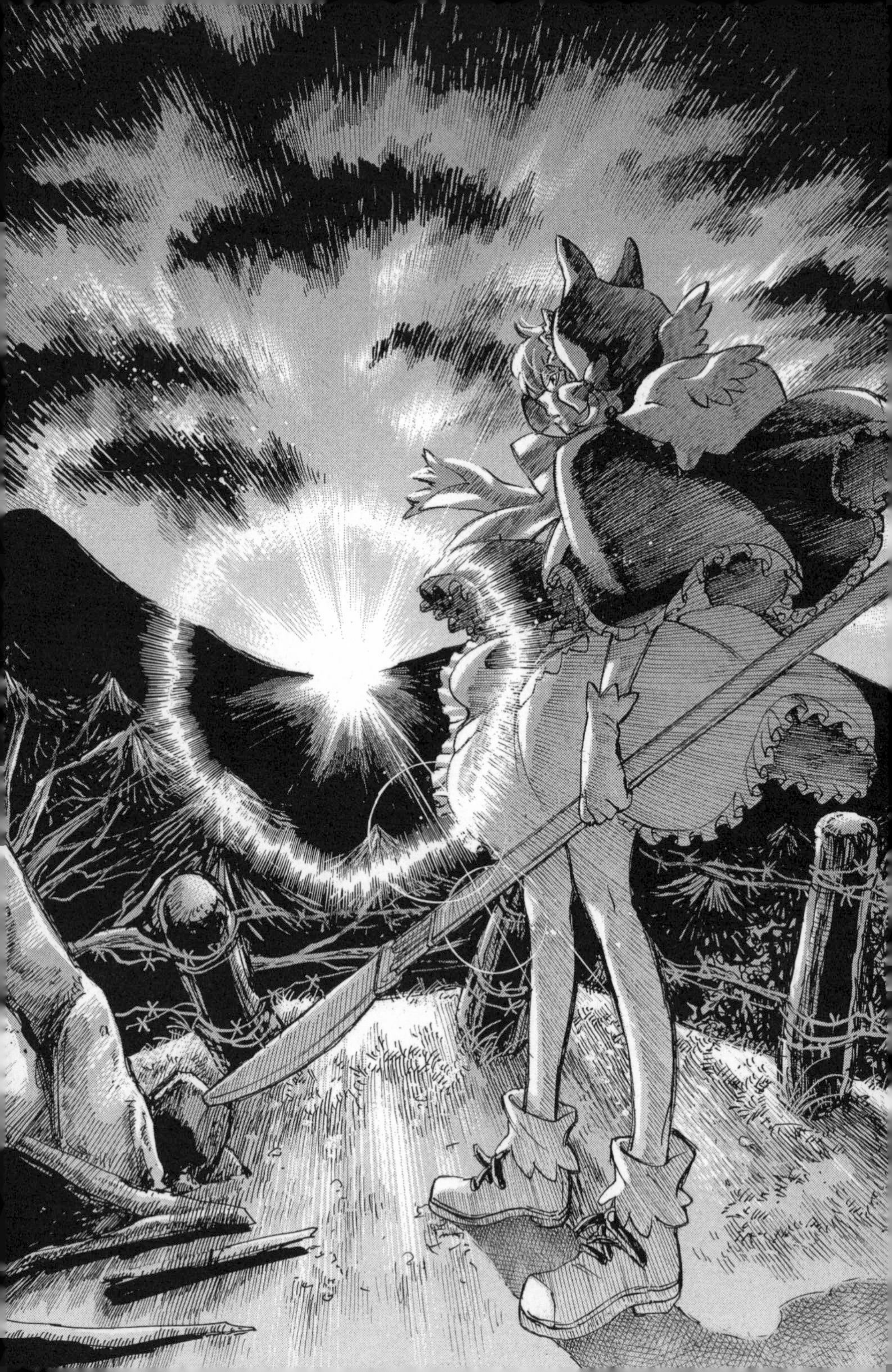

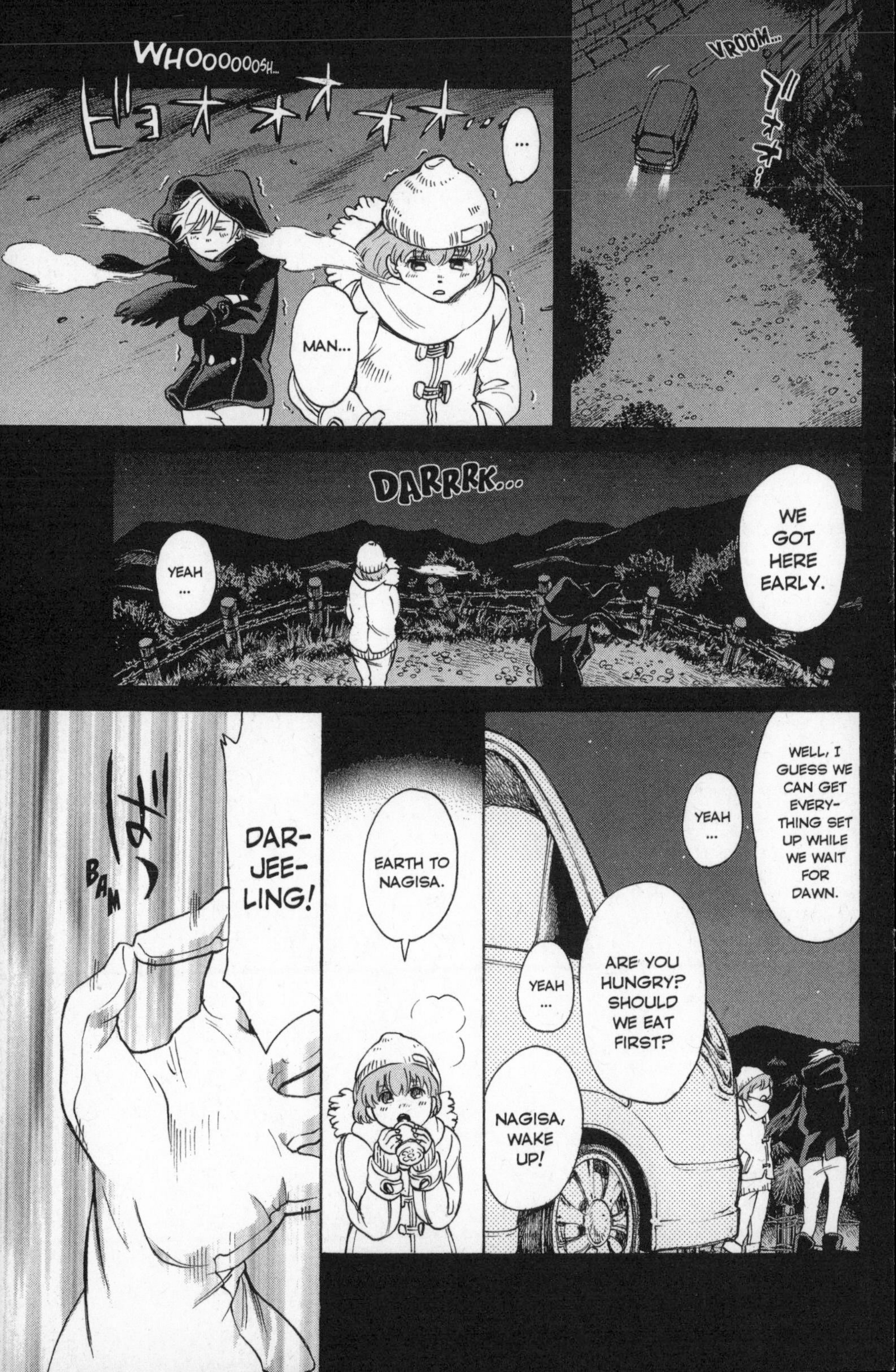
VROOM...
WHOOOOOOSH...
ビョオオオオオ...
...
MAN...
DARRRK...
WE GOT HERE EARLY.
YEAH ...
WELL, I GUESS WE CAN GET EVERYTHING SET UP WHILE WE WAIT FOR DAWN.
YEAH ...
ARE YOU HUNGRY? SHOULD WE EAT FIRST?
YEAH ...
NAGISA, WAKE UP!
EARTH TO NAGISA.
DAR-JEE-LING!
BAM

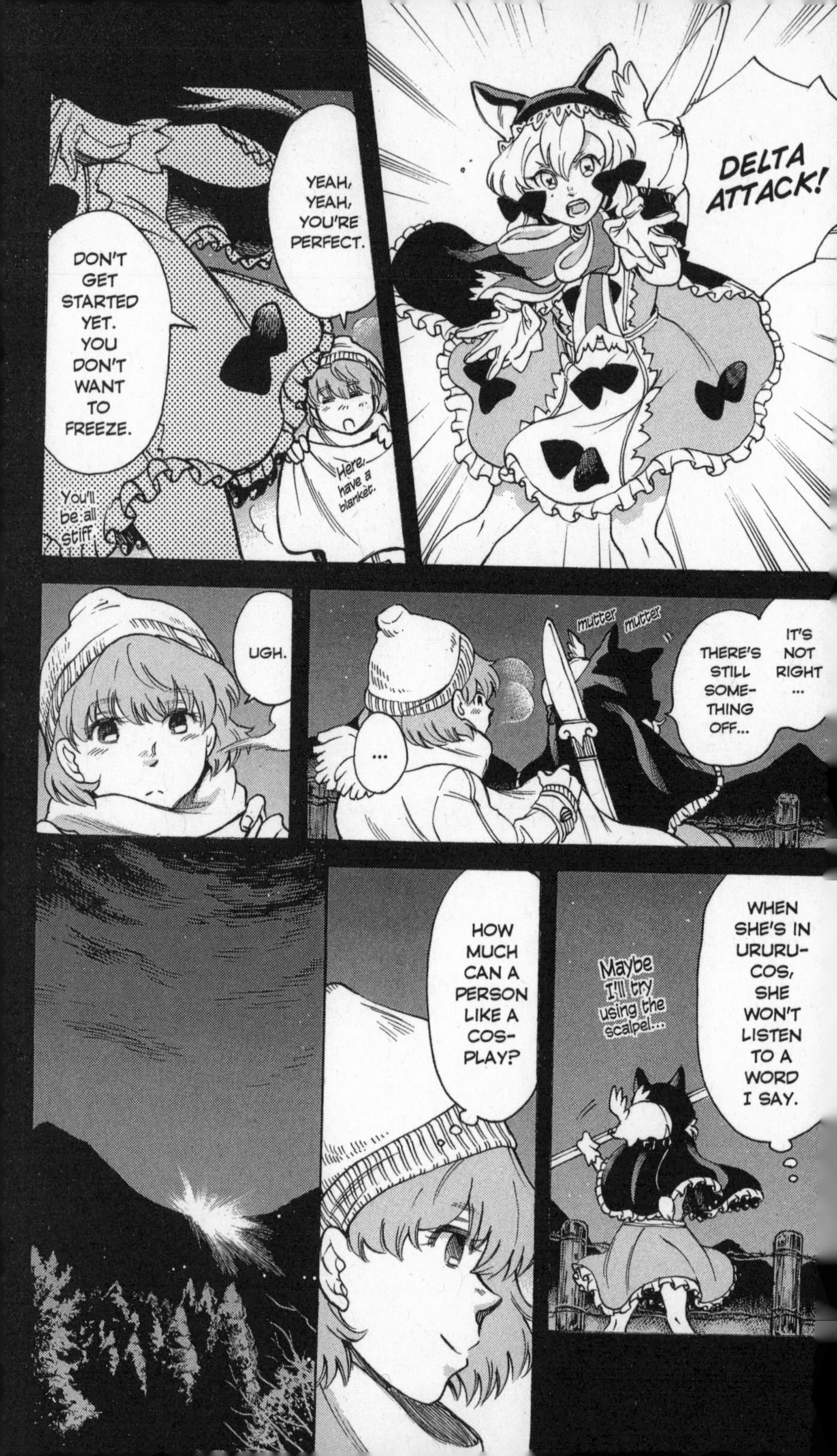
DELTA ATTACK!
YEAH, YEAH, YOU'RE PERFECT.
DON'T GET STARTED YET. YOU DON'T WANT TO FREEZE.
Here, have a blanket.
You'll be all stiff.
IT'S NOT RIGHT...
THERE'S STILL SOME-THING OFF...
mutter mutter
...
UGH.
WHEN SHE'S IN URURU-COS, SHE WON'T LISTEN TO A WORD I SAY.
Maybe I'll try using the scalpel...
HOW MUCH CAN A PERSON LIKE A COS-PLAY?

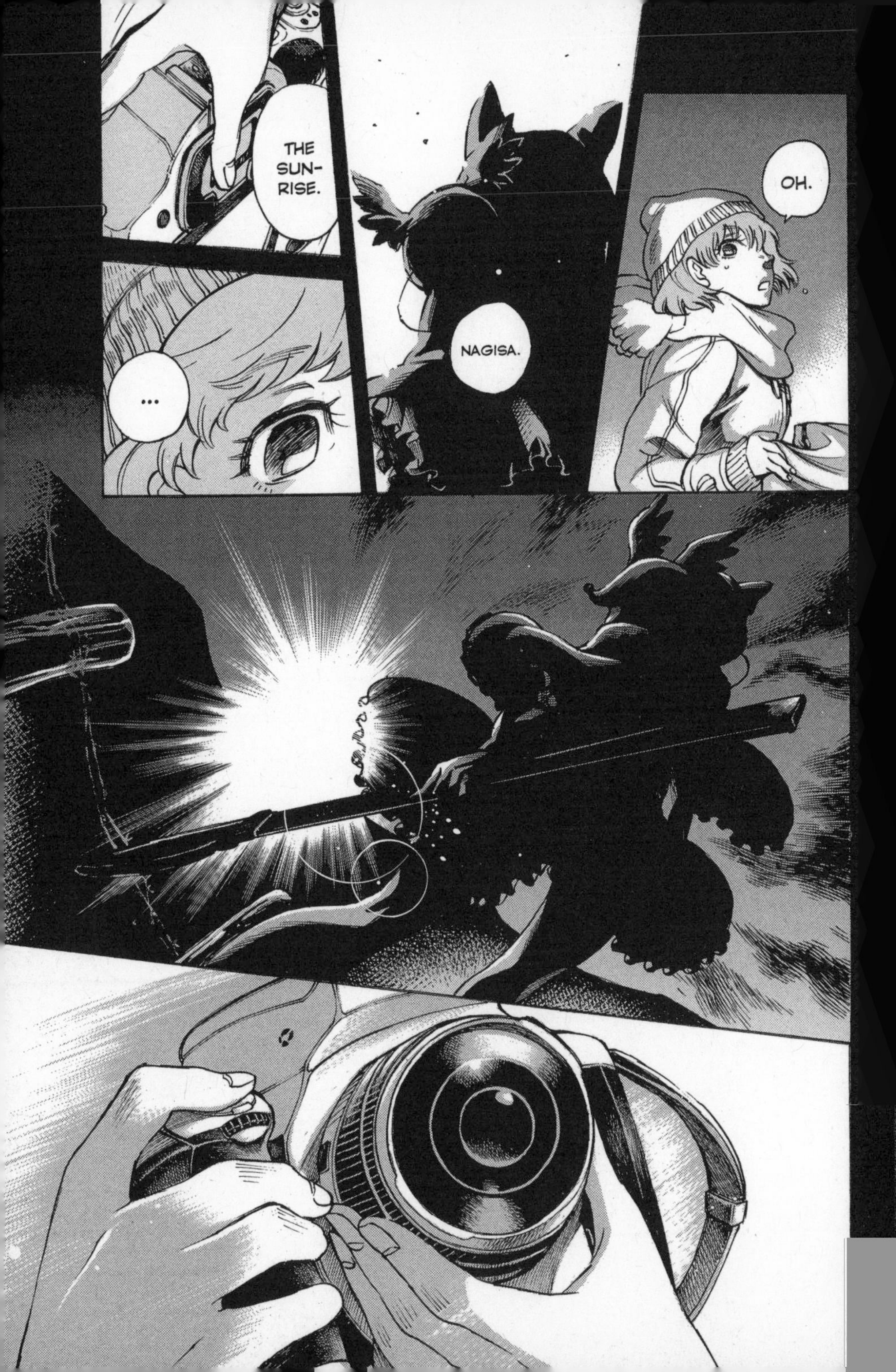
OH.
NAGISA.
THE SUN-RISE.
...

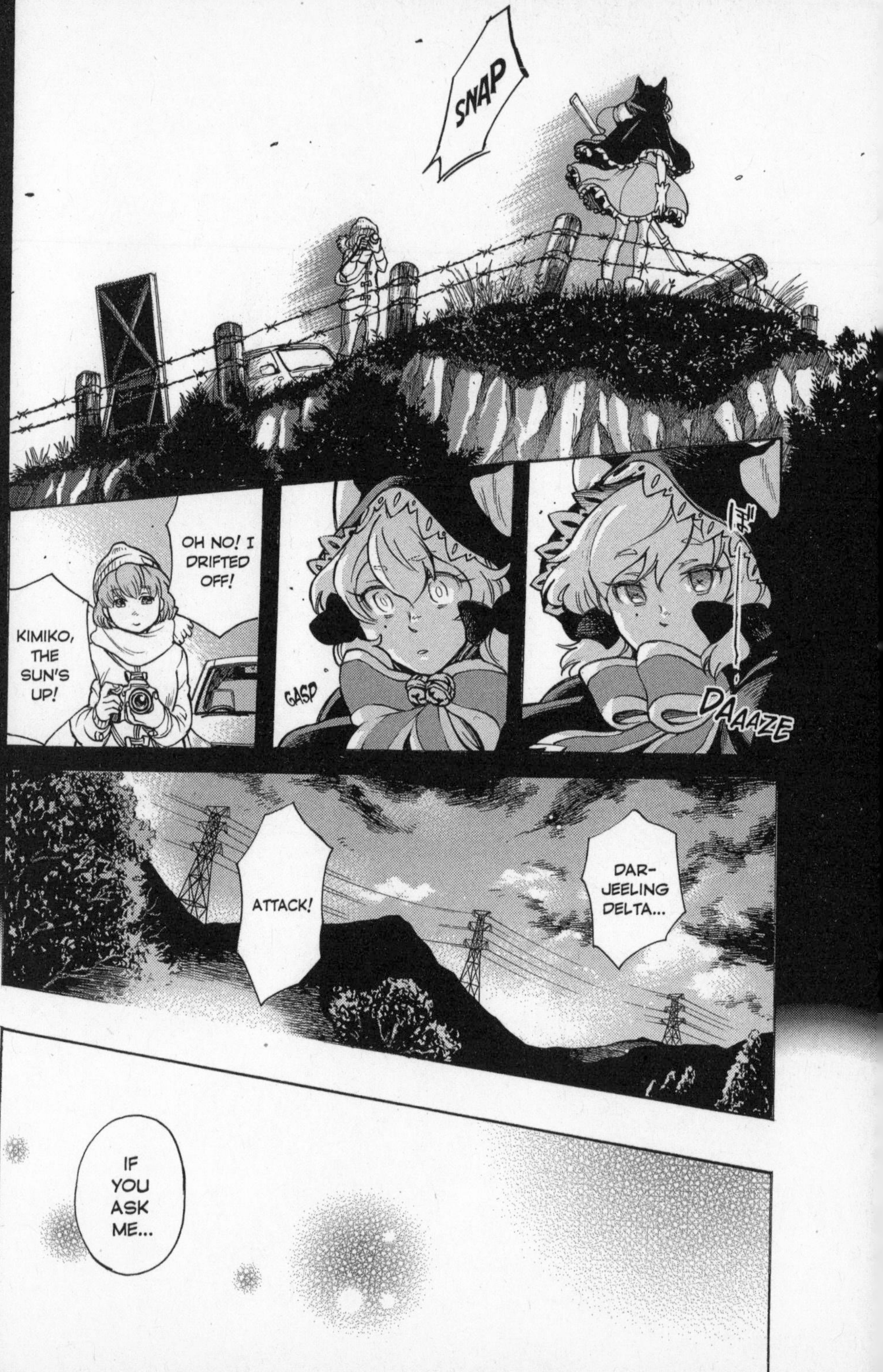
SNAP
DAAAZE
GASP
OH NO! I DRIFTED OFF!
KIMIKO, THE SUN'S UP!
DAR-JEELING DELTA...
ATTACK!
IF YOU ASK ME...

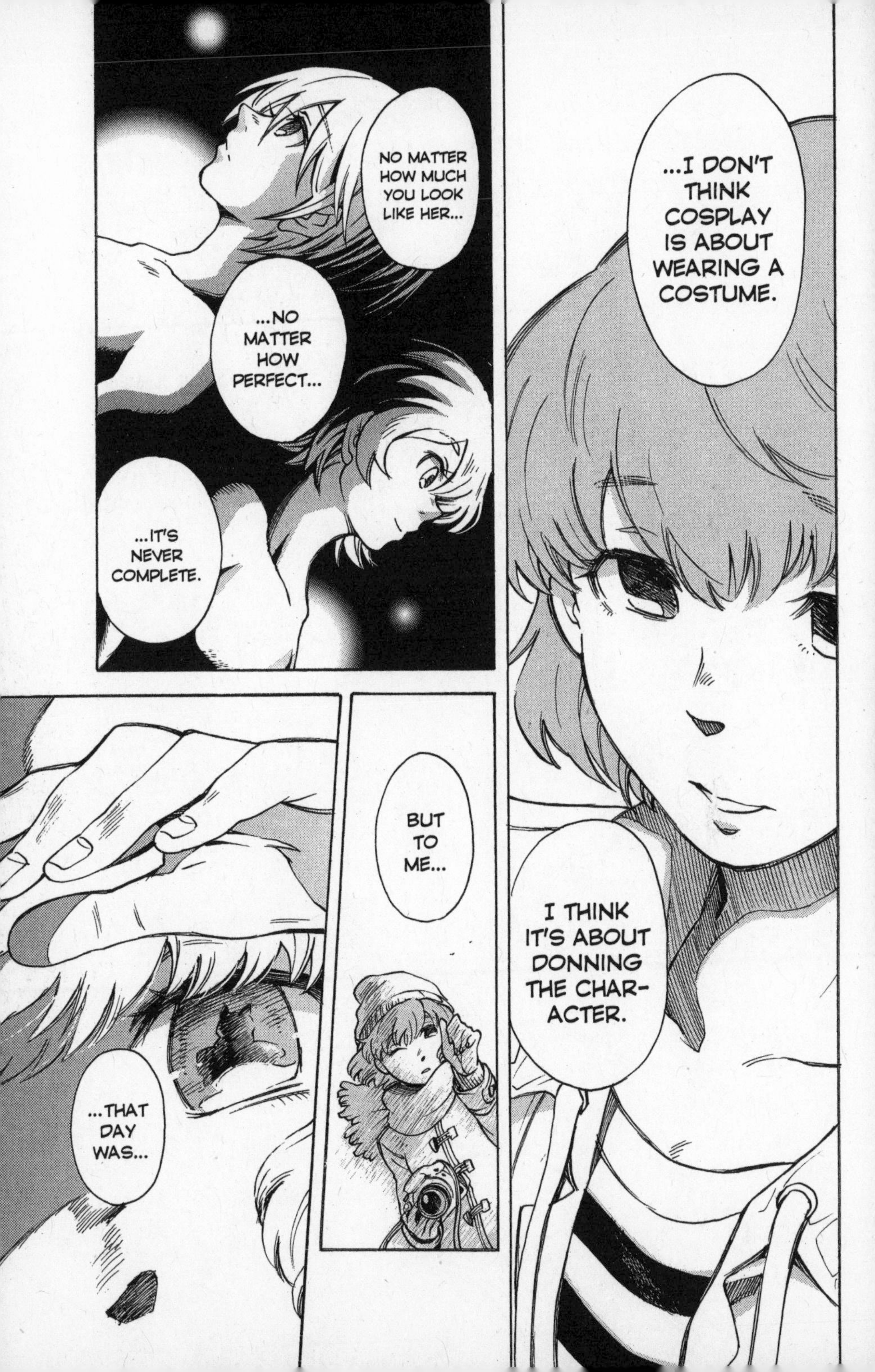
...I DON'T THINK COSPLAY IS ABOUT WEARING A COSTUME.
I THINK IT'S ABOUT DONNING THE CHAR-ACTER.
NO MATTER HOW MUCH YOU LOOK LIKE HER...
...NO MATTER HOW PERFECT...
...IT'S NEVER COMPLETE.
BUT TO ME...
...THAT DAY WAS...

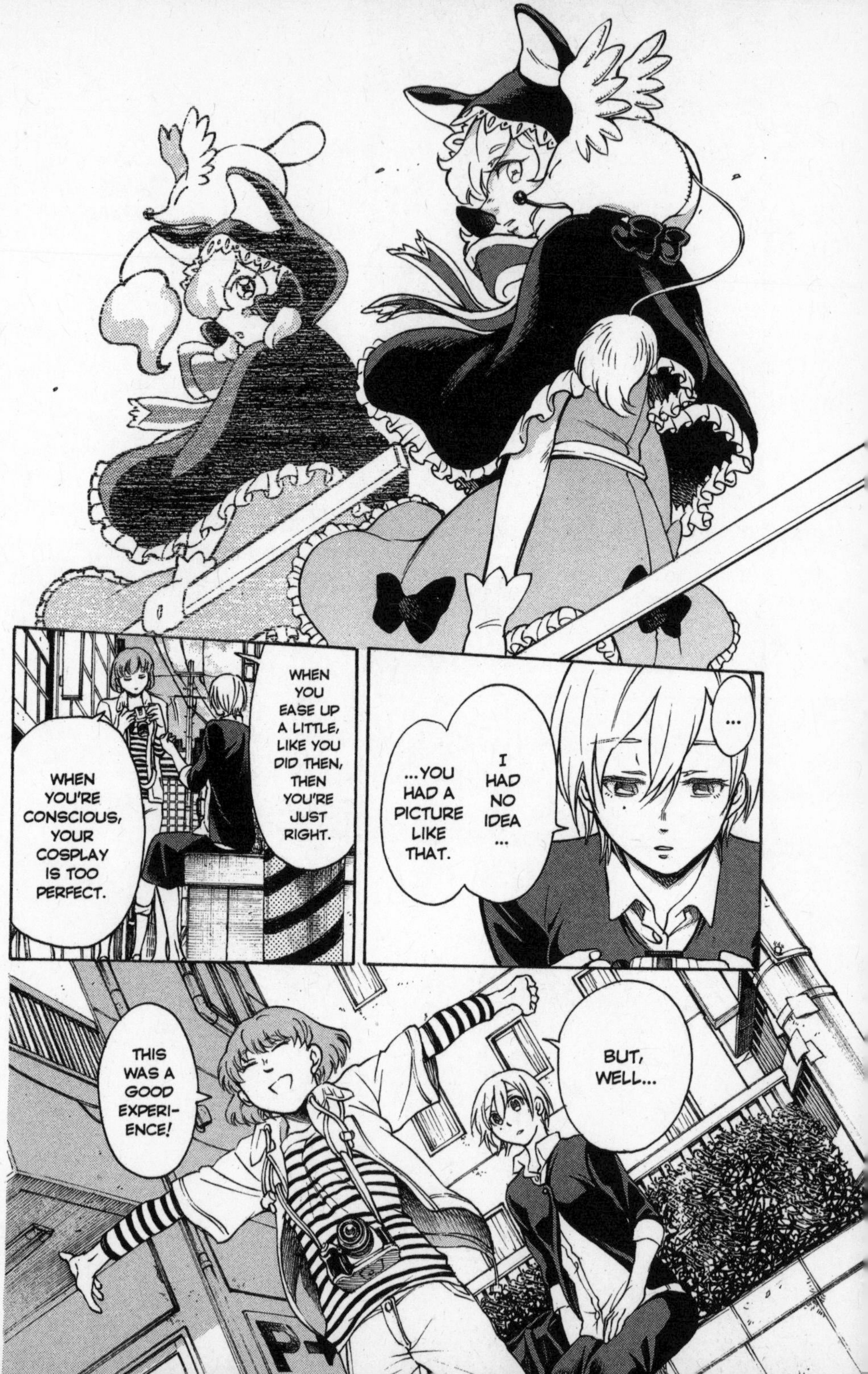
...
I HAD NO IDEA...
...YOU HAD A PICTURE LIKE THAT.
WHEN YOU EASE UP A LITTLE, LIKE YOU DID THEN, THEN YOU'RE JUST RIGHT.
WHEN YOU'RE CONSCIOUS, YOUR COSPLAY IS TOO PERFECT.
BUT, WELL...
THIS WAS A GOOD EXPERIENCE!

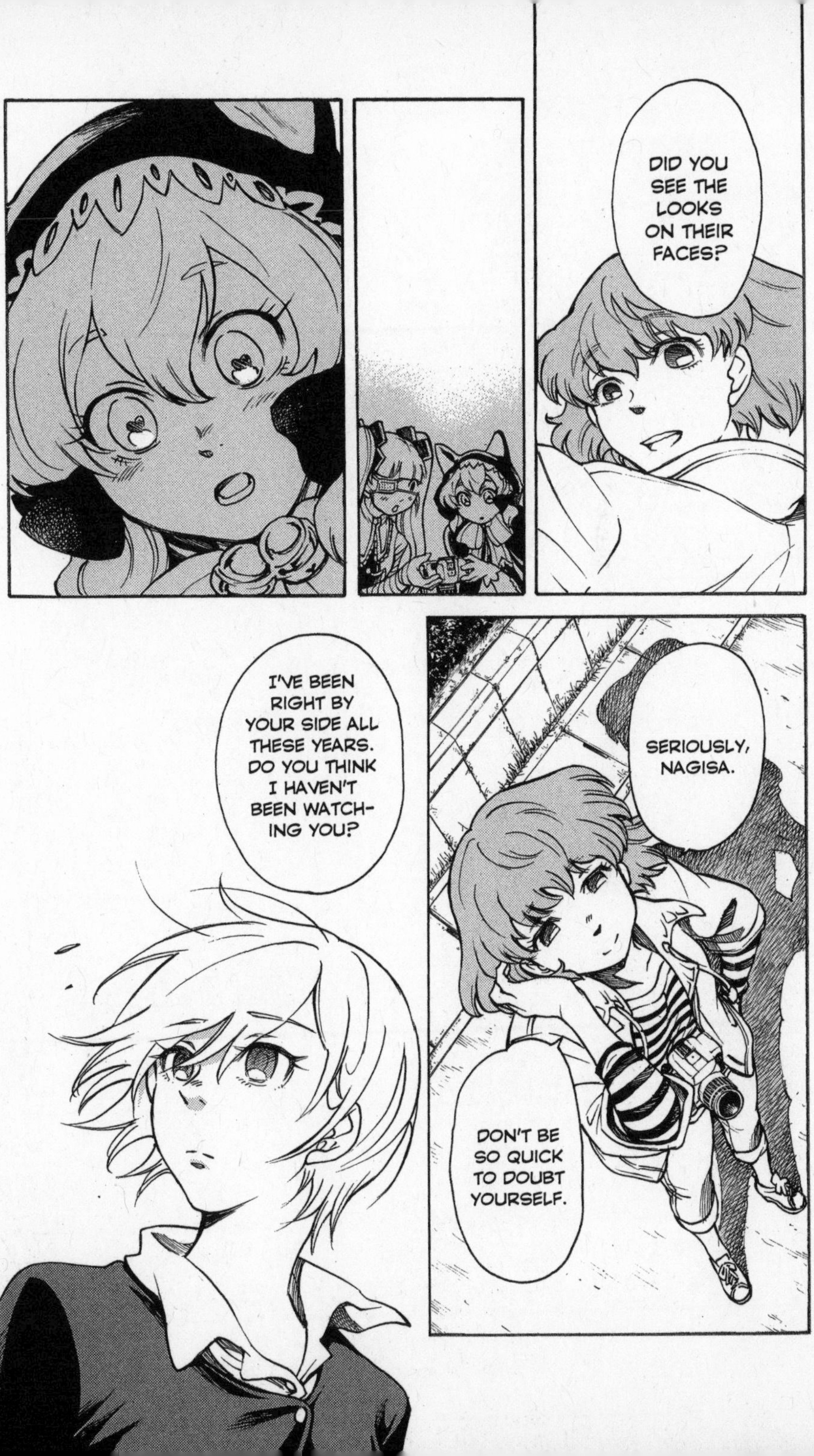
DID YOU SEE THE LOOKS ON THEIR FACES?
SERIOUSLY, NAGISA.
I'VE BEEN RIGHT BY YOUR SIDE ALL THESE YEARS. DO YOU THINK I HAVEN'T BEEN WATCHING YOU?
DON'T BE SO QUICK TO DOUBT YOURSELF.

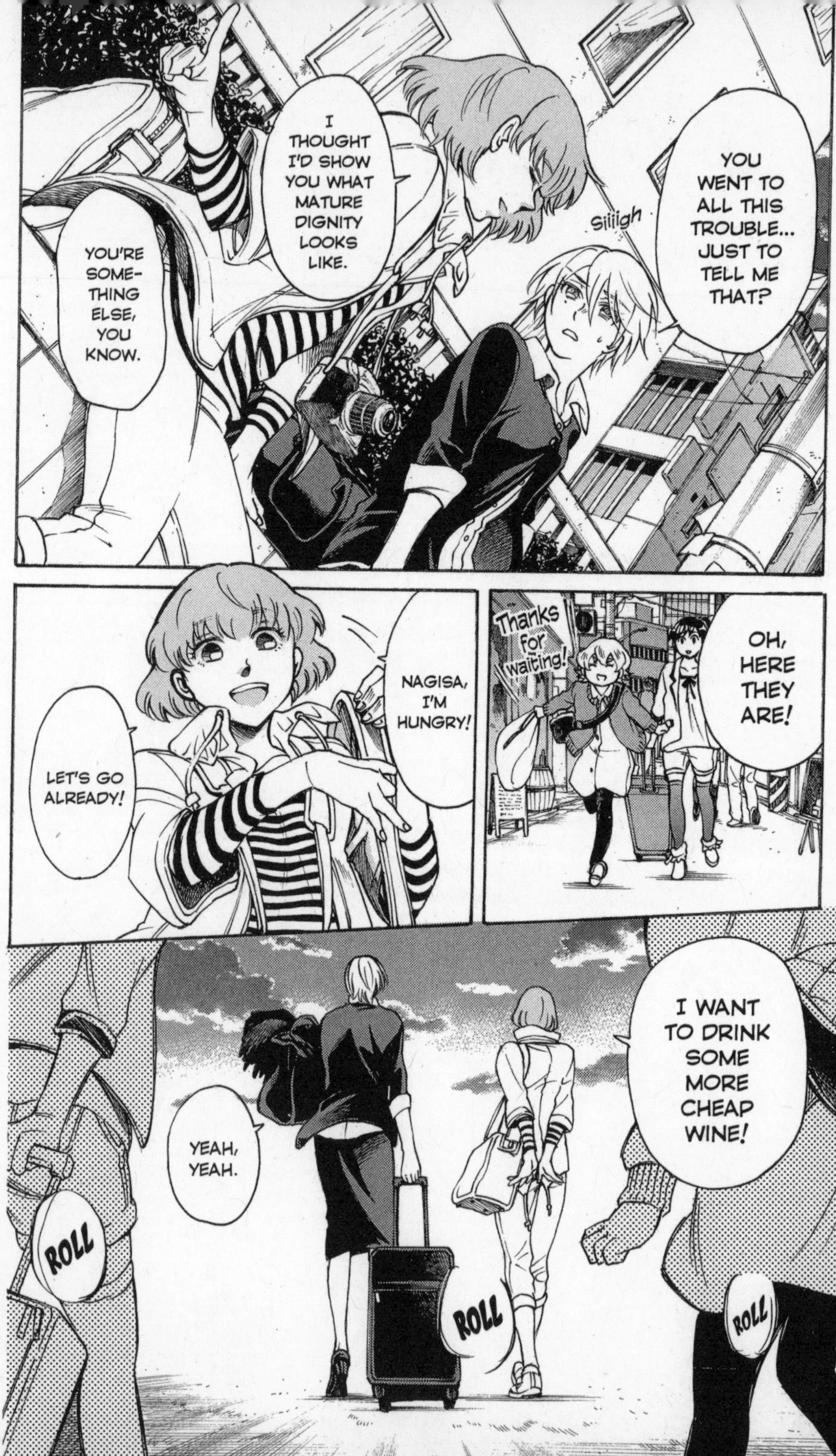
YOU WENT TO ALL THIS TROUBLE... JUST TO TELL ME THAT?
Siiiigh
I THOUGHT I'D SHOW YOU WHAT MATURE DIGNITY LOOKS LIKE.
YOU'RE SOME-THING ELSE, YOU KNOW.
OH, HERE THEY ARE!
Thanks for waiting!
NAGISA, I'M HUNGRY!
LET'S GO ALREADY!
I WANT TO DRINK SOME MORE CHEAP WINE!
YEAH, YEAH.
ROLL
ROLL
ROLL

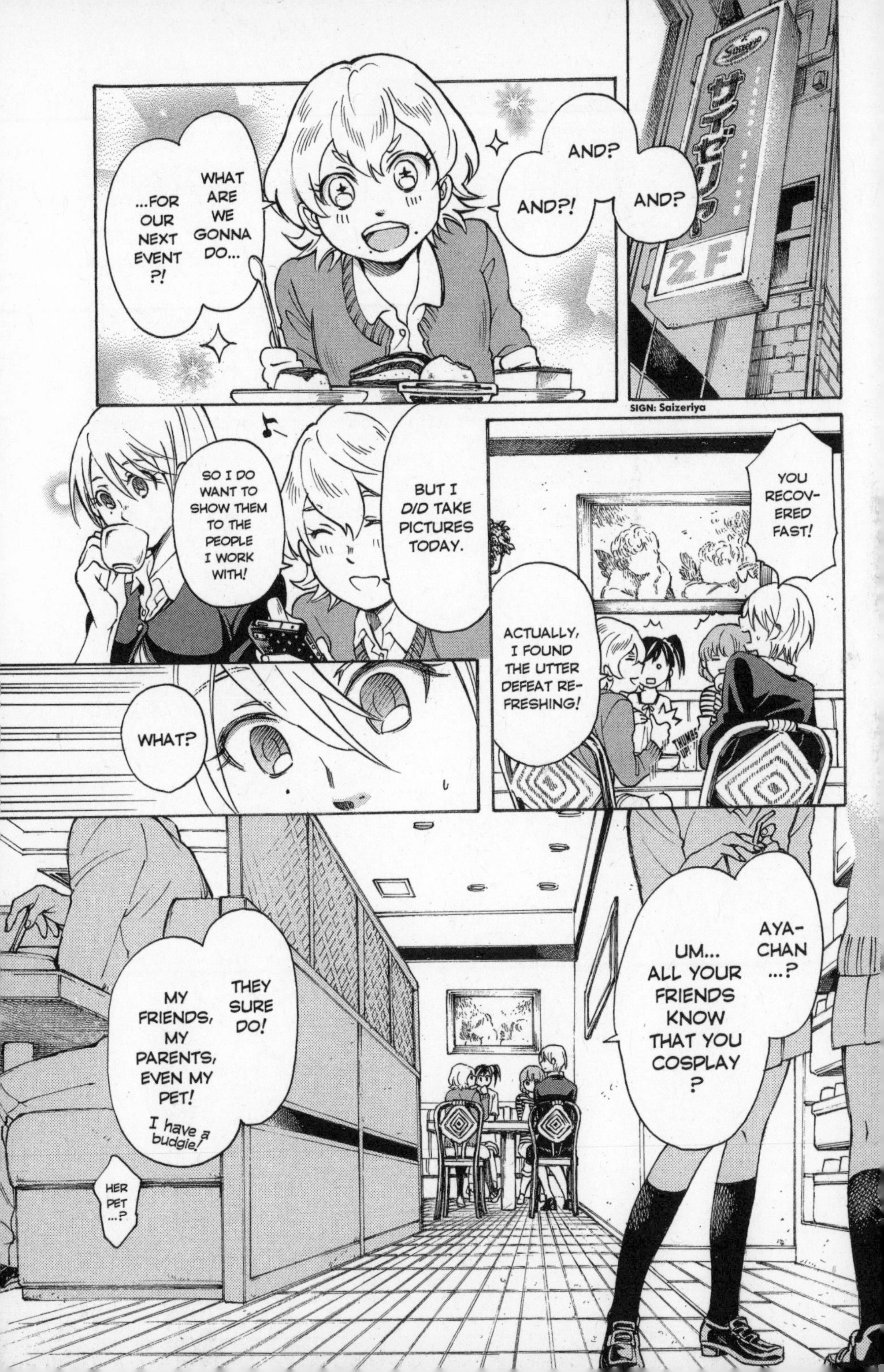
SIGN: Saizeriya
...FOR OUR NEXT EVENT?!
WHAT ARE WE GONNA DO...
AND? AND? AND?!
YOU RECOVERED FAST!
ACTUALLY, I FOUND THE UTTER DEFEAT REFRESHING!
THUMBS UP!
BUT I *DID* TAKE PICTURES TODAY.
SO I DO WANT TO SHOW THEM TO THE PEOPLE I WORK WITH!
WHAT?
AYA-CHAN...?
UM... ALL YOUR FRIENDS KNOW THAT YOU COSPLAY?
THEY SURE DO!
MY FRIENDS, MY PARENTS, EVEN MY PET!
I have a budgie!
HER PET...?

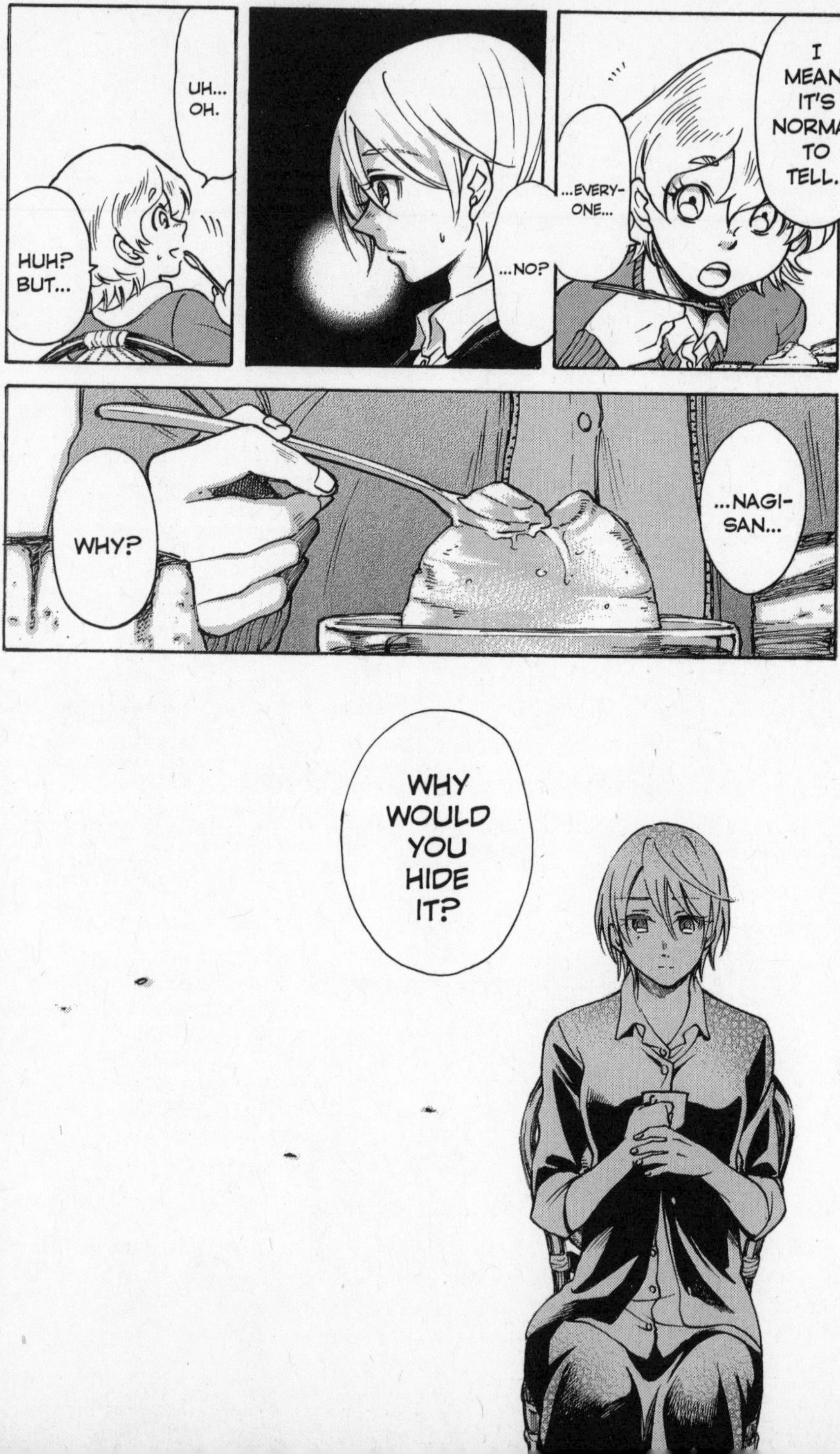
I MEAN, IT'S NORMAL TO TELL...
...EVERY-ONE...
...NO?
UH... OH.
HUH? BUT...
...NAGI-SAN...
WHY?
WHY WOULD YOU HIDE IT?

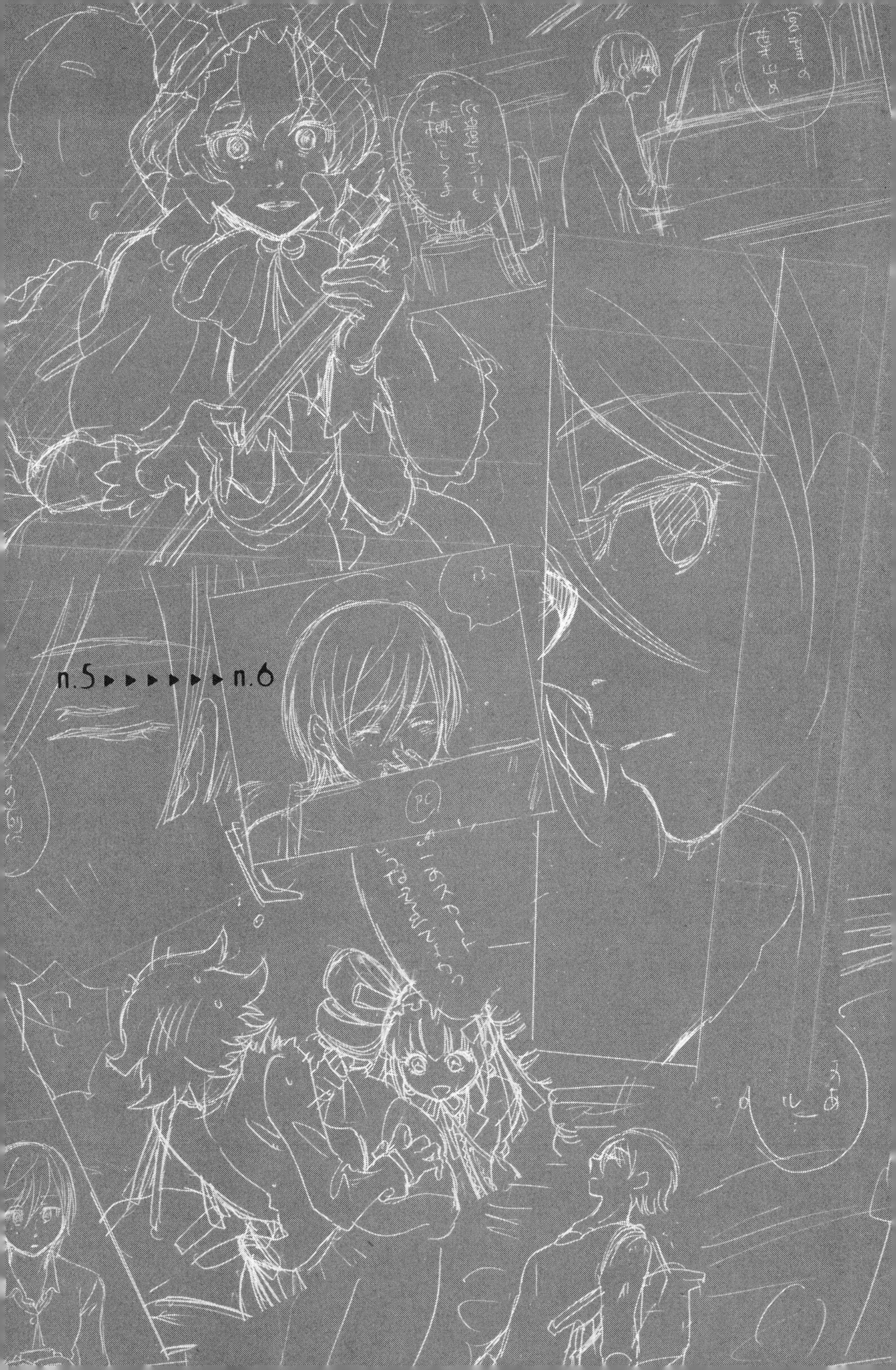
n.5 ▶▶▶▶▶▶ n.6

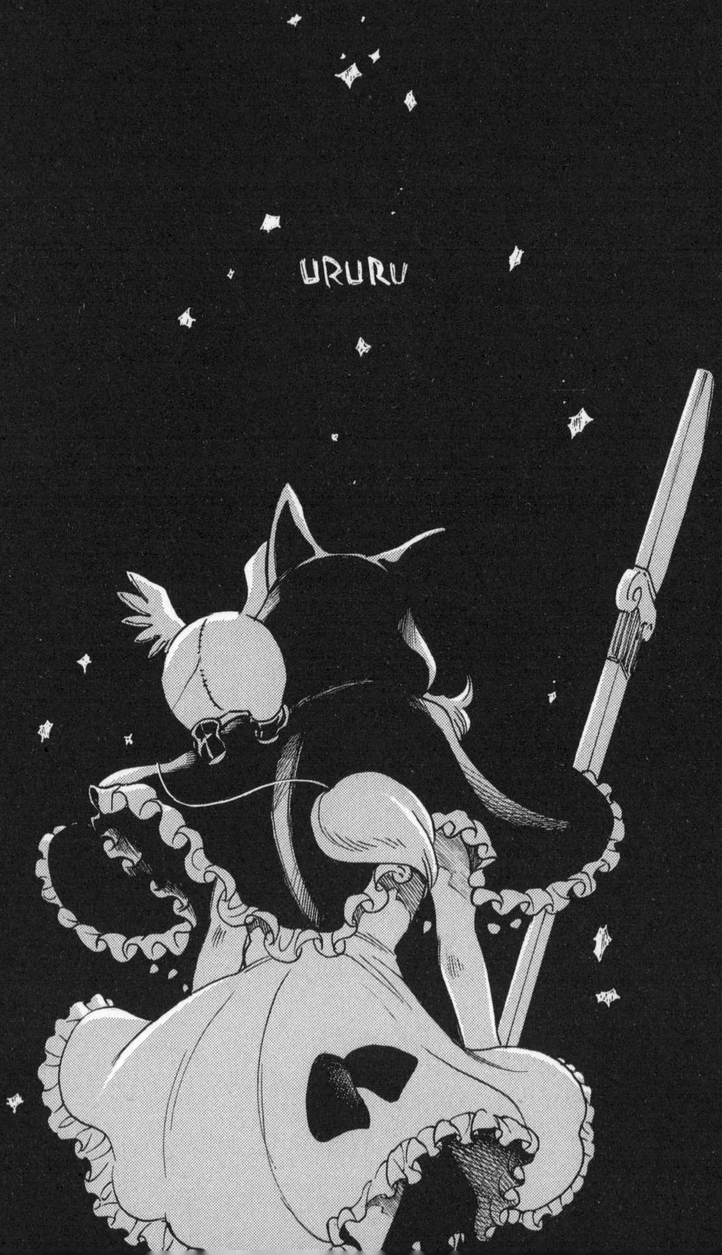
URURU

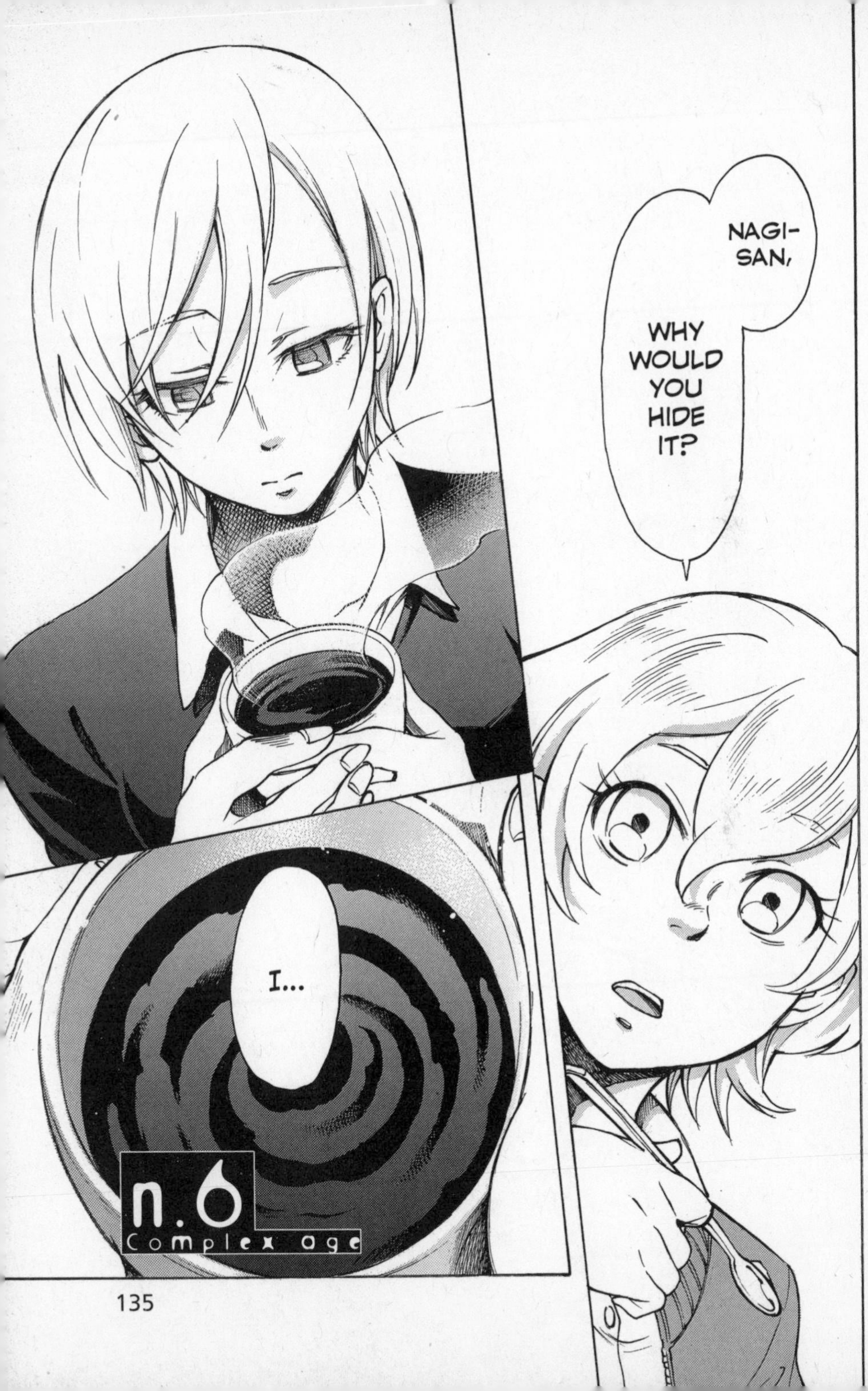
NAGI-SAN,
WHY WOULD YOU HIDE IT?
I...
n.6
Complex age

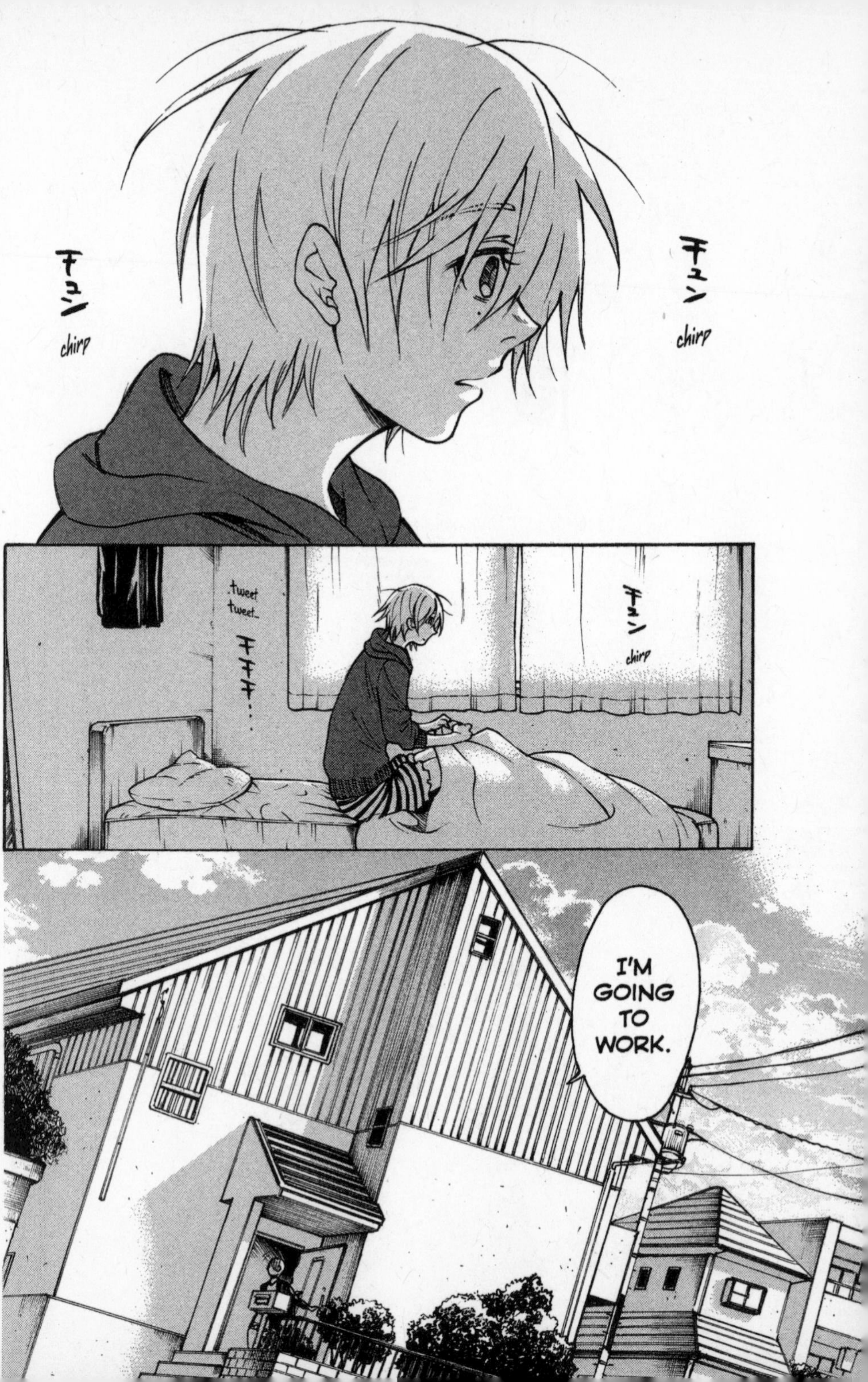
チュン
chirp
チュン
chirp
チュン
chirp
チチチ…
tweet tweet…
I'M GOING TO WORK.

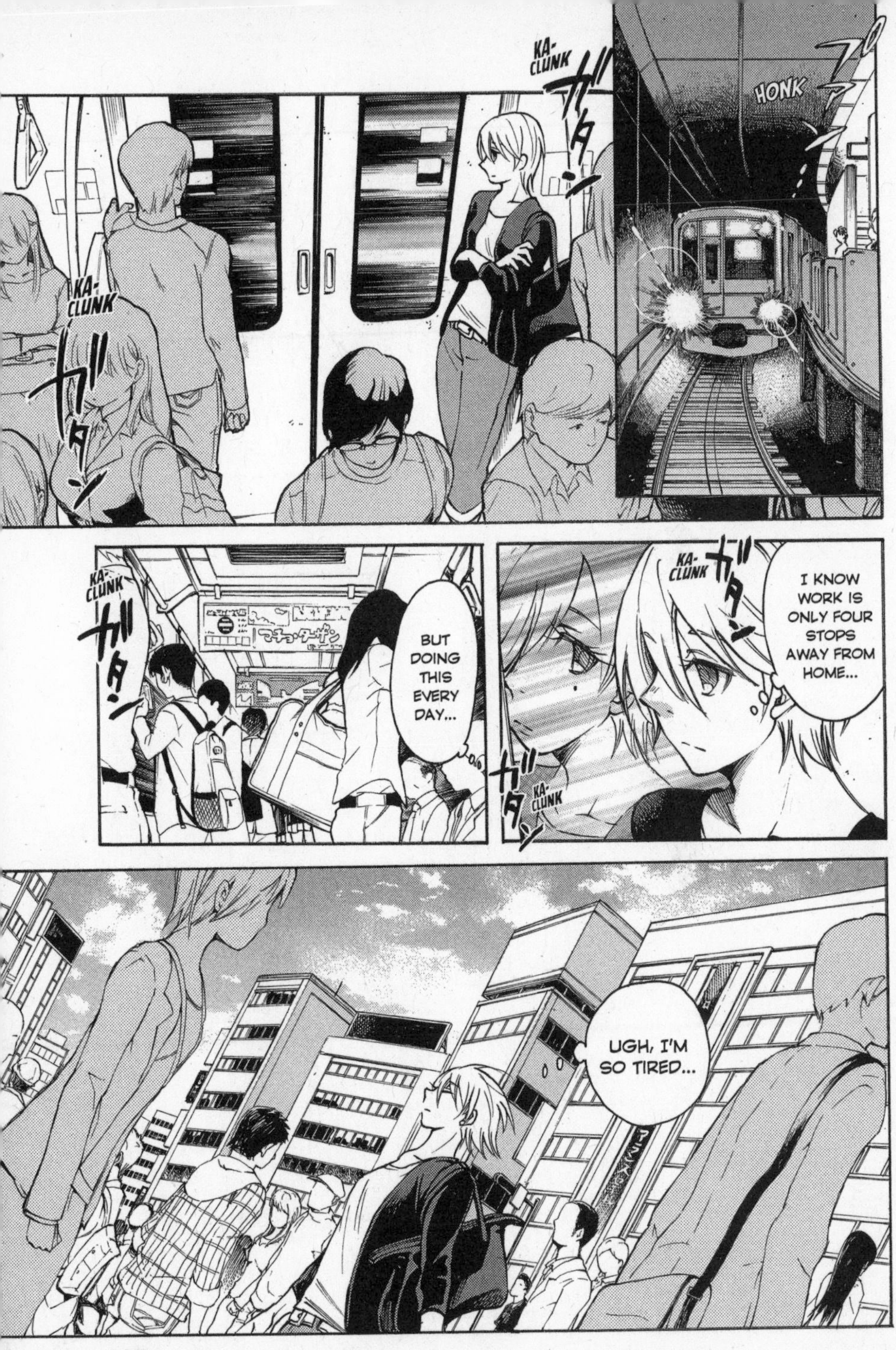
HONK
KA-CLUNK
KA-CLUNK
KA-CLUNK
I KNOW WORK IS ONLY FOUR STOPS AWAY FROM HOME...
KA-CLUNK
KA-CLUNK
BUT DOING THIS EVERY DAY...
UGH, I'M SO TIRED...

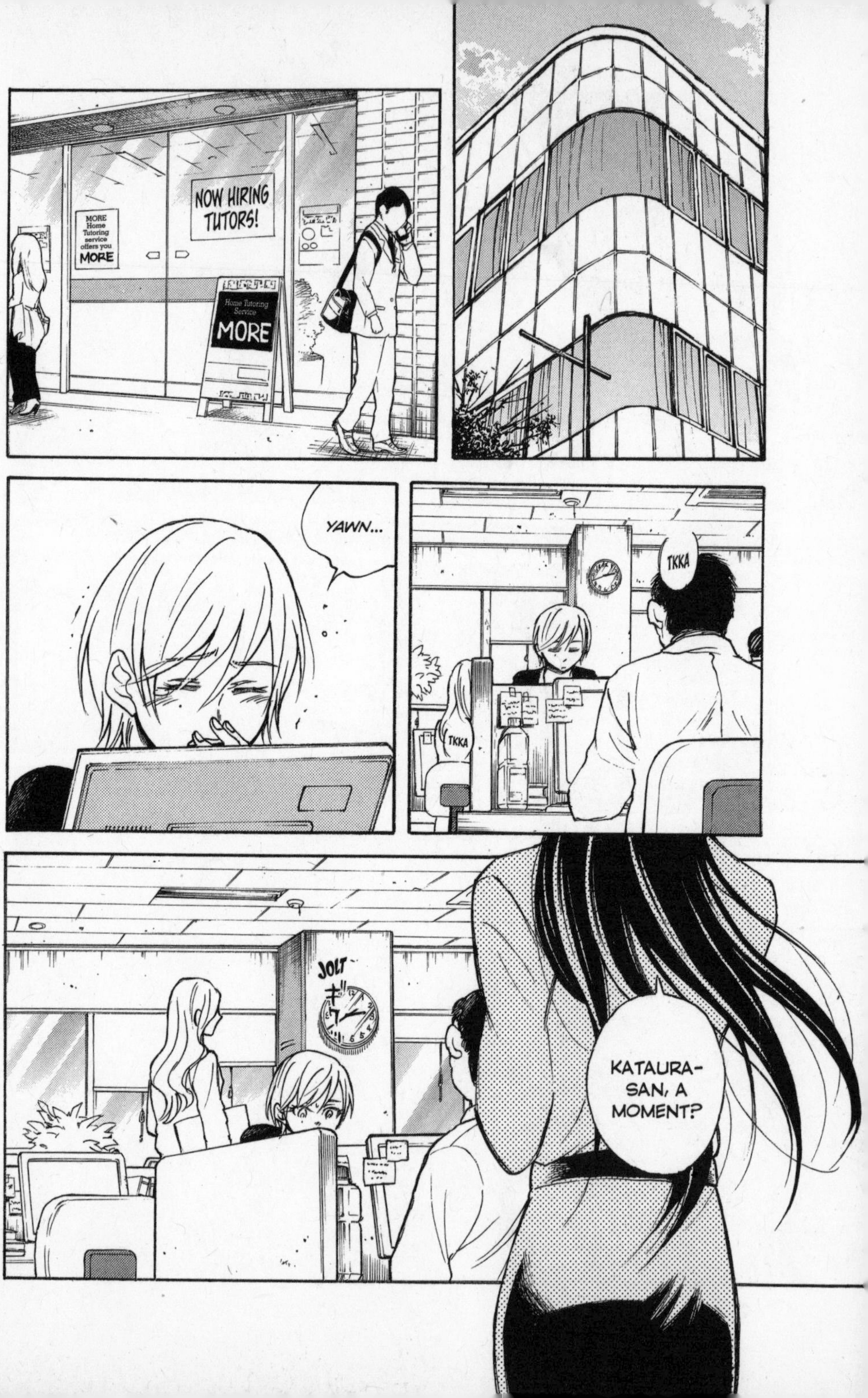
NOW HIRING TUTORS!
MORE Home Tutoring service offers you MORE
Home Tutoring Service MORE
TKKA
TKKA
YAWN...
JOLT
KATAURA-SAN, A MOMENT?

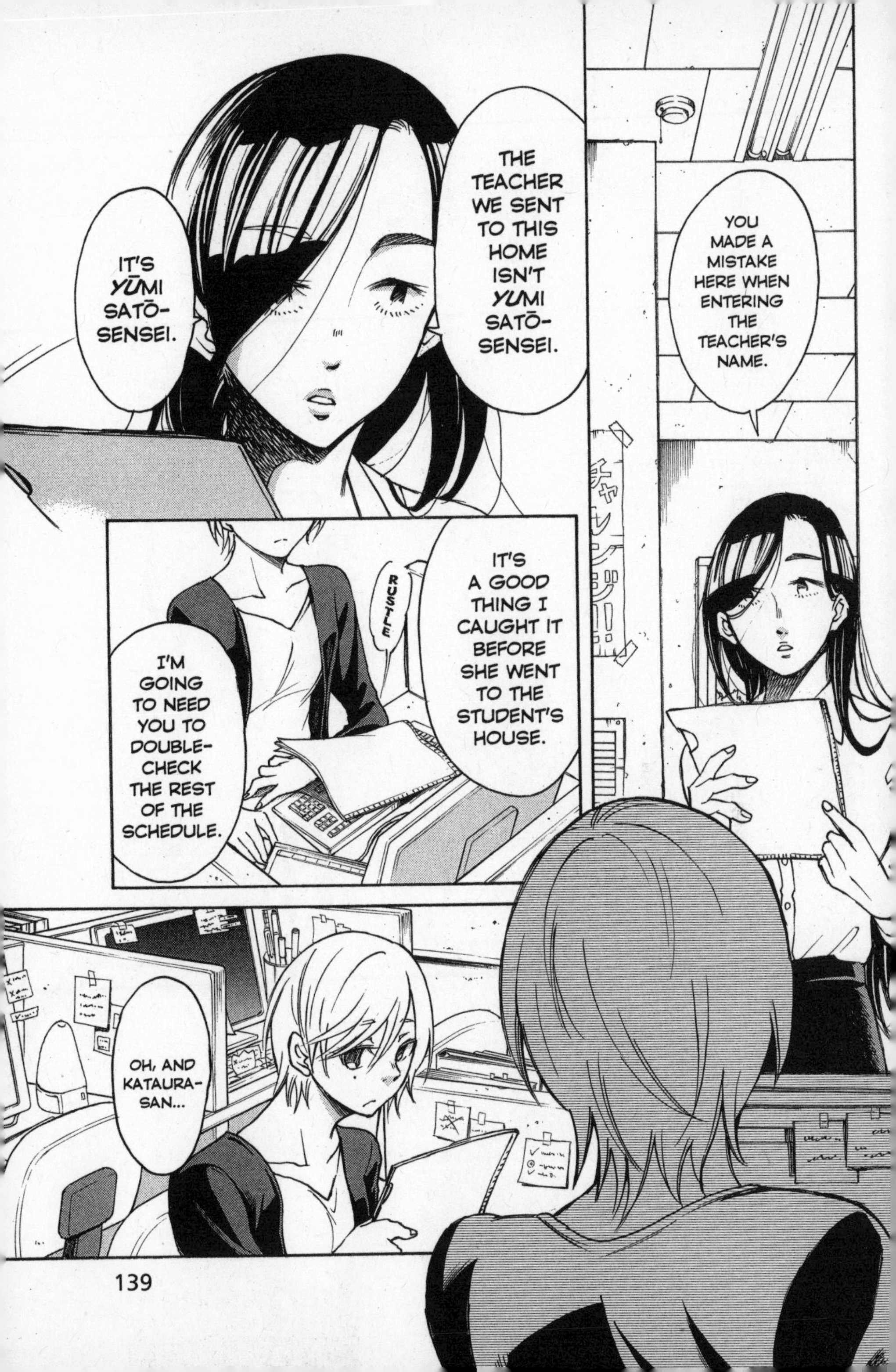
YOU MADE A MISTAKE HERE WHEN ENTERING THE TEACHER'S NAME.
THE TEACHER WE SENT TO THIS HOME ISN'T YUMI SATŌ-SENSEI.
IT'S YŪMI SATŌ-SENSEI.
チャレンジ!!
IT'S A GOOD THING I CAUGHT IT BEFORE SHE WENT TO THE STUDENT'S HOUSE.
RUSTLE
I'M GOING TO NEED YOU TO DOUBLE-CHECK THE REST OF THE SCHEDULE.
OH, AND KATAURA-SAN...

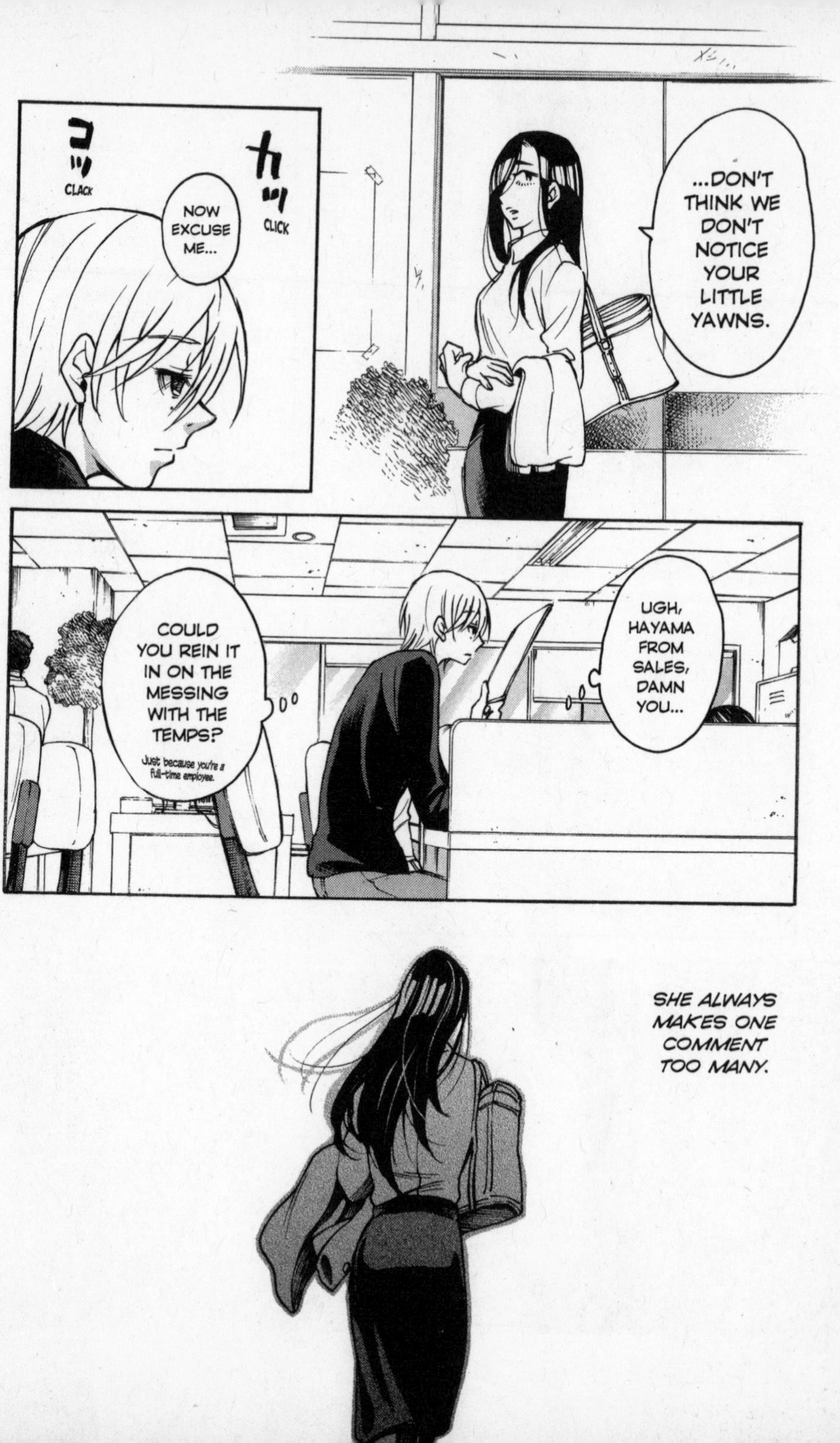
...DON'T THINK WE DON'T NOTICE YOUR LITTLE YAWNS.
カッ
CLICK
NOW EXCUSE ME...
コッ
CLACK
UGH, HAYAMA FROM SALES, DAMN YOU...
COULD YOU REIN IT IN ON THE MESSING WITH THE TEMPS?
Just because you're a full-time employee.
SHE ALWAYS MAKES ONE COMMENT TOO MANY.

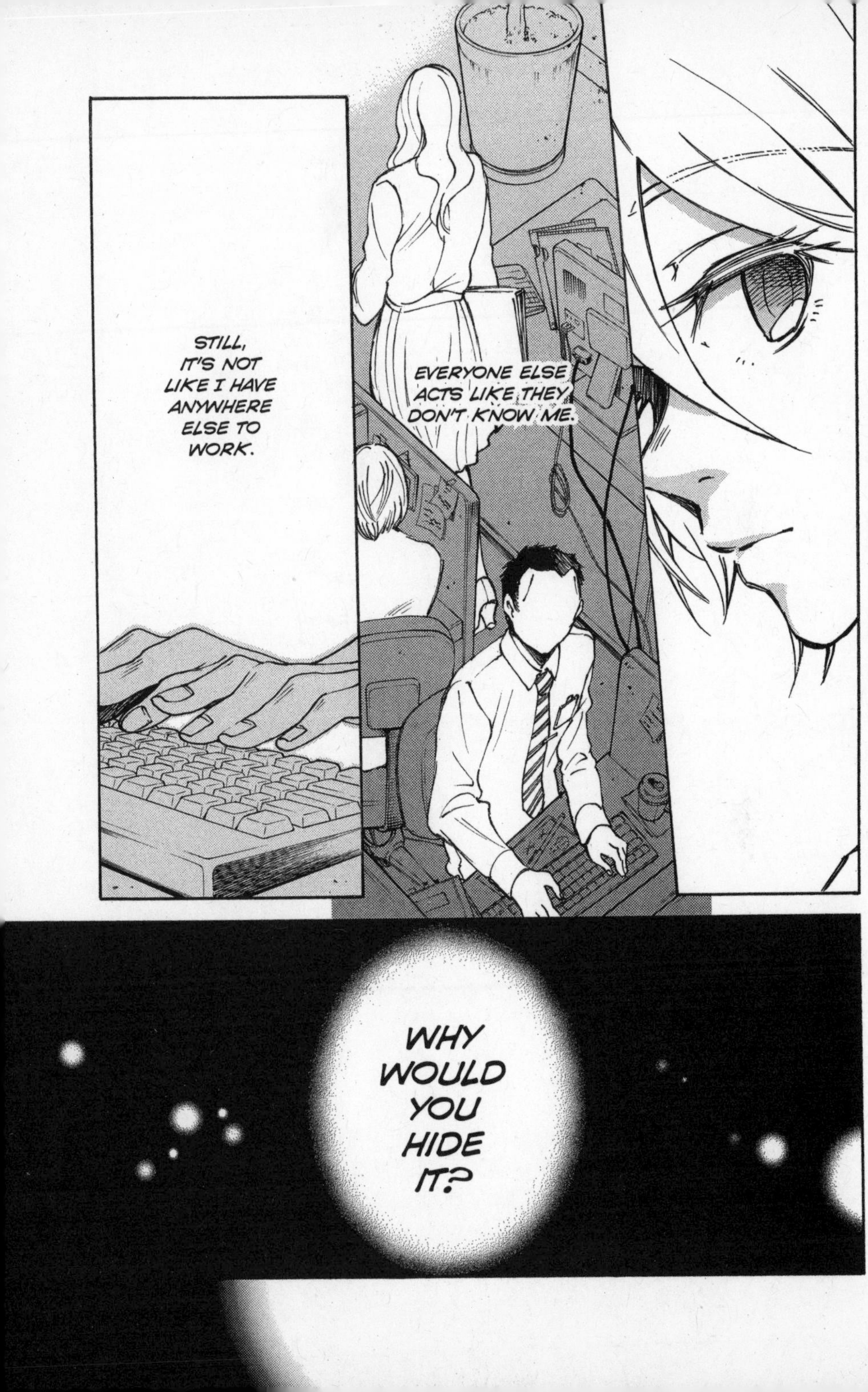
EVERYONE ELSE ACTS LIKE THEY DON'T KNOW ME.
STILL, IT'S NOT LIKE I HAVE ANYWHERE ELSE TO WORK.
WHY WOULD YOU HIDE IT?

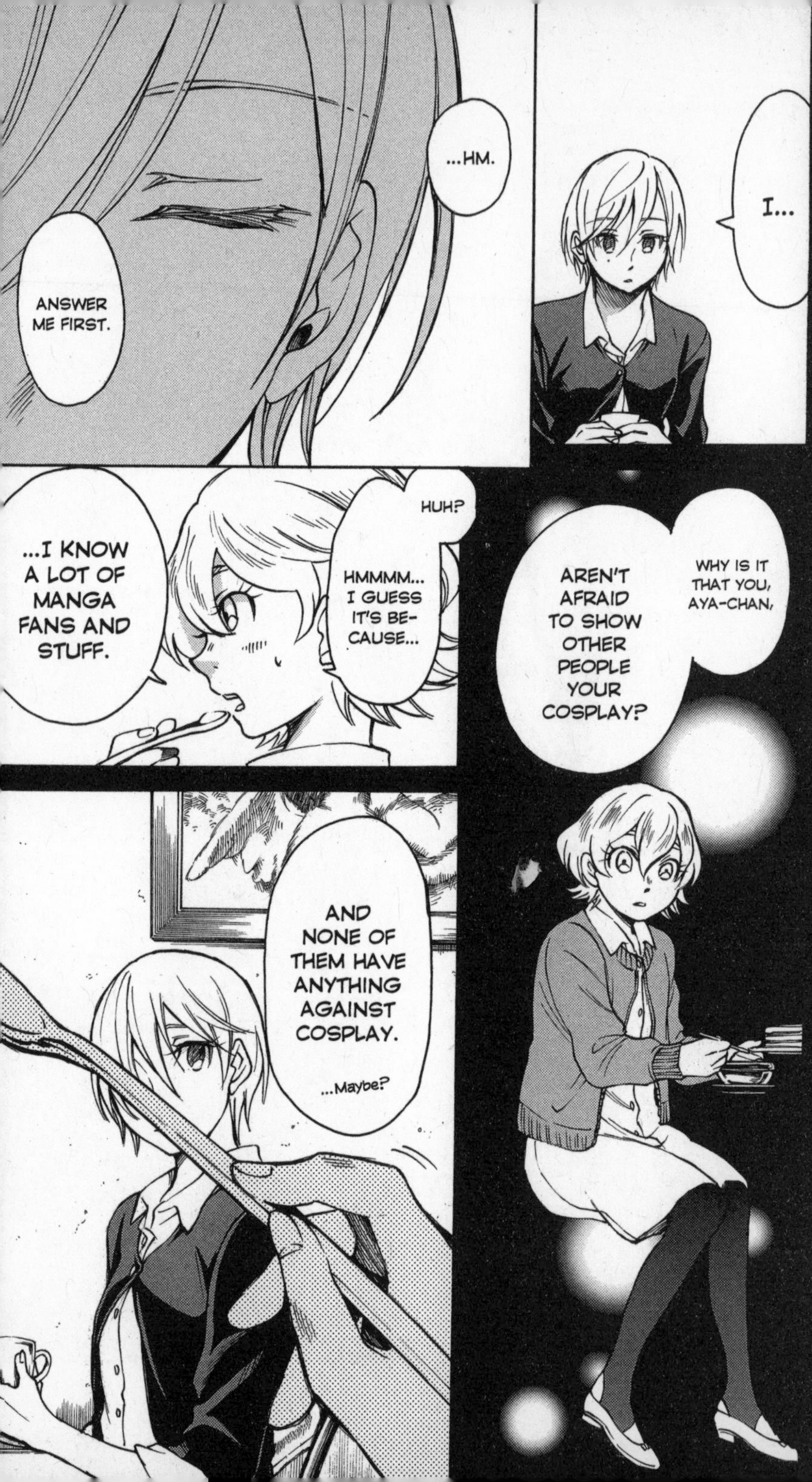
I...
...HM.
ANSWER ME FIRST.
WHY IS IT THAT YOU, AYA-CHAN,
AREN'T AFRAID TO SHOW OTHER PEOPLE YOUR COSPLAY?
HUH?
HMMMM... I GUESS IT'S BE-CAUSE...
...I KNOW A LOT OF MANGA FANS AND STUFF.
AND NONE OF THEM HAVE ANYTHING AGAINST COSPLAY.
...Maybe?

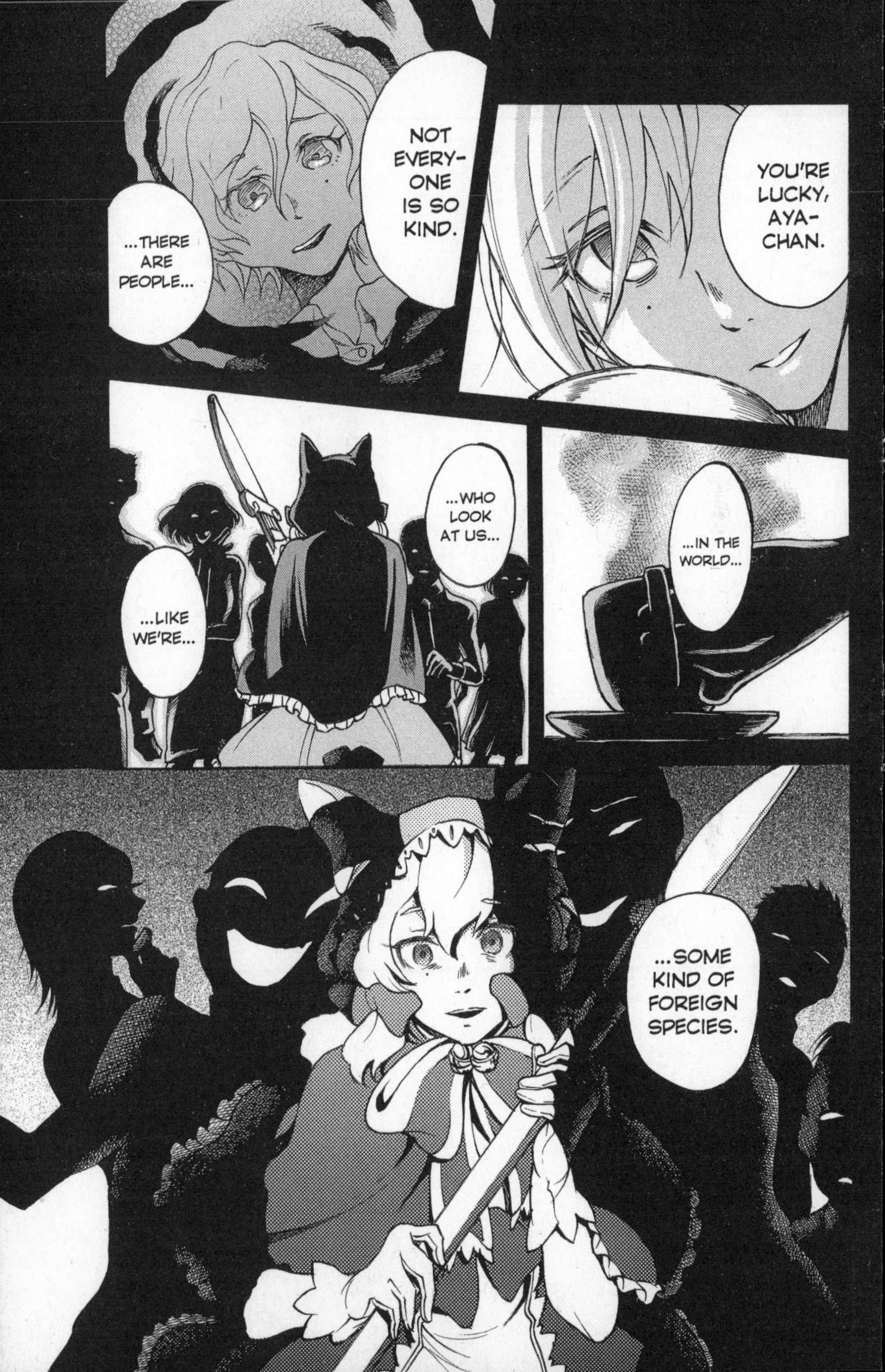
YOU'RE LUCKY, AYA-CHAN.
NOT EVERY-ONE IS SO KIND.
...THERE ARE PEOPLE...
...IN THE WORLD...
...WHO LOOK AT US...
...LIKE WE'RE...
...SOME KIND OF FOREIGN SPECIES.

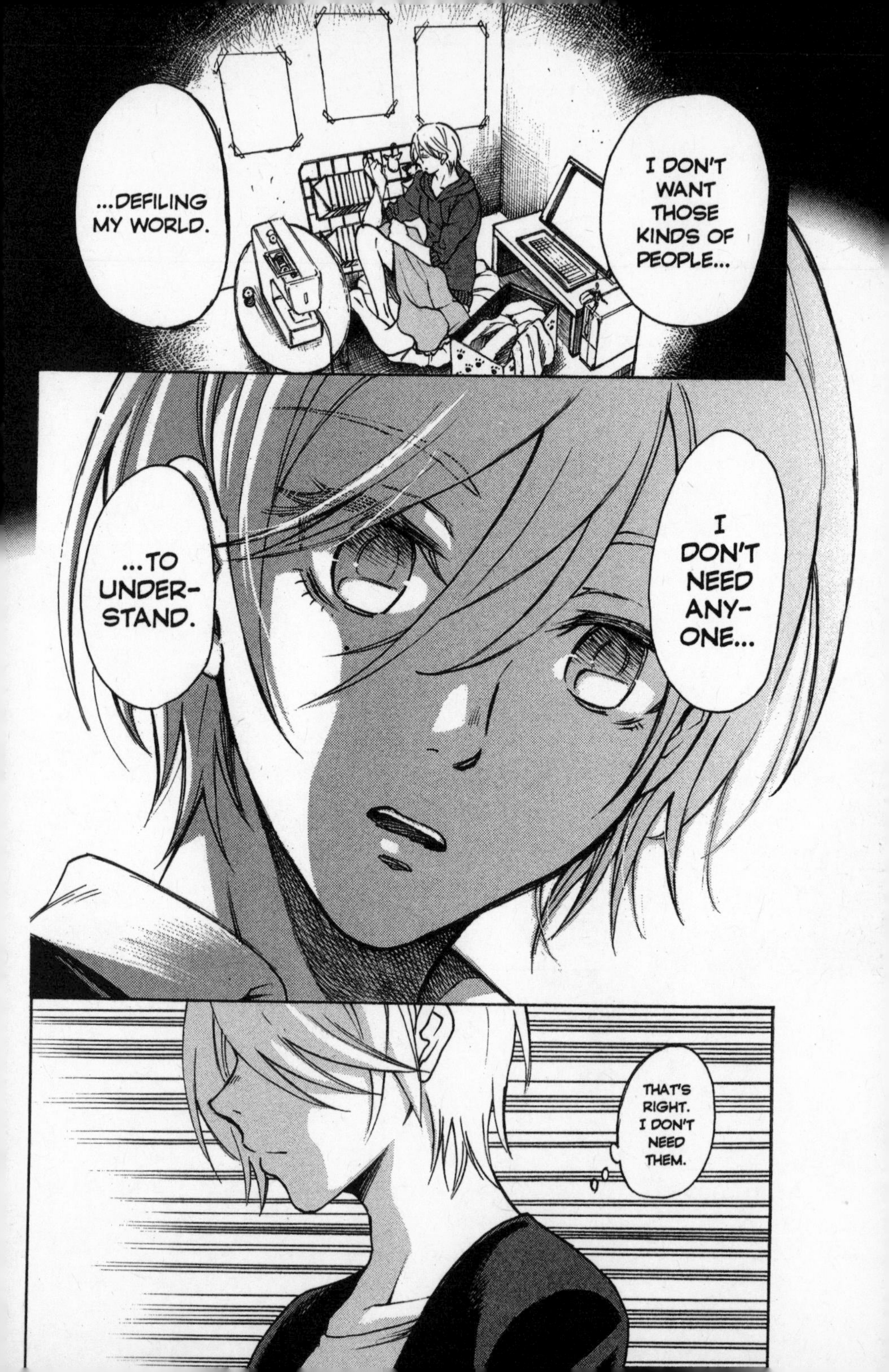
I DON'T WANT THOSE KINDS OF PEOPLE...
...DEFILING MY WORLD.
I DON'T NEED ANY-ONE...
...TO UNDER-STAND.
THAT'S RIGHT. I DON'T NEED THEM.

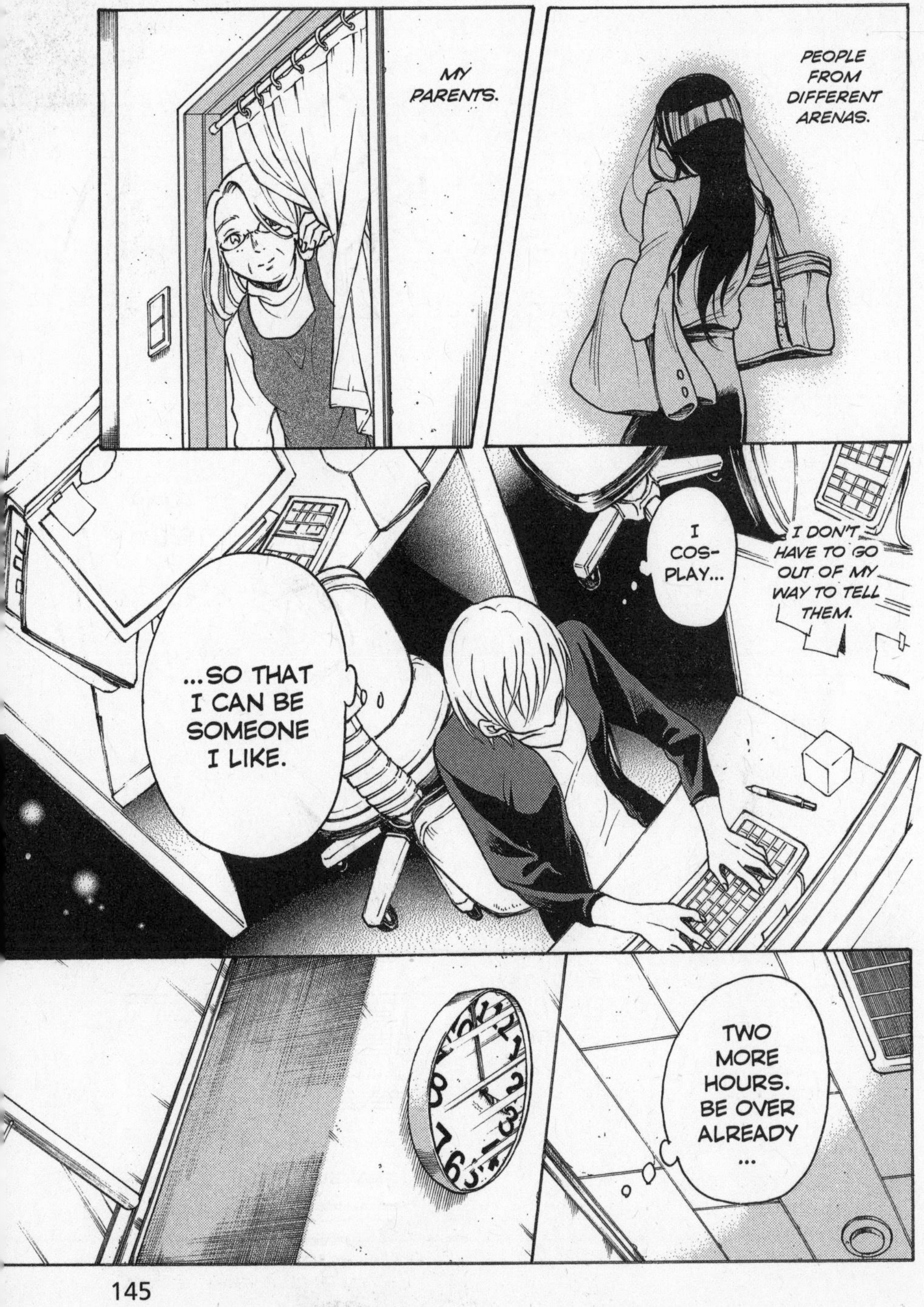
PEOPLE FROM DIFFERENT ARENAS.
MY PARENTS.
I DON'T HAVE TO GO OUT OF MY WAY TO TELL THEM.
I COS-PLAY...
...SO THAT I CAN BE SOMEONE I LIKE.
TWO MORE HOURS. BE OVER ALREADY ...

SIGN (TOP HALF):
Danganronpa Only Event
Trial of Despair Island

SIGN (BOTTOM HALF):
Court's in session!
Pu hu hu hu hu

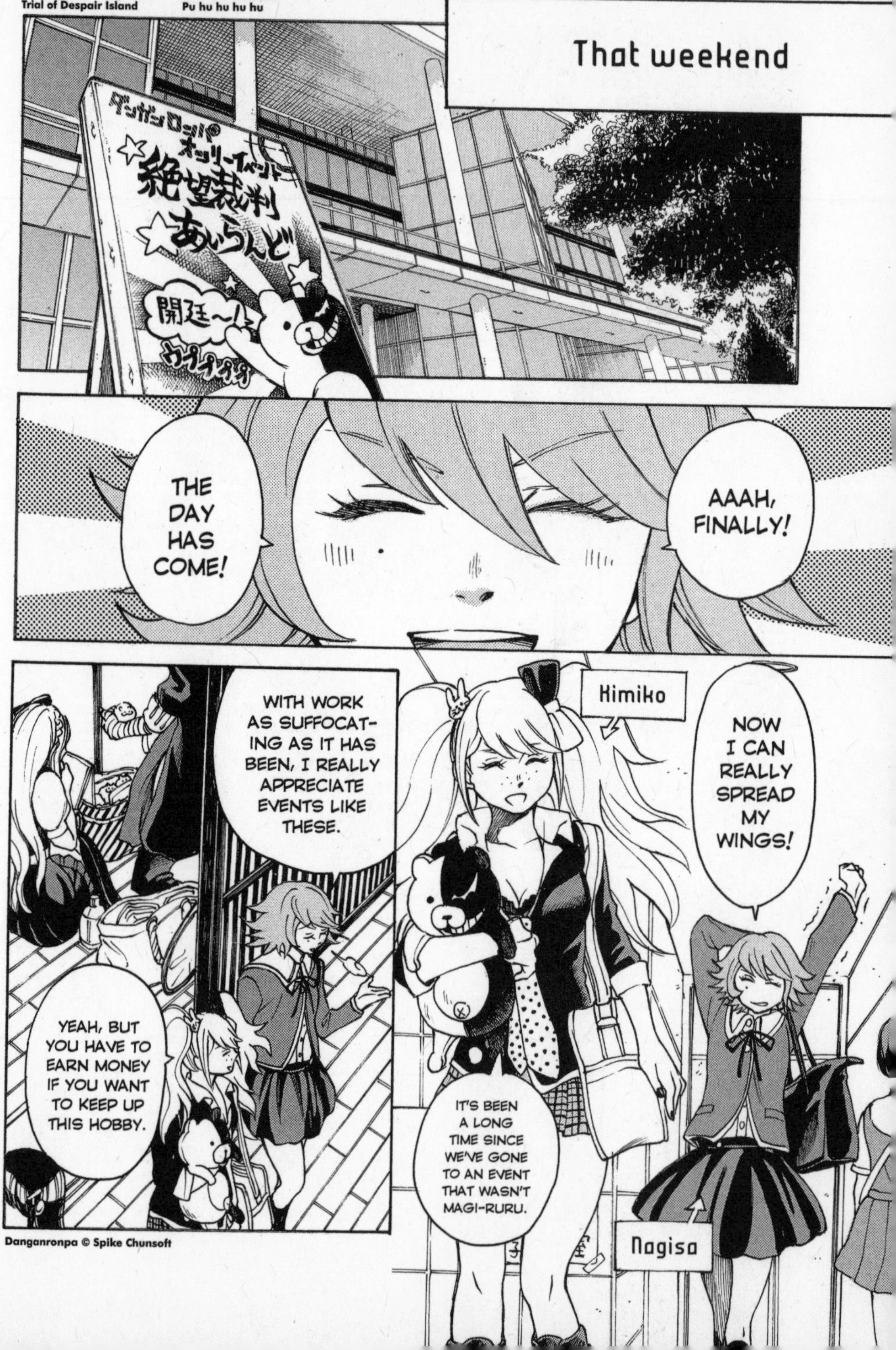

That weekend
AAAH, FINALLY!
THE DAY HAS COME!
Kimiko
NOW I CAN REALLY SPREAD MY WINGS!
WITH WORK AS SUFFOCATING AS IT HAS BEEN, I REALLY APPRECIATE EVENTS LIKE THESE.
Nagisa
IT'S BEEN A LONG TIME SINCE WE'VE GONE TO AN EVENT THAT WASN'T MAGI-RURU.
YEAH, BUT YOU HAVE TO EARN MONEY IF YOU WANT TO KEEP UP THIS HOBBY.

DANGANRONPA A murder mystery adventure game series sold by Spike Chunsoft.

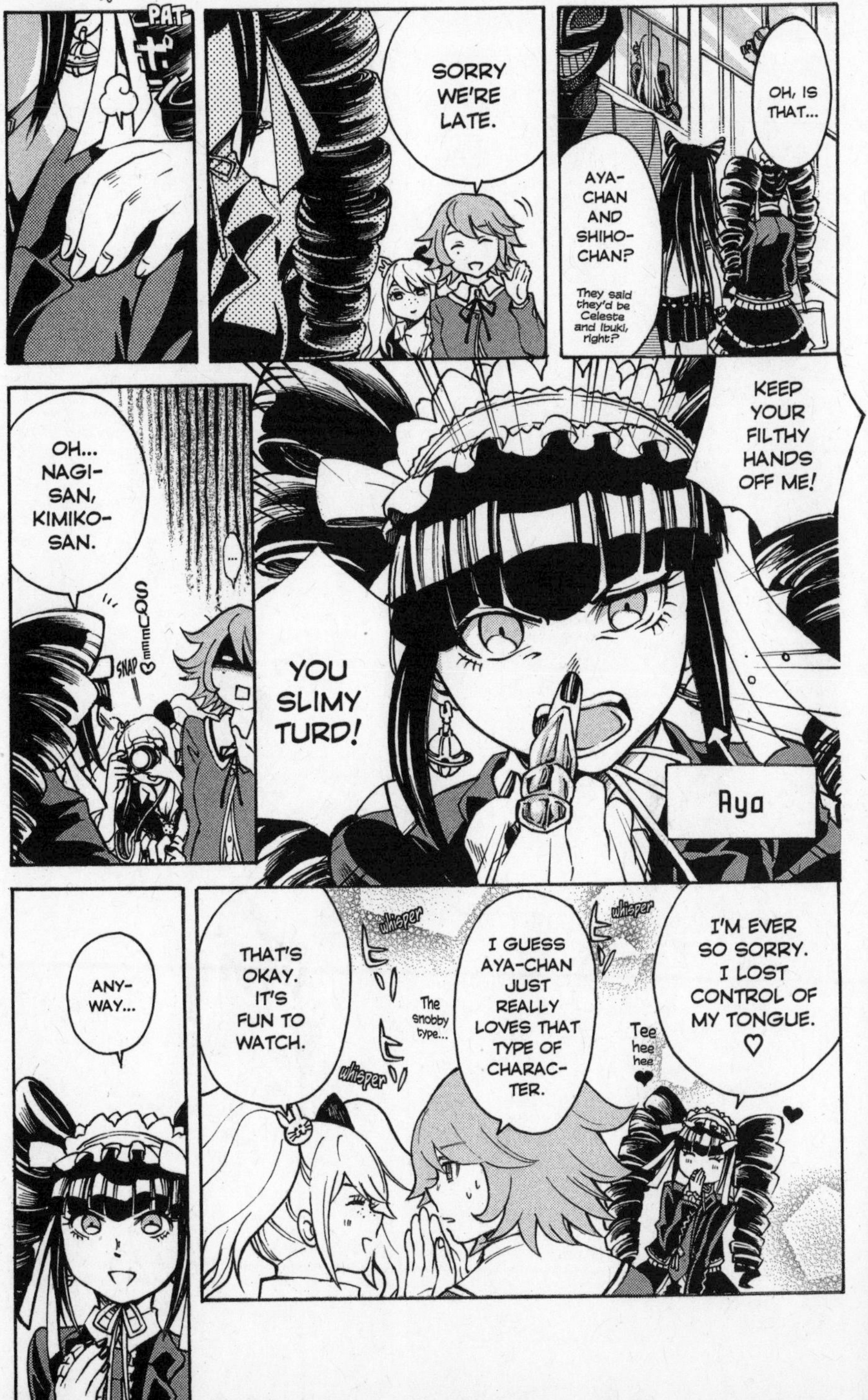
OH, IS THAT...
AYA-CHAN AND SHIHO-CHAN?
They said they'd be Celeste and Ibuki, right?
SORRY WE'RE LATE.
PAT
KEEP YOUR FILTHY HANDS OFF ME!
YOU SLIMY TURD!
Aya
...
OH... NAGI-SAN, KIMIKO-SAN.
SQUEEE
SNAP
I'M EVER SO SORRY. I LOST CONTROL OF MY TONGUE. ♡
Tee hee hee
whisper
I GUESS AYA-CHAN JUST REALLY LOVES THAT TYPE OF CHARACTER.
The snobby type...
whisper
THAT'S OKAY. IT'S FUN TO WATCH.
whisper
ANY-WAY...

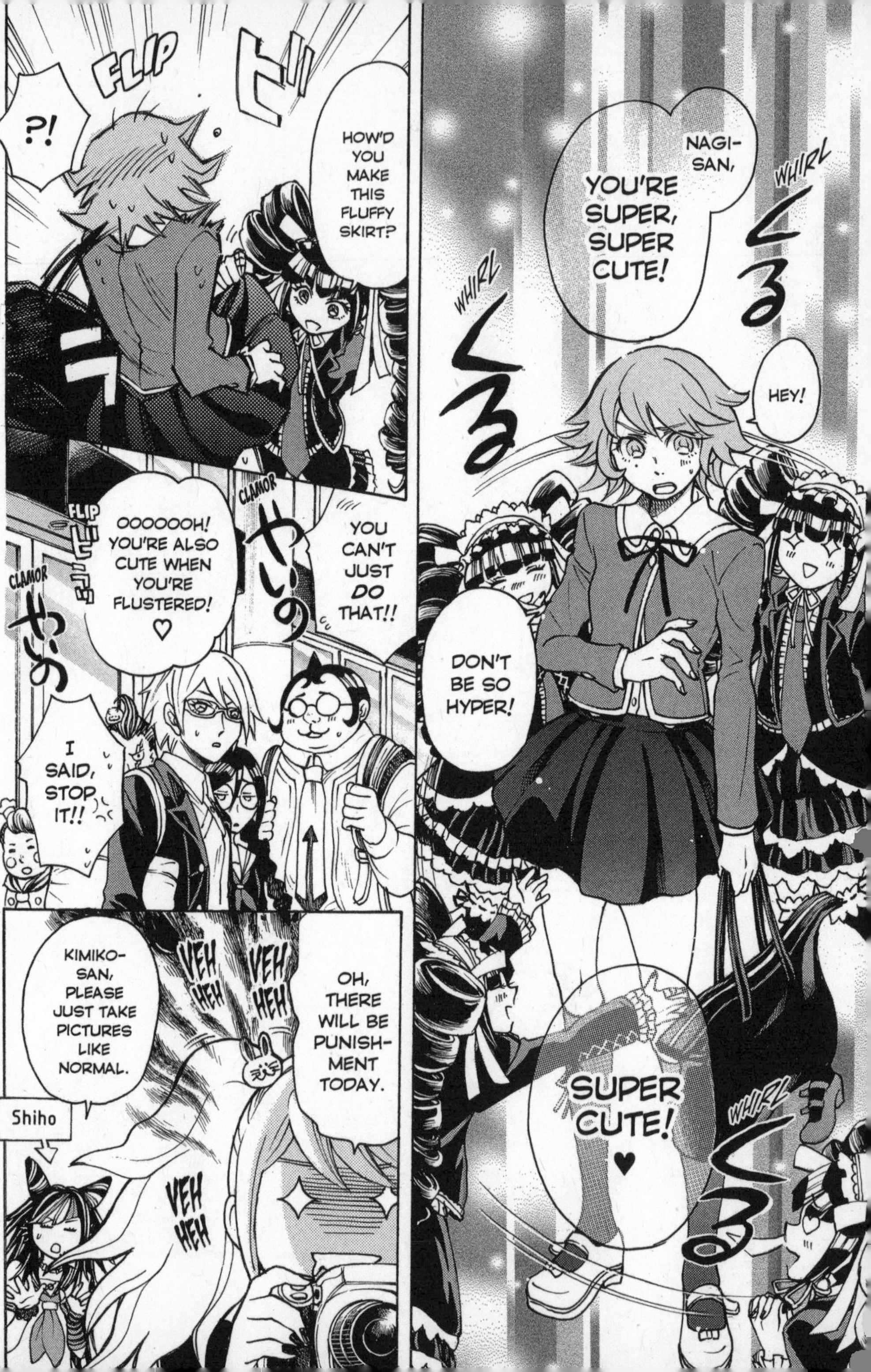
NAGI-SAN,
YOU'RE SUPER, SUPER CUTE!
WHIRL
くる
WHIRL
くる
HEY!
DON'T BE SO HYPER!
SUPER CUTE! ♥
WHIRL
くる
FLIP
HOW'D YOU MAKE THIS FLUFFY SKIRT?
?!
YOU CAN'T JUST DO THAT!!
CLAMOR
OOOOOOH! YOU'RE ALSO CUTE WHEN YOU'RE FLUSTERED! ♡
FLIP
CLAMOR
I SAID, STOP IT!!
OH, THERE WILL BE PUNISHMENT TODAY.
VEH HEH
VEH HEH
KIMIKO-SAN, PLEASE JUST TAKE PICTURES LIKE NORMAL.
VEH HEH
Shiho

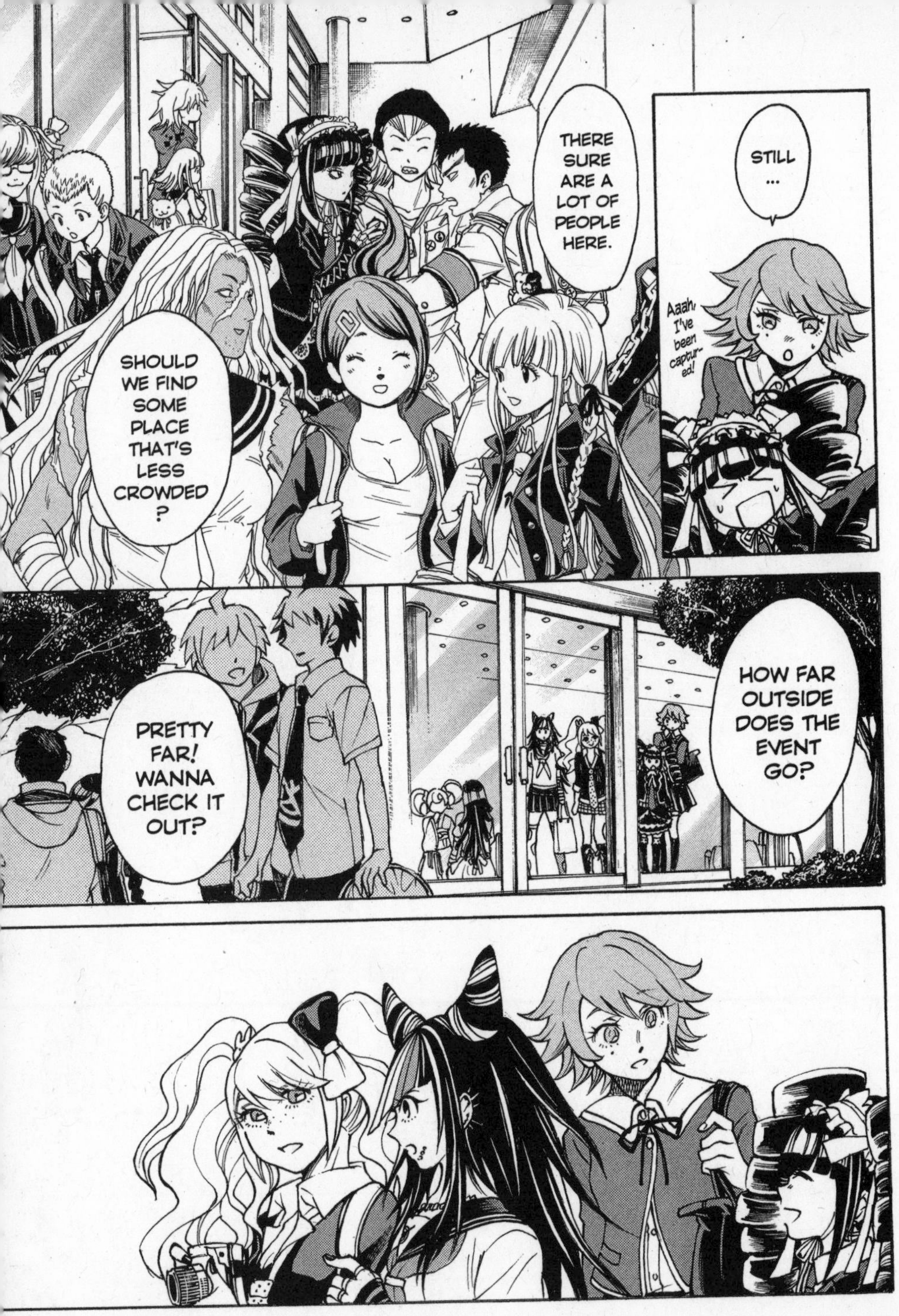
STILL ...
Aaah, I've been captur-ed!
THERE SURE ARE A LOT OF PEOPLE HERE.
SHOULD WE FIND SOME PLACE THAT'S LESS CROWDED ?
HOW FAR OUTSIDE DOES THE EVENT GO?
PRETTY FAR! WANNA CHECK IT OUT?

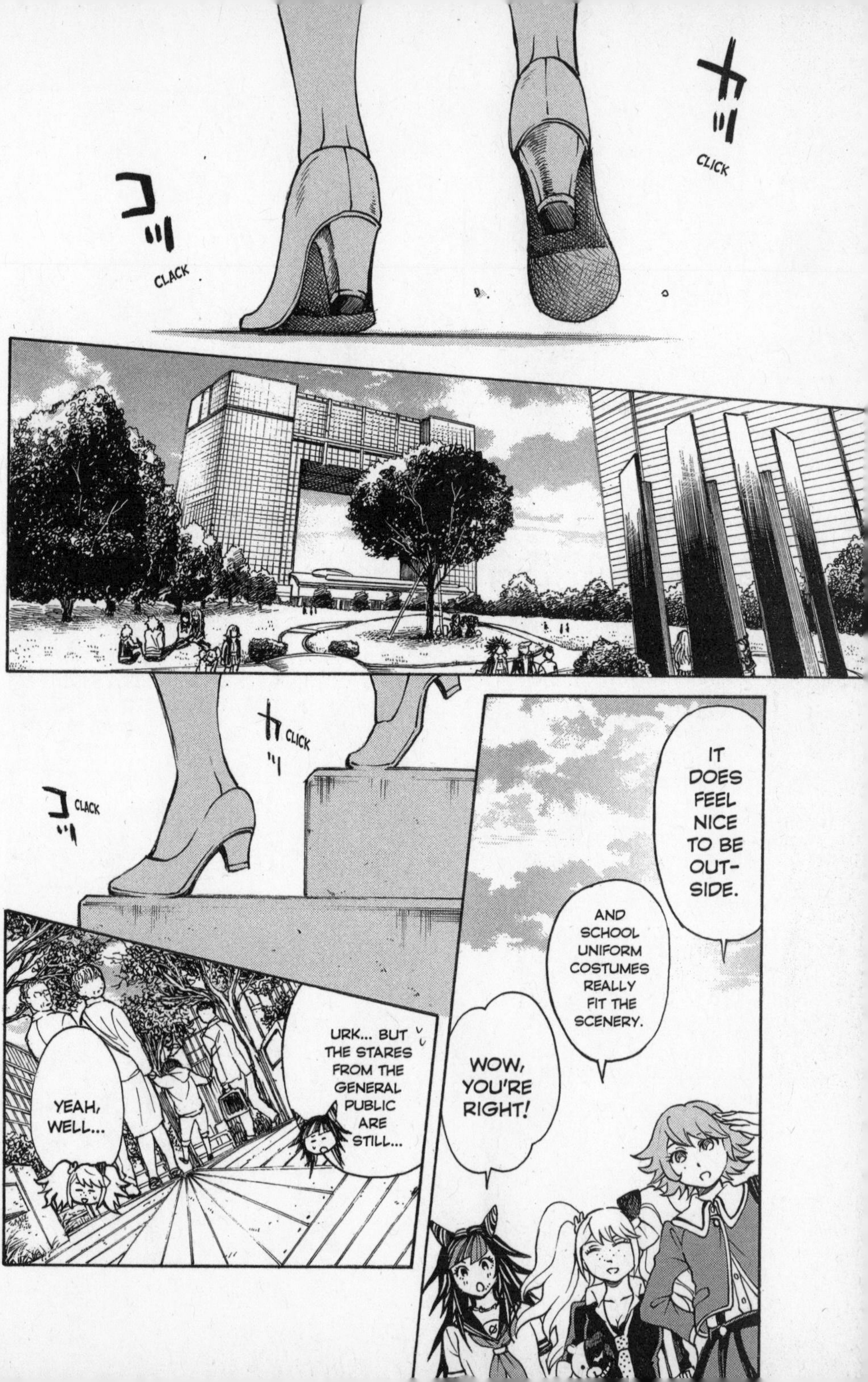
カッ
CLICK
コッ
CLACK
IT DOES FEEL NICE TO BE OUT-SIDE.
AND SCHOOL UNIFORM COSTUMES REALLY FIT THE SCENERY.
WOW, YOU'RE RIGHT!
カッ CLICK
コッ CLACK
URK... BUT THE STARES FROM THE GENERAL PUBLIC ARE STILL...
YEAH, WELL...

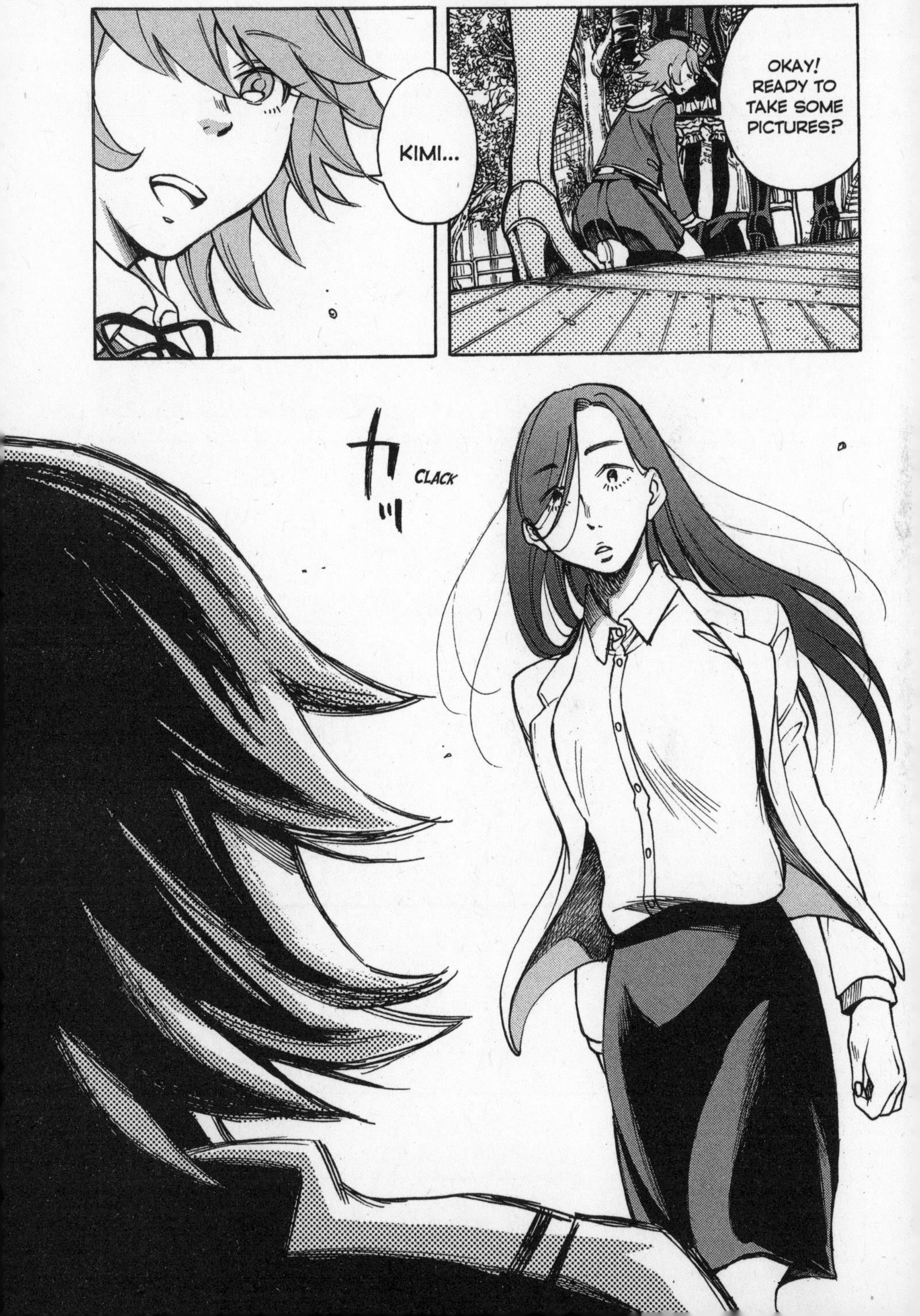
OKAY! READY TO TAKE SOME PICTURES?
KIMI...
カッ
CLACK

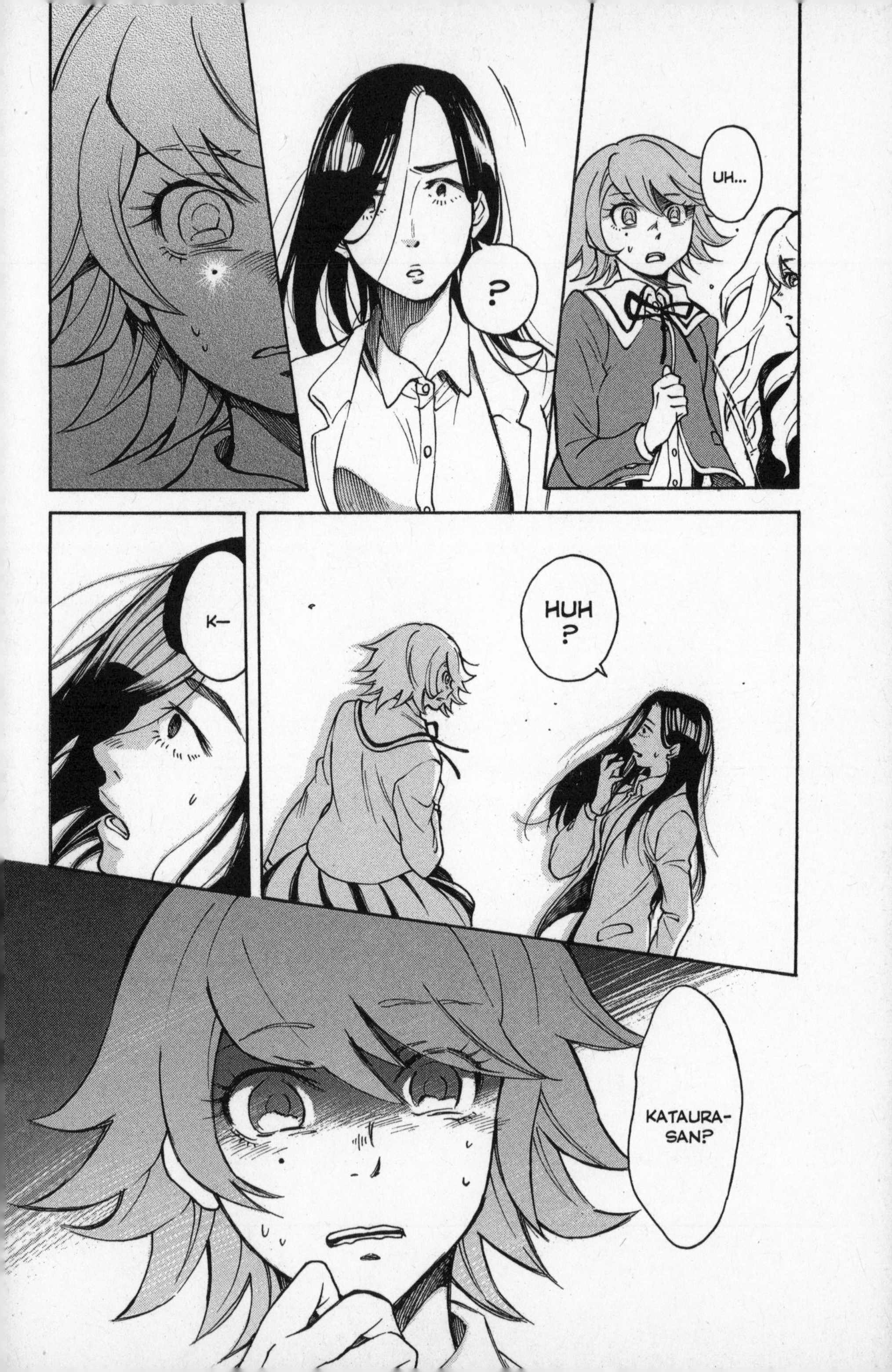
UH...
?
HUH ?
K–
KATAURA-SAN?

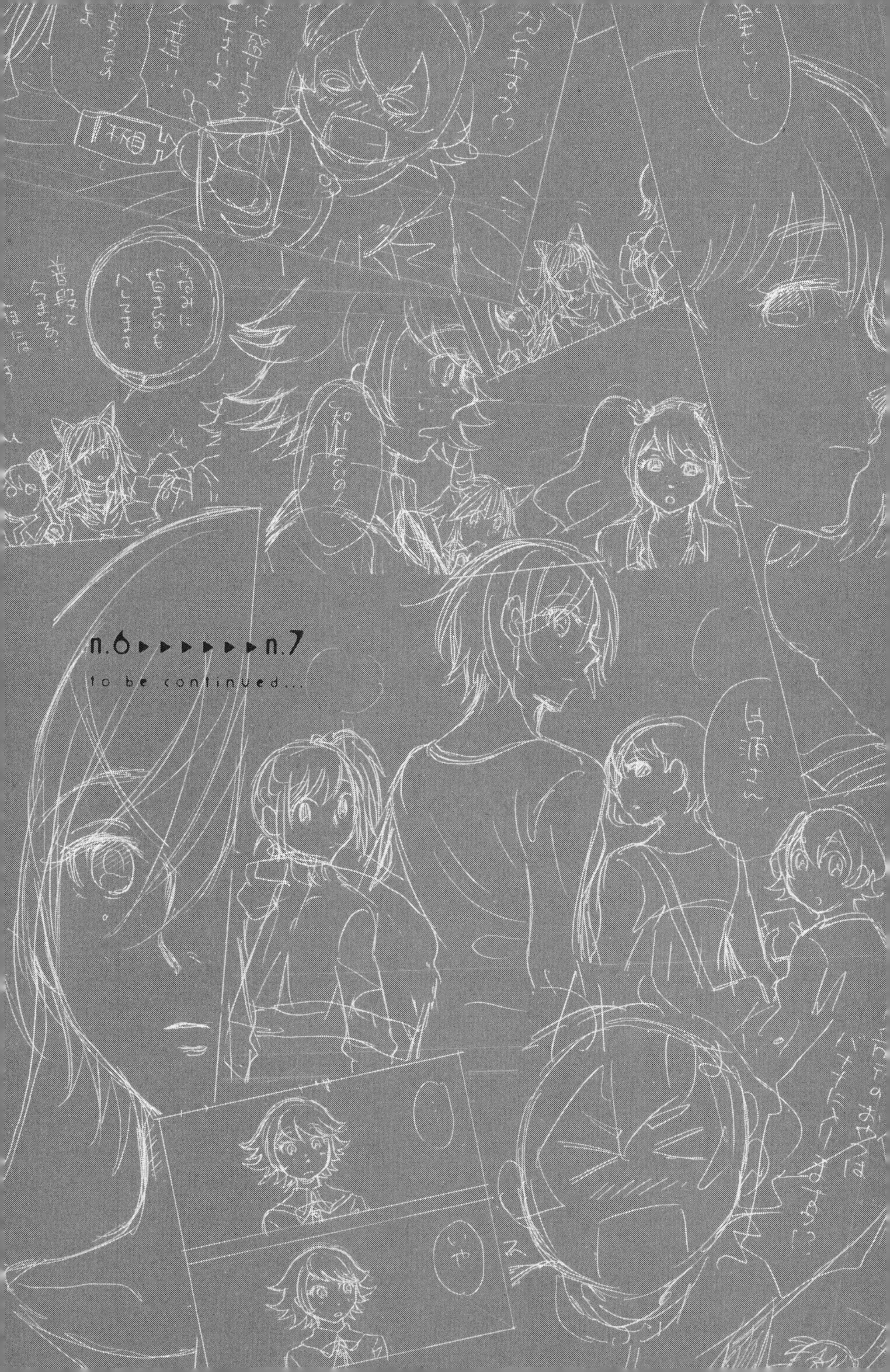
n.6▸▸▸▸▸▸▸▸n.7
to be continued...

Starting on the next page, you can read the one-shot version of Complex Age.

It's the one that won the 63rd Tetsuya Chiba Award.

This story is near and dear to my heart. It led me to my first series, so I published it here without making any corrections. (One part of it has been changed.)

I hope you can get some enjoyment out of it.

Yui
Sakuma

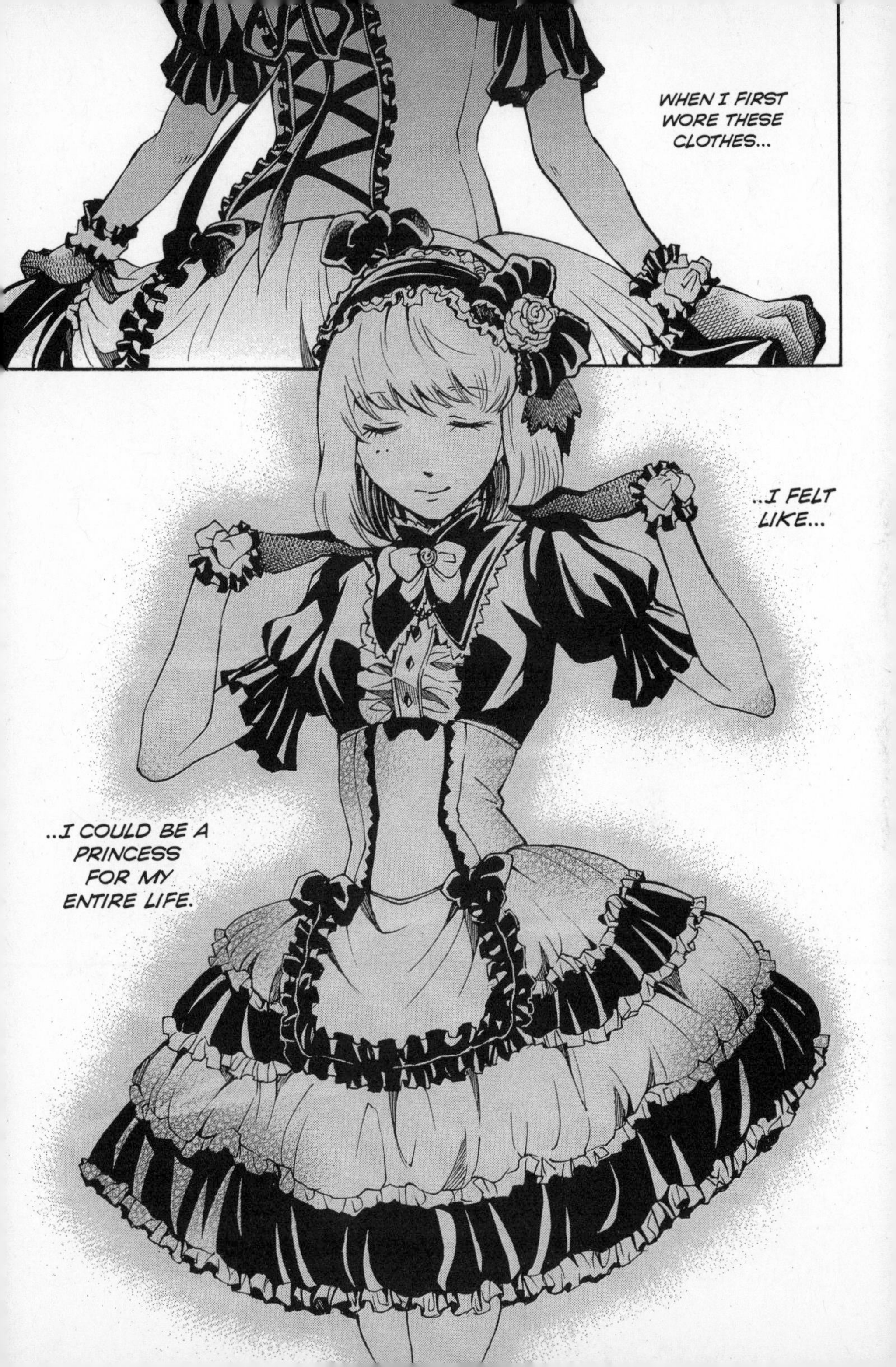
WHEN I FIRST WORE THESE CLOTHES...
...I FELT LIKE...
...I COULD BE A PRINCESS FOR MY ENTIRE LIFE.

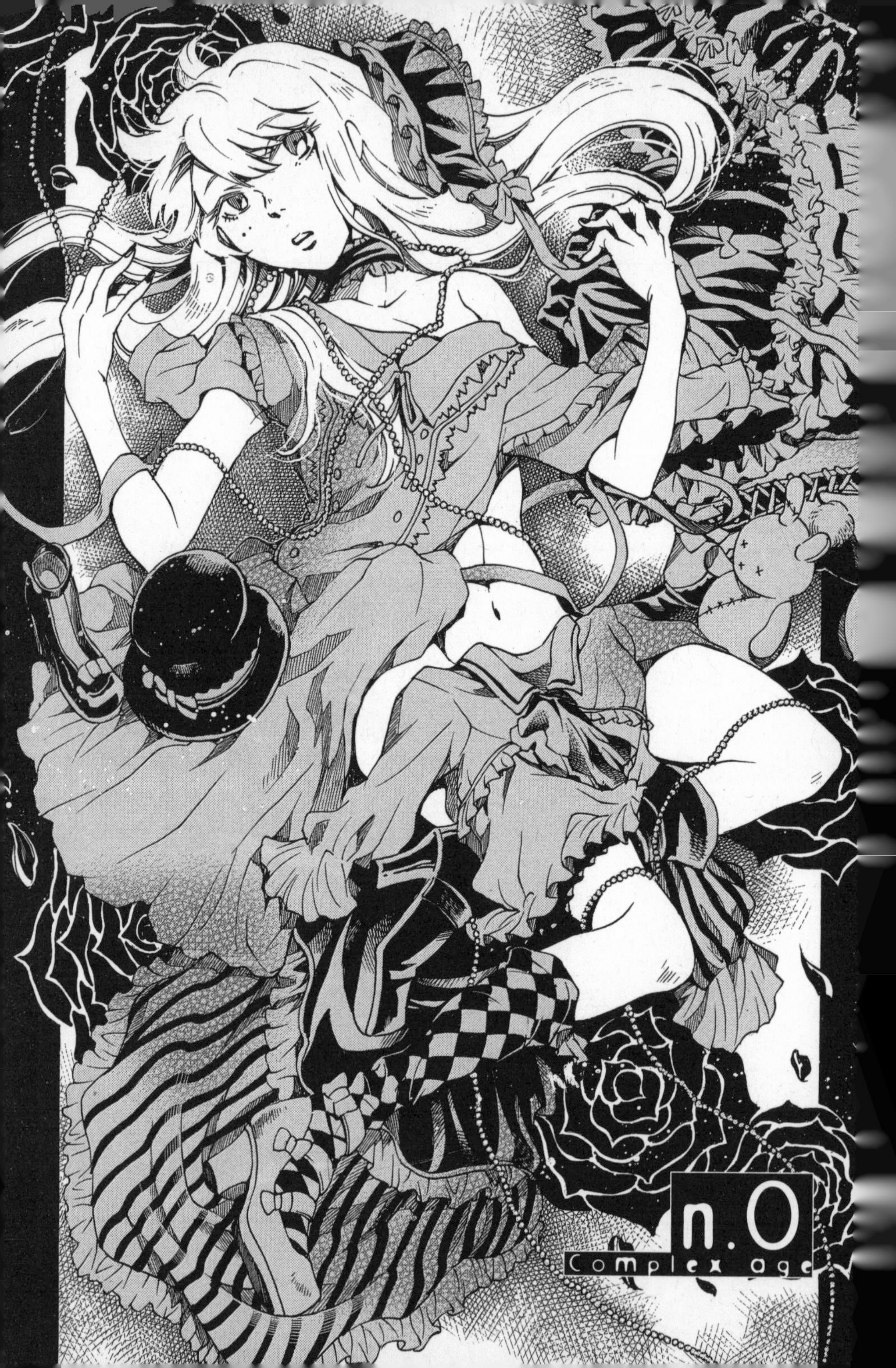
n.O
Complex age

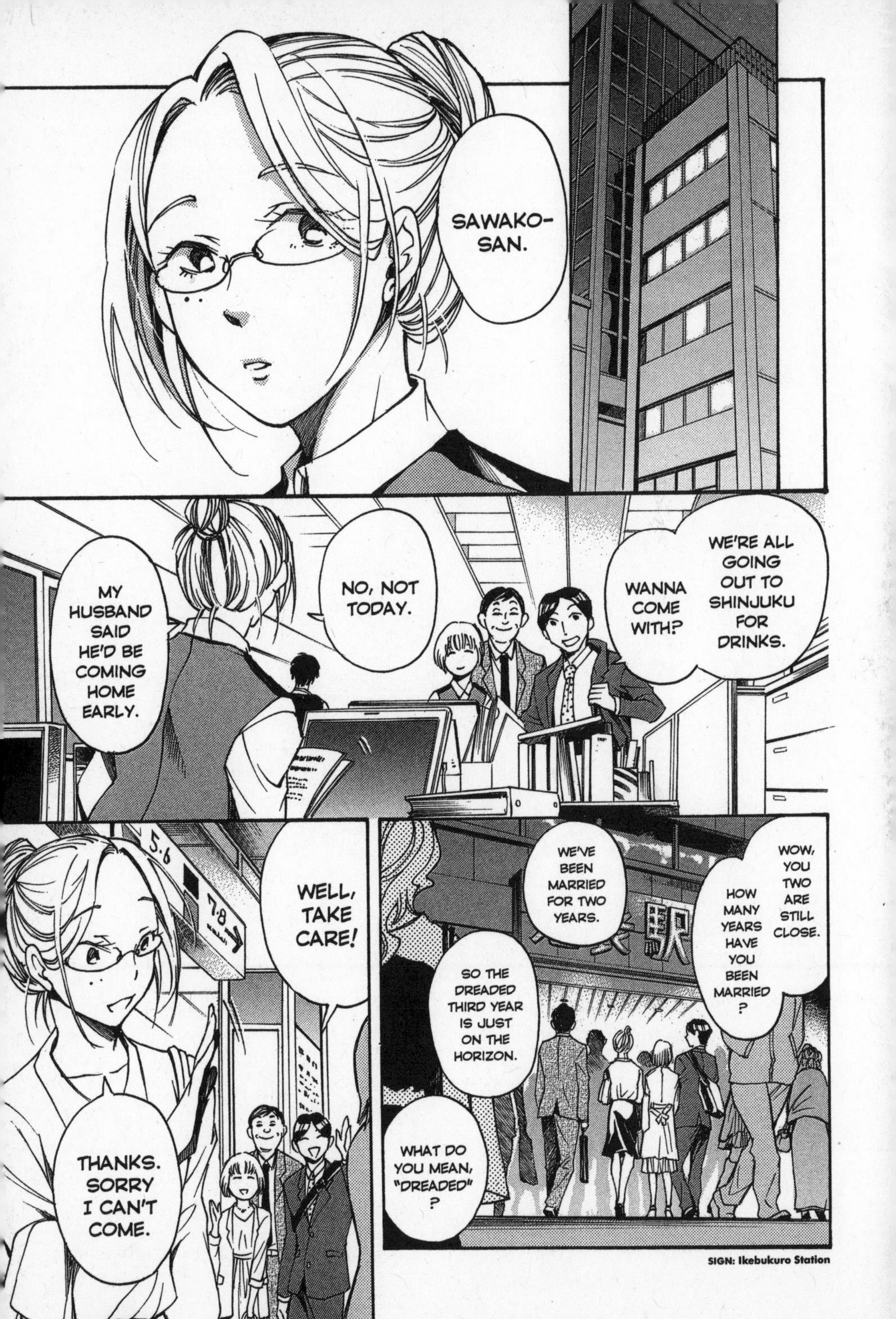
SAWAKO-SAN.
WE'RE ALL GOING OUT TO SHINJUKU FOR DRINKS.
WANNA COME WITH?
NO, NOT TODAY.
MY HUSBAND SAID HE'D BE COMING HOME EARLY.
WOW, YOU TWO ARE STILL CLOSE.
HOW MANY YEARS HAVE YOU BEEN MARRIED?
WE'VE BEEN MARRIED FOR TWO YEARS.
SO THE DREADED THIRD YEAR IS JUST ON THE HORIZON.
WHAT DO YOU MEAN, "DREADED"?
駅
5·6
7·8
WELL, TAKE CARE!
THANKS. SORRY I CAN'T COME.

SIGN: Ikebukuro Station

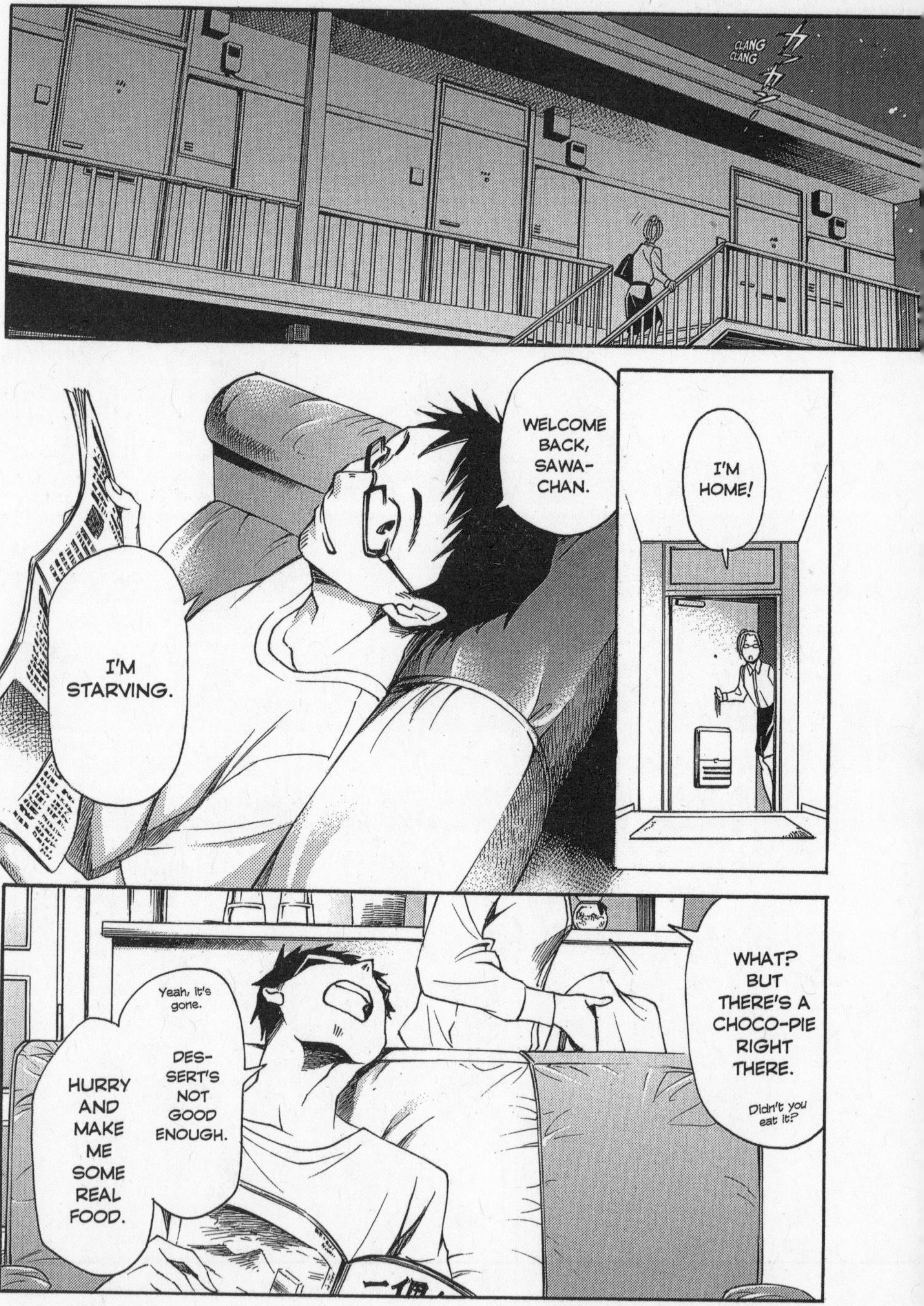
CLANG CLANG
I'M HOME!
WELCOME BACK, SAWA-CHAN.
I'M STARVING.
WHAT? BUT THERE'S A CHOCO-PIE RIGHT THERE.
Didn't you eat it?
Yeah, it's gone.
DES-SERT'S NOT GOOD ENOUGH.
HURRY AND MAKE ME SOME REAL FOOD.

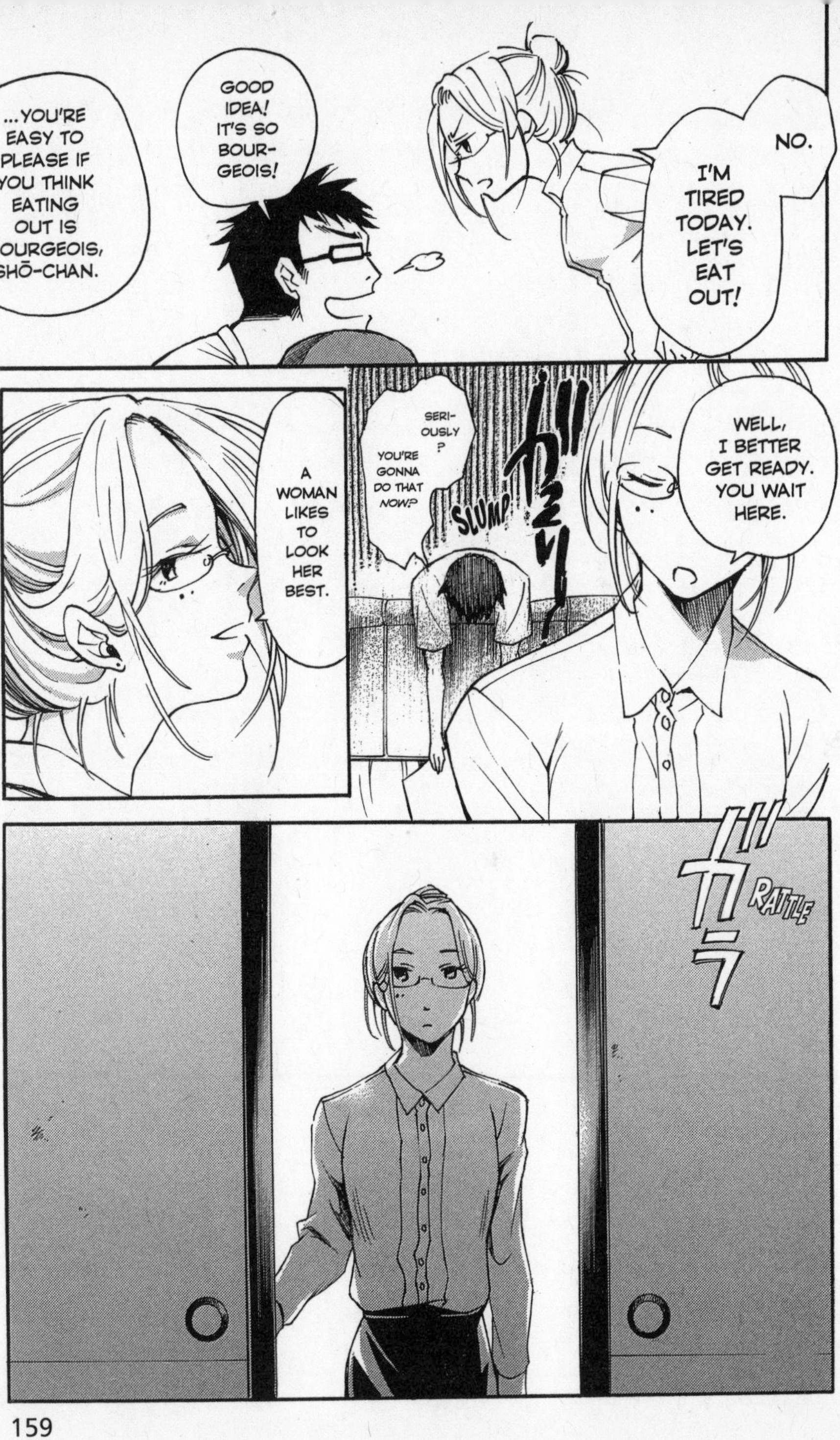
NO. I'M TIRED TODAY. LET'S EAT OUT!
GOOD IDEA! IT'S SO BOURGEOIS!
...YOU'RE EASY TO PLEASE IF YOU THINK EATING OUT IS BOURGEOIS, SHŌ-CHAN.
WELL, I BETTER GET READY. YOU WAIT HERE.
SLUMP
SERIOUSLY? YOU'RE GONNA DO THAT *NOW?*
A WOMAN LIKES TO LOOK HER BEST.
RATTLE

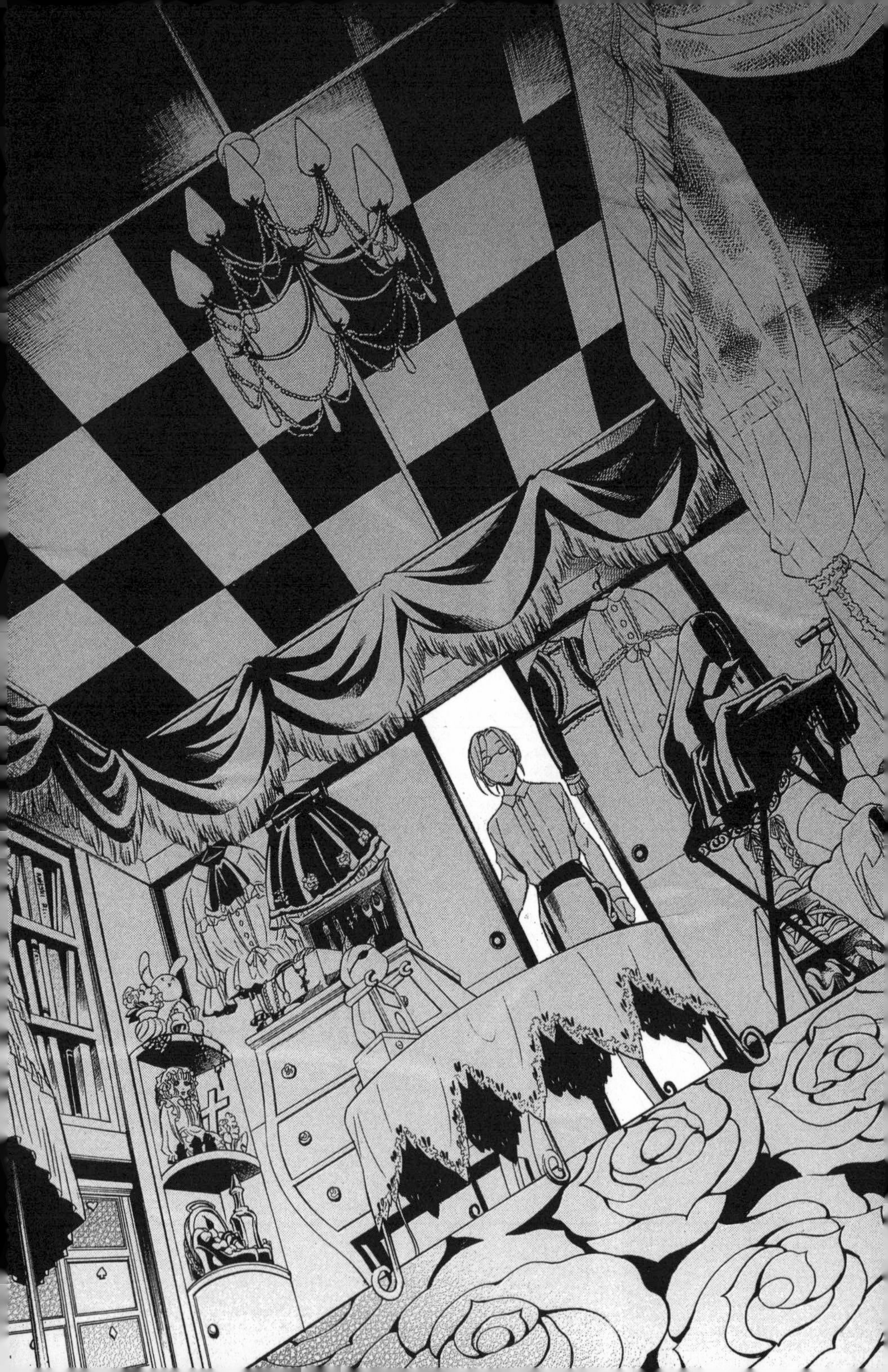

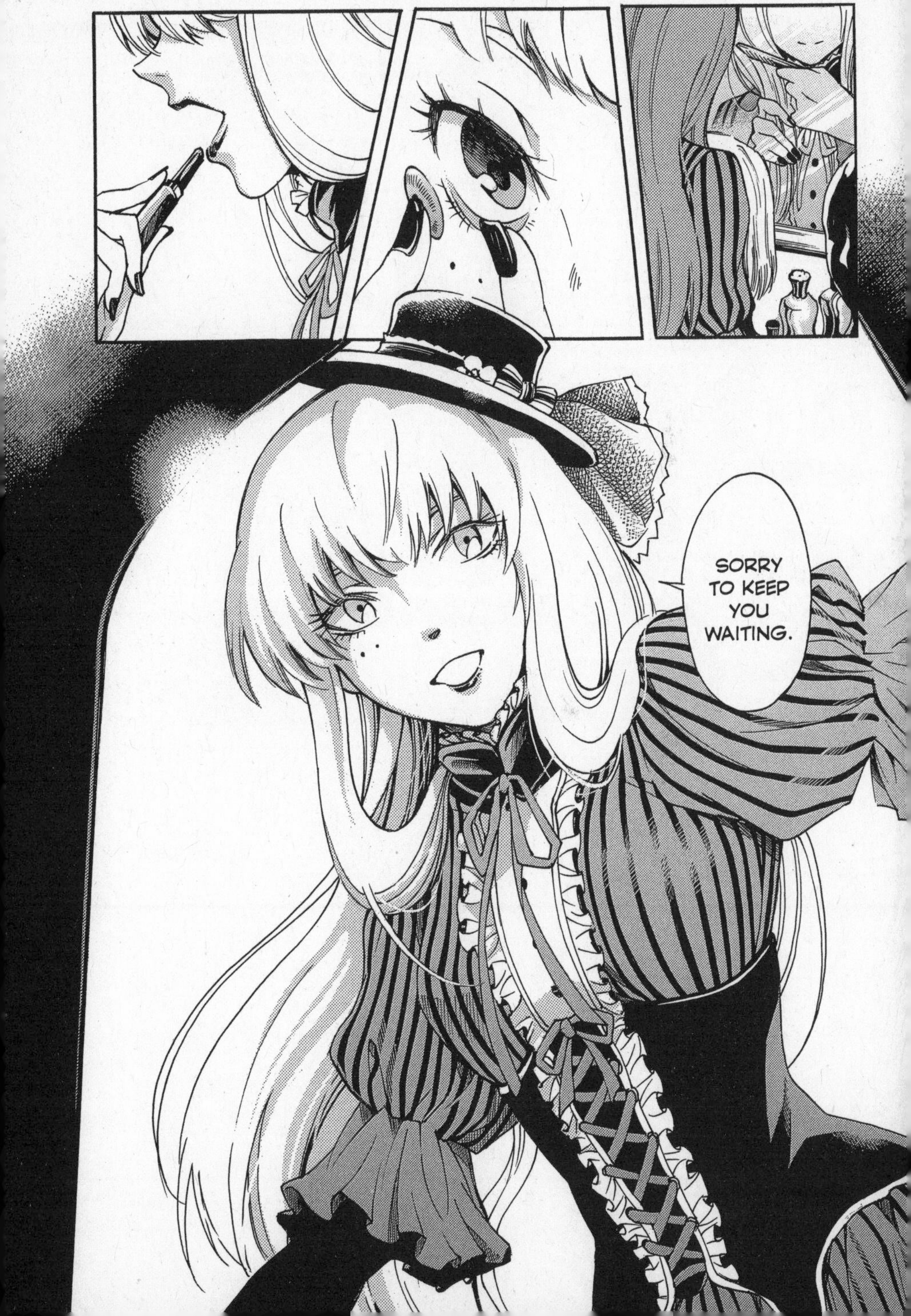
SORRY TO KEEP YOU WAITING.

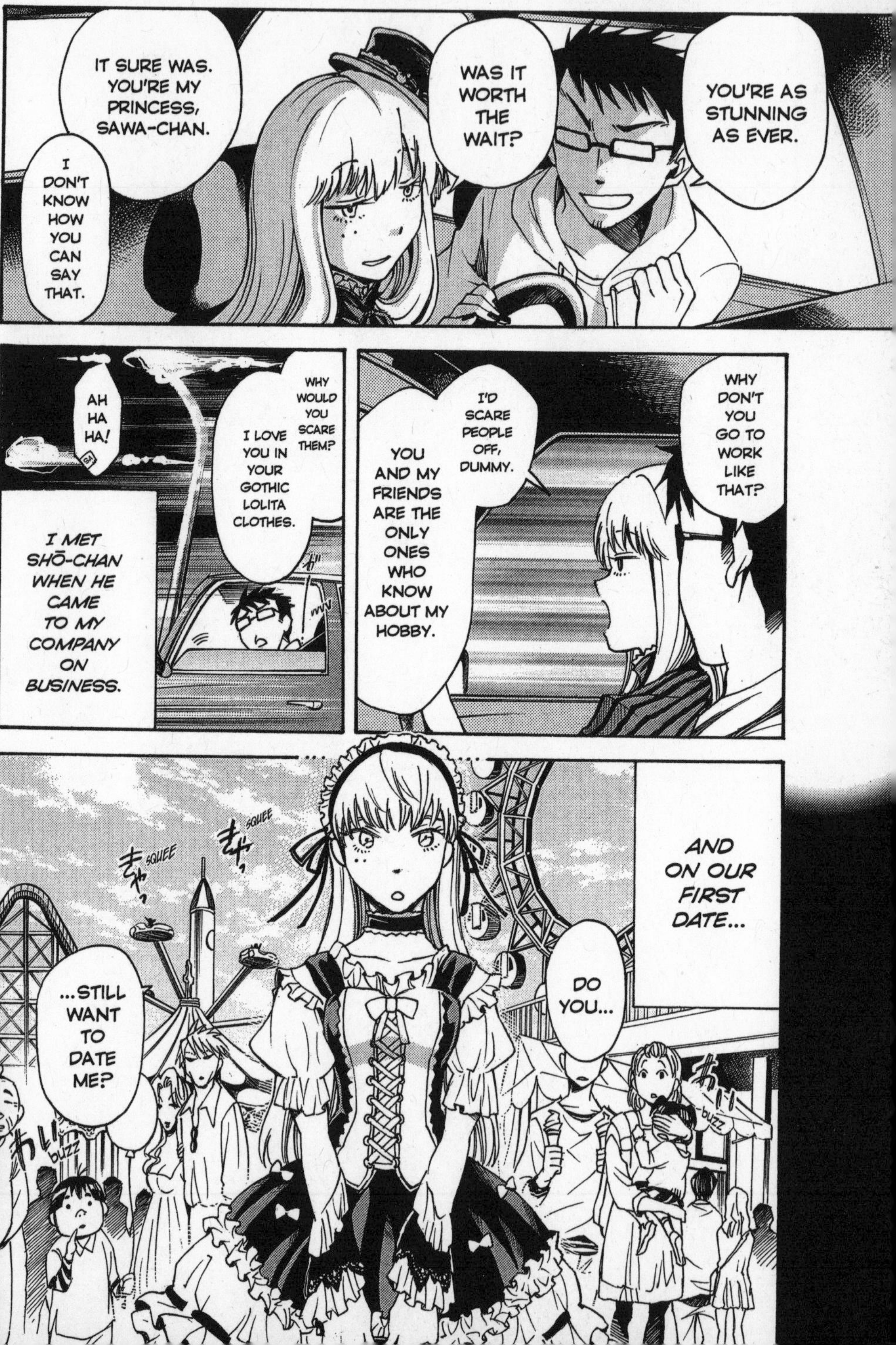
YOU'RE AS STUNNING AS EVER.
WAS IT WORTH THE WAIT?
IT SURE WAS. YOU'RE MY PRINCESS, SAWA-CHAN.
I DON'T KNOW HOW YOU CAN SAY THAT.
WHY DON'T YOU GO TO WORK LIKE THAT?
I'D SCARE PEOPLE OFF, DUMMY.
YOU AND MY FRIENDS ARE THE ONLY ONES WHO KNOW ABOUT MY HOBBY.
WHY WOULD YOU SCARE THEM?
I LOVE YOU IN YOUR GOTHIC LOLITA CLOTHES.
AH HA HA!
I MET SHŌ-CHAN WHEN HE CAME TO MY COMPANY ON BUSINESS.
...
AND ON OUR FIRST DATE...
SQUEE
SQUEE
DO YOU...
...STILL WANT TO DATE ME?
BUZZ
BUZZ

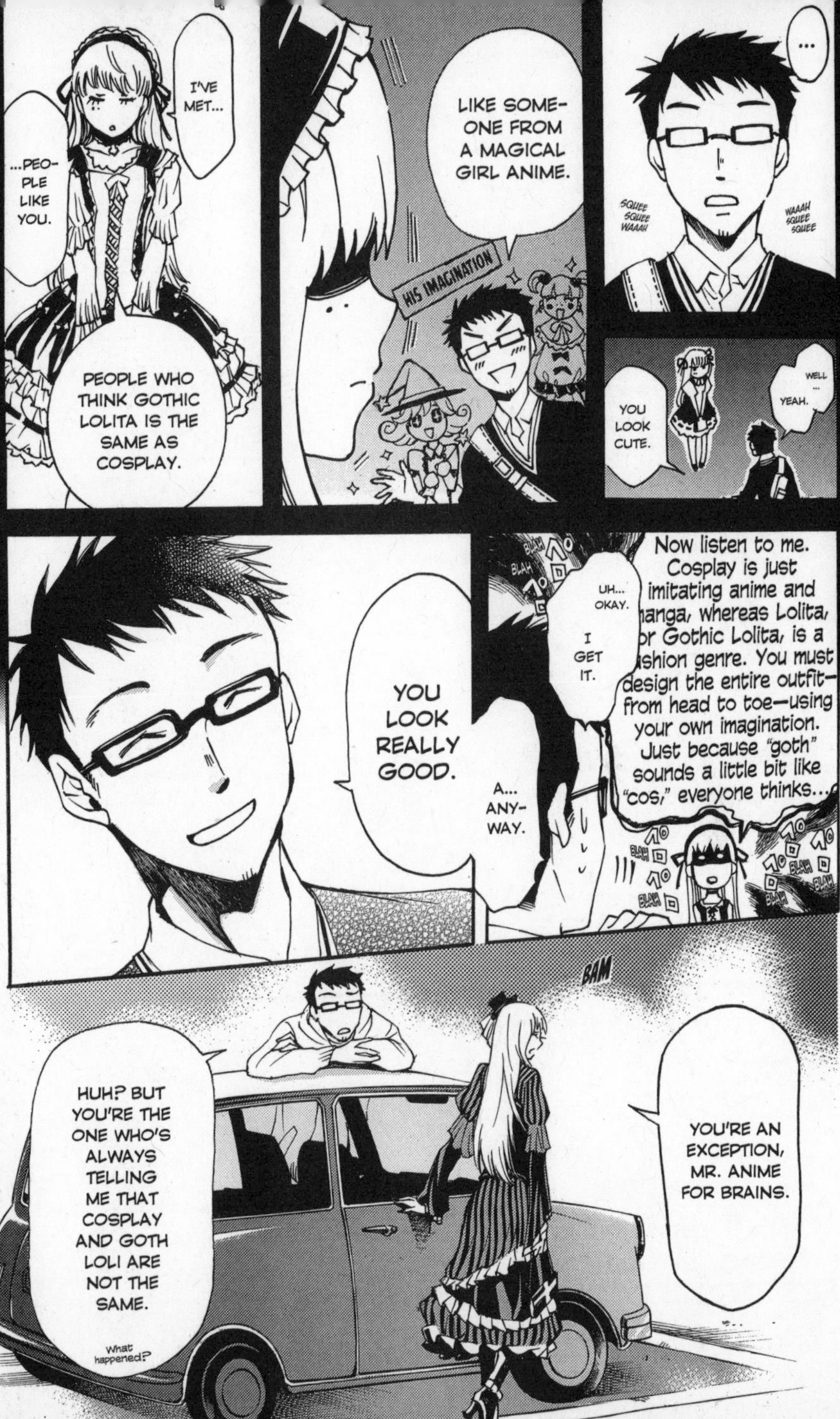
...
SQUEE SQUEE WAAAH
WAAAH SQUEE SQUEE
WELL ... YEAH.
YOU LOOK CUTE.
LIKE SOME-ONE FROM A MAGICAL GIRL ANIME.
HIS IMAGINATION
I'VE MET...
...PEO-PLE LIKE YOU.
PEOPLE WHO THINK GOTHIC LOLITA IS THE SAME AS COSPLAY.
Now listen to me. Cosplay is just imitating anime and nanga, whereas Lolita, or Gothic Lolita, is a ashion genre. You must design the entire outfit—from head to toe—using your own imagination. Just because "goth" sounds a little bit like "cos," everyone thinks...
BLAH BLAH
UH... OKAY.
I GET IT.
A... ANY-WAY.
YOU LOOK REALLY GOOD.
BAM
YOU'RE AN EXCEPTION, MR. ANIME FOR BRAINS.
HUH? BUT YOU'RE THE ONE WHO'S ALWAYS TELLING ME THAT COSPLAY AND GOTH LOLI ARE NOT THE SAME.
What happened?

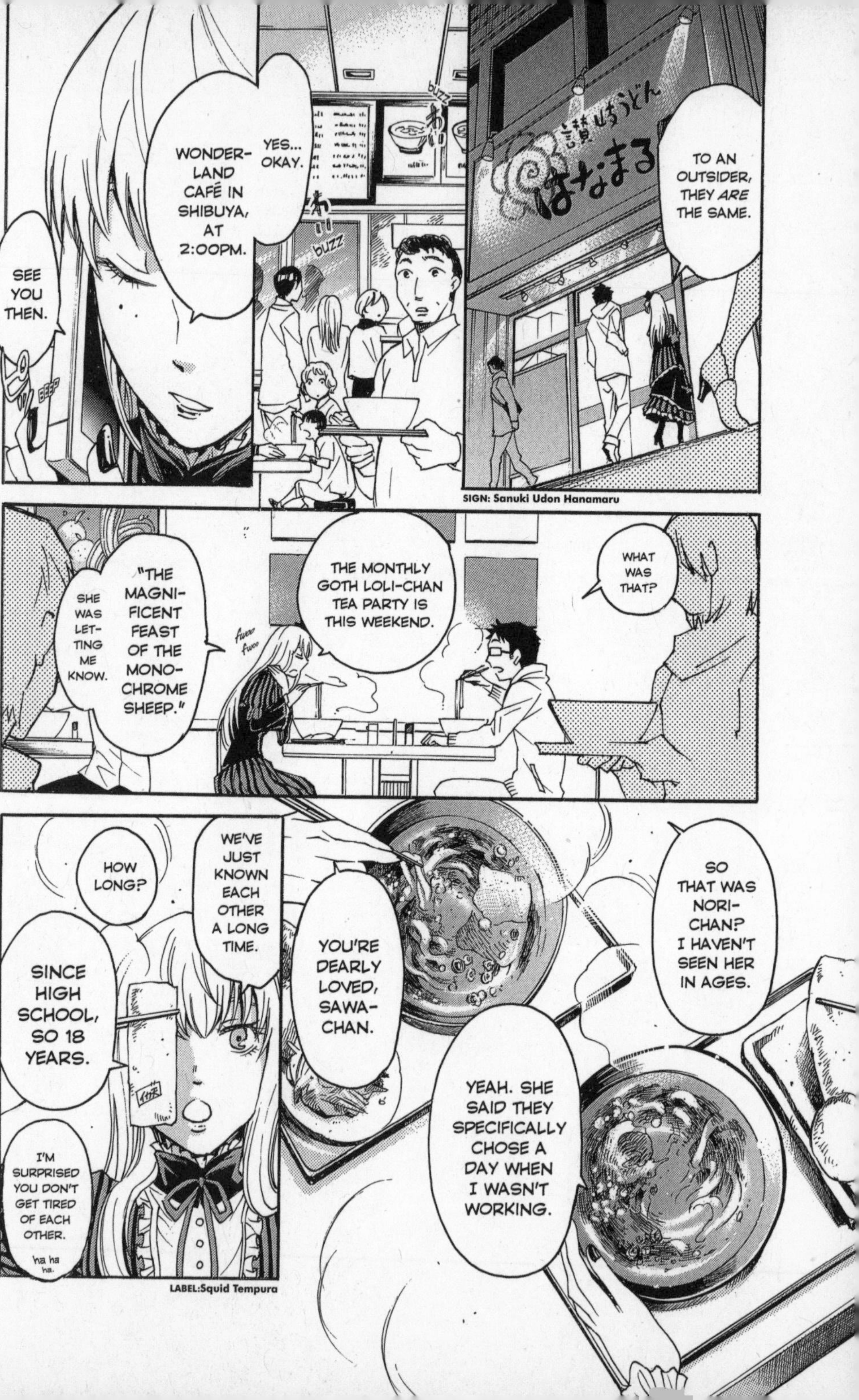
TO AN OUTSIDER, THEY *ARE* THE SAME.
YES... OKAY.
buzz
buzz
WONDER-LAND CAFÉ IN SHIBUYA, AT 2:00PM.
SEE YOU THEN.
BEEP
WHAT WAS THAT?
THE MONTHLY GOTH LOLI-CHAN TEA PARTY IS THIS WEEKEND.
fwoo fwoo
"THE MAGNI-FICENT FEAST OF THE MONO-CHROME SHEEP."
SHE WAS LET-TING ME KNOW.
SO THAT WAS NORI-CHAN? I HAVEN'T SEEN HER IN AGES.
YEAH. SHE SAID THEY SPECIFICALLY CHOSE A DAY WHEN I WASN'T WORKING.
WE'VE JUST KNOWN EACH OTHER A LONG TIME.
YOU'RE DEARLY LOVED, SAWA-CHAN.
HOW LONG?
SINCE HIGH SCHOOL, SO 18 YEARS.
I'M SURPRISED YOU DON'T GET TIRED OF EACH OTHER.
ha ha ha.

SIGN: Sanuki Udon Hanamaru

LABEL: Squid Tempura

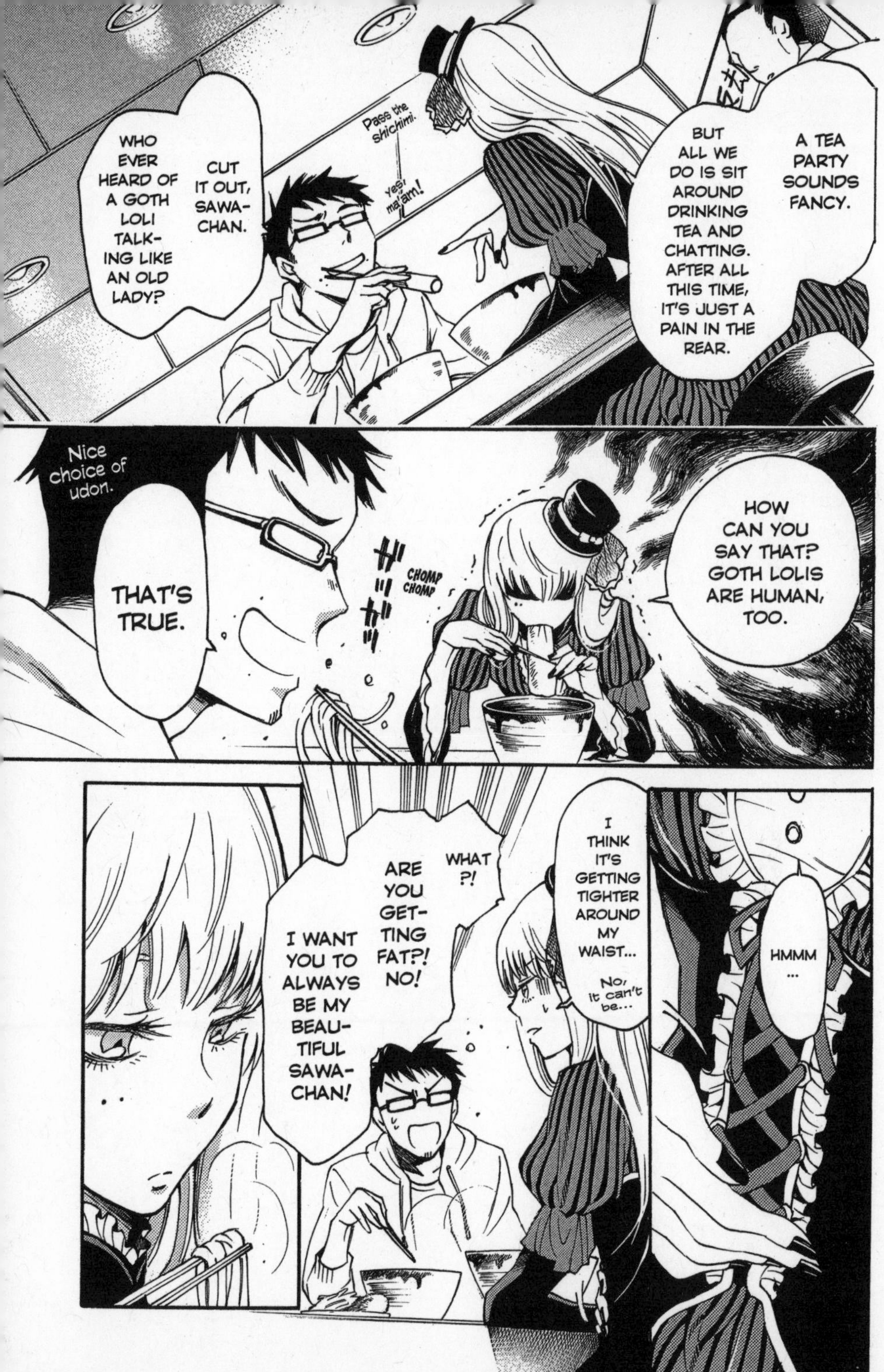
A TEA PARTY SOUNDS FANCY.
BUT ALL WE DO IS SIT AROUND DRINKING TEA AND CHATTING. AFTER ALL THIS TIME, IT'S JUST A PAIN IN THE REAR.
Pass the shichimi.
Yes, ma'am!
CUT IT OUT, SAWA-CHAN.
WHO EVER HEARD OF A GOTH LOLI TALKING LIKE AN OLD LADY?
HOW CAN YOU SAY THAT? GOTH LOLIS ARE HUMAN, TOO.
CHOMP CHOMP
THAT'S TRUE.
Nice choice of udon.
HMMM ...
I THINK IT'S GETTING TIGHTER AROUND MY WAIST...
No, it can't be...
WHAT?!
ARE YOU GETTING FAT?! NO!
I WANT YOU TO ALWAYS BE MY BEAUTIFUL SAWA-CHAN!

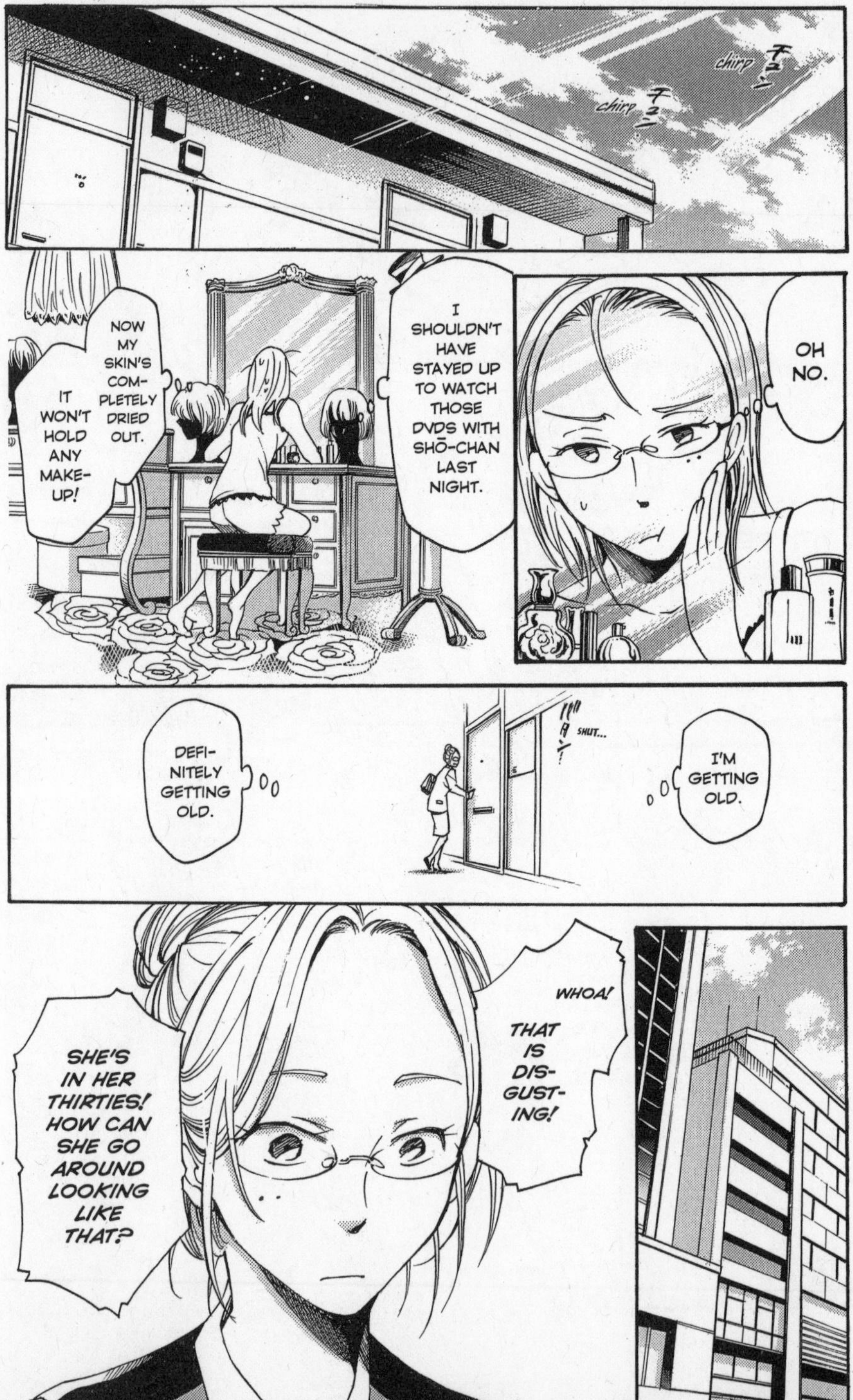
chirp
chirp
OH NO.
I SHOULDN'T HAVE STAYED UP TO WATCH THOSE DVDS WITH SHŌ-CHAN LAST NIGHT.
NOW MY SKIN'S COMPLETELY DRIED OUT.
IT WON'T HOLD ANY MAKE-UP!
I'M GETTING OLD.
SHUT...
DEFINITELY GETTING OLD.
WHOA!
THAT IS DISGUSTING!
SHE'S IN HER THIRTIES! HOW CAN SHE GO AROUND LOOKING LIKE THAT?

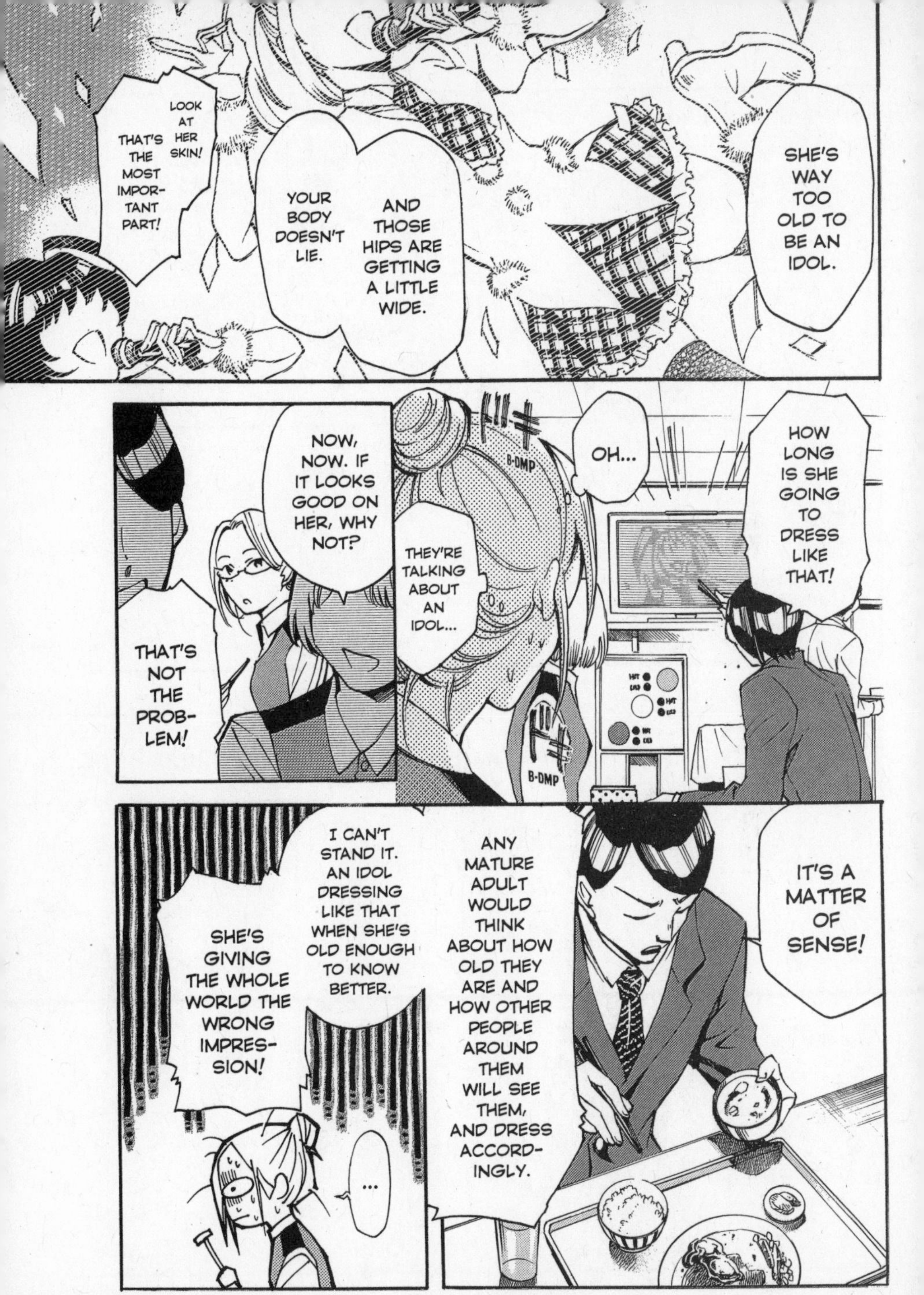
SHE'S WAY TOO OLD TO BE AN IDOL.
AND THOSE HIPS ARE GETTING A LITTLE WIDE.
YOUR BODY DOESN'T LIE.
LOOK AT HER SKIN!
THAT'S THE MOST IMPORTANT PART!
HOW LONG IS SHE GOING TO DRESS LIKE THAT!
OH...
B-DMP
THEY'RE TALKING ABOUT AN IDOL...
B-DMP
NOW, NOW. IF IT LOOKS GOOD ON HER, WHY NOT?
THAT'S NOT THE PROBLEM!
IT'S A MATTER OF SENSE!
ANY MATURE ADULT WOULD THINK ABOUT HOW OLD THEY ARE AND HOW OTHER PEOPLE AROUND THEM WILL SEE THEM, AND DRESS ACCORDINGLY.
I CAN'T STAND IT. AN IDOL DRESSING LIKE THAT WHEN SHE'S OLD ENOUGH TO KNOW BETTER.
SHE'S GIVING THE WHOLE WORLD THE WRONG IMPRESSION!
...

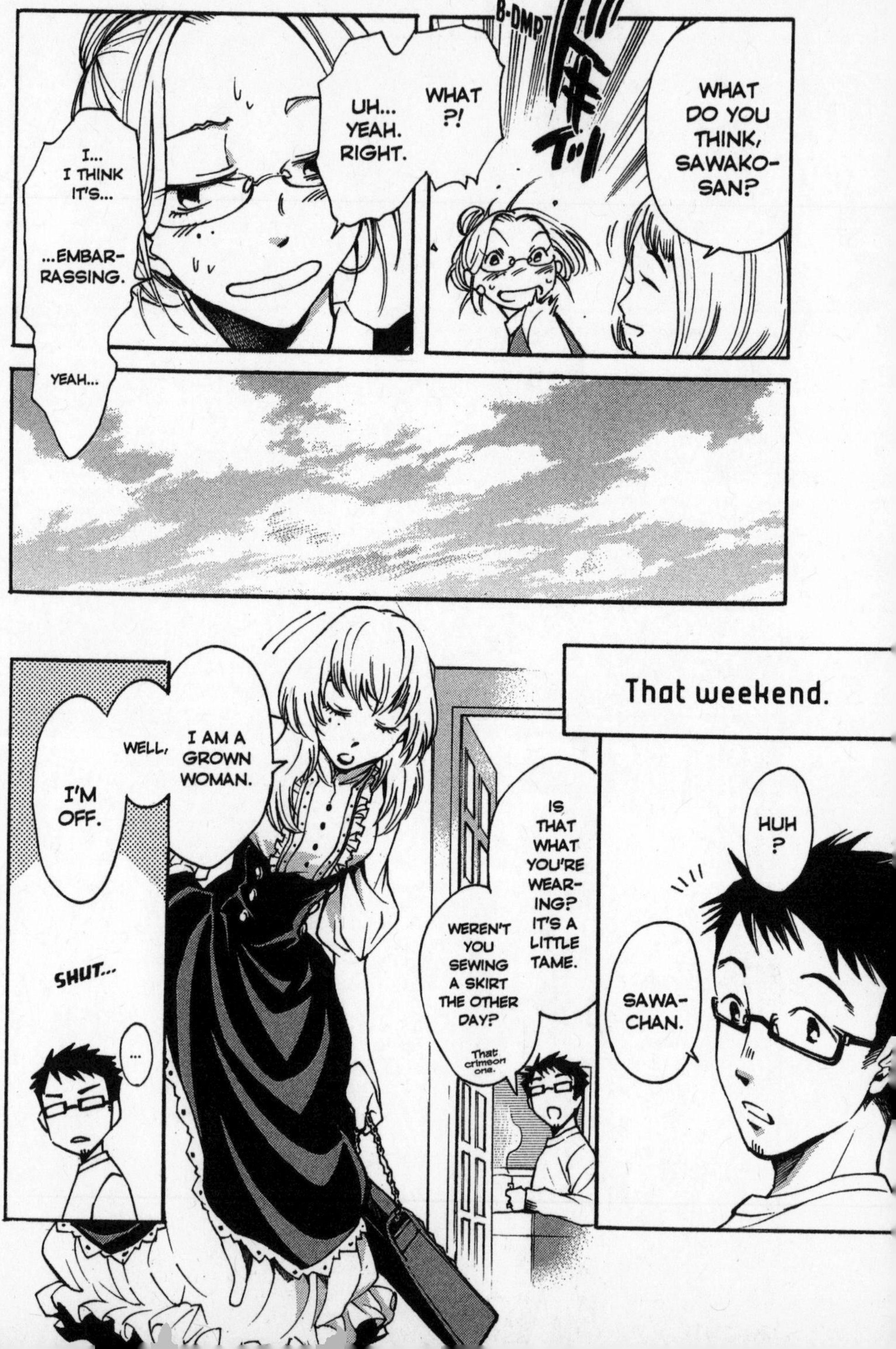
WHAT DO YOU THINK, SAWAKO-SAN?
B-DMP
WHAT ?!
UH... YEAH. RIGHT.
I... I THINK IT'S...
...EMBARRASSING.
YEAH...
That weekend.
HUH ?
SAWA-CHAN.
IS THAT WHAT YOU'RE WEARING? IT'S A LITTLE TAME.
WEREN'T YOU SEWING A SKIRT THE OTHER DAY?
That crimson one.
WELL, I AM A GROWN WOMAN.
I'M OFF.
SHUT...
...

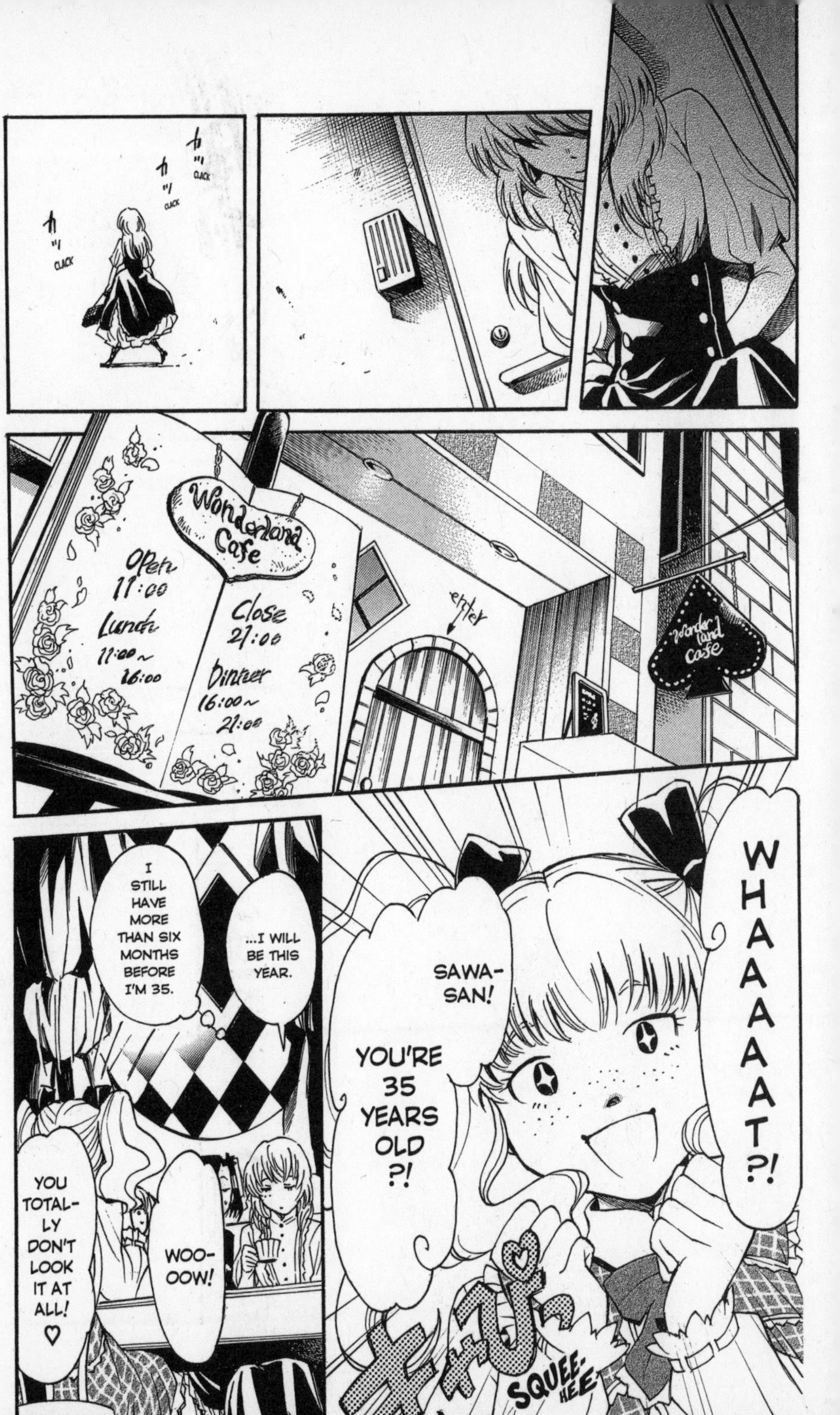
CLACK
CLACK
CLACK
Wonderland Cafe
Open 11:00
Lunch 11:00~16:00
Close 21:00
Dinner 16:00~21:00
enter
Wonder land Cafe
WHAAAAAAT?!
SAWA-SAN!
YOU'RE 35 YEARS OLD?!
SQUEE-HEE
...I WILL BE THIS YEAR.
I STILL HAVE MORE THAN SIX MONTHS BEFORE I'M 35.
WOO-OOW!
YOU TOTALLY DON'T LOOK IT AT ALL! ♡

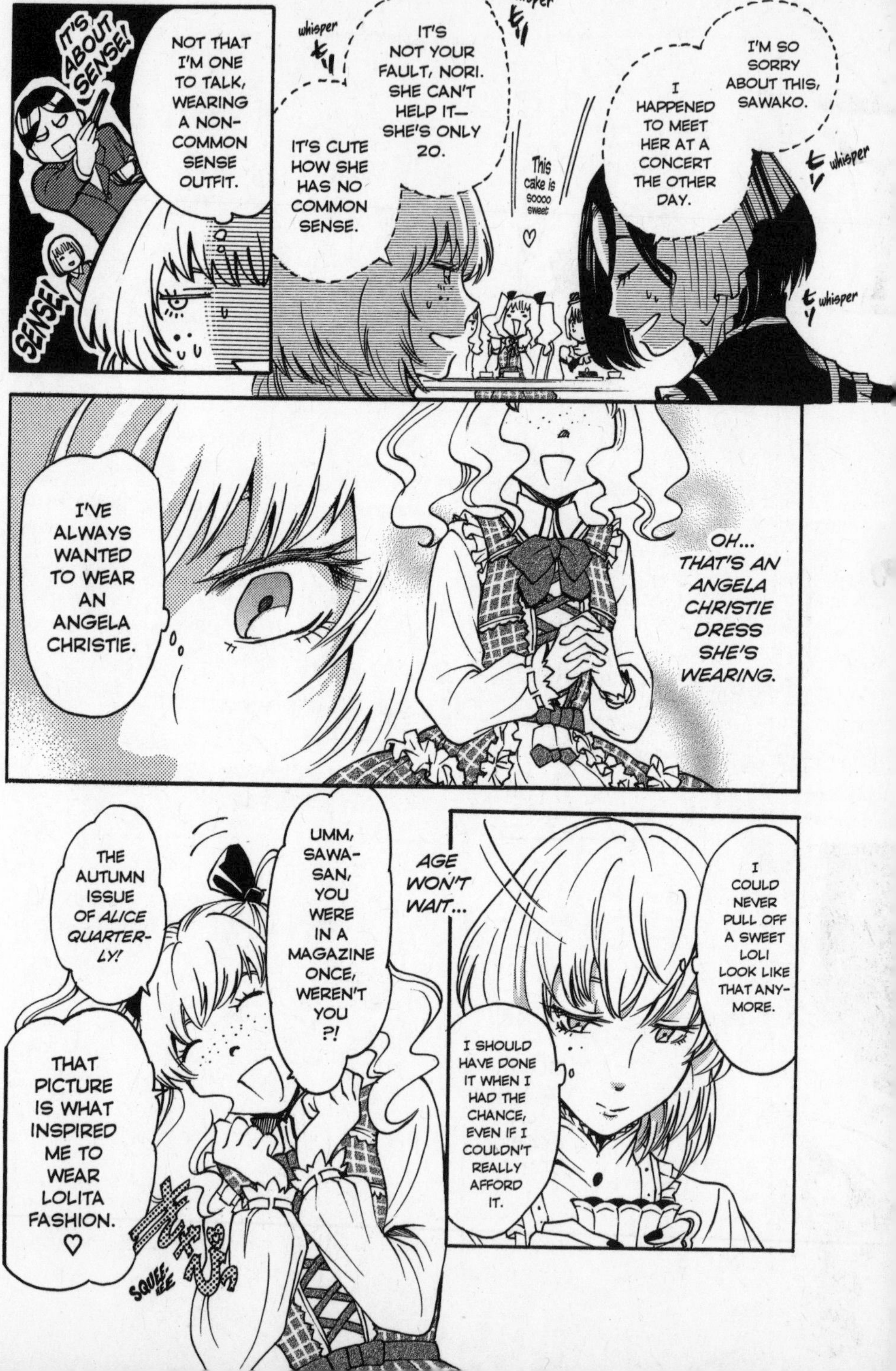

whisper
I'M SO SORRY ABOUT THIS, SAWAKO.
I HAPPENED TO MEET HER AT A CONCERT THE OTHER DAY.
whisper
whisper
This cake is soooo sweet ♡
IT'S NOT YOUR FAULT, NORI. SHE CAN'T HELP IT— SHE'S ONLY 20.
whisper
IT'S CUTE HOW SHE HAS NO COMMON SENSE.
NOT THAT I'M ONE TO TALK, WEARING A NON-COMMON SENSE OUTFIT.
IT'S ABOUT SENSE!
SENSE!
OH... THAT'S AN ANGELA CHRISTIE DRESS SHE'S WEARING.
I'VE ALWAYS WANTED TO WEAR AN ANGELA CHRISTIE.
I COULD NEVER PULL OFF A SWEET LOLI LOOK LIKE THAT ANYMORE.
I SHOULD HAVE DONE IT WHEN I HAD THE CHANCE, EVEN IF I COULDN'T REALLY AFFORD IT.
AGE WON'T WAIT...
UMM, SAWA-SAN, YOU WERE IN A MAGAZINE ONCE, WEREN'T YOU ?!
THE AUTUMN ISSUE OF *ALICE QUARTERLY!*
THAT PICTURE IS WHAT INSPIRED ME TO WEAR LOLITA FASHION. ♡
SQUEE-EE

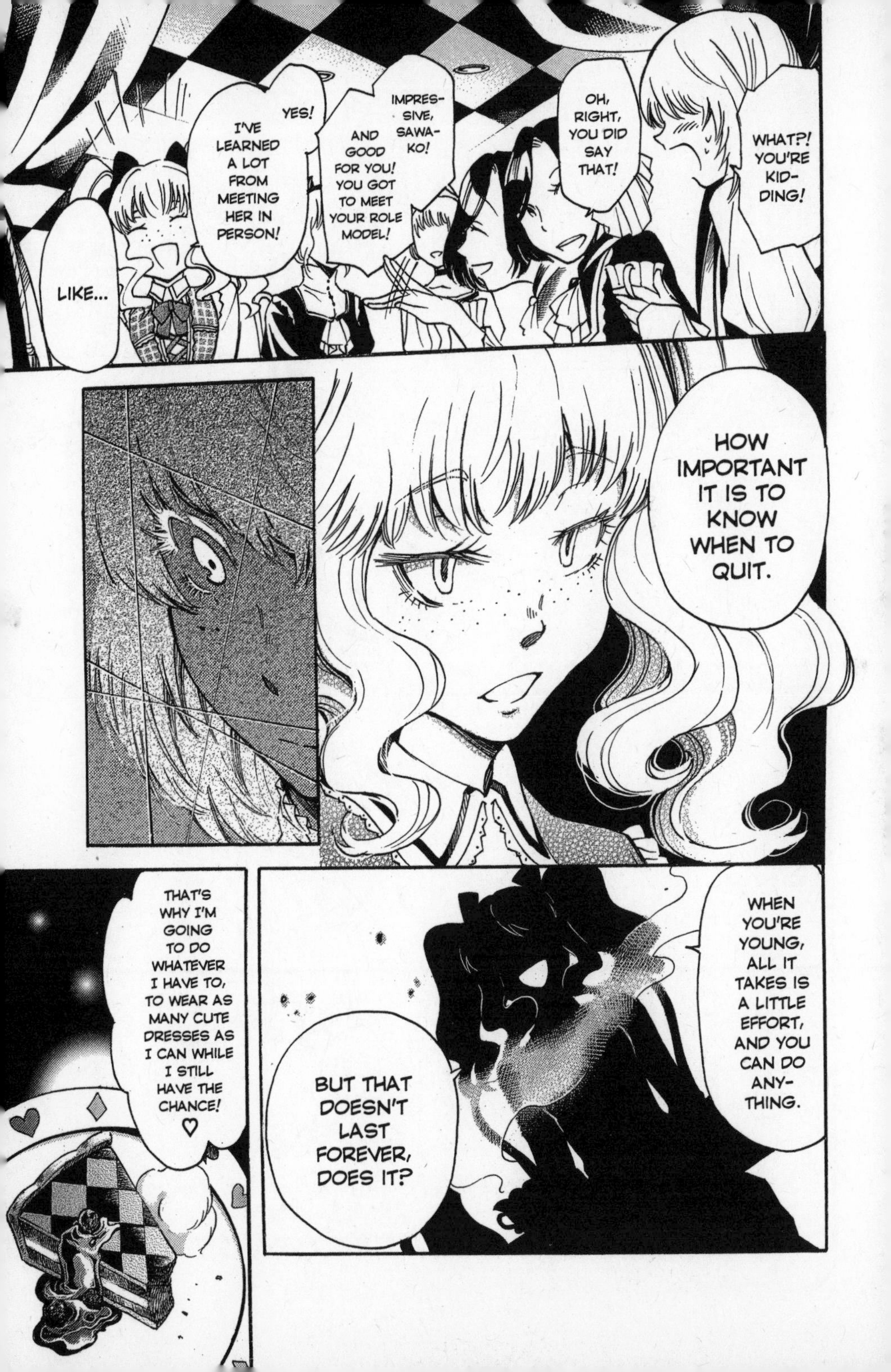
WHAT?! YOU'RE KIDDING!
OH, RIGHT, YOU DID SAY THAT!
IMPRESSIVE, SAWAKO!
AND GOOD FOR YOU! YOU GOT TO MEET YOUR ROLE MODEL!
YES!
I'VE LEARNED A LOT FROM MEETING HER IN PERSON!
LIKE...
HOW IMPORTANT IT IS TO KNOW WHEN TO QUIT.
WHEN YOU'RE YOUNG, ALL IT TAKES IS A LITTLE EFFORT, AND YOU CAN DO ANYTHING.
BUT THAT DOESN'T LAST FOREVER, DOES IT?
THAT'S WHY I'M GOING TO DO WHATEVER I HAVE TO, TO WEAR AS MANY CUTE DRESSES AS I CAN WHILE I STILL HAVE THE CHANCE! ♡

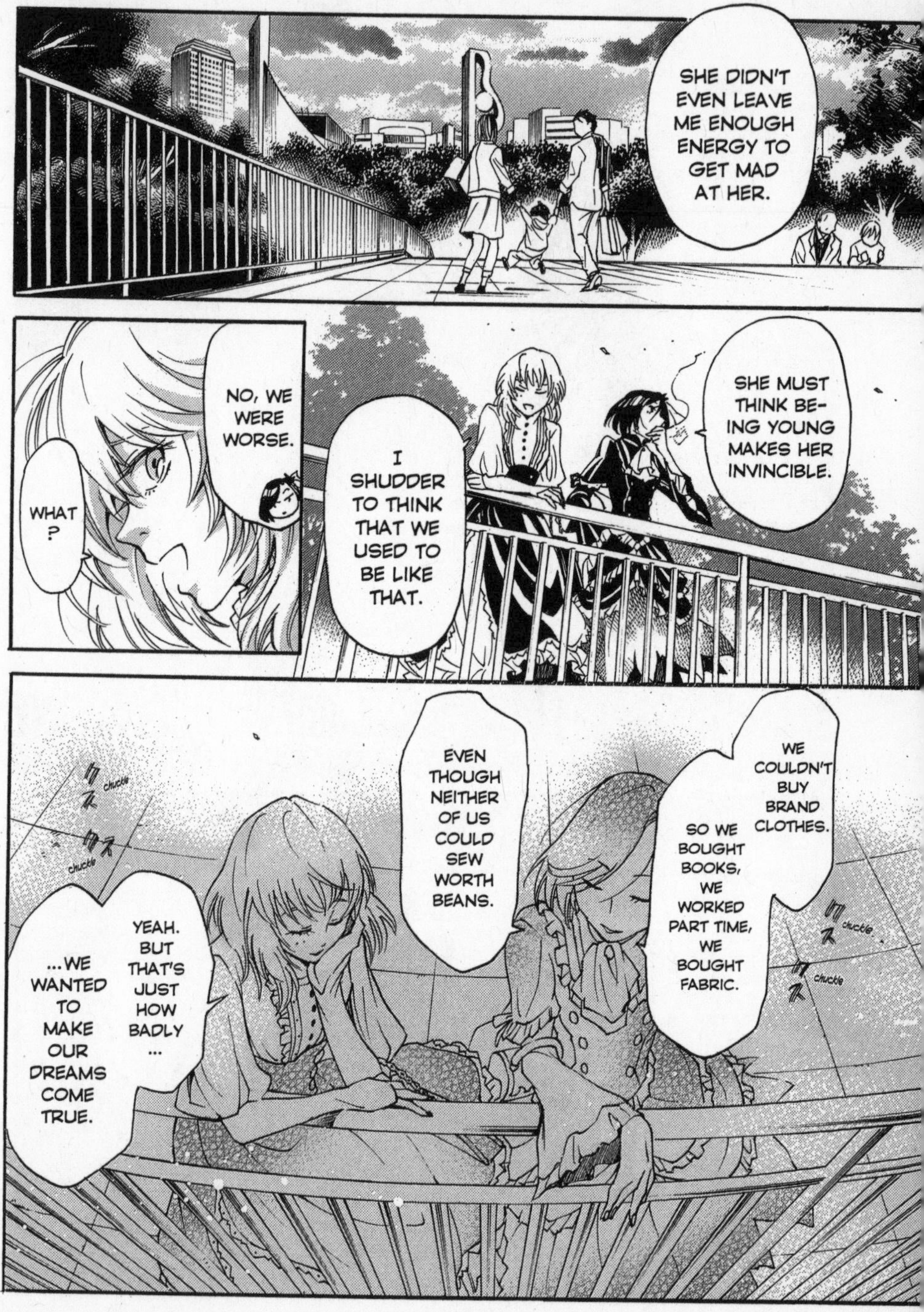
SHE DIDN'T EVEN LEAVE ME ENOUGH ENERGY TO GET MAD AT HER.
SHE MUST THINK BE-ING YOUNG MAKES HER INVINCIBLE.
I SHUDDER TO THINK THAT WE USED TO BE LIKE THAT.
NO, WE WERE WORSE.
WHAT?
WE COULDN'T BUY BRAND CLOTHES.
SO WE BOUGHT BOOKS, WE WORKED PART TIME, WE BOUGHT FABRIC.
chuckle
chuckle
EVEN THOUGH NEITHER OF US COULD SEW WORTH BEANS.
YEAH. BUT THAT'S JUST HOW BADLY...
...WE WANTED TO MAKE OUR DREAMS COME TRUE.
chuckle
chuckle

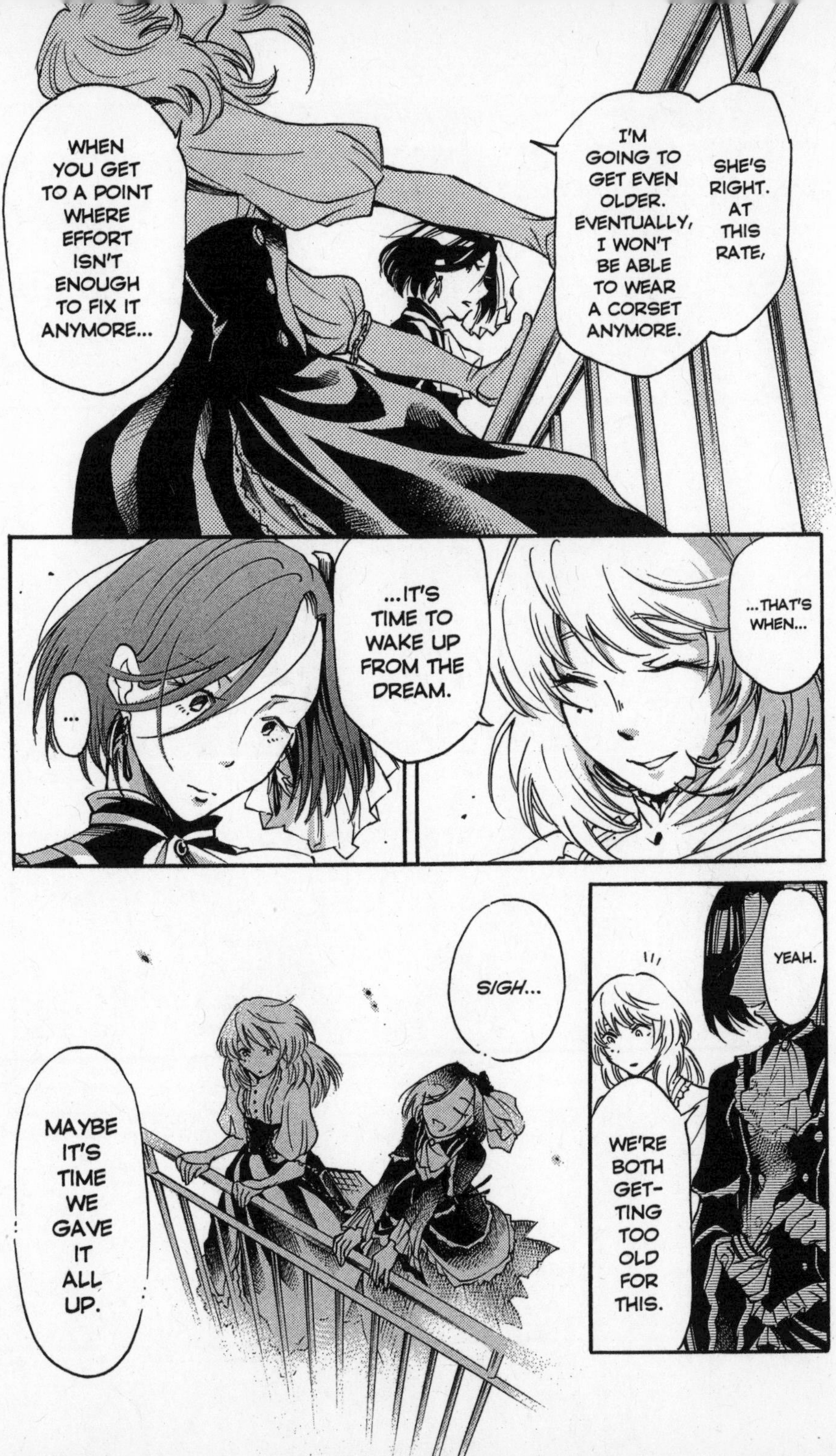
SHE'S RIGHT. AT THIS RATE,
I'M GOING TO GET EVEN OLDER. EVENTUALLY, I WON'T BE ABLE TO WEAR A CORSET ANYMORE.
WHEN YOU GET TO A POINT WHERE EFFORT ISN'T ENOUGH TO FIX IT ANYMORE...
...THAT'S WHEN...
...IT'S TIME TO WAKE UP FROM THE DREAM.
...
YEAH.
WE'RE BOTH GET-TING TOO OLD FOR THIS.
SIGH...
MAYBE IT'S TIME WE GAVE IT ALL UP.

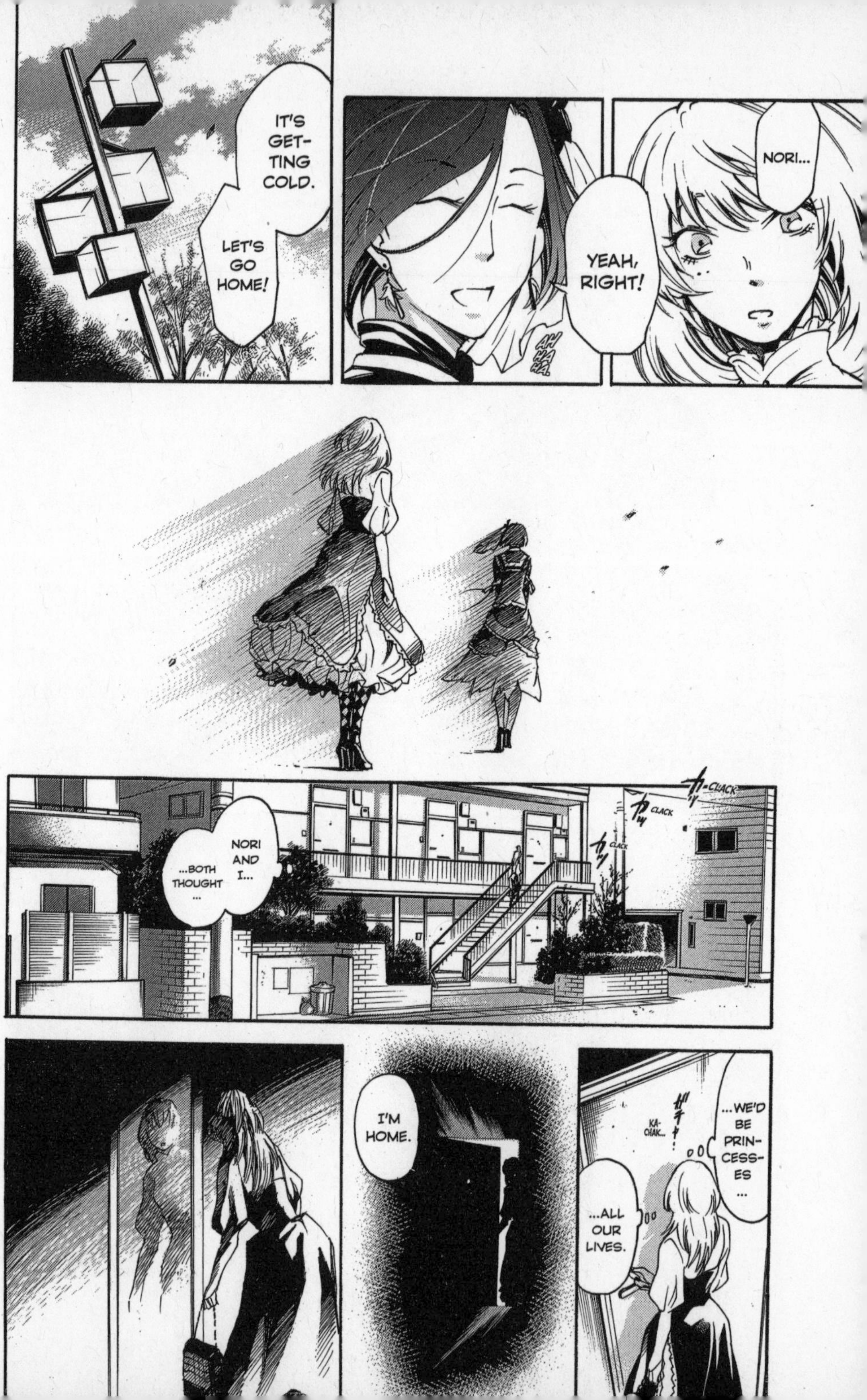
NORI...
YEAH, RIGHT!
AH HA HA.
IT'S GETTING COLD.
LET'S GO HOME!
CLACK
CLACK
CLACK
NORI AND I...
...BOTH THOUGHT...
KA-CHAK...
...WE'D BE PRINCESSES...
...ALL OUR LIVES.
I'M HOME.

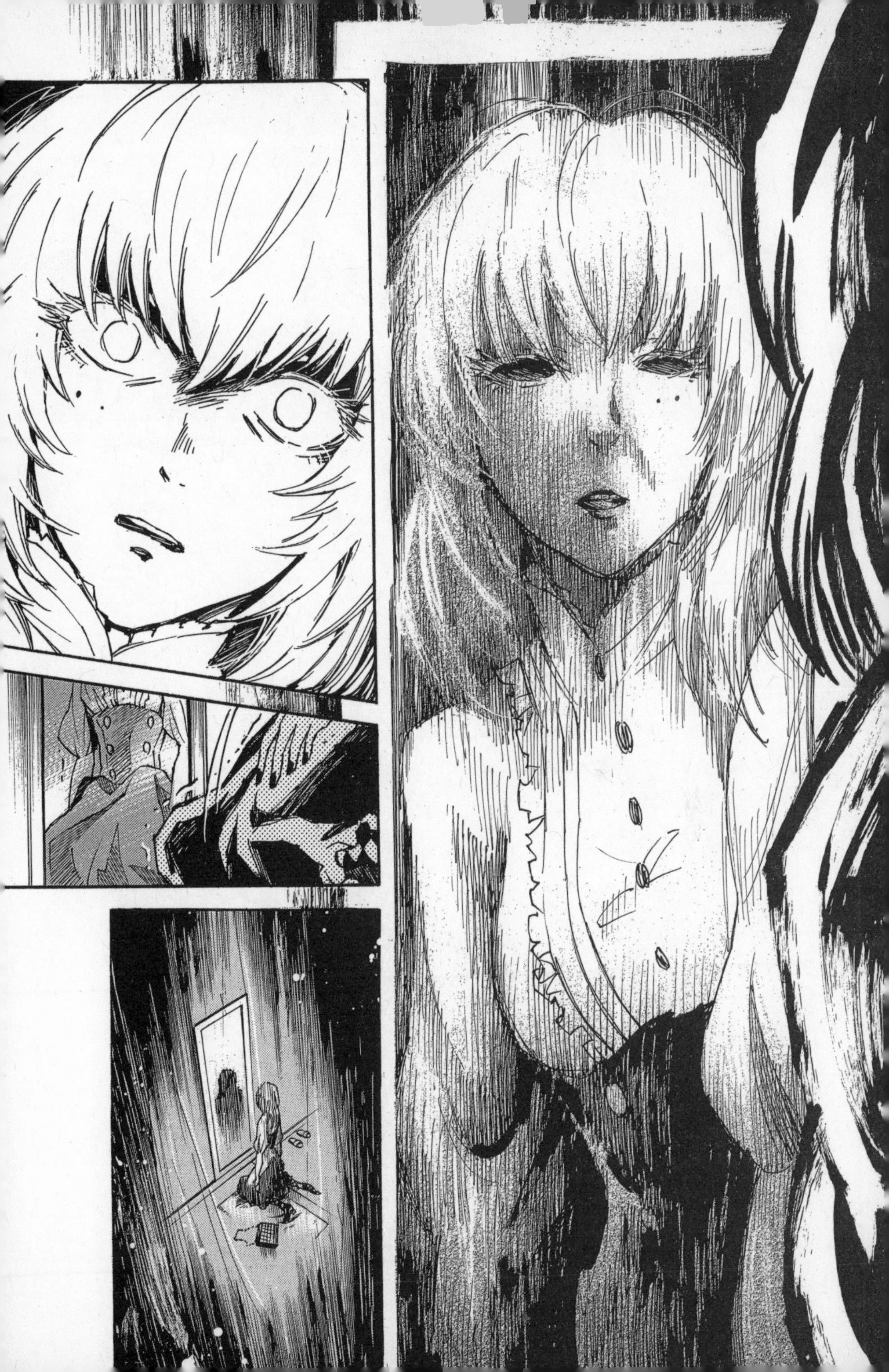

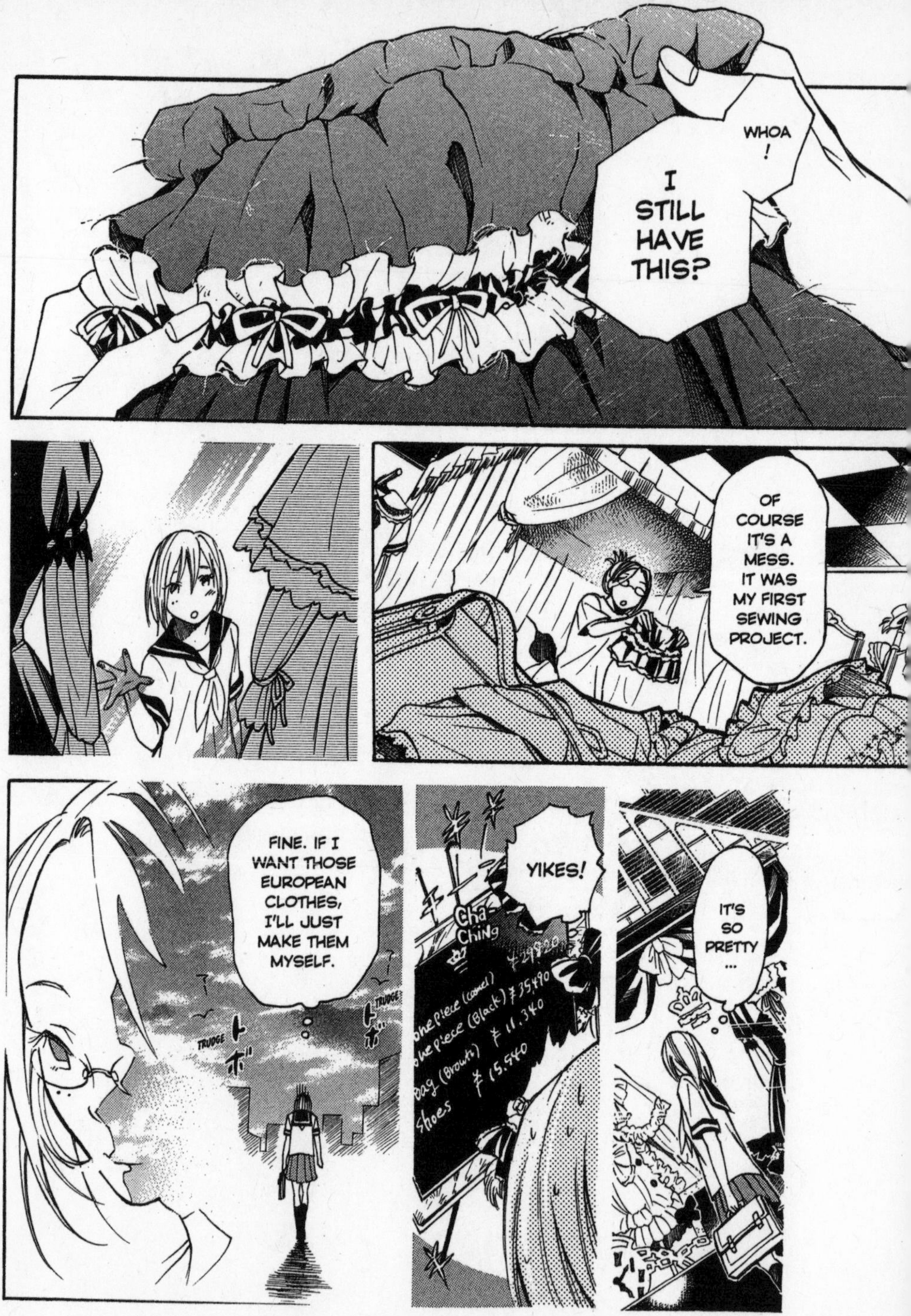
WHOA!
I STILL HAVE THIS?
OF COURSE IT'S A MESS. IT WAS MY FIRST SEWING PROJECT.
IT'S SO PRETTY ...
YIKES!
Cha-ChiNg
¥29820
one piece (camel)
one piece (Black) ¥35,490
bag (Brown) ¥11.340
shoes ¥15.540
FINE. IF I WANT THOSE EUROPEAN CLOTHES, I'LL JUST MAKE THEM MYSELF.
TRUDGE
TRUDGE

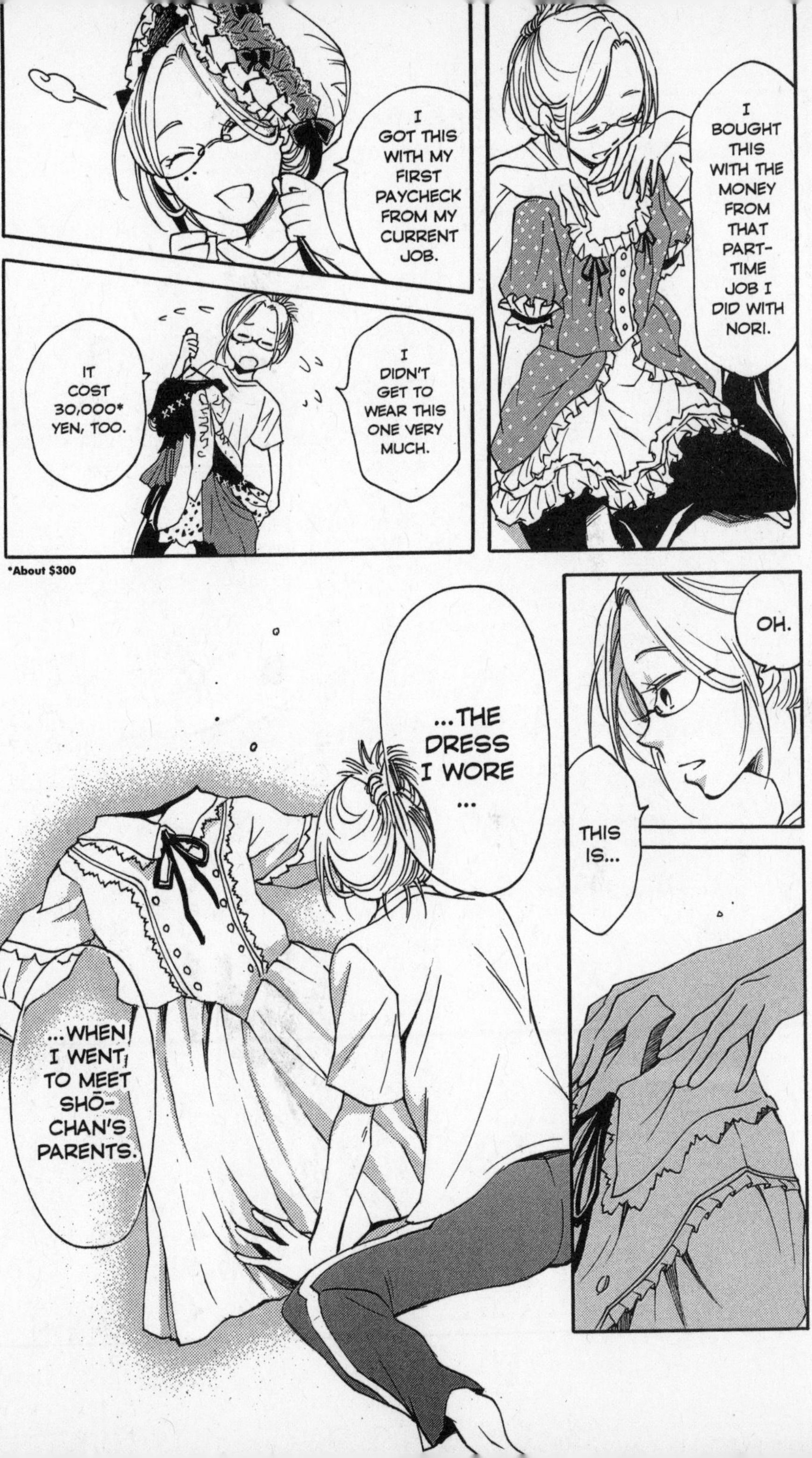
I BOUGHT THIS WITH THE MONEY FROM THAT PART-TIME JOB I DID WITH NORI.
I GOT THIS WITH MY FIRST PAYCHECK FROM MY CURRENT JOB.
I DIDN'T GET TO WEAR THIS ONE VERY MUCH.
IT COST 30,000* YEN, TOO.
OH.
THIS IS...
...THE DRESS I WORE ...
...WHEN I WENT TO MEET SHŌ-CHAN'S PARENTS.
*About $300

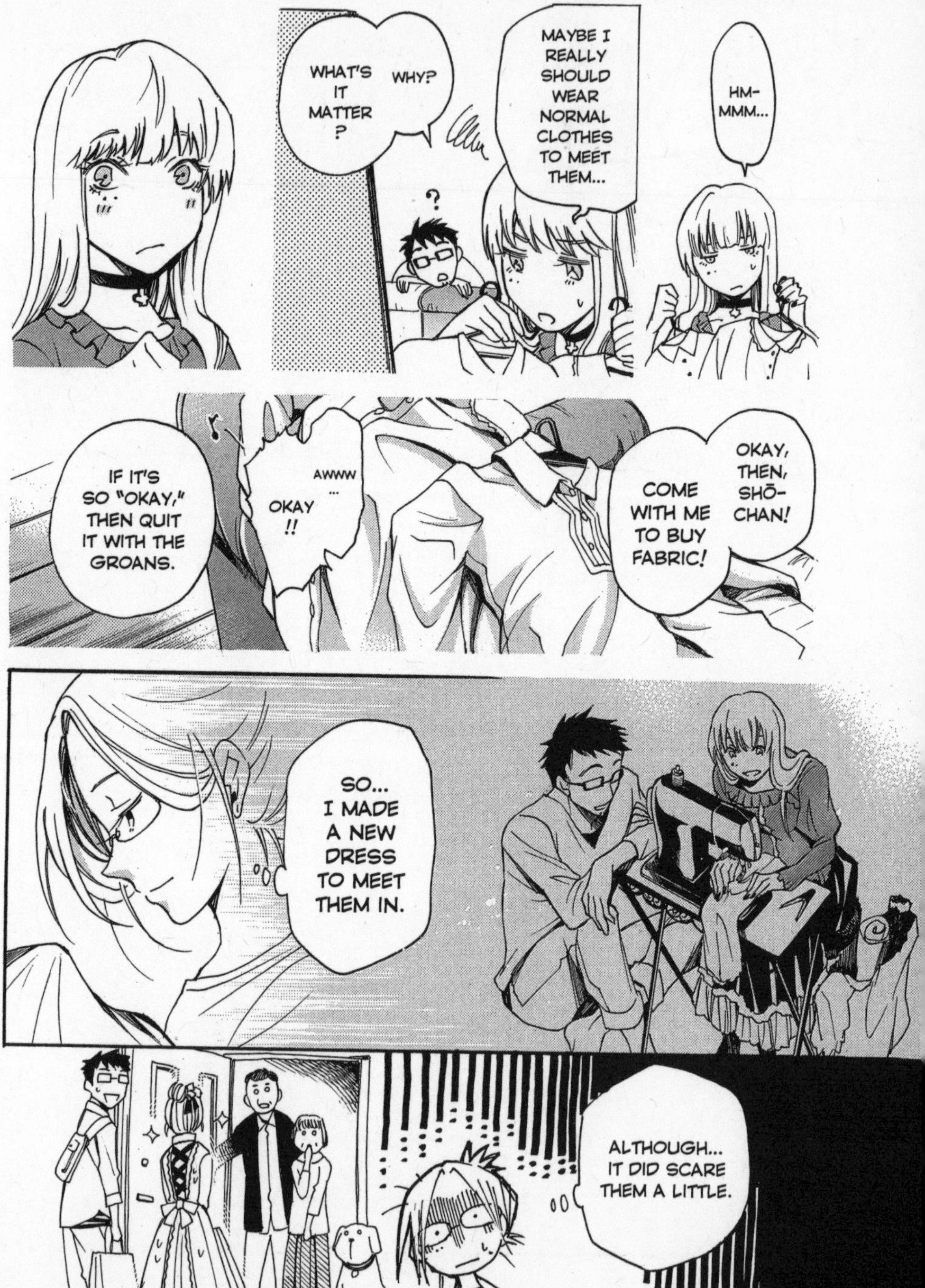
HM-MMM...
MAYBE I REALLY SHOULD WEAR NORMAL CLOTHES TO MEET THEM...
WHY?
WHAT'S IT MATTER?
?
OKAY, THEN, SHŌ-CHAN!
COME WITH ME TO BUY FABRIC!
AWWW...
OKAY!!
IF IT'S SO "OKAY," THEN QUIT IT WITH THE GROANS.
SO... I MADE A NEW DRESS TO MEET THEM IN.
ALTHOUGH... IT DID SCARE THEM A LITTLE.

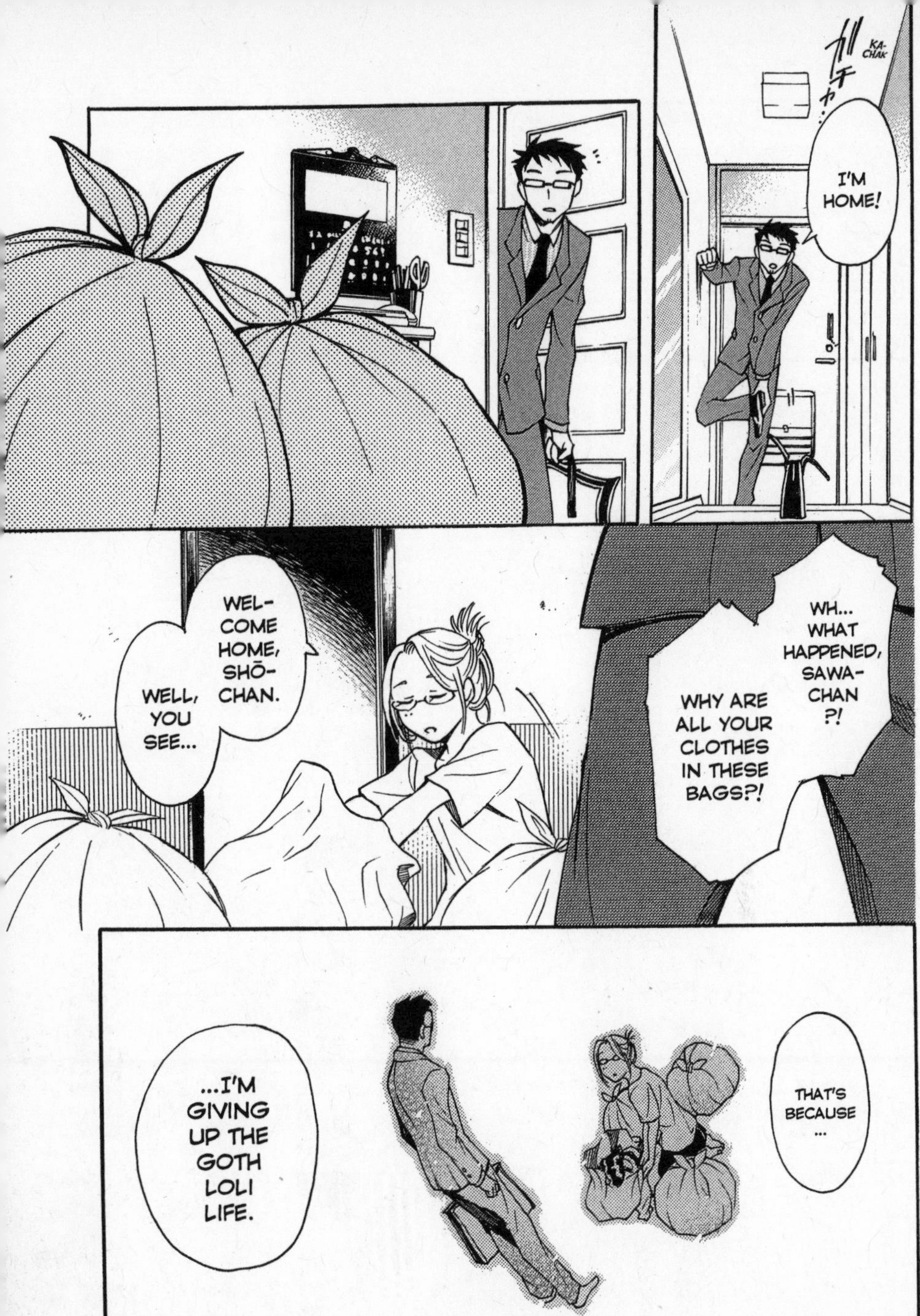
ガチャ
KA-CHAK
I'M HOME!
WH... WHAT HAPPENED, SAWA-CHAN?!
WHY ARE ALL YOUR CLOTHES IN THESE BAGS?!
WELCOME HOME, SHŌ-CHAN.
WELL, YOU SEE...
THAT'S BECAUSE ...
...I'M GIVING UP THE GOTH LOLI LIFE.

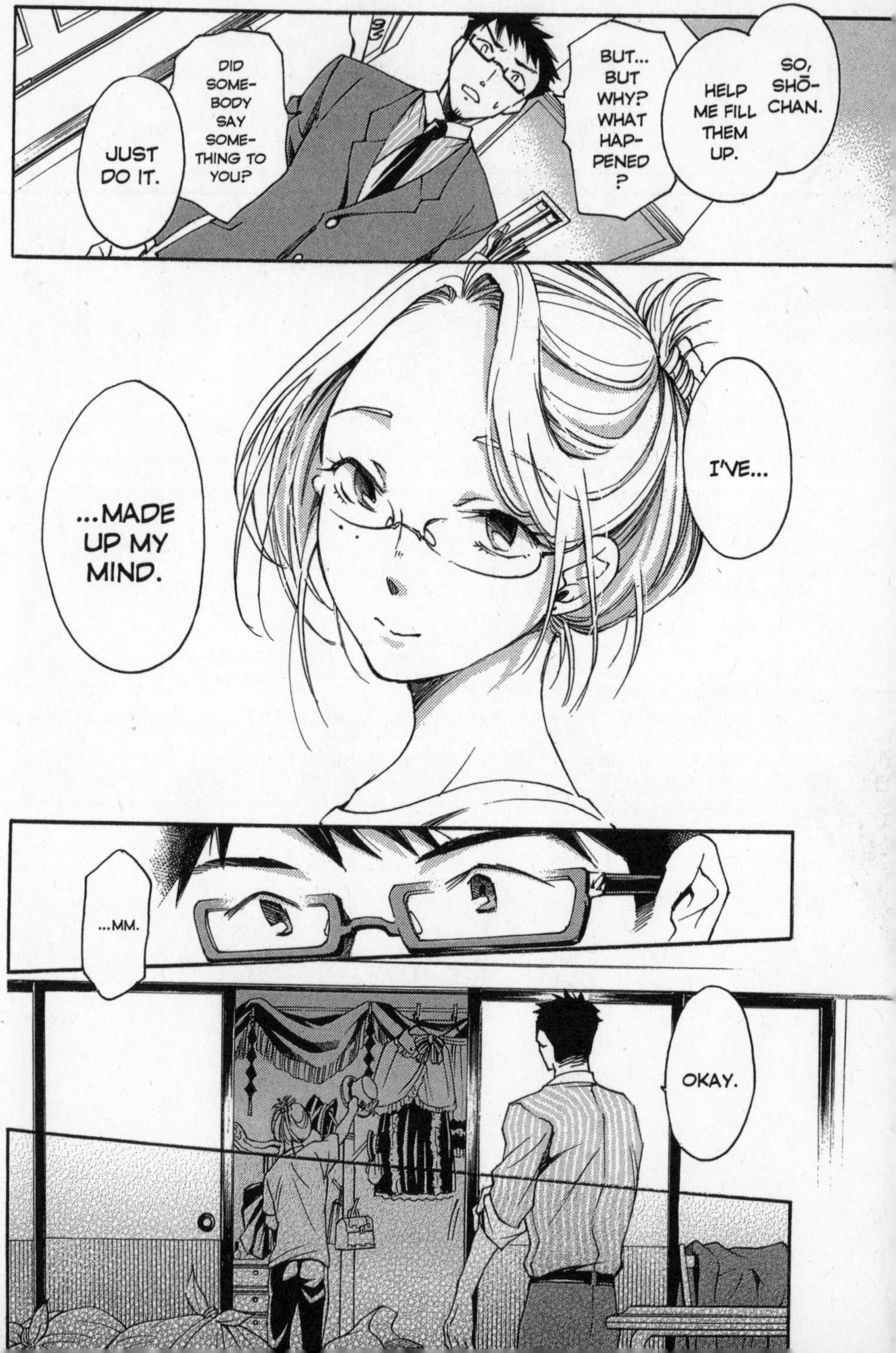
SO, SHŌ-CHAN.
HELP ME FILL THEM UP.
BUT... BUT WHY? WHAT HAPPENED?
DID SOMEBODY SAY SOMETHING TO YOU?
JUST DO IT.
I'VE...
...MADE UP MY MIND.
...MM.
OKAY.

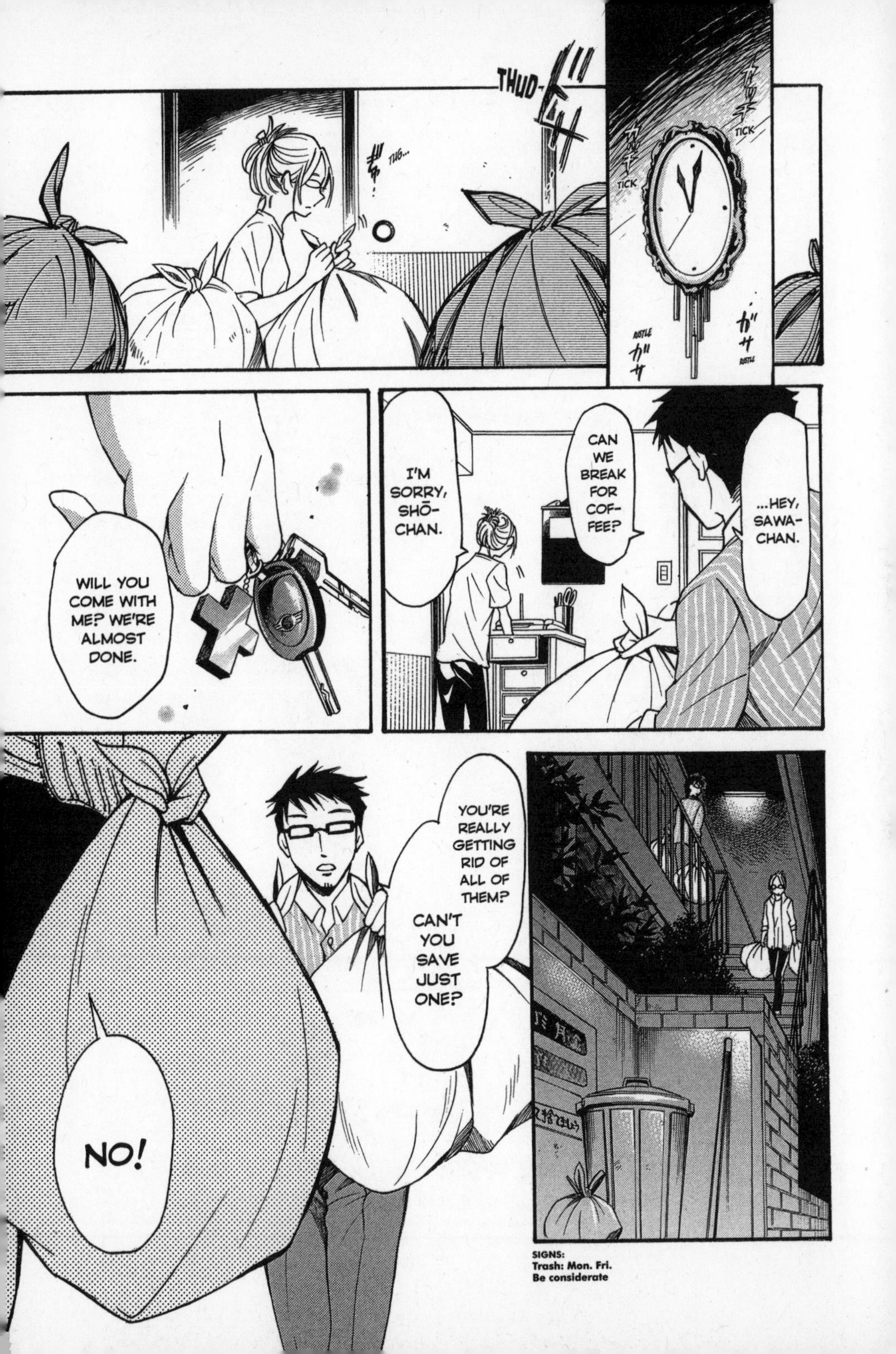
TICK
TICK
RUSTLE
RUSTLE
THUD-
TUG...
...HEY, SAWA-CHAN.
CAN WE BREAK FOR COF-FEE?
I'M SORRY, SHŌ-CHAN.
WILL YOU COME WITH ME? WE'RE ALMOST DONE.
SIGNS:
Trash: Mon. Fri.
Be considerate
YOU'RE REALLY GETTING RID OF ALL OF THEM?
CAN'T YOU SAVE JUST ONE?
NO!

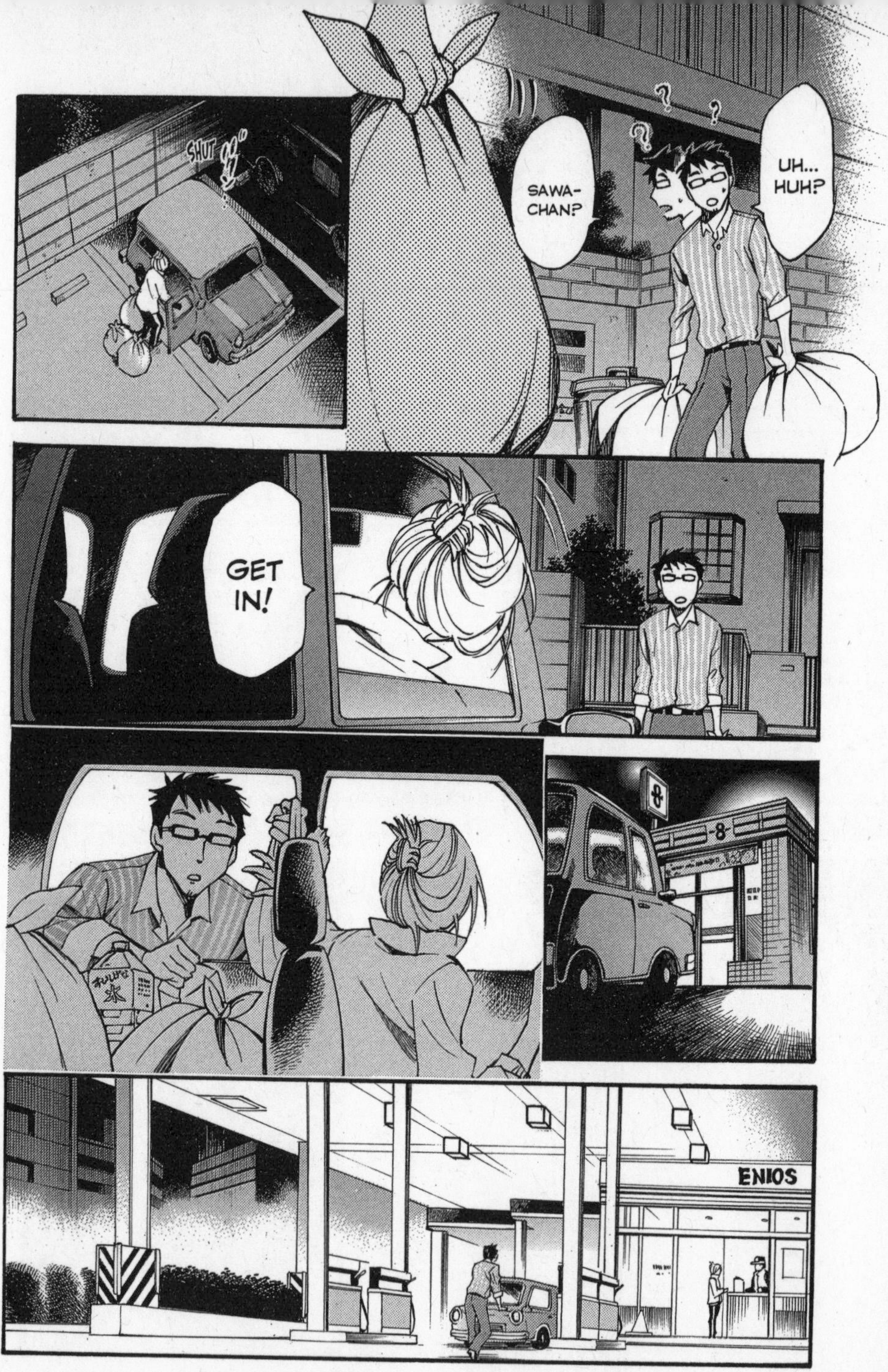
UH... HUH?
SAWA-CHAN?
SHUT
GET IN!
ENIOS

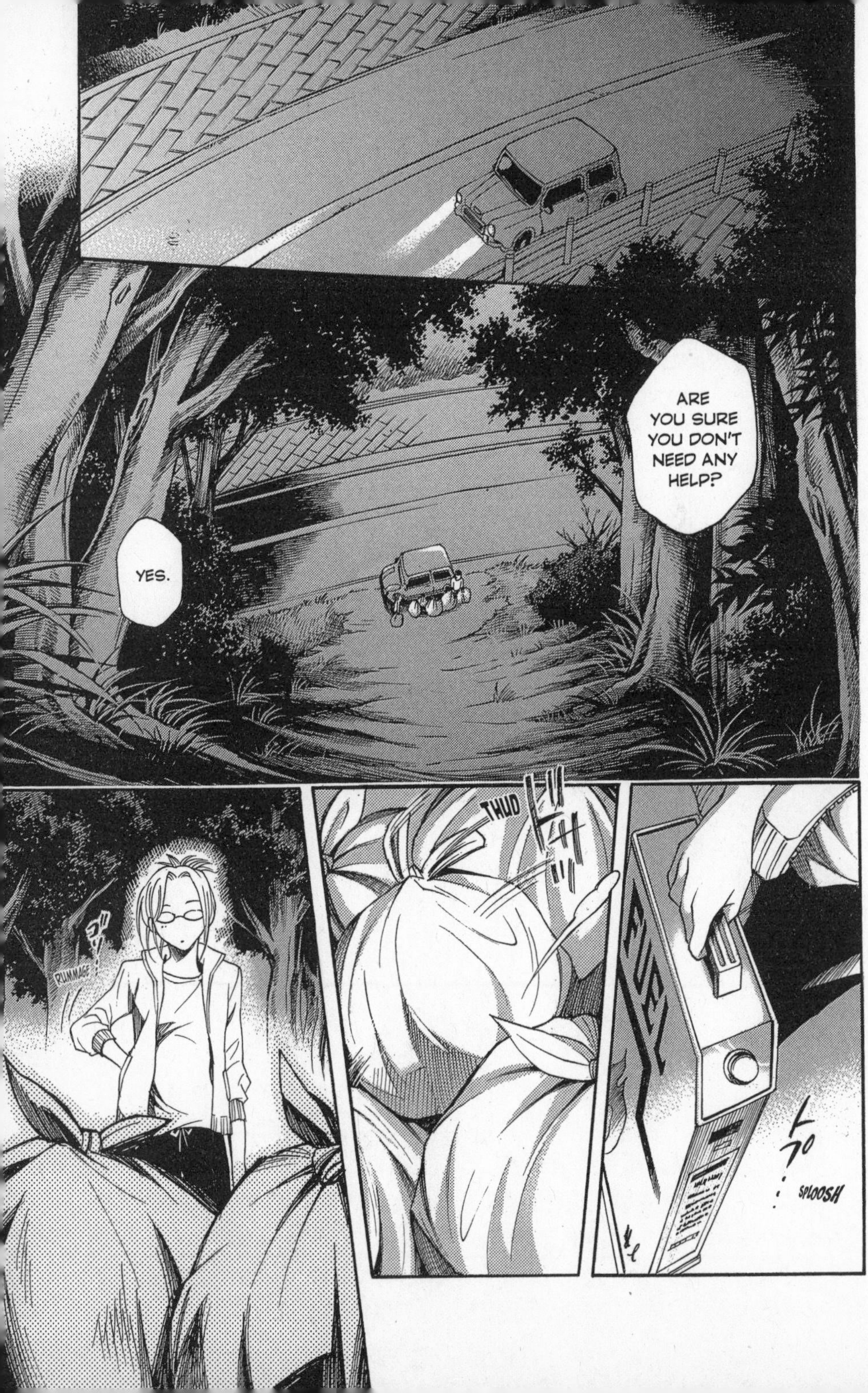
ARE YOU SURE YOU DON'T NEED ANY HELP?
YES.
SPLOOSH
THUD
RUMMAGE

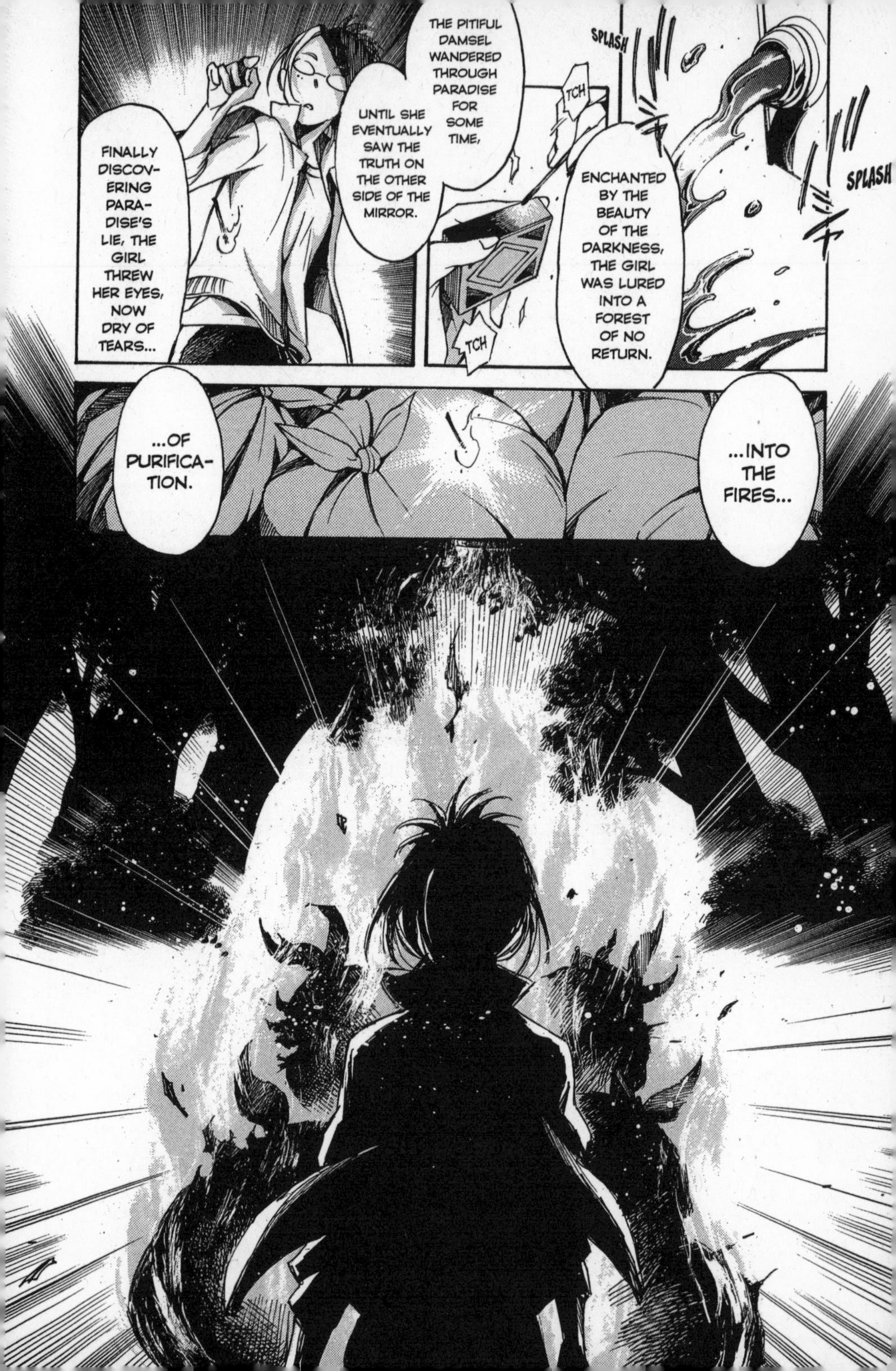
SPLASH
SPLASH
TCH
ENCHANTED BY THE BEAUTY OF THE DARKNESS, THE GIRL WAS LURED INTO A FOREST OF NO RETURN.
TCH
THE PITIFUL DAMSEL WANDERED THROUGH PARADISE FOR SOME TIME,
UNTIL SHE EVENTUALLY SAW THE TRUTH ON THE OTHER SIDE OF THE MIRROR.
FINALLY DISCOVERING PARADISE'S LIE, THE GIRL THREW HER EYES, NOW DRY OF TEARS...
...INTO THE FIRES...
...OF PURIFICATION.

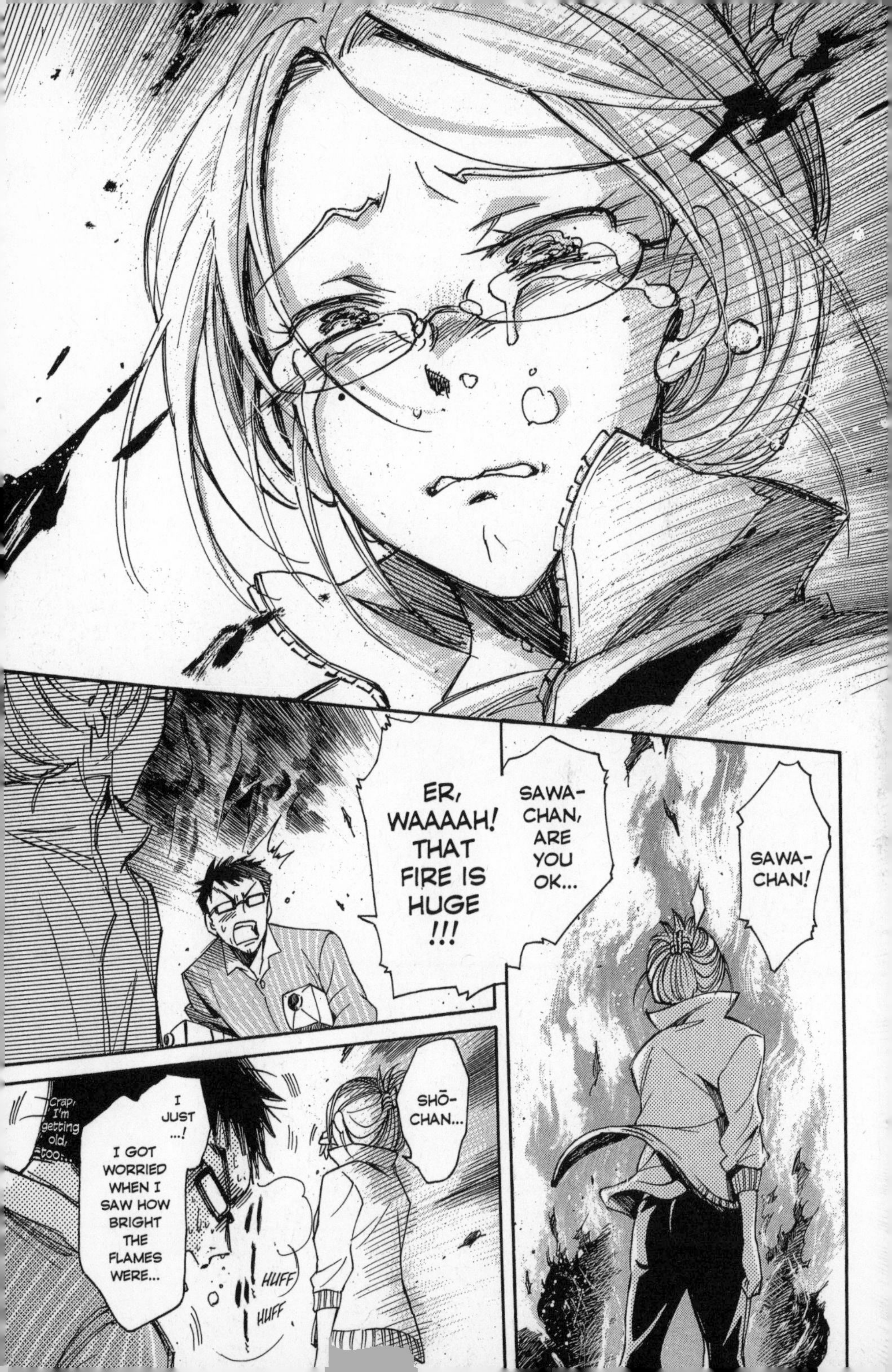
SAWA-CHAN!
SAWA-CHAN, ARE YOU OK...
ER, WAAAAH! THAT FIRE IS HUGE!!!
SHŌ-CHAN...
I JUST ...!
I GOT WORRIED WHEN I SAW HOW BRIGHT THE FLAMES WERE...
HUFF
HUFF
Crap, I'm getting old, too...

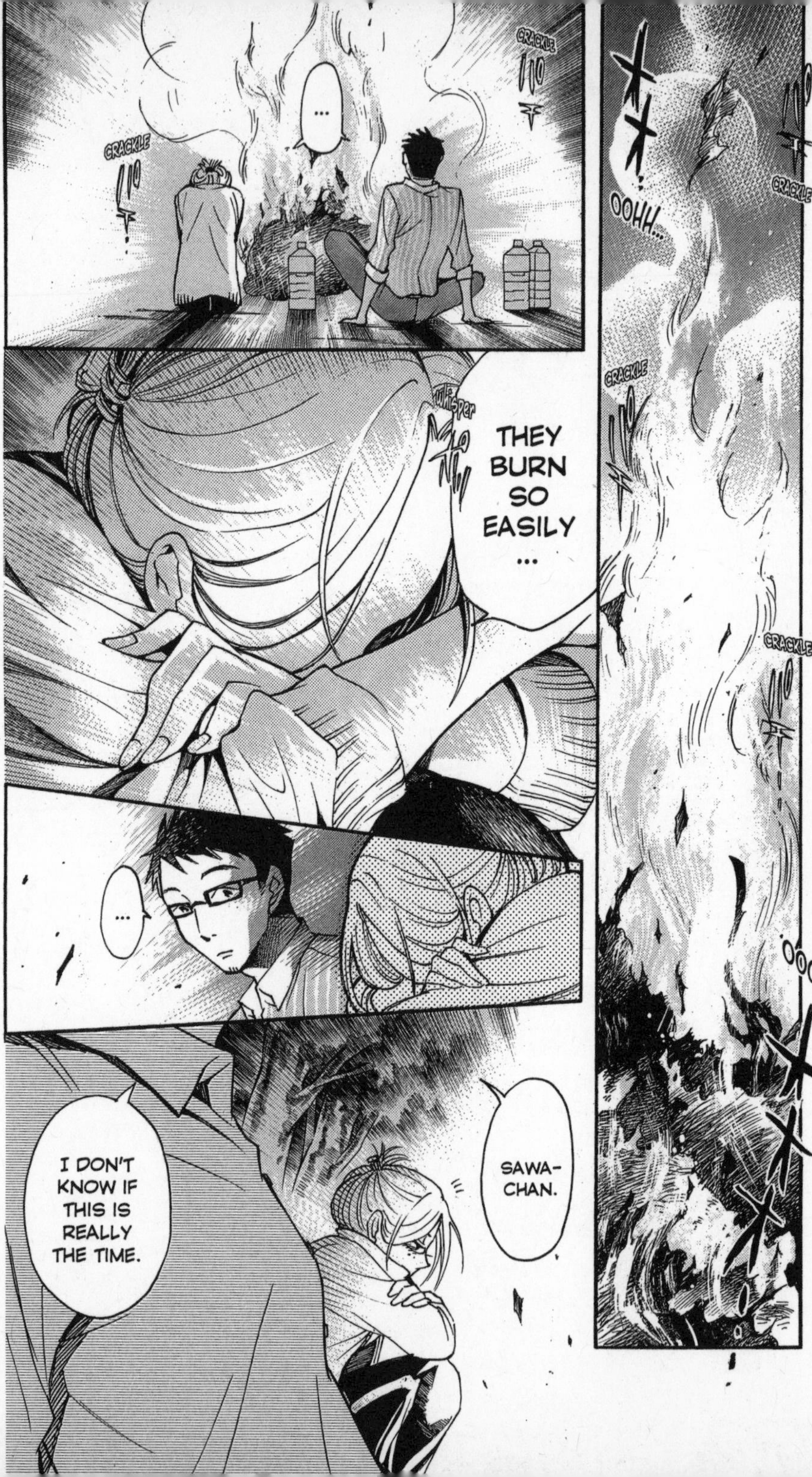
CRACKLE
OOHH...
CRACKLE
CRACKLE
OOOHHH...
CRACKLE
...
CRACKLE
whisper
THEY BURN SO EASILY ...
...
SAWA-CHAN.
I DON'T KNOW IF THIS IS REALLY THE TIME.

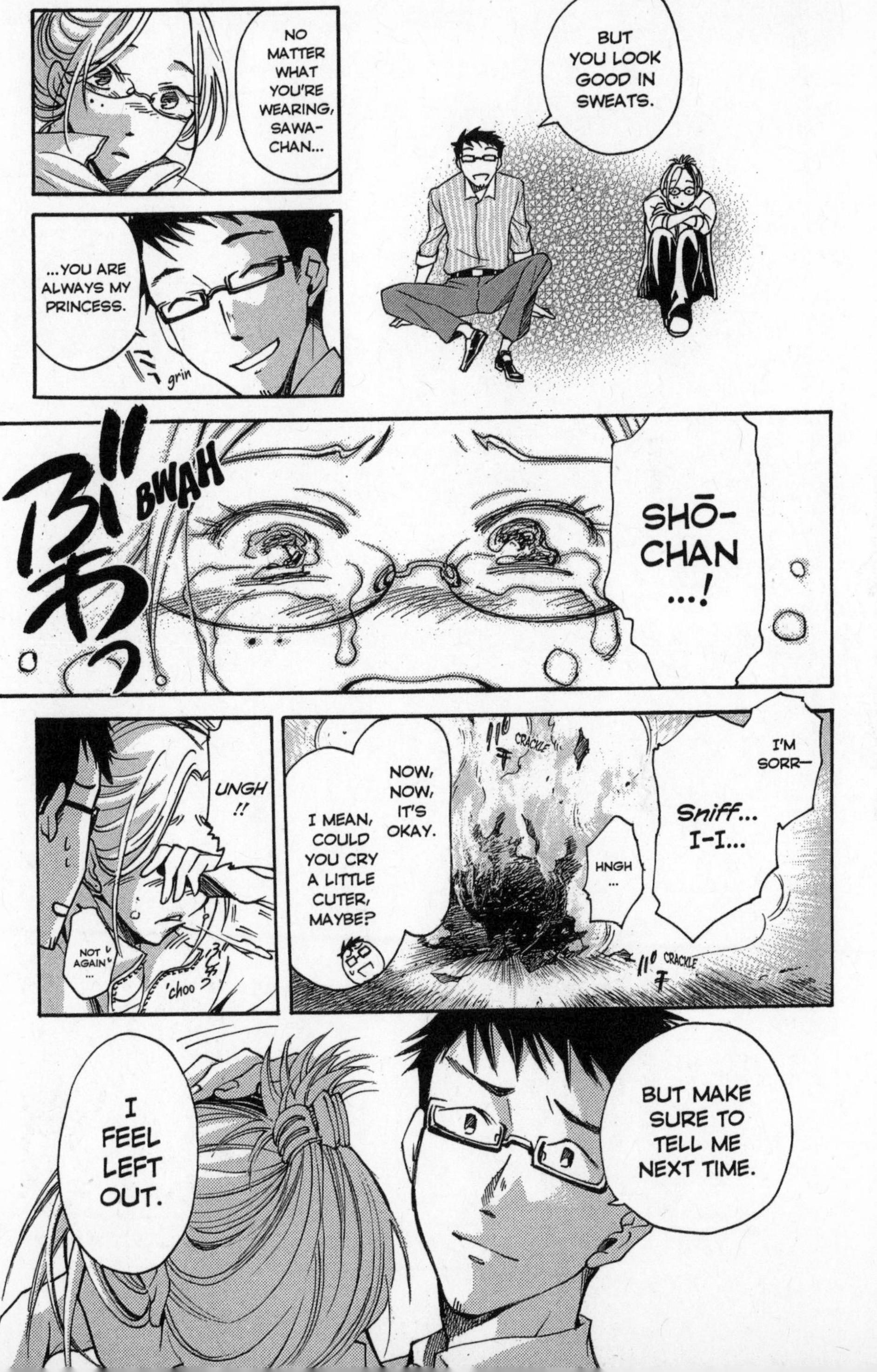
BUT YOU LOOK GOOD IN SWEATS.
NO MATTER WHAT YOU'RE WEARING, SAWA-CHAN...
...YOU ARE ALWAYS MY PRINCESS.
grin
SHŌ-CHAN...!
BWAH
I'M SORR—
Sniff... I-I...
HNGH...
CRACKLE
NOW, NOW, IT'S OKAY.
I MEAN, COULD YOU CRY A LITTLE CUTER, MAYBE?
CRACKLE
UNGH!!
NOT AGAIN...
'choo
BUT MAKE SURE TO TELL ME NEXT TIME.
I FEEL LEFT OUT.

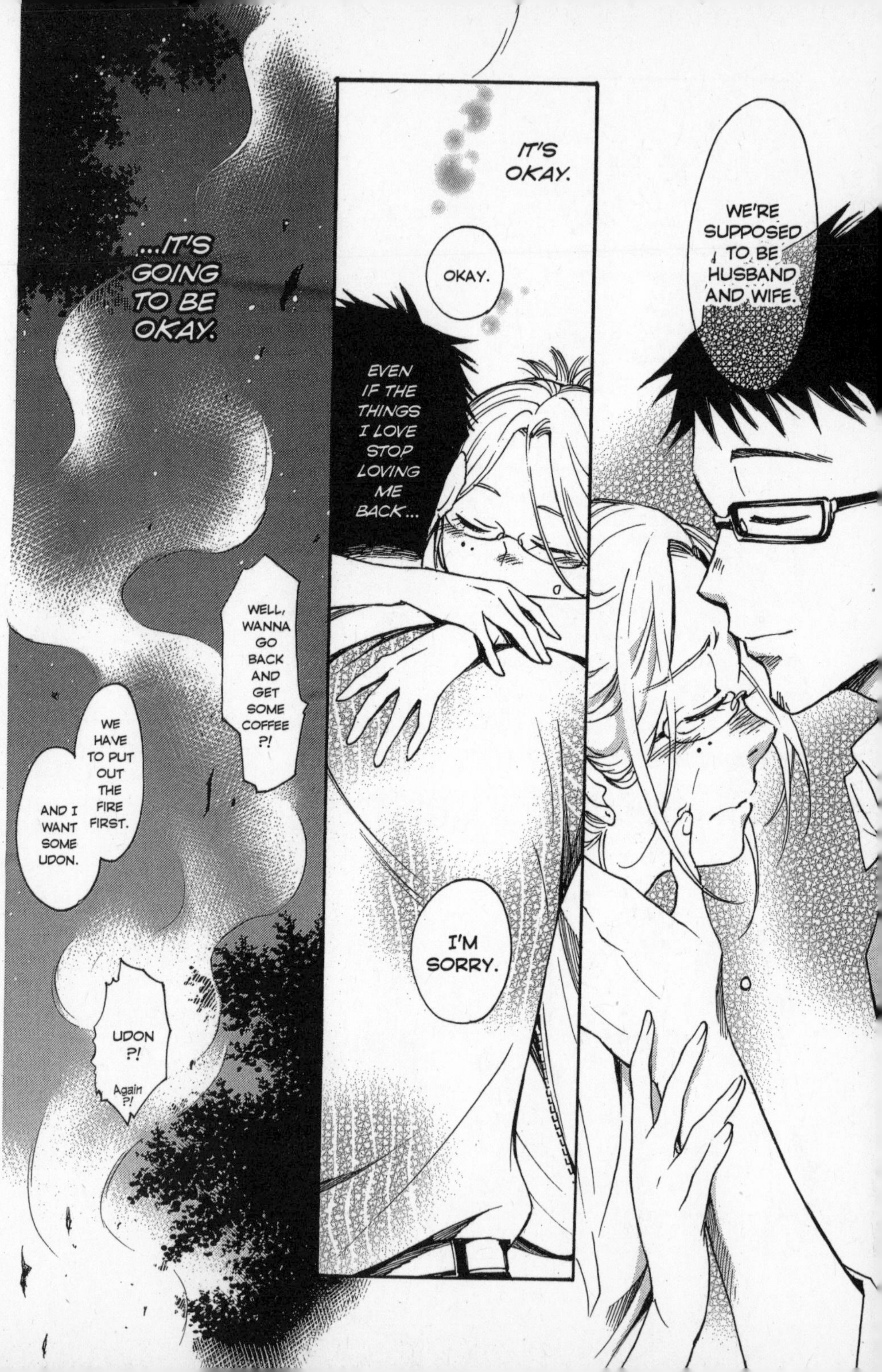
WE'RE SUPPOSED TO BE HUSBAND AND WIFE.
IT'S OKAY.
OKAY.
EVEN IF THE THINGS I LOVE STOP LOVING ME BACK...
I'M SORRY.
...IT'S GOING TO BE OKAY.
WELL, WANNA GO BACK AND GET SOME COFFEE?!
WE HAVE TO PUT OUT THE FIRE FIRST.
AND I WANT SOME UDON.
UDON?!
Again?!

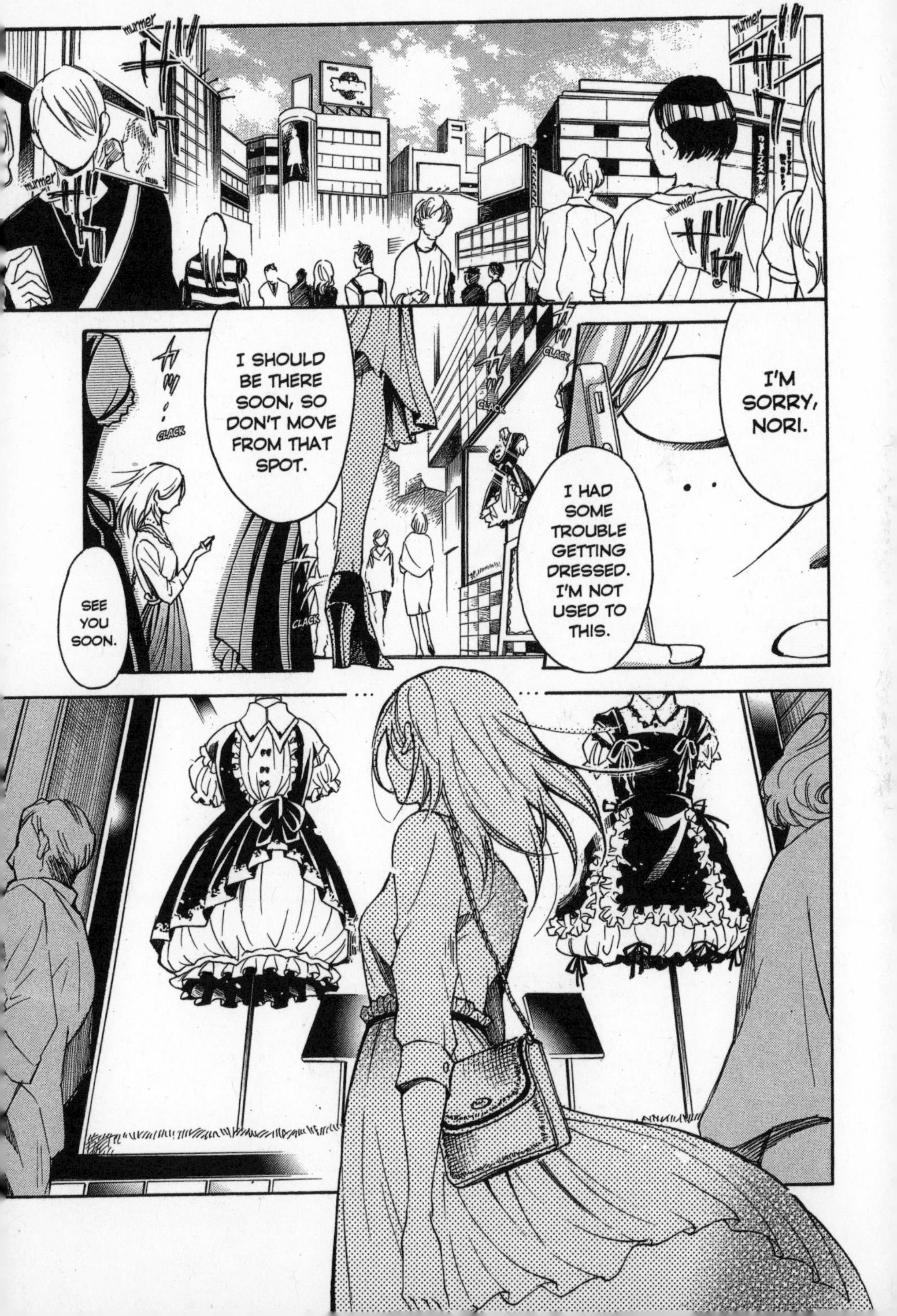
murmer
murmer
murmer
murmer
I'M SORRY, NORI.
I HAD SOME TROUBLE GETTING DRESSED. I'M NOT USED TO THIS.
CLACK
CLACK
I SHOULD BE THERE SOON, SO DON'T MOVE FROM THAT SPOT.
CLACK
CLACK
SEE YOU SOON.
...
...

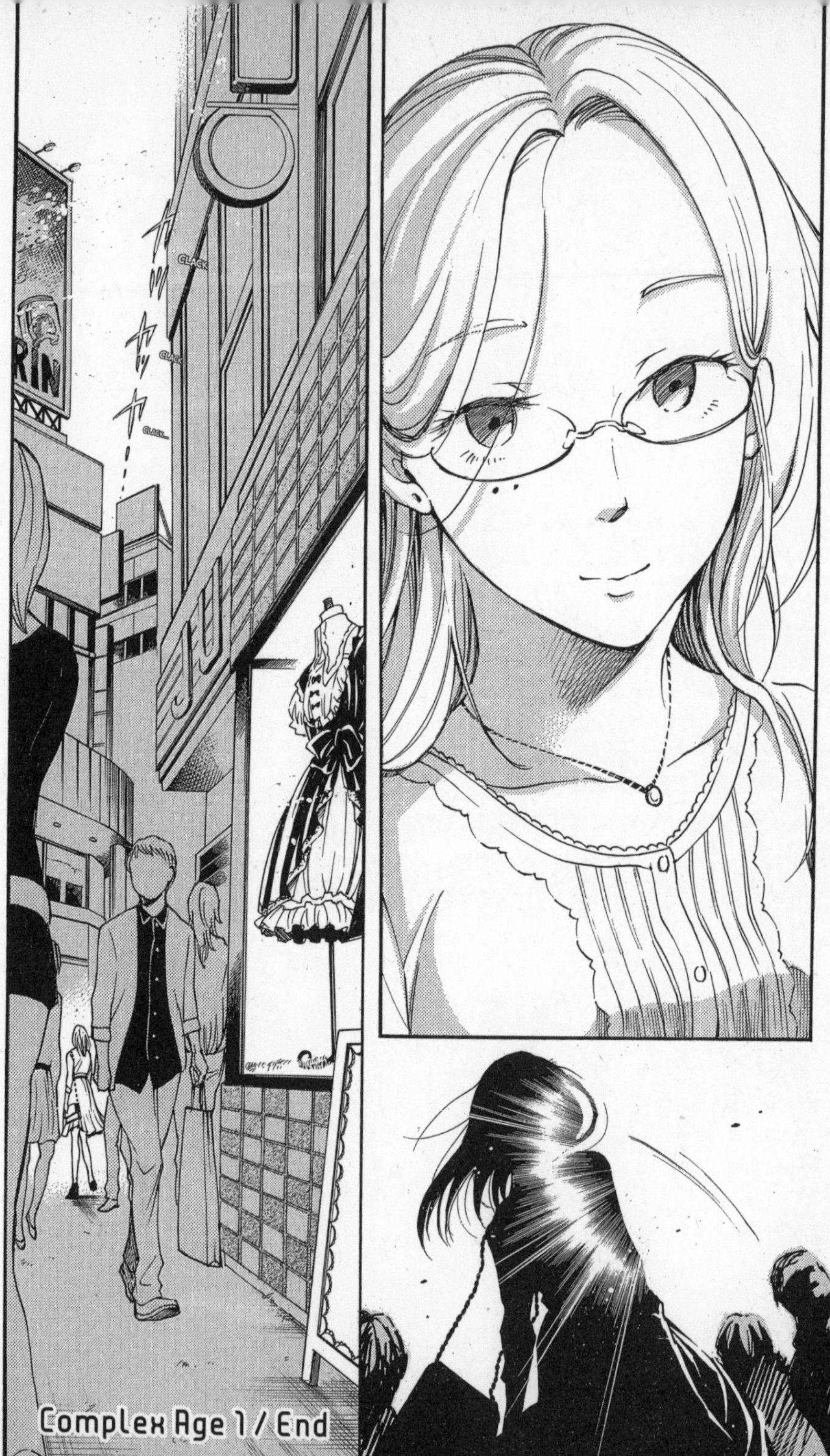
ガッ
CLACK
カッ
CLACK
カ…
CLACK...
Complex Age 1 / End

コンプレックス・エイジ

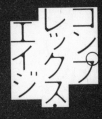

Complex age

Yui Sakuma

THANK YOU FOR READING THIS FAR!

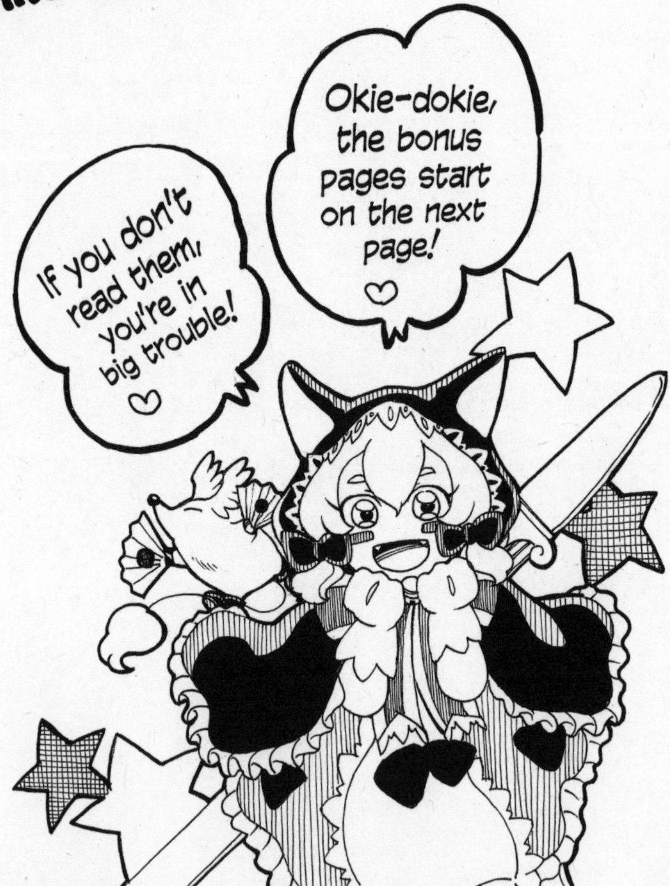
Okie-dokie, the bonus pages start on the next page!
If you don't read them, you're in big trouble!

orz.1 Bonus Original Manga

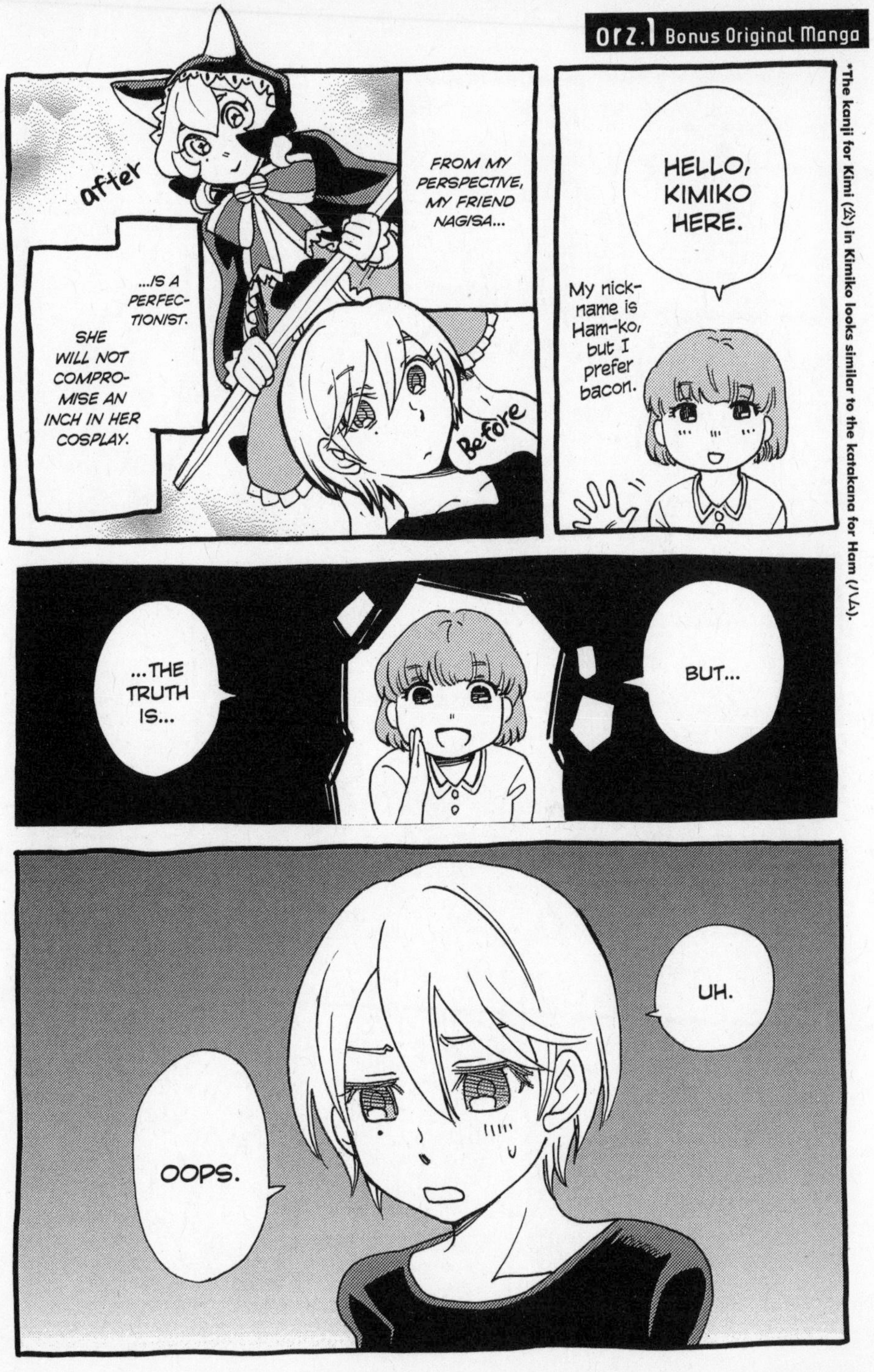
HELLO, KIMIKO HERE.
My nick-name is Ham-ko, but I prefer bacon.
FROM MY PERSPECTIVE, MY FRIEND NAGISA...
after
Before
...IS A PERFECTIONIST.
SHE WILL NOT COMPROMISE AN INCH IN HER COSPLAY.
BUT...
...THE TRUTH IS...
UH.
OOPS.

*The kanji for Kimi (公) in Kimiko looks similar to the katakana for Ham (ハム).

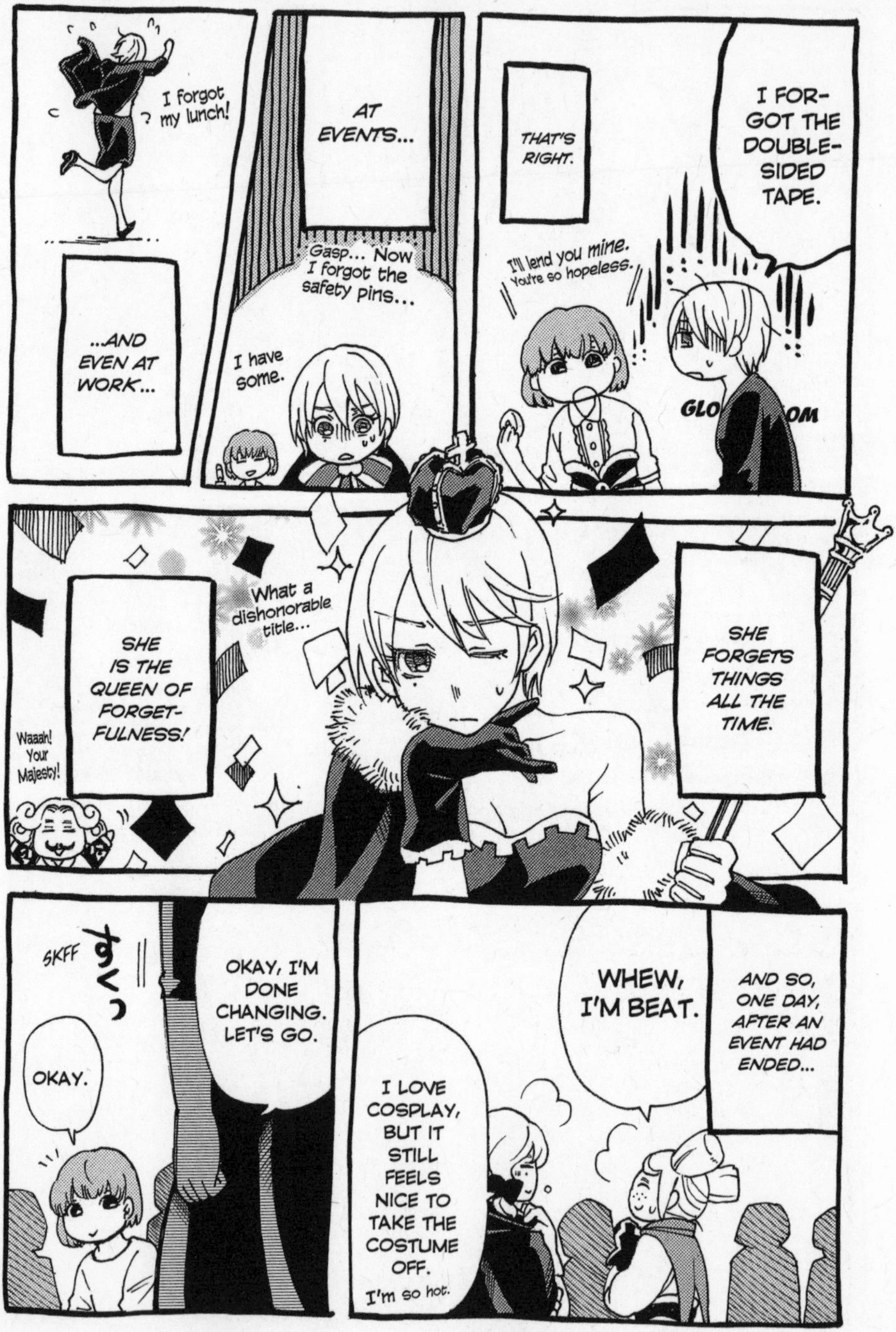

I FOR-GOT THE DOUBLE-SIDED TAPE.
THAT'S RIGHT.
I'll lend you mine. You're so hopeless.
GLO OM
AT EVENTS...
Gasp... Now I forgot the safety pins...
I have some.
I forgot my lunch!
...AND EVEN AT WORK...
SHE FORGETS THINGS ALL THE TIME.
What a dishonorable title...
SHE IS THE QUEEN OF FORGET-FULNESS!
Waaah! Your Majesty!
AND SO, ONE DAY, AFTER AN EVENT HAD ENDED...
WHEW, I'M BEAT.
I LOVE COSPLAY, BUT IT STILL FEELS NICE TO TAKE THE COSTUME OFF.
I'm so hot.
OKAY, I'M DONE CHANGING. LET'S GO.
SKFF すくっ
OKAY.

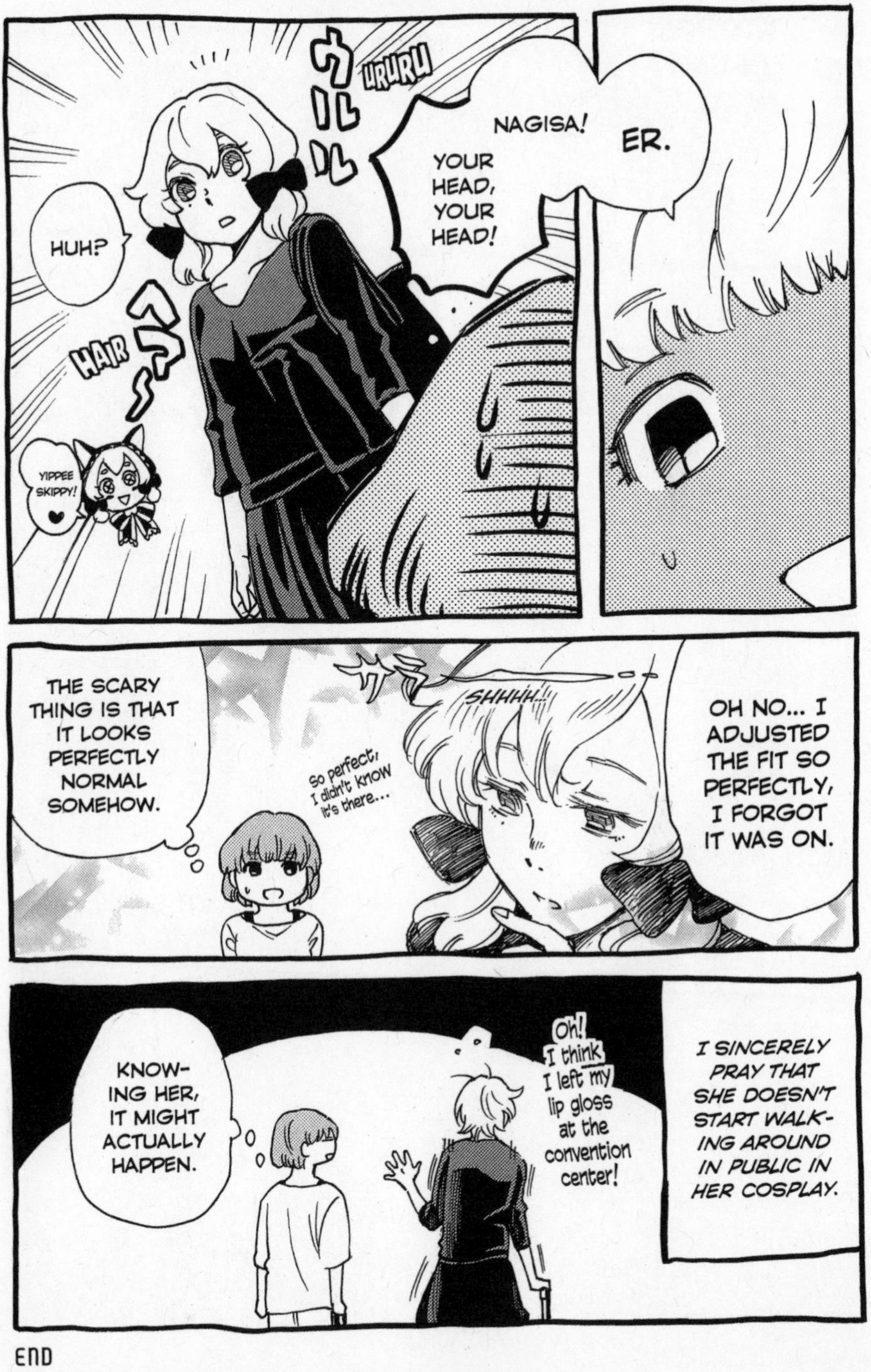
ER.
NAGISA! YOUR HEAD, YOUR HEAD!
ウルル URURU
HUH?
HAIR
YIPPEE SKIPPY!
OH NO... I ADJUSTED THE FIT SO PERFECTLY, I FORGOT IT WAS ON.
SHHHH...
So perfect, I didn't know it's there...
THE SCARY THING IS THAT IT LOOKS PERFECTLY NORMAL SOMEHOW.
I SINCERELY PRAY THAT SHE DOESN'T START WALKING AROUND IN PUBLIC IN HER COSPLAY.
Oh! I think I left my lip gloss at the convention center!
KNOWING HER, IT MIGHT ACTUALLY HAPPEN.

END

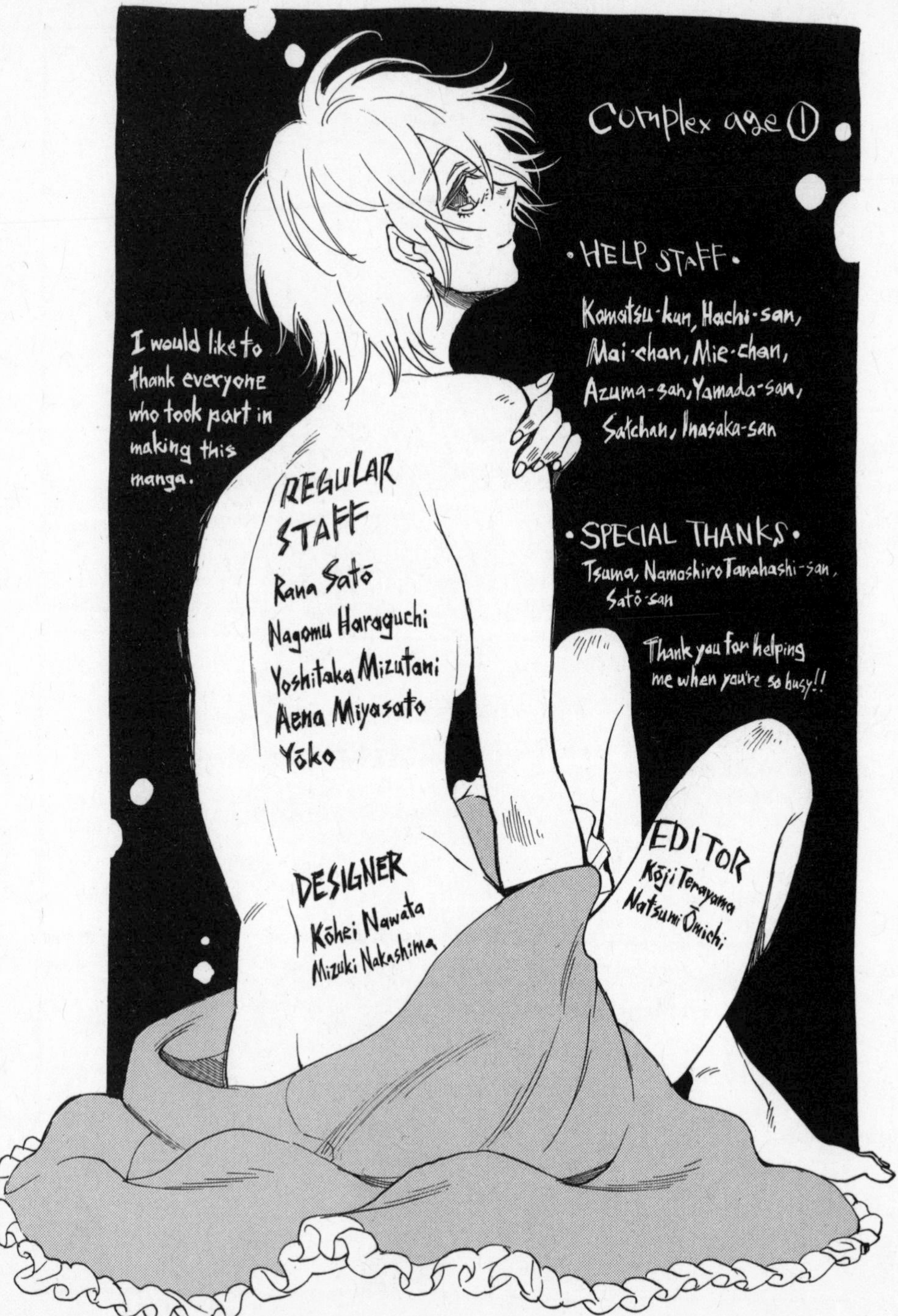
Complex age ①
I would like to thank everyone who took part in making this manga.
•HELP STAFF•
Komatsu-kun, Hachi-san, Mai-chan, Mie-chan, Azuma-san, Yamada-san, Satchan, Inasaka-san
•SPECIAL THANKS•
Tsuma, Namashiro Tanahashi-san, Satō-san
Thank you for helping me when you're so busy!!
REGULAR STAFF
Rana Satō
Nagomu Haraguchi
Yoshitaka Mizutani
Aena Miyasato
Yōko
DESIGNER
Kōhei Nawata
Mizuki Nakashima
EDITOR
Kōji Terayama
Natsumi Ōmichi

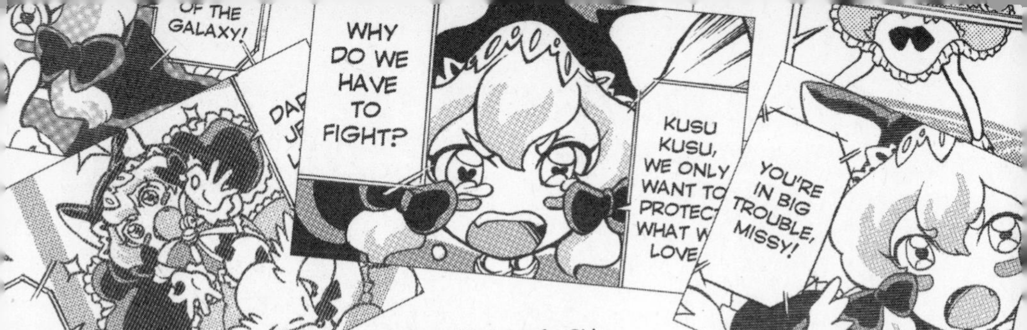
YOU'RE IN BIG TROUBLE, MISSY!
KUSU KUSU, WE ONLY WANT TO PROTECT WHAT W LOVE
WHY DO WE HAVE TO FIGHT?
OF THE GALAXY!
DELTA ATTACK!

Mega Hit Anime for Girls

Magical Riding Hood Ururu

マジカルずきん☆ウルル

CHARACTER DESIGN COLLECTION

Magical Riding Hood Ururu is an anime which airs every Saturday morning at 8:00. This season marks the beginning of its second year. It is the tale of Ururu, who, in a world where girls battle from morning till night, fights her hardest to be friends with everyone on the planet. Although its target demographic is young girls, a lot of effort has gone into its action scenes, and some of its fans call it "*Moé of the North Star.*" Each girl, starting with Ururu, pairs up with a Friend Monster (or Friendster) to fight her battles. And when her heart syncs with her Friendster, they can use a powerful magic attack. All the special attacks have names based on tea (e.g. Darjeeling Delta Attack).

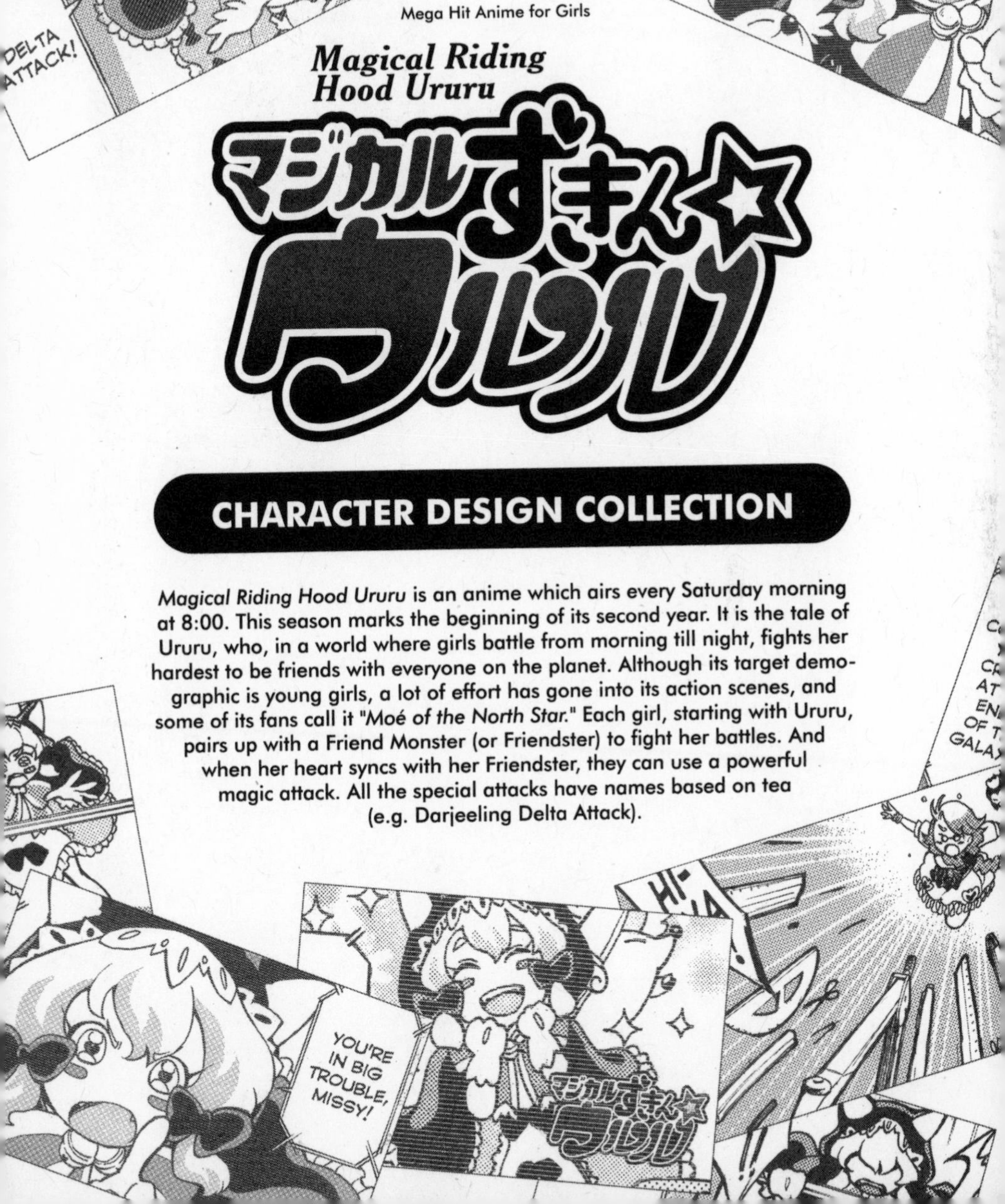
YOU'RE IN BIG TROUBLE, MISSY!
マジカルずきん☆ウルル

ウルル

URURU

The heroine of the series. Saddened by a world of constant fighting, this girl aims to be friends with everyone. She's more straightforward than anyone, and more easily hurt. Her Friendster is Mukuku. Her weapon is a giant scalpel. Her special move is Darjeeling Delta Attack.

COMMENTS

As you can see, she was modeled after Little Red Riding Hood. She was born from the simple concept that "the leader in a power rangers(?) show always wears red!" (Sakuma)

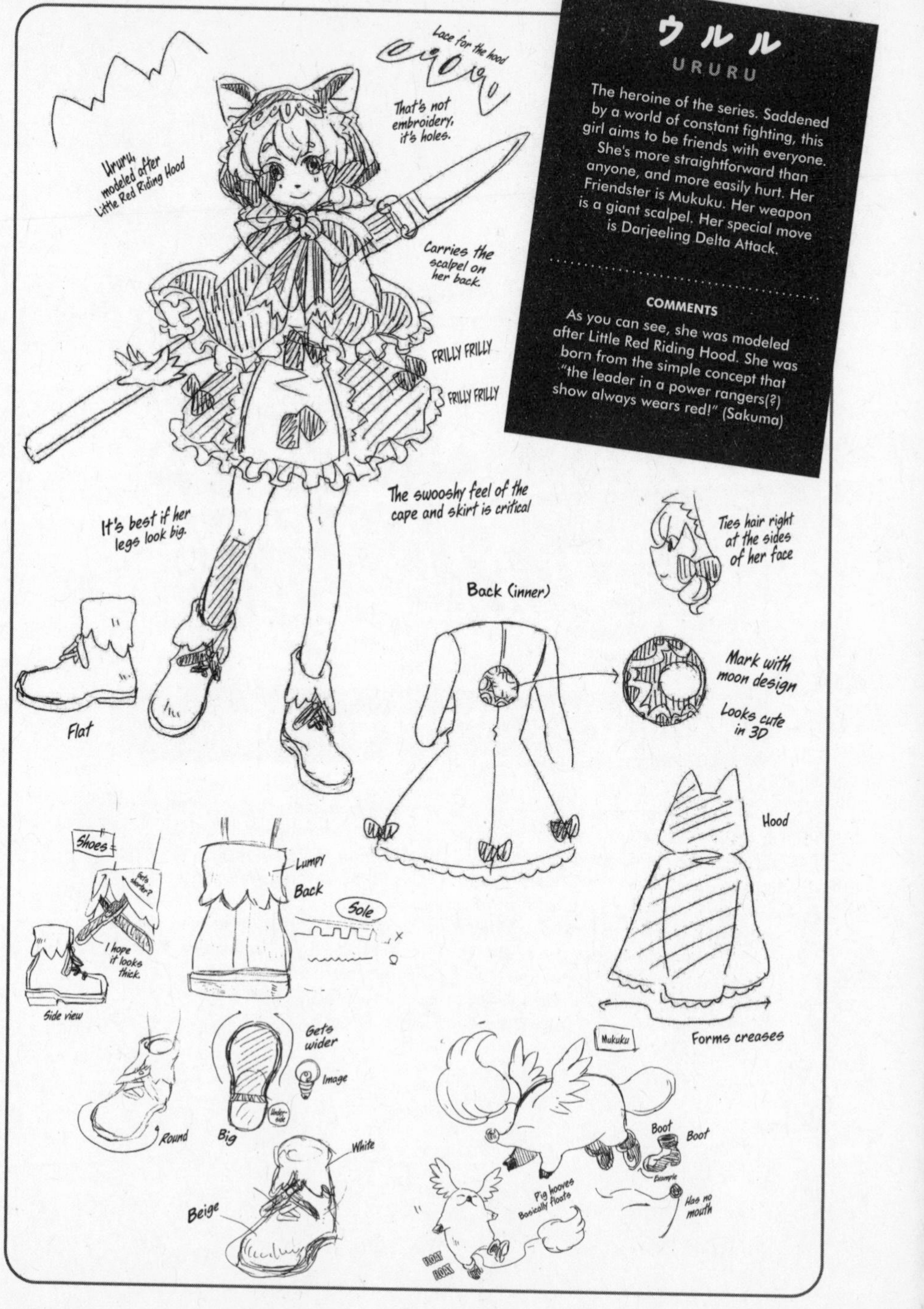

Lace for the hood
That's not embroidery, it's holes.
Ururu, modeled after Little Red Riding Hood
Carries the scalpel on her back.
FRILLY FRILLY
FRILLY FRILLY
The swooshy feel of the cape and skirt is critical
It's best if her legs look big.
Ties hair right at the sides of her face
Back (inner)
Mark with moon design
Looks cute in 3D
Flat
Hood
Shoes
Gets shorter?
I hope it looks thick.
Side view
Lumpy
Back
Sole
Forms creases
Gets wider
Image
Under-side
Round
Big
White
Beige
Mukuku
Boot
Boot
Example
Pig hooves
Basically floats
Has no mouth
FLOAT
FLOAT

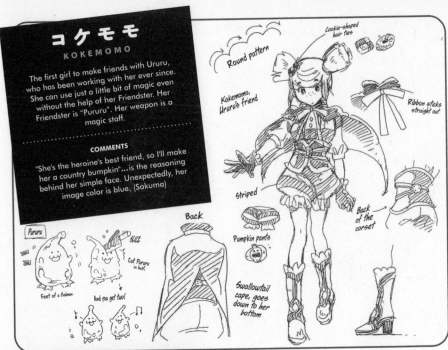

コケモモ

KOKEMOMO

The first girl to make friends with Ururu, who has been working with her ever since. She can use just a little bit of magic even without the help of her Friendster. Her Friendster is "Pururu". Her weapon is a magic staff.

COMMENTS

"She's the heroine's best friend, so I'll make her a country bumpkin"...is the reasoning behind her simple face. Unexpectedly, her image color is blue. (Sakuma)

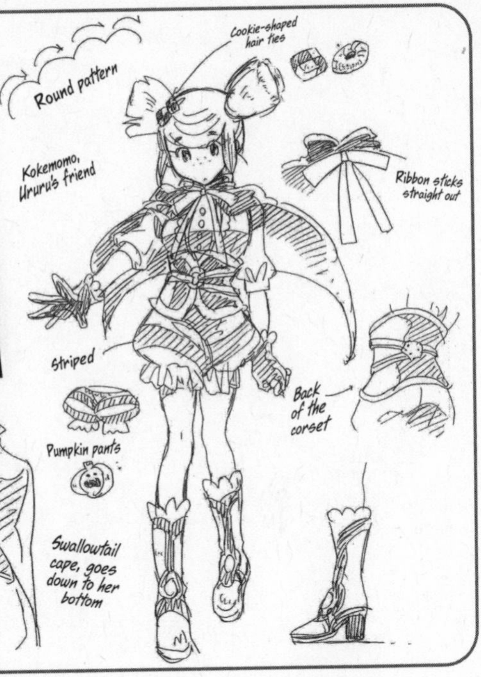

Round pattern
Cookie-shaped hair ties
Kokemomo, Ururu's friend
Ribbon sticks straight out
Striped
Back of the corset
Pumpkin pants
Swallowtail cape, goes down to her bottom

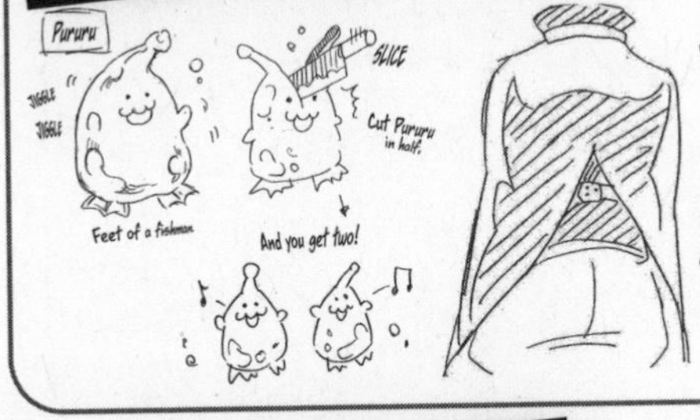

Pururu
JIGGLE
JIGGLE
SLICE
Cut Pururu in half.
Feet of a fishman
And you get two!
Back

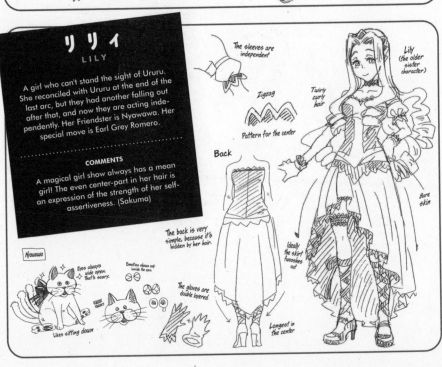

リリィ

LILY

A girl who can't stand the sight of Ururu. She reconciled with Ururu at the end of the last arc, but they had another falling out after that, and now they are acting independently. Her Friendster is Nyawawa. Her special move is Earl Grey Romero.

COMMENTS

A magical girl show always has a mean girl! The even center-part in her hair is an expression of the strength of her self-assertiveness. (Sakuma)

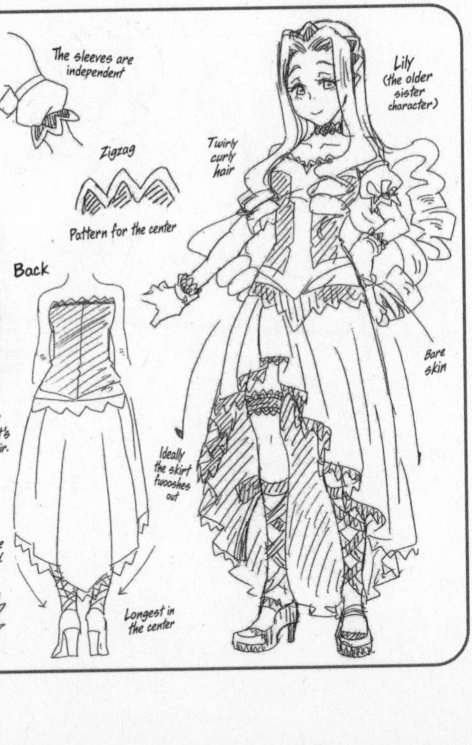

The sleeves are independent
Lily (the older sister character)
Zigzag
Twirly curly hair
Pattern for the center
Back
Bare skin
The back is very simple, because it's hidden by her hair.
Ideally the skirt twooshes out
Longest in the center

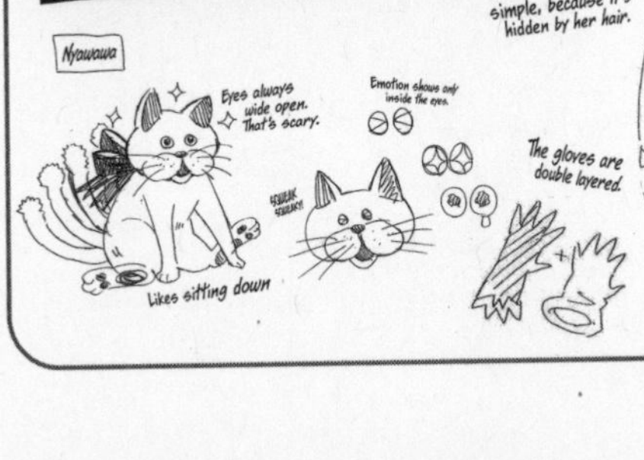

Nyawawa
Eyes always wide open. That's scary.
Emotion shows only inside the eyes.
The gloves are double layered.
Likes sitting down

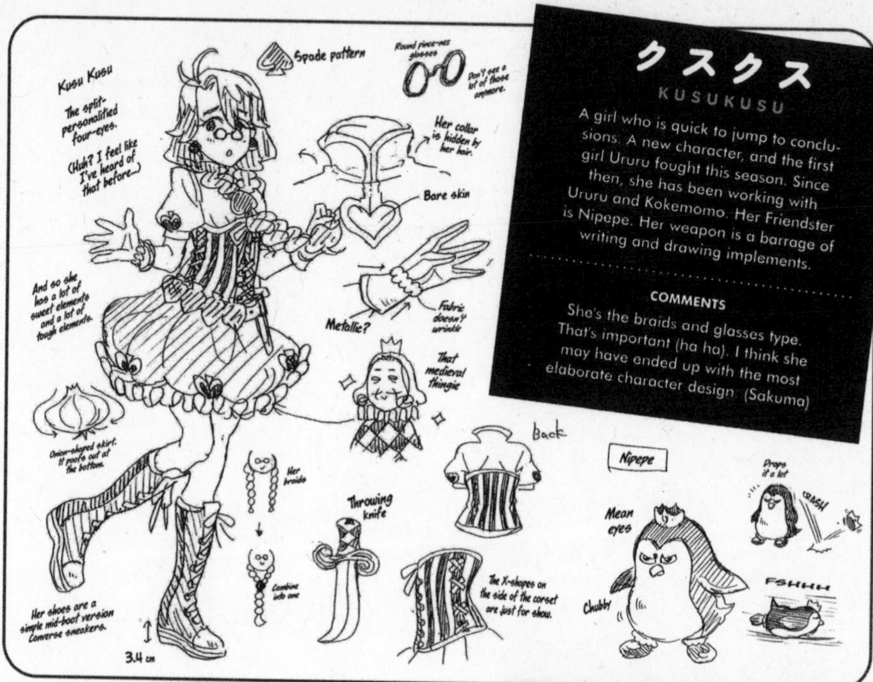

Kusu Kusu
The split-personalitied four-eyes.
(Huh? I feel like I've heard of that before...)
Spade pattern
Round pince-nez glasses
Don't see a lot of those anymore.
Her collar is hidden by her hair.
Bare skin
And so she has a lot of sweet elements and a lot of tough elements.
Metallic?
Fabric doesn't wrinkle
That medieval thingie
Onion-shaped skirt. It poofs out at the bottom.
Her braids
Combine into one
Throwing knife
Back
The X-shapes on the side of the corset are just for show.
Nipepe
Drops it a lot
CRASH
Mean eyes
Chubby
FSHHH
Her shoes are a simple mid-boot version Converse sneakers.
3.4 cm

クスクス

KUSUKUSU

A girl who is quick to jump to conclusions. A new character, and the first girl Ururu fought this season. Since then, she has been working with Ururu and Kokemomo. Her Friendster is Nipepe. Her weapon is a barrage of writing and drawing implements.

COMMENTS

She's the braids and glasses type. That's important (ha ha). I think she may have ended up with the most elaborate character design. (Sakuma)

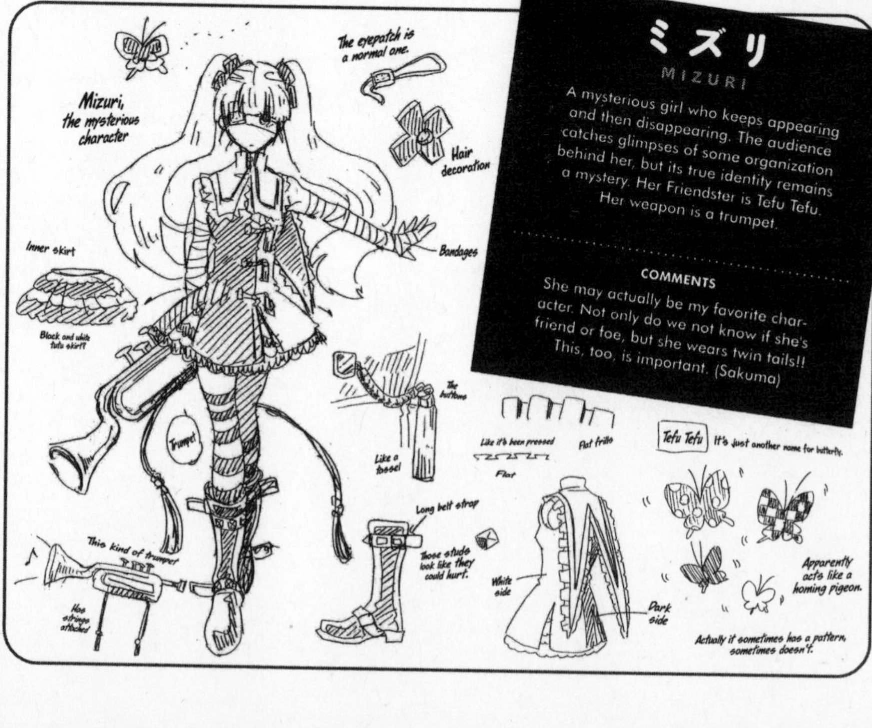

Mizuri, the mysterious character
The eyepatch is a normal one.
Hair decoration
Bandages
Inner skirt
Black and white tutu skirt?
Trumpet
The buttons
Like a tassel
Like it's been pressed
Flat frills
Flat
Tefu Tefu
It's just another name for butterfly.
Long belt strap
Those studs look like they could hurt.
This kind of trumpet
Has strings attached
White side
Dark side
Apparently acts like a homing pigeon.
Actually it sometimes has a pattern, sometimes doesn't.

ミズリ

MIZURI

A mysterious girl who keeps appearing and then disappearing. The audience catches glimpses of some organization behind her, but its true identity remains a mystery. Her Friendster is Tefu Tefu. Her weapon is a trumpet.

COMMENTS

She may actually be my favorite character. Not only do we not know if she's friend or foe, but she wears twin tails!! This, too, is important. (Sakuma)

Cospedia

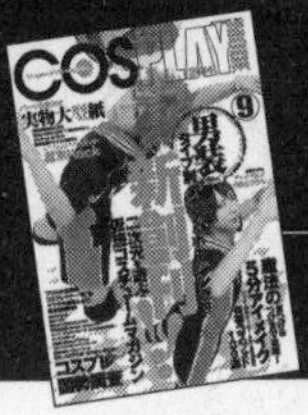

[GLOSSARY OF COSPLAY TERMS]

Supervisor: COSPLAY MODE

The cosplay magazine that has taken over the reins of Cosmode magazine, which ran until spring 2014. It publishes everything related to cosplay, including pinup photos, fan-submitted cosplay photos, and information on costumes, makeup, photography, armor and prop building, and cosplay culture. Released on the 3rd of every even-numbered month. (Published by Famima.com)

General

Cosplay
To dress up like a character from anime, manga, video games, etc. by imitating their clothing and hairstyle. The word was coined in Japan, using the English words "costume play," as in to act something out (like a play) in costume, but the word "cosplay" as written in English is understood throughout the world. People who take part in cosplay are called cosplayers, or layers for short.

---

n.1

▶ Page 3
"I am perfect."
When a cosplayer attempts a faithful re-creation of her character, like Nagisa has, it is called *kan-cos* [complete cosplay]. However, the definition of *kan-cos* is determined by personal preference, and opinions are divided on how far a cosplayer must go to achieve *kan-cos*.

▶ Page 9
"I'm still adjusting the waist."
To make them look more beautiful, characters in anime and manga are generally drawn with high waists and long legs. To recreate this effect, cosplay costumes are often made with the waist in the highest possible position.

Event
A general term for events related to cosplay, such as *dōjinshi* fairs (for selling fan-made comics known as *dōjinshi*), cosplay-only events, and dance parties that play mostly anime and game music (*danpa*). In recent years, events of every kind can be found in various places across the country on any given weekend.

▶ Page 12
"It's a new opening!"
The animation sequence that plays with the theme song at the beginning of an anime is called the "opening." Sometimes, certain cuts will be changed out to match new developments in the story. For long-running series, the entire sequence may change, including the song.

▶ Page 13
"She has a mark there?"
Sometimes, new details will be added to a character without warning, especially in long-running anime. Not many series publish a book of detailed character designs, so layers are constantly fighting to keep up.

▶ Page 15
Tokyo Big Sight
The popular nickname for (and name of the company that manages) the Tokyo International Exhibition Center in Ariake. It's Japan's biggest convention center, hosting such events as the world's largest *dōjinshi* fair, Comic Market (Comiket). Cosplay events are also frequently held at the TFT (Tokyo Fashion Town Building) Hall nearby.

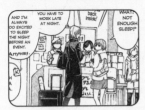

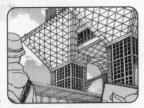

Cosplayers XX yen, Non Cosplayers XX yen
At *dōjinshi* fairs, cosplayers will often have to pay a separate fee on top of stand admission, to cover the cost of changing rooms and photo shoot registration. On the other hand, at a cosplay event, people who ***don't*** cosplay may have to pay more.

WHAT!? NOT ENOUGH SLEEP?
back inside!
YOU HAVE TO WORK LATE AT NIGHT.
AND I'M ALWAYS OO EXCITED TO SLEEP THE NIGHT BEFORE AN EVENT. Anyway.

▶ Page 17
"I would die before painting it on."
"I didn't have time to buy batting, so I stuffed it with tissue (weep)."
There are layers who, like Nagisa, would die before painting a flat version of a 3D pattern on their costume. Nevertheless, the day of the event remains the same. It's a fight against time, so sometimes emergency measures must be taken behind the scenes.

Ururu-Cos
Ururu cosplay. A character's name with the suffix "-cos" becomes the word for cosplaying that character.

"Did you remember to put hand warmers in your socks?"
"Want some miso soup before we hit the hall?"
Tokyo Big Sight is cold in the winter. The temperature gets especially low before the doors open (the recorded low for December 28, 2013 in Tokyo was 2.7°C (36.9°F)), and many people bring disposable heaters and warm things to drink with them to combat the chill. However, after opening, the body heat from the

include using multiple bra pads; stuffing a bra with cotton, towels, pantyhose, or gloves; and wearing two bras.

▶ Page 53
"As a basic rule,, you're not allowed to bring wax or hair-spray into the convention center."
Many event venues prohibit bringing or using anything that might dirty the venue (hairspray, color spray, fake blood, etc.). Wax is allowed as long as it's not granulated.

▶ Page 54
Custom-Made
It varies depending on the maker and levels of perfectionism, but some custom-made items cost up to 100,000 yen (about $1,000).

▶ Page 70
Handle
The name one uses on the internet instead of one's real name.

But the girl on the left looks more awkward than Ururu-san. lol You all look great! Good job getting the whole Magi-Ruru Cast!

Handle Nekosuke

▶ Page 72
"The picture was right there for the taking. lolol" (unauthorized photo)
Slimy photographers who shoot from low angles in the hopes of getting a panty shot are called "low anglers." The picture referred to here was likely taken by one of that ilk (unauthorized photography is a crime!).

n.3

▶ Page 77
Show-panties (boy shorts)
Short for "panties you don't mind showing people." Worn when cosplaying a character whose skirt is so short it is a given that her underwear will be seen. Many layers also prefer to wear leggings or tights to prevent unauthorized photography. Depending on the event, sometimes a cosplayer will be required to wear something underneath, and there are even cases where they will not be allowed inside the venue unless they are wearing leggings or tights.

Yuzawaya and Tokyu Hands, which are located close to Shinjuku Station, making this a priceless treasure of convenience for the working cosplayer, who can stop by on the way home from a job in the heart of Tokyo.

▶ Page 36
Only Event
Refers to an event that focuses only on one work, genre, or theme. They are also called "Onlies."

▶ Page 40
TRC
The Tokyo Ryutsu Center in Heiwajima. It consists of distribution centers, offices, and an exhibition hall, which hosts events of all kinds, including cosplay events and dōjinshi fairs.

▶ Page 43
Materials Cost
The cost of cosplay materials is generally dominated by the price of the fabric used in the costume, so a cosplayer must develop the skill of finding the cheapest material that will most closely catch the spirit of the original. Also, constructing the costume takes a lot of time and labor. When asking someone to make a costume for you, never forget to also pay the labor fee.

n.2

▶ Page 50
"We're gonna change clothes here?"
The places available for changing into costume vary depending on the event venue. Some use a large room for changing, others partition off just a part of the venue, some use warehouses, storerooms, restrooms, kitchens, etc.

▶ Page 52
"I'm filling you out."
One trick for becoming a large-breasted character when the cosplayer's natural shape is smaller in that area. The methods vary from one cosplayer to the next, and

crowds can make it quite hot inside the building, so layers must take caution.

▶ Page 18
"Nagi-san!"
Nagi is Nagisa's cosplay name, the name a cosplayer uses when cosplaying. In Japanese, the names look much different, because they are written with different Chinese characters, but they still sound similar. The benefits of using a cosplay name include the ability to separate your daily life from your cosplay life, protection of personal information, etc.

"Will you let me take a picture?"
It is bad manners to take a picture of a layer without permission (taking pictures without consent can be seen as unauthorized photography). Make sure to ask first! Also, at recent events, to prevent trouble, many places have started requiring camera registration and a photography permit, so check before you go.

▶ Page 20
Wig
In cosplay, they are used to recreate the character's hairstyle and color. Because of the increase in the cosplay population, there are more completed wigs on the market and the price is comparatively lower, but many layers insist on creating their own. When transporting a wig, it is placed on a mannequin head (these days they are sold at 100 yen stores), and put in a cardboard or other box to help it keep its shape.

▶ Page 21
Group cosplay
Taking pictures with multiple cosplayers cosplaying the same work (such as *Magical Riding Hood Ururu*), series (such as the Persona games), or theme (such as the Special Operations Squad from Attack on Titan).

▶ Page 32
Second Dimension
Refers to all things enjoyed on a flat, two-dimensional medium, such as anime, manga, and video games. Its antonym is the Third Dimension, which refers to the real world.

▶ Page 35
"I'd rather look around for something cheaper. But since I don't have time, it's nice that I can come here."
Takashimaya Times Square is a shopping complex composed of a department store (Takashimaya) and specialty stores. These stores include

▶ Page 79
"How many box sets do you need to release?!"
Spoken by people whose lives are controlled by the so-called "bonus feature marketing" in which DVDs and Blu-ray discs (BDs) are sold in new sets with various bonus features added. (This is the cry of their hearts.) Many fans who already own the DVDs nevertheless rejoice at the Blu-ray release with its higher picture quality...but the damage to their bank accounts goes unabated.

▶ Page 80
Cameko
A general term for photographers and picture takers, from the term "camera *kozō*," meaning "camera boy." The shortened version is especially used for women, as *ko* by itself can also mean "girl."

▶ Page 82
Saizeriya
An Italian wine & cafe restaurant that originated in the city of Ichikawa in Chiba Prefecture. It sets itself apart from other family restaurants by its substantial low-price menu and plentiful selection of wines. Incidentally, the Kita-Shukugawa Saizeriya that appeared in the movie *The Disappearance of Haruhi Suzumiya*, unfortunately shut its doors on February 23, 2014.

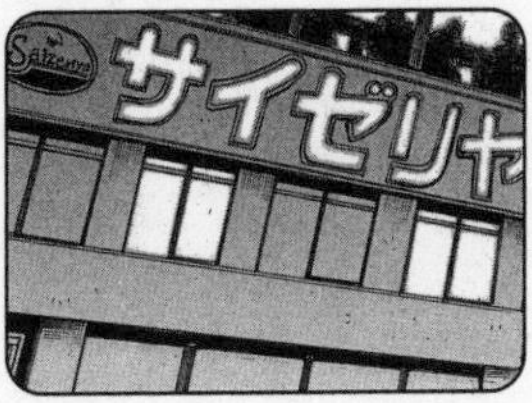
サイゼリヤ

▶ Page 90
"Let's rent a studio!"
"Studio" refers to a photography studio of any kind, from standard studio to a cosplay-specific one. In recent years, there has been an increase in the number of studios run by cosplay-related businesses, and different sets, props, etc. can be found in abundance.

n.4

▶ Page 100
Location Scouting
This usually refers to looking for outdoor locations, but in this story it's used to refer to checking out a photo shoot location before the shoot.

▶ Page 101
Chacott
The brand of Chacott co. Ltd., which specializes in ballet and dance products. Their makeup is made for stage performers, but it earned a reputation for durability, and so more and more layers have started using Chacott finishing powder.

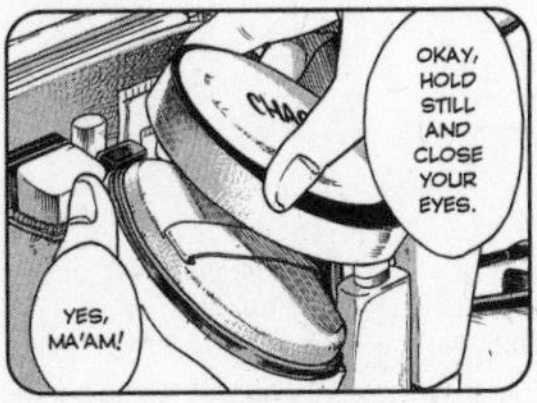
OKAY, HOLD STILL AND CLOSE YOUR EYES.
YES, MA'AM!

n.5

▶ Page 122
Outdoor Shoot
To do photo shoots outside of events, a cosplayer needs permission from whoever manages the location or building (wherever you do your photo shoot, doing it without permission can lead to trouble, so don't even think about it!).

n.6

▶ Page 146
Telecom Center
The Tokyo Teleport Center building in Aomi. The first through fifth floors are like large event halls, and the top floor has an observation deck. When an event is held there, cosplayers can also go to the neighboring park.

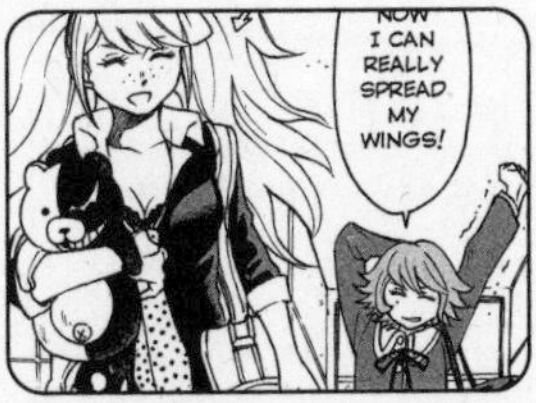
NOW I CAN REALLY SPREAD MY WINGS!

Danganronpa
An adventure game series sold by Spike Chunsoft. Its genre is "high speed murder mystery adventure." An anime hit the airwaves in 2013, gaining it even more popularity among layers.

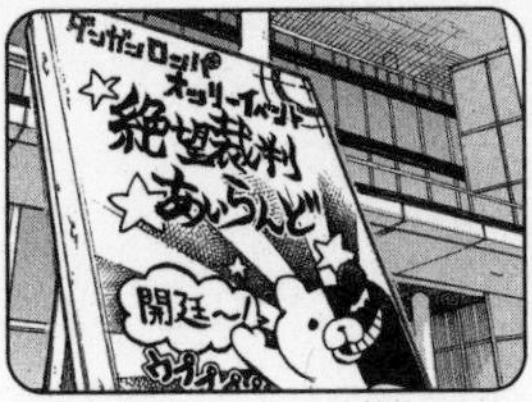
ダンガンロンパ
オンリーイベント
絶望裁判
あいらんど
開廷〜!

Translation
Notes

PAGE 12

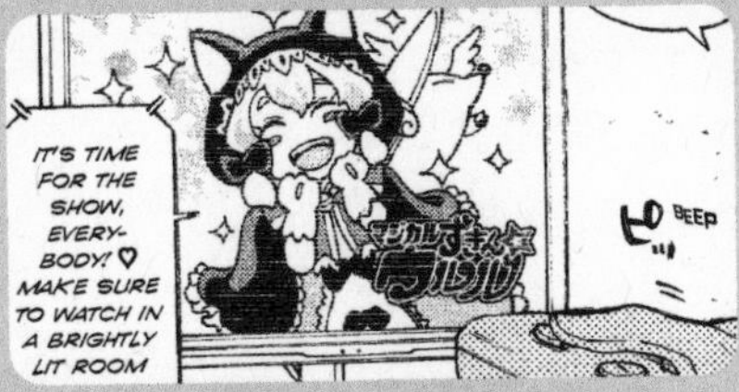
BEEP
IT'S TIME FOR THE SHOW, EVERYBODY! ♡ MAKE SURE TO WATCH IN A BRIGHTLY LIT ROOM

MAKE SURE TO WATCH IN A BRIGHTLY LIT ROOM

In Japan, anime—especially anime aimed at young children—is required to warn viewers to watch in a brightly lit room, and not to sit too close to the TV screen. This may be because of an incident in 1997 when an episode of the immensely popular *Pokémon* TV series caused hundreds of epileptic seizures with its strobing light effects.

PAGE 16

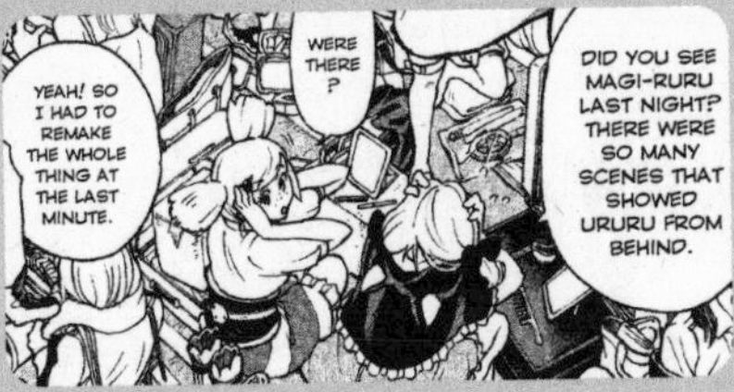
DID YOU SEE MAGI-RURU LAST NIGHT? THERE WERE SO MANY SCENES THAT SHOWED URURU FROM BEHIND.
WERE THERE ?
YEAH! SO I HAD TO REMAKE THE WHOLE THING AT THE LAST MINUTE.

MAGI-RURU

The Japanese writing system doesn't really have initials, so it's more common to abbreviate long titles by sticking a couple of syllables of the important words (like "magical" and "Ururu") together to make a shorter word, like Magi-Ruru. Incidentally, the Japanese title of *Magical Riding Hood Ururu* is *Majikaru Zukin Ururu*, where "*maji-karu*" is the English word "magical."

PAGE 18

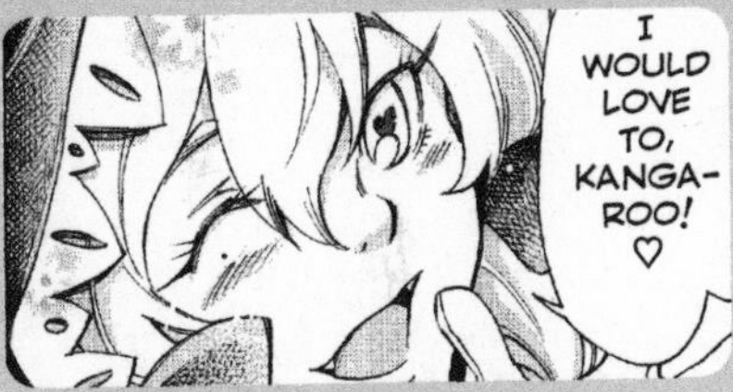
I WOULD LOVE TO, KANGAROO! ♡

I WOULD LOVE TO, KANGAROO

Ururu, and therefore any good Ururu cosplayer, ends many of her sentences with a hearty *nano~*. Because of the way Japanese works, it's easy to add a little spice to a character's dialogue by giving them a special sentence ender. This one is a cutesy way of emphasizing sentences, and as far as meaning goes, it can be translated simply to an exclamation point. But it also makes Ururu sound childlike and feminine. The translators are attempting to replicate this effect by having the character use a simple rhyme, in the vein of "no way, José" and "see you later, alligator."

PAGE 38

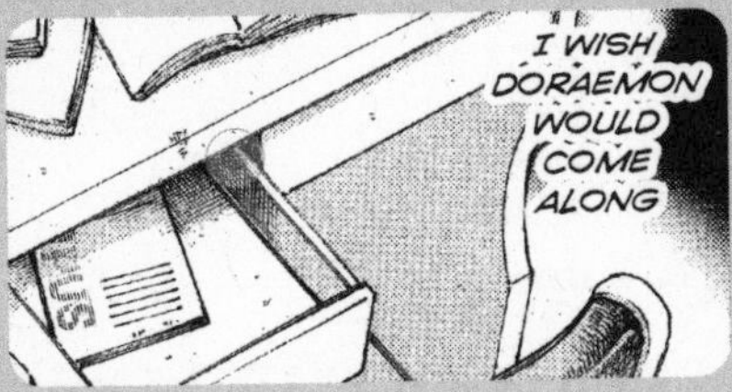
I WISH DORAEMON WOULD COME ALONG

DORAEMON

Doraemon, from the popular anime of the same name, is a robot cat who helps his friend Nobita by pulling various gadgets out of his magic pocket. As the reader may have guessed, one of these gadgets is a shrink ray.

PAGE 62

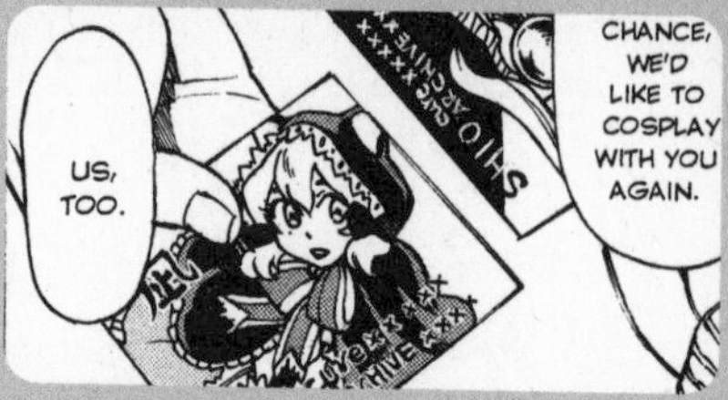
CHANCE, WE'D LIKE TO COSPLAY WITH YOU AGAIN.
US, TOO.

COSCARD

The cards Nagisa and Shiho trade with each other are called CosCards. They're like business cards, but for cosplayers. As you can see, they have pictures of the layers in costume, along with their contact information.

PAGE 58

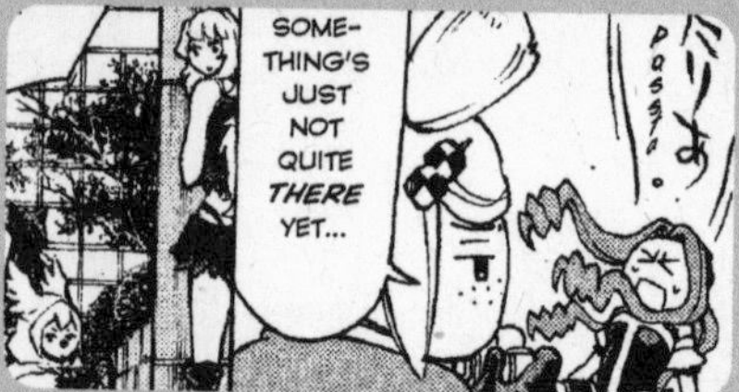
Passta.
SOME-THING'S JUST NOT QUITE *THERE* YET...

PASSTA

This is an unusual way of representing the sound of falling listlessly to the floor, which the translators may ordinarily have rendered as "fwump." But in this case, instead of using the usual *hetaaa*, the author of the manga went for a long version, *hetaria*, which, uncoincidentally, sounds very much like the title of a popular-among-cosplayers series about anthropomorphized countries, in which the main character has a fondness for pasta.

PAGE 99

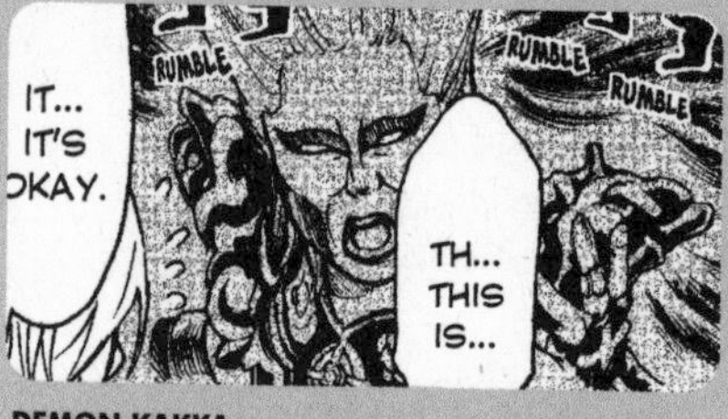
RUMBLE
RUMBLE
TH... THIS IS...
RUMBLE
IT... IT'S OKAY.

DEMON KAKKA

The chaos in Kimiko's notebook is apparently so bad that it summoned Demon Kakka, or His Excellency Lord Demon. Formerly known as Demon Kogure, this heavy metal singer purportedly descended upon the earth when Zeus's seal over hell weakened enough for him to break out. He seeks to conquer the world through heavy metal music.

PAGE 85

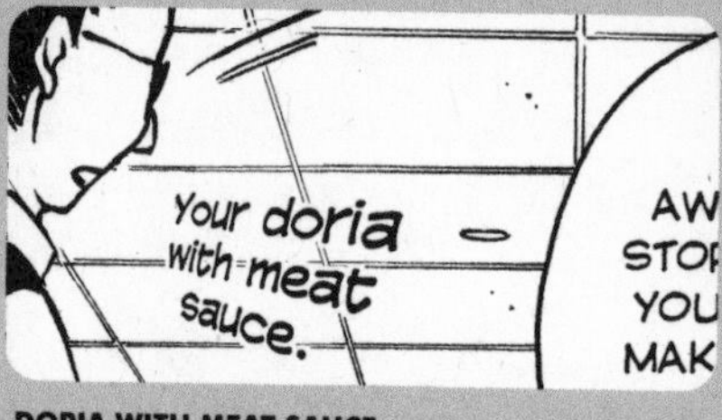
AW STO YOU MAK
Your doria with meat sauce.

DORIA WITH MEAT SAUCE

Doria is a type of *yōshoku*, which in this case refers to the European-inspired dishes that were invented in Japan. Doria is roasted pilaf that is usually served with white sauce, but this particular dish is the Milanese-style of doria, which is served with meat sauce.

PAGE 163

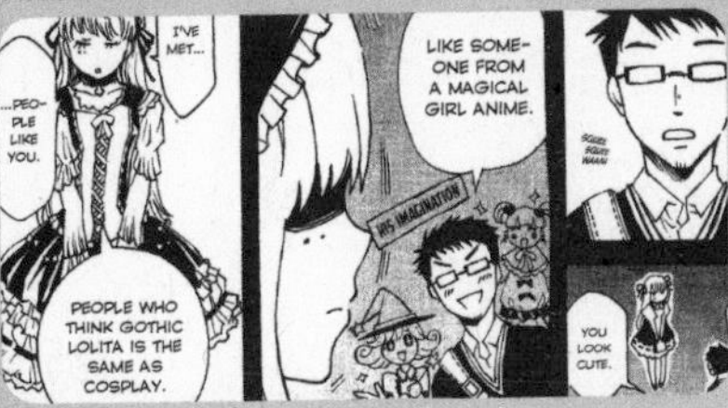
LIKE SOME-ONE FROM A MAGICAL GIRL ANIME.
HIS IMAGINATION
YOU LOOK CUTE.
I'VE MET...
...PEOPLE LIKE YOU.
PEOPLE WHO THINK GOTHIC LOLITA IS THE SAME AS COSPLAY.

GOTH LOLI

Goth Loli, a romanization of the nickname for Gothic Lolita in Japan, *gosurori*, is being used here to refer to Lolita fashion in general. Although the gothic substyle of Lolita fashion was the most popular in the late 1990s and early 2000s to the extent that *gosurori* became a shorthand for the entire fashion subculture, characters with "sweet" and "classic" styles can also be found in this chapter. In the English language Lolita community, fans of the fashion simply use "Lolita" to describe themselves and their clothes, not "Goth Loli."

PAGE 139

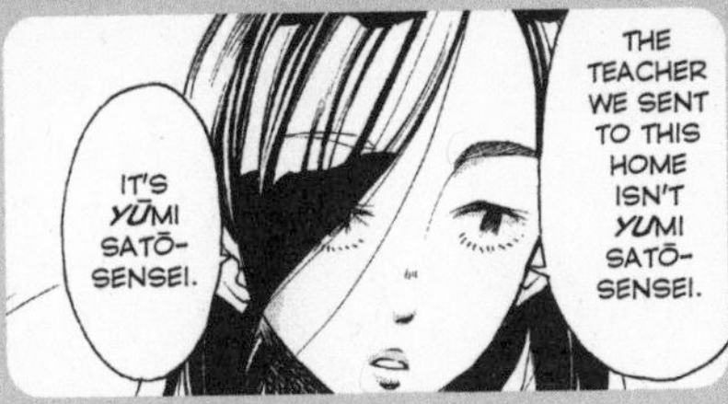
THE TEACHER WE SENT TO THIS HOME ISN'T *YUMI* SATŌ-SENSEI.
IT'S *YŪMI* SATŌ-SENSEI.

THE INFAMOUS YŪMI SATŌ-SENSEI

For those of you who may be as picky about correct name entry as Hayama (and those of you who might be interested), the mistake Nagisa made in entering the teacher's name was different in the original Japanese. Originally, she entered the wrong *kanji* character for the name, calling her Yūmi meaning "fruit of friendship" instead of Yūmi meaning "beauty of friendship." Either way, the name would be pronounced Yūmi. Incidentally, the characters for "fruit" and "beauty" look very similar.

PAGE 165

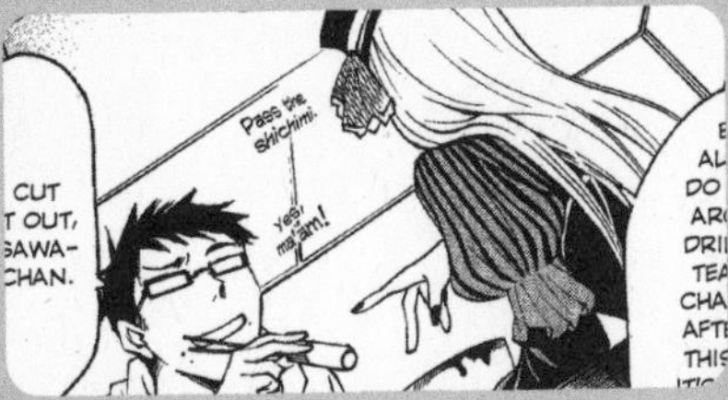
Pass the shichimi.
Yes, ma'am!
CUT

SHICHIMI

Shichimi is a Japanese condiment, like a seasoning salt. It consists of seven different Japanese spices, hence the name *shichimi*, meaning "seven flavors."

PAGE 164

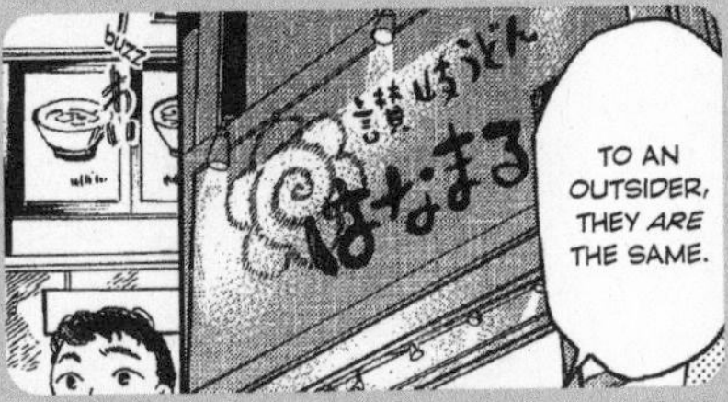
TO AN OUTSIDER, THEY *ARE* THE SAME.
讃岐うどん
はなまる
buzz

HANAMARU

Hanamaru is a restaurant chain that specializes in sanuki udon, a noodle dish that uses flat, square noodles that were once mainly eaten in western Japan. The mission of Hanamaru is to bring the joy of sanuki udon to the entire country of Japan.

PAGE 197

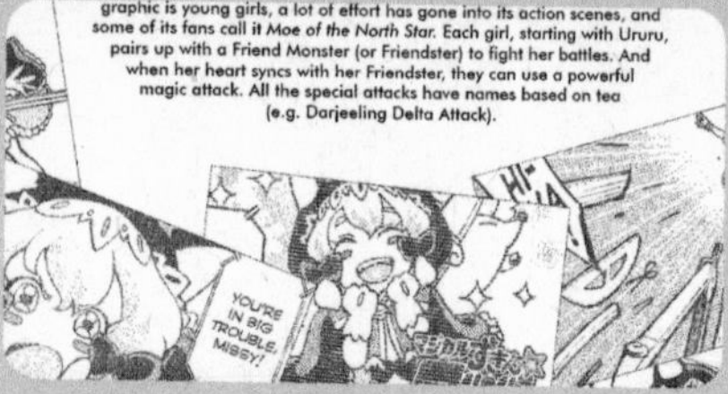
graphic is young girls, a lot of effort has gone into its action scenes, and some of its fans call it *Moe of the North Star.* Each girl, starting with Ururu, pairs up with a Friend Monster (or Friendster) to fight her battles. And when her heart syncs with her Friendster, they can use a powerful magic attack. All the special attacks have names based on tea (e.g. Darjeeling Delta Attack).
YOU'RE IN BIG TROUBLE, MISSY!

MOÉ OF THE NORTH STAR

A play on the title *Fist of the North Star*, a famous action anime from the 1980s. In this case, the term *moé* is most likely used to refer to the cutesy nature of the character designs.

Praise for the anime:

"The show provides a pleasant window on the highs and lows of young love with two young people who are first timers at the real thing."

-The Fandom Post

"Always it is smarter, more poetic, more touching, just plain better than you think it is going to be."

-Anime News Network

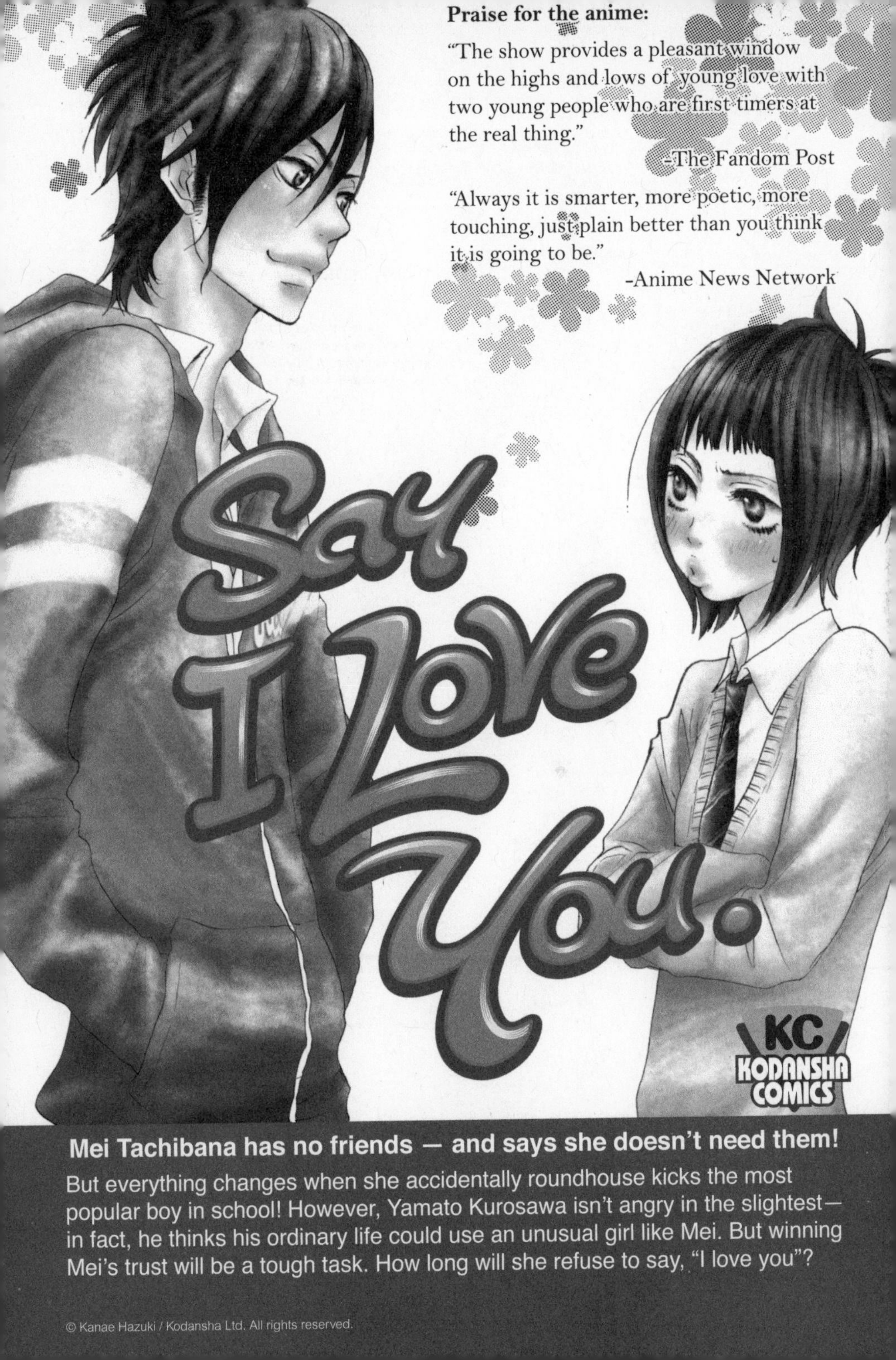
Say I Love You.
KC
KODANSHA COMICS

Mei Tachibana has no friends — and says she doesn't need them!

But everything changes when she accidentally roundhouse kicks the most popular boy in school! However, Yamato Kurosawa isn't angry in the slightest—in fact, he thinks his ordinary life could use an unusual girl like Mei. But winning Mei's trust will be a tough task. How long will she refuse to say, "I love you"?

My Little Monster

OPPOSITES ATTRACT...MAYBE?

Haru Yoshida is feared as an unstable and violent "monster." Mizutani Shizuku is a grade-obsessed student with no friends. Fate brings these two together to form the most unlikely pair. Haru firmly believes he's in love with Mizutani and she firmly believes he's insane.

KC KODANSHA COMICS

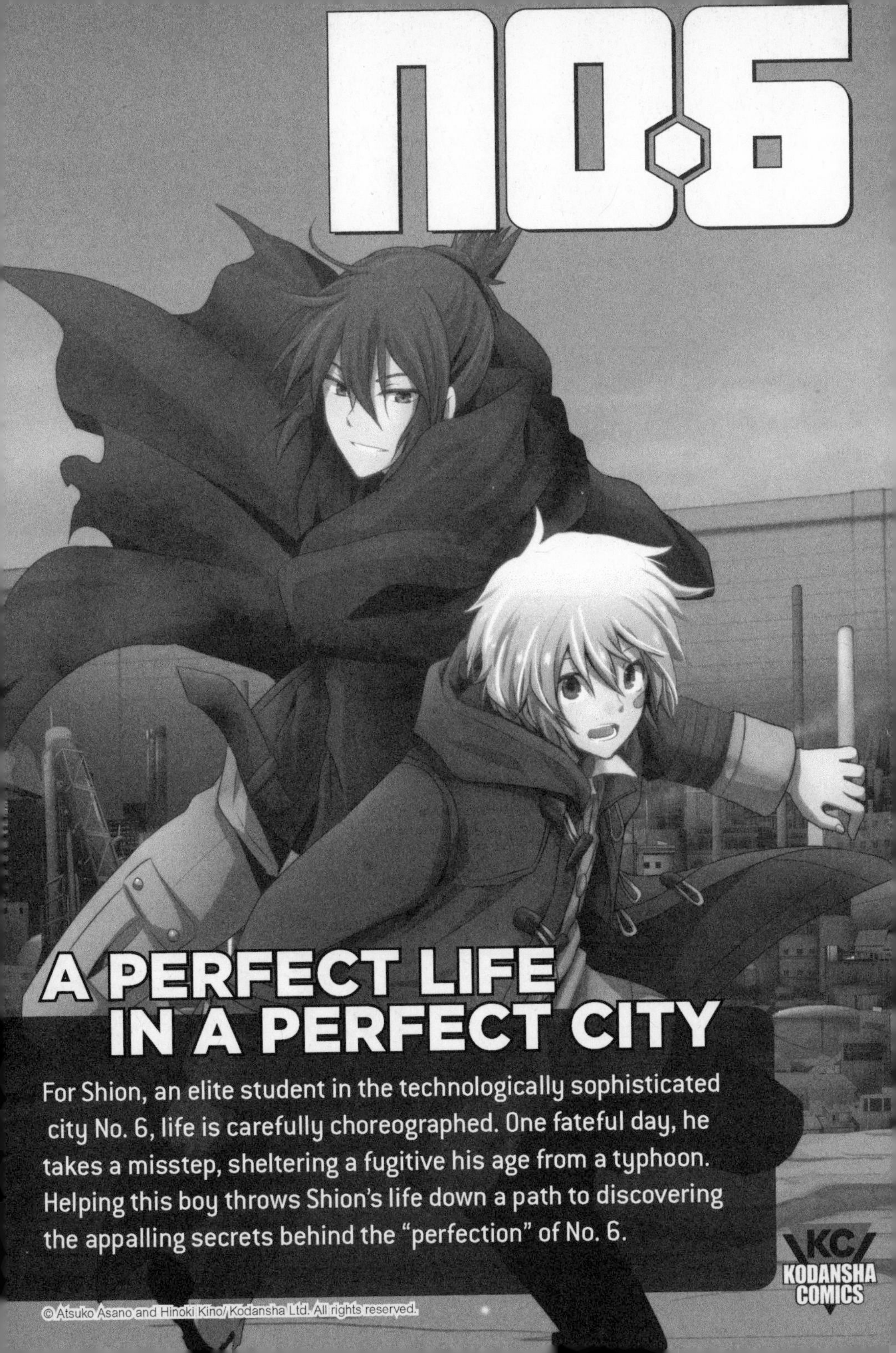
NO.6
A PERFECT LIFE
IN A PERFECT CITY
For Shion, an elite student in the technologically sophisticated city No. 6, life is carefully choreographed. One fateful day, he takes a misstep, sheltering a fugitive his age from a typhoon. Helping this boy throws Shion's life down a path to discovering the appalling secrets behind the "perfection" of No. 6.
KC
KODANSHA
COMICS
© Atsuko Asano and Hinoki Kino/ Kodansha Ltd. All rights reserved.

Maria THE VIRGIN WITCH

"Maria's brand of righteous justice, passion and plain talking make for one of the freshest manga series of 2015. I dare any other book to top it."
—UK Anime Network

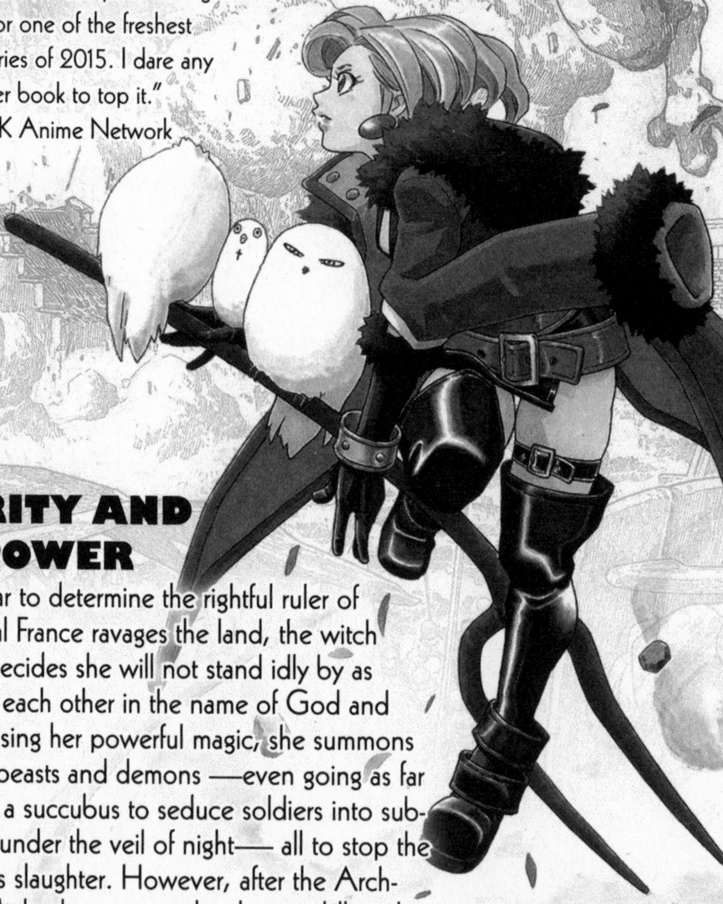

PURITY AND POWER

As a war to determine the rightful ruler of medieval France ravages the land, the witch Maria decides she will not stand idly by as men kill each other in the name of God and glory. Using her powerful magic, she summons various beasts and demons —even going as far as using a succubus to seduce soldiers into submission under the veil of night— all to stop the needless slaughter. However, after the Archangel Michael puts an end to her meddling, he curses her to lose her powers if she ever gives up her virginity. Will she forgo the forbidden fruit of adulthood in order to bring an end to the merciless machine of war?
Available now in print and digitally!

KODANSHA COMICS

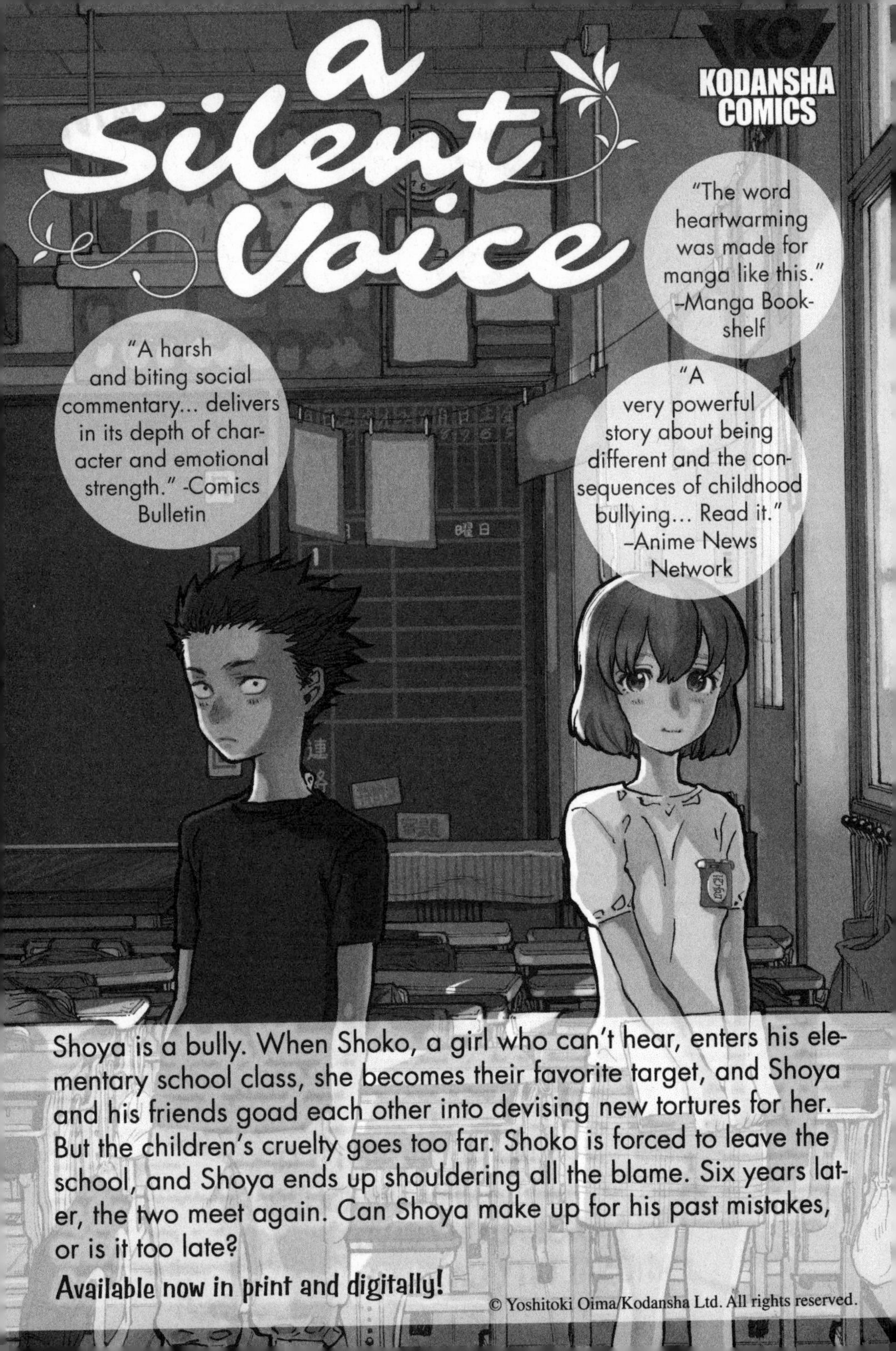
a Silent Voice
KODANSHA COMICS
"The word heartwarming was made for manga like this." –Manga Bookshelf
"A harsh and biting social commentary... delivers in its depth of character and emotional strength." -Comics Bulletin
"A very powerful story about being different and the consequences of childhood bullying... Read it." –Anime News Network
Shoya is a bully. When Shoko, a girl who can't hear, enters his elementary school class, she becomes their favorite target, and Shoya and his friends goad each other into devising new tortures for her. But the children's cruelty goes too far. Shoko is forced to leave the school, and Shoya ends up shouldering all the blame. Six years later, the two meet again. Can Shoya make up for his past mistakes, or is it too late?
Available now in print and digitally!
© Yoshitoki Oima/Kodansha Ltd. All rights reserved.

Complex Age volume 1 is a work of fiction. Names, characters, places, and incidents are the products of the author's imagination or are used fictitiously. Any resemblance to actual events, locales, or persons, living or dead, is entirely coincidental.

A Kodansha Comics Trade Paperback Original.

Published in the United States by Kodansha Comics, an imprint of Kodansha USA Publishing, LLC, New York.

Publication rights for this English edition arranged through Kodansha Ltd., Tokyo.

First published in Japan in 2014 by Kodansha Ltd., Tokyo, as *Complex Age* volume 1.

ISBN 978-1-63236-248-3

Printed in the United States of America.

www.kodanshacomics.com

9 8 7 6 5 4 3 2 1

Translation: Alethea Nibley & Athena Nibley
Lettering: Evan Hayden
Editing: Ajani Oloye
Kodansha Comics Edition Cover Design: Phil Balsman